Oracle Database 10g

High Availability with RAC,
Flashback & Data Guard

Matthew Hart
Scott Jesse

McGraw-Hill/Osborne

New York Chicago San Francisco
Lisbon London Madrid Mexico City Milan
New Delhi San Juan Seoul Singapore Sydney Toronto

The McGraw-Hill Companies

McGraw-Hill/Osborne
2100 Powell Street, 10th Floor
Emeryville, California 94608
U.S.A.

To arrange bulk purchase discounts for sales promotions, premiums, or fund-raisers, please contact **McGraw-Hill**/Osborne at the above address. For information on translations or book distributors outside the U.S.A., please see the International Contact Information page immediately following the index of this book.

Oracle Database 10*g* High Availability with RAC, Flashback & Data Guard

1234567890 FGR FGR 01987654

ISBN 0-07-225428-9

Publisher
  Brandon A. Nordin

Vice President & Associate Publisher
  Scott Rogers

Acquisitions Editor
  Lisa McClain

Project Editor
  Jennifer Malnick

Acquisitions Coordinator
  Athena Honore

Technical Editors
  Soumendra Paik, Bill Burton, Ed Magoffin

Copy Editor
  Dennis Weaver

Proofreader
  Linda Medoff

Indexer
  Claire Splan

Composition
  Lucie Ericksen

Illustrators
  Kathleen Edwards, Melinda Lytle

Series Design
  Jani Beckwith, Peter F. Hancik

Cover Designer
  Damore Johann Design, Inc.

This book was composed with Corel VENTURA™ Publisher.

This book is dedicated to Beth's strength, Lily's curiosity, and Thomas's beginning.

—Matt

This book is dedicated to my wife, Tricia, and my children, Erica (9), Amanda (7), and Mitchell (5).

—Scott

About the Authors

Matthew Hart was last spotted in a dungeon of his own making, coaxing life out of five-year-old Linux conversion boxes with too many Oracle instances running simultaneously. It is rumored that he lives in the middle of the country now, and leads a normal life with a wife and two children. There is some evidence that indicates he has been employed by Oracle Corporation for the past six years. Mr. Hart can be reached for questions or comments on this book by yelling loudly into a tin can, or by e-mailing mhart@mingram.com.

Scott Jesse is a full-time father of three, and a part-time husband (aspiring for a full-time position). Scott is also a brother, a son, a grandson, a cousin, an uncle and friend—these are the defining jobs and roles that stick with you for life, and make one's life incredibly full and rich. Scott has also been an avid Denver Broncos fan his entire life, and an avid Colorado Rockies and Colorado Avalanche fan their entire lives. He has also been known to occasionally hit a golf ball past the Ladies tees (at least once per 18 holes). Aside from these endeavors, Scott has moonlighted as an Oracle Support Professional for the past 7+ years, where he currently holds the title of Principal Support Engineer.

About the Contributor

Michael T. Smith has worked with Oracle for over five years and is the Global Technical Lead for Data Guard. Michael currently lives in Florida with his wife, two kids, two guinea pigs, and a four-pound dog.

Contents at a Glance

PART IV
Distributed Database Solutions

Contents

PART I
Logical Availability

PART II
Real Application Clusters

PART III
Disaster Planning

PART IV
Distributed Database Solutions

Acknowledgments

Matt:

I love big words. Big words and long, overly complicated sentences with plenty of punctuation marks. I dig dangling modifiers. Seriously. I am also a fan of petty asides, pointless indications of emotion, and the phonetic spelling of slang words.

And so it is with the deepest gratitude that I thank the team at Osborne for allowing me to write technical books, putting up with my wildly unappealing prose, and, in the end, fixing it all so that people can read it. Lisa McClain, our fearless acquisitions editor, met with us at OracleWorld and agreed to a contract, and since then she has seen us through every step of the process, including last-minute chapter revisions, rewrites, and hand-wringing overstyle. It has been a real pleasure having her as a sounding board as well as a shaper of amorphous ideas. I must also thank Athena Honore for her ability to gently but firmly hold us all to the deadlines we ourselves set. This is a more difficult task than it sounds. I must thank our technical editor, Soumendra Paik, who kept us honest throughout the book and pointed out when we had cut corners or completely messed up a technical example. And, of course, thanks must go out to the project editor, Jenny Malnick, and her team of copyeditors; to them goes the most difficult work. That whole dangling modifier thing.

I've known Scott Jesse since I began working at Oracle six years ago, and he has been a mentor to me both professionally and personally. And I must come clean: Scott Jesse is the real High Availability guru on this project, people. My name comes first on the book only because I suckered him into this book, not the other way round. And I cannot thank him enough for agreeing to write this with me. It would be tiresome to list all the reasons for my gratitude to Scott, but here's the Cliff's Notes: his willingness to dig into each new challenge, regardless of the complexity; the patience to test workshops with questionable beta code, and then rebuild and test again; a complete and total dedication to technical accuracy; and the desire to have a little fun. It is on this last point that I failed Scott—my deepest apologies for wussing out on the first write of Chapter 1. Maybe we'll do an extended director's cut version down the road.

I was discussing the possibility of writing this book with Scott Jesse over pints at Vesuvio's in San Francisco. We were both working the floors at OracleWorld 2003, and had recused ourselves to the little bar to cool our heels and flesh out the details. At the table happened to be a colleague of ours from the Orlando office, Mike Smith. As we discussed the book, I bought Mike a beer and asked him if he would do the tech edit of the Data Guard chapter, as he is the primary Data Guard resource in Oracle Support. He amiably agreed. After about three or four more pints, I asked him if he'd write the Data Guard chapter. He amiably agreed. The surprising part, really, is that when I asked him after he sobered up, he still said yes. Mike went on to not only write the Data Guard chapter in this book, but put in long hours doing the 10*g* testing that it required, and reading other chapters for me, and in general acting like the best damn guy a person could have the opportunity to work with. My deepest gratitude must go out to Mike for his fortitude on this project.

A book of this scope isn't written by two or even three people. They are just compilers of information that comes from a hundred different sources. Awards for excellence in technical assistance go to John Sobecki for getting me out of Linux jams; Kerry O'Brien and Mark Richwine for Linux and Solaris bail-outs; Ed Magoffin for teching my Streams chapter; Bill Burton for teching Mike's Data Guard chapter; Matt Arrocha, for being my second pair of RMAN eyes; Tammy Bednar for reviewing both the RMAN and Flashback bits; Martin Ingram and Terri Beckleheimer for Enterprise Manager help; and, of course, Mike Smith, not just for writing a better Data Guard chapter than I ever could have, but also for providing all kinds of installation and configuration help with 10*g*.

Outside of the technical arena, support came in many forms. I must thank my good friend and mentor Martin Ingram for his continual support and encouragement. Since I have known him, Martin has been nothing short of the best kind of friend to me and my family.

I need to thank my Kansas City support network: for last-minute babysitting and other care of my wife and daughter, thanks goes to Clare and Anne. Without them, this book would still be half done. I want to thank Alex for Sunday brunch and dinners out. And thanks to the entire Flemington clan for making this place feel like home to an imported Westerner.

I must extend my gratitude to my Colorado support network: Martin, Tonja, and Tucker in Colorado Springs, along with Molly Gross, Ed Magoffin, Bill Davis, and John and Rhonda Sobecki; in Denver, Brennan and Courtney Dodson; in Fort Collins, Eric, Airica, and the new little Aiden. Good friends are hard to find, and geography is the least of my concerns.

Finally, I must thank my unbelievable wife, Beth. This is the second time I have undertaken one of these books while she was pregnant, which is telling if you consider I only have two children. She never hesitated when I approached her about it, and she has been my greatest fan and most ardent supporter through the entire process.

I must defer all praise to her for providing me an opportunity to write yet another book she'll never read. Such a leap of faith is startling to me at times.

Scott:

This book would not have been possible without the never-ending support of my wife, Tricia. She has faithfully kept our family on course, through the long hours, days, weeks, and months it has taken to complete this book, and put many other things on hold as well while awaiting its completion. Tricia is the rock in my life, and nothing would be possible without her support. I also want to thank my wonderful children, Erica, Amanda, and Mitchell, for putting up with me as I was ignoring them, and yet still always being there for me, unquestioning. I love you guys. Each passing day reminds me of how important family is in so many ways— and so I also want to thank my own parents and Tricia's parents and our extended families for always being so supportive of us.

Aside from my family, I want to also thank Matt Hart, who took the lead on this project and made it happen, dragging me kicking and screaming behind him. Matt is a tireless individual with an insatiable appetite for knowledge, which I greatly admire. Congratulations to Matt, his wife, Beth, and their daughter, Lily, on the new addition to their family, Thomas, who was born on March 13, 2004, before the ink on this project was barely dry. In addition, thanks to Michael Smith for his outstanding contributions in the Data Guard arena. Mike is the quintessential authority on Data Guard, as well as having expertise in so many other areas, and we could not have found a better choice for filling that role. Also, thanks to Soumendra Paik, Ed Magoffin, and Bill Burton for their roles in doing the technical reviews for the chapters in this book. Their timely and crucial input has been invaluable in the making of this book. Over the years, many other people at Oracle have contributed to my growth and knowledge, as well as contributing to my keeping my sanity. Those folks include friends and colleagues Joe Donnelly, Peter Trent, Steve Correia, Dan Braddock, George Angster, and many others. In addition, members of my own management staff, including Chip Brown, Martin Ingram, Lauren Verno, Cathy Scully, and Andy Taylor have provided invaluable support to this project and others. Thank you for that support.

Along the lines of making this book happen, we are also forever indebted to Lisa McClain for again having faith in us to do this. Thank you, Lisa, for helping us to put this all together. In addition, thanks to Athena Honore, Jenny Malnick, Dennis Weaver, and all the folks at Osborne. Thank you for your patience, your gentle prodding and timely work, and advice.

Finally, a closing word for Horatio, the inspiration behind it all. Late nights working on this tome were made more bearable by thoughts of Horatio, slaving away at his own job, all the while giving us respite from our own daily grind. Horatio gave us the chance to laugh at ourselves, and at the same time put things in perspective in our own lives. He was the quintessential HA DBA in training, yet Horatio moved on before he ever earned his stripes. Hats off to all the Horatios out there, and know that we are with you in your struggles. Alas, poor Horatio—a fellow of infinite jest, of most excellent fancy. We barely knew him.

Introduction

igh Availability, as a term bandied about among database administrators, has been around for many years and can be used in all kinds of situations to describe nearly anything that involves keeping your business up and running, every minute of every day. But High Availability (HA) as a generally recognizable set of technologies and practices has undergone a radical transformation over the past few years. Gone may be the dot com buzz and the e-business hype, but a lasting legacy remains from the salad days of the fin de siecle: your systems should be available 24 hours a day, 7 days a week.

The parameters surrounding this simple principle are wide and complex, but the reality is simple: availability is defined, ultimately, by end users of your systems who have no notion of what HA requires, but simply want to buy books at midnight, or check their 401(k) over the weekend, or run financial intelligence reports at the end of every month. What that means is that any true availability solution must encompass the entire technology stack, from the database to the application server to the network. This requires the cooperation of nearly every aspect of a company's technology staff.

Gone, of course, are the oversized budgets to make availability happen at any cost, and technology providers and solution peddlers have gone out of their way to offer the modern DBA and the modern System Administrator affordable options in the epic battle against the enemies of uptime: hardware failure, database corruption, user error, even natural disasters. Most of these modern solutions usually come in the form of proprietary hardware configurations or costly software add-ons to systems you already have in place. And, honestly, most of them are pitched to a System Administrator audience. But High Availability for the database remains a problem best tackled by the database administrator, who is ultimately responsible for the well-being of the data.

What Is High Availability?

Like it or not, availability is more and more the rule, not the exception. As a database administrator, HA refers to a number of related issues that must be planned and prepared for:

- Uptime
- Performance
- Disasters
- Manageability

Uptime literally refers to the fact that the database must be assumed to stay open around the clock. Database maintenance and administration has to occur on the fly, with no down windows.

A slow database is an unavailable database. Performance must be accounted for at all times, and performance increases must be accessible without downtime. This means scaling up, scaling out, and reorganizing in-flight.

Whether man-made or of the natural type, disasters happen and must be taken into account when preparing a database for production go-live. This means having a fail-over system in case of complete system loss, but it also means having the technologies in place that help recover from the more minor tragedies: user errors, bad memory, or database corruption.

If a HA solution is overly complex, it can become too top-heavy and collapse in upon itself and the management costs can outweigh the benefits of availability. So manageability must be considered a critical component of HA.

A DBA-Centric Approach to Availability

Which brings us to the book you hold in your hands. We have written this book based on what can be called a DBA-centric approach to availability. We concentrate on explaining technologies and practices common to the a database administrator, and that cover database uptime, database performance, and disaster planning.

This is not to say that we ignore hardware or application needs entirely; the web of HA is too interwoven for that. But a database-centered approach reveals many cost-effective approaches to availability that take into account the specific requirements and unique challenges presented by an enterprise-level relational database system. We want to help you in the transformation from a DBA to the HADBA: the High Availability Database Administrator.

Leverage What You Have

Oracle provides a wide spectrum of HA technologies built in to the core RDBMS that you already use. What we offer in this book is a guide to leveraging those technologies that you have in your toolkit already but may not be using yet. While there are a multitude of HA options on the market, if you already paid for your Oracle license, there's a vested interested in exploring how much of the base functionality you can employ before widening your scope of inquiry.

Granted, there is a certain "six or half dozen" argument that can be made: Oracle provides solutions that cost licensing fees, so money saved on hardware solutions might just be redirected. But we feel that leveraging database-centric HA technologies provides the most cost-effective approach to HA, as well as making the tech stack manageable by database administrators.

Integration Oriented

Besides leveraging technologies already waiting at your fingertips, the DBA-centric approach to HA provides more opportunities to focus on the integration of multiple aspects of availability, instead of dealing with them in isolation. This book focuses on explaining the individual HA technologies separately, so that you can pick and choose that that fit your needs.

But we also emphasize the fully integrated package that can be provided by a database-centric HA strategy. We put Real Applications Cluster (RAC) and Data Guard together and discuss the unique challenges provided by this solution. We put a media backup strategy into the mix as well, showing how Recovery Manager (RMAN) and RAC and Data Guard work together to provide a full solution. We put Oracle Flashback technologies together with Data Guard so that you can leverage a database flashback quickly to reinstantiate after failover. The list goes on and on. When you focus on database availability tools, the challenges of integration quickly disappear.

Welcome to "The Grid"...

If you haven't been barraged by the publicity yet, you should probably know that the little "g" in Oracle Database 10g stands for "grid." Grid Computing is a philosophy of computing that posits, simply, that computing needs should operate on the same principle as utility grids. You do not know where your electricity comes from, or how it is managed; all you know is that you can plug your appliances in and you get as much electricity as you need, from a single lamp to an entire house of washers, dryers, and water heaters. Your computing needs should be the same: you plug in to the grid and you get your computational needs, your information needs, your application needs. You get as much as you need and do not worry where the computers are or how it is managed.

Such a grid would be based, of course, on the kind of availability that we have come to expect from the utility grid. When the electricity grid goes down, even for a single day, it makes headlines all over the country *because it only happens every 30 years or so.* Thus, for Grid Computing, one of the foundational pillars must be high availability.

...And Then Back to Reality

For the Grid to become a reality, there are imminent challenges to uptime, and database administrators need existing solutions. The Grid guides us, but business dictates our actions. And to that end Oracle Database 10*g* provides real solutions for current availability challenges. In all actuality, these solutions are a natural evolution of concepts and technologies that Oracle has been building toward since the release of Oracle8*i*. While we have written a book that discusses how to use Oracle Database 10*g*, many of the options are available in Oracle9*i* or earlier. Rest assured, we are now officially done writing about "The Grid."

What's Inside This Book

This book is specifically about the Oracle technologies that are provided with the Oracle RDBMS to help achieve a highly available database. We have grouped these technologies into four sections:

- General Availability

- Real Application Clusters

- Disaster Planning and Recovery

- Distributed Database Solutions

General Availability

General Availability refers to those features and techniques that encompass basic database configuration and administration: init.ora parameters, memory tuning, datafile storage, database object reorganization, and others immediately available to you in your existing Oracle Database 10*g* database.

We begin in Chapter 1, "Oracle and Availability: Illustrated Downtime Scenarios," by going through a hypothetical series of downtime situations that happen to a fictional company that sells woodscrews. With each downtime scenario we offer a box that directs you to the technology that would assist the DBA for that particular problem. This is a way for us to show how the technologies discussed in Chapters 2–11 (the rest of the book) apply to very real uptime challenges. We also introduce the embarrassingly simple database tables that will be used throughout the book to illustrate examples of high availability database administration.

We embark on the journey into the world of dba-centric availability in Chapter 2, "RDBMS Features for Availability." Chapter 2 is dedicated to the Oracle options you can currently find hiding in the woodwork of your databases: dynamic parameter modifications, architectural availability options such as partitions and materialized views, logminer, and transportable tablespaces. We spend time discussing the benefits of Oracle's reworked Enterprise Manager suite, a one-stop interface meant to make your life easier.

Chapter 3, "Tuning Your Database for Availability," is a more in-depth look at tuning a database for maximum uptime. This includes a look at memory considerations for the database and utilizing the new Automatic Storage Management to get better use out of available disk space while minimizing the management of disk resources. We also spend time discussing online database performance tuning, including usage of the new Automatic Workload Repository—the offshoot of the existing Statspack software.

Real Application Clusters (RAC)

Part 2 is dedicated in its entirety to the setup, configuration, and administration of Real Application Clusters (RAC). The centerpiece of Oracle's availability offerings, RAC provides a clustering solution that found its footing in Oracle9*i* and now mushrooms into the next generation of enterprise database computing in Oracle Database 10*g*.

Chapter 4, "RAC Setup and Configuration," is the definitive guide to RAC Setup, starting with a beginner's guide to the basic architecture, as well as a hands-on lab for configuring a low-cost test cluster to allow you to get your hands dirty with minimal investment. It covers moving through the OS setup, including the setup of Oracle's Cluster File System, as well as raw files. The database configuration is coded step by step for quick RAC implementations, including the options for how to configure the archive logs.

Chapter 5, "Database Administration in a RAC Environment," delves deeper into the RAC stack, discussing the finer points of administration and upkeep unique to clustered databases. A closer look at RAC-specific redo and undo processing can be found here. This chapter talks to such availability requisites as rolling patch upgrades, dropping nodes, and adding nodes.

Chapter 6, "Utility Computing: Applications as Services," is dedicated to the implementation of services in a RAC environment—viewing applications as Services— a first step toward utility computing. The concepts of services are discussed along with the more important steps for configuration and rollout: services and work distribution.

Disaster Planning and Recovery

Part 3 deals with those technologies provided to minimize downtime due to unforeseen problems. This can be complete site loss due to natural disaster or power outage, or a smaller outage due to a burned-out hard drive or memory failure. Problems can also come in the form of user error: incorrect updates, logical application errors, or dropped tables. In the case of these types of problems, the goal must always be to have prepared successfully, and then have all the pieces in place to deal with different types of disasters appropriately.

Chapter 7, "Oracle Data Guard: Surviving the Disaster," is an extensive look at the configuration and administration of Oracle's most frequently overlooked feature: Data Guard. Provided as a complete disaster recovery solution, Data Guard provides a rich toolkit for using a database's existing architecture to mirror a complete database to another site. Combined with RAC and the new Flashback Recovery, Data Guard is a superior business continuity tool at times of total site loss or blackout.

Chapter 8, "Backup and Recovery for High-Availability Environments," takes us through the usage of Oracle's server managed recovery utility, RMAN, and how the usage of RMAN for media backups provides a necessary partner to RAC and Data Guard in the fight against down-time. Topics include a primer on RMAN configuration and usage, Enterprise Manager integration, new Oracle Database 10*g* features such as the Flashback Recovery Area, and performing backups and recoveries when required. Advanced topics include the integration of RMAN into RAC clusters, and using RMAN to help build Data Guard environments.

Chapter 9, "Oracle Flashback: Surviving User-Induced Trauma," focuses entirely on the new suite of technologies that Oracle collectively refers to as "Flashback Recovery." This suite has been developed to provide minimal loss of time and data during those most dreaded of accidents: human error. Flashback Recovery comes in four related types: Flashback Query (as seen in Oracle9*i*), Flashback Transaction, Flashback Drop (for undoing a dropped object), and Flashback Database.

Distributed Database Solutions

In the brief Part 4, we discuss the benefits of exploring a distributed database solution to provide availability. In certain environments it often proves most useful to forego single-site availability and instead use a software solution to push tables to multiple sites, so that everyone sees the same table locally. This act of distributing database operations across a multitude of independent databases can provide a powerful availability solution with fringe benefits that match business requirements for independent site data.

Chapter 10, "Oracle Streams for High Availability," discusses Oracle Streams, a queue-based solution that provides a way to stream updates at independent sites to each other. Here we provide an overview, focusing on the use of Streams to provide a High Availability solution, as well as for Replication of Replica Databases.

Chapter 11, "Oracle Net Configuration for Failover," is a brief discussion of Network Configuration at the Oracle listener for various availability solutions. This includes setting up the listener for Transparent Application Failover (TAF), RAC, Data Guard, and Streams.

HA Workshops

This book is organized in such a way as to provide a conceptual understanding of how the Oracle High Availability technologies work. We also strive to provide a real-world scenario in which to place the functionality of these integrated offerings so that you can see the worth demonstrated.

There's more than a fair amount of how-to, step-by-step instructions that walk through configuration and setup of different products. As readers of technical books ourselves, we know that these tried-and-tested cookbook recipes can be invaluable when a configuration is not something you run through every day. We also understand that reading for comprehension and understanding is not always the use of a good book. Sometimes you just need the step-by-step instructions.

That is why we have instituted the "HA Workshops" in this book. Here's how it works: Whenever we get to a point where we step through instructions to achieve a certain end, such as transporting a tablespace from a database on Solaris to a database on Linux, we will break out the instructions into a box with the heading "HA Workshop." When you see this, you will know that the following steps have been freed of any conceptual explanation and will get you through the process.

So that you can access the HA Workshops quickly and easily, when you need them, every one in the book has been catalogued with its starting page number in the section at the beginning of this book entitled "Table of Contents: At a Glance." So, after you read this book cover to cover and have found what you need, you can later return to the configuration steps for a quick guide to setup, configuration, or administration technique.

A Note on Worked Examples

When we began to put this book together, we took a look at the breadth of topics involved and, after much hand-wringing, made a touch decision: all examples that we will work for this book have been done on Linux.

We understand that, more likely than not, your production system may not be on Linux, and some of the configuration for high availability include OS-specific steps, particularly when it comes to using RAC with a third-party clusterware product.

A couple of things guided our thinking: first, we are emphasizing a database-centric view of availability, and the strong majority of the technology we discuss in this book act identical on all operating systems. So the code is portable, and is not affected by our test environment.

Second, many of the aspects of an OS-specific configuration can be eliminated through usage of Oracle-provided add-ons: Oracle Cluster File System for RAC, Automated Storage Management for volume management, and RMAN for media backups.

Third, we wanted to write a book that you can take into a small testing environment, that has been configured on the cheap to do proof-of-concept on some of the availability techniques in this book. For such environments, it only makes sense to use a cost-sensitive OS such as Linux, running on commodity-priced hardware. It also means that you can teach yourself how to use complex enterprise-computing concepts in the basement of your own home. Being self-taught DBAs ourselves, we understand the value of tinkering for comprehension.

Finally, Linux is emerging as an operating system that large enterprises are taking seriously as the strategic platform of the future. This includes Oracle Corporation, which sees low-priced operating systems and commodity-priced hardware as the key that will unlock the potential of grid computing and make high availability a reality for all databases.

A Note, Then, on Linux Versions

Oracle Database 10*g* does not work on all versions of Linux. While this seems unfortunate at first glance, the reality is such that the Linux kernel has a high degree of volatility due to its open source nature. To avoid unsupportable kernel upgrades, Oracle worked with the major Linux distribution providers to get an Enterprise Linux developed that can be guaranteed to work with Oracle Database 10*g*.

Oracle is perhaps most cozy with Red Hat, which has two products that Oracle Database 10*g* is supported on: Red Hat Advanced Server 2.1 and Red Hat Enterprise Linux 3.0. In fact, if you have a registered copy of these operating systems and a licensed copy of Oracle, you can get OS support for the Red Hat product from Oracle.

Oracle is also supported on UnitedLinux 1.0, an enterprise-ready Linux that comes from a collaboration between SuSe, Turbo, and other distributors. However, Oracle does not provide OS support for United Linux.

We worked our examples on Red Hat Enterprise Linux 3.0. While it costs a bit more to purchase even the low-end RHEL, we recommend it. While you may be able to get Oracle to work on non-supported distributions, it will take more work, and you will be laboring alone.

Get Ready for Rock-Solid Availability

We are done with the introductions, so it's time to discover the power of a DBA-centric approach to High Availability. The tech stack is often complex, and you will have a few setbacks, but the results will be impressive and worth all the effort. Happy tinkering!

PART
I

Logical Availability

CHAPTER
1

Oracle and Availability: Illustrated Downtime Scenarios

s you have already discovered, or perhaps are about to discover, maintaining the high-availability database is a tricky prospect. There are hundreds of possible sources of downtime hiding in the crooks and crannies of your enterprise. Many outage situations cascade into each other, where an attempt to resolve a problem creates another outage and quickly spirals further and further out of control. But almost all downtime scenarios can be prevented with careful planning or swift corrective action.

Throughout this book, we discuss numerous technologies that prevent or drastically reduce different database outages. But what are these downtime scenarios? Which possible outages can you protect yourself against? In order to illustrate the various types of situations that threaten the availability of your database, we will illustrate various database problems that can be prevented using the technologies outlined in this book. We have typically provided a worst-case scenario, but we wanted to place the high-availability technologies in Chapters 2 through 11 in a real-world context prior to exploring the configuration and administration of these technologies.

After each downtime scenario, a text box will describe which piece of technology could be employed to prevent the outage, or to recover from it quickly. If you are not interested in reading through the situations, you can skim through this chapter and just look for the boxes. The boxes provide a road map to the available technologies that are discussed in the rest of this book.

Horatio's Woodscrews

For the situations in this chapter, and for the workshops and examples throughout the book, we will use the database from the company Horatio's Woodscrews, Inc. This is a fictitious company that sells…well…woodscrews. This company has a primary database that holds millions of records concerning woodscrews, woodscrew inventory, and woodscrew orders. The following is the code to create the application owner in the oracle database, along with the three primary tables: Woodscrew, woodscrew_inventory, and woodscrew_orders. These tables will be used throughout the book for all examples, so you might want to make note of this information. After building the tables, a few rows are added so we can manipulate them for labs, like this:

```
create tablespace ws_app_data datafile
'/u01/product/oracle/oradata/orcl/ws_app_data01.dbf' size 100m;
create tablespace ws_app_idx datafile
'/u01/product/oracle/oradata/orcl/ws_app_idx01.dbf' size 100m;

create user ws_app identified by ws_app
default tablespace ws_app_data
temporary tablespace temp;

grant connect, resource to ws_app;
connect ws_app/ws_app;
```

```
create table woodscrew (
scr_id          number not null,
manufactr_id    varchar2(20) not null,
scr_type        varchar2(20),
thread_cnt      number,
length          number,
head_config     varchar2(20),
constraint pk_woodscrew primary key (scr_id, manufactr_id)
using index tablespace ws_app_idx);

create index woodscrew_identity
   on woodscrew(scr_type, thread_cnt, length, head_config)
tablespace ws_app_idx;

create table woodscrew_inventory (
scr_id          number not null,
manufactr_id    varchar2(20) not null,
warehouse_id    number not null,
region          varchar2(20),
count           number,
lot_price     number);

create table woodscrew_orders (
ord_id          number not null,
ord_date        date,
cust_id         number not null,
scr_id          number not null,
ord_cnt         number,
warehouse_id    number not null,
region          varchar2(20),
constraint pk_wdscr_orders primary key (ord_id, ord_date)
using index tablespace ws_app_idx);

---- Now, add rows to the tables.

insert into woodscrew values (
1000, 'Tommy Hardware', 'Finish', 30, 1.5, 'Phillips');
insert into woodscrew values (
1000, 'Balaji Parts, Inc.', 'Finish', 30, 1.5, 'Phillips');
insert into woodscrew values (
1001, 'Tommy Hardware', 'Finish', 30, 1, 'Phillips');
insert into woodscrew values (
1001, 'Balaji Parts, Inc.', 'Finish', 30, 1, 'Phillips');
insert into woodscrew values (
1002, 'Tommy Hardware', 'Finish', 20, 1.5, 'Phillips');
insert into woodscrew values (
1002, 'Balaji Parts, Inc.', 'Finish', 20, 1.5, 'Phillips');
insert into woodscrew values (
1003, 'Tommy Hardware', 'Finish', 20, 1, 'Phillips');
```

```
insert into woodscrew values (
1003, 'Balaji Parts, Inc.', 'Finish', 20, 1, 'Phillips');
insert into woodscrew values (
1004, 'Tommy Hardware', 'Finish', 30, 2, 'Phillips');
insert into woodscrew values (
1004, 'Balaji Parts, Inc.', 'Finish', 30, 2, 'Phillips');
insert into woodscrew values (
1005, 'Tommy Hardware', 'Finish', 20, 2, 'Phillips');
insert into woodscrew values (
1005, 'Balaji Parts, Inc.', 'Finish', 20, 2, 'Phillips');

insert into woodscrew_inventory values (
1000, 'Tommy Hardware', 200, 'NORTHEAST', 3000000, .01);
insert into woodscrew_inventory values (
1000, 'Tommy Hardware', 350, 'SOUTHWEST', 1000000, .01);
insert into woodscrew_inventory values (
1000, 'Balaji Parts, Inc.', 450, 'NORTHWEST', 1500000, .015);
insert into woodscrew_inventory values (
1005, 'Balaji Parts, Inc.', 450, 'NORTHWEST', 1700000, .017);

insert into woodscrew_orders values (
20202, '2003-09-22 00:02:02', 2001, 1000, 20000, 64114, 'NORTHEAST');
insert into woodscrew_orders values (
20203, '2003-09-22 00:02:04', 2001, 1001, 10000, 64114, 'NORTHEAST');
insert into woodscrew_orders values (
20204, '2003-09-22 00:02:06', 2002, 1002, 10000, 64114, 'NORTHWEST');
insert into woodscrew_orders values (
20205, '2003-09-22 00:02:08', 2002, 1003, 30000, 64114, 'NORTHWEST');
insert into woodscrew_orders values (
20206, '2003-10-04 00:02:12', 2002, 1004, 10000, 80903, 'SOUTHWEST');
insert into woodscrew_orders values (
20207, '2003-10-04 00:02:14', 2001, 1003, 20000, 80903, 'SOUTHWEST');
insert into woodscrew_orders values (
20208, '2003-10-04 00:02:16', 2002, 1002, 30000, 64114, 'SOUTHWEST');
insert into woodscrew_orders values (
20209, '2003-10-04 00:02:18', 2003, 1001, 40000, 90210, 'NORTHWEST');
insert into woodscrew_orders values (
20210, '2003-11-04 00:02:20', 2005, 1000, 10000, 83401, 'SOUTHEAST');
insert into woodscrew_orders values (
20211, '2003-11-04 00:02:22', 2002, 1005, 10000, 83401, 'SOUTHEAST');
insert into woodscrew_orders values (
20212, '2003-11-04 00:02:24', 2001, 1004, 10000, 64114, 'NORTHEAST');
insert into woodscrew_orders values (
20213, '2003-11-04 00:02:26', 2003, 1003, 10000, 64114, 'NORTHEAST');
insert into woodscrew_orders values (
20214, '2003-12-04 00:02:28', 2002, 1001, 20000, 64114, 'SOUTHEAST');
insert into woodscrew_orders values (
20215, '2003-12-04 00:02:30', 2001, 1000, 10000, 80903, 'NORTHWEST');
insert into woodscrew_orders values (
```

```
20216, '2003-12-04 00:02:32', 2005, 1001, 50000, 80903, 'SOUTHWEST');
insert into woodscrew_orders values (
20217, '2003-12-04 00:02:34', 2003, 1003, 70000, 90210, 'SOUTHWEST');
commit;
```

User-Defined Availability

Sometimes database availability is not defined by the database administrator. Even if the DBA can connect to the database and select against tables, users may not be having the same experience from their application.

Take the example of Horatio's Woodscrews. Due to massive transaction processing that occurs over the course of the day against the woodscrew_orders table, thousands of new rows could be added over the course of a day. When the CEO goes to check on his reports which show how many woodscrews are being sold, and to which customers, the report is creating an ad hoc SQL query against the entire table. Because of the amount of data, and the simplistic data design, these queries might not return in what the CEO envisions as a reasonable amount of time. The DBA of the company is inundated with uncomfortable calls from impatient executives wondering why the database is "down."

The CEO has a button on his desktop application, see, that says nothing more than woodscrew_orders_by_customer. He has no interest in hearing about how long-running queries against massive amounts of data might take a little longer than his expectations. He just wants the report to be available.

Test and Development Availability

Just as with CEOs demanding faster reports, sometimes availability is defined more by a human resource issue than actual data availability. At Horatio's Woodscrews, they run all their production systems on Solaris, but are investigating Linux as an alternative. The first step of the investigation is to set up the test and development shop with Linux servers, and then move a copy of production data to the new Linux servers for application testing.

Partitioning, mviews, and Index-Organized-Tables

Sometimes availability has as much to do with user perception as it does with database reality. When upper management complains, even brand new DBAs must take measures to improve performance for them. In this situation, the HA DBA will be best served by looking to reformulate some of the tables used by his boss, or by creating materialized views to subset the data appropriately. This is covered in Chapter 2, in the section "Materialized Views."

Cross-Platform Transportable Tablespaces

Availability isn't always about the production database, and an outage may simply be defined by "idle developers twiddling their thumbs." But a move of database information to a new platform has always been a huge undertaking involving the tried and true export and import utilities to logically extract data. However, this always came with huge resource issues at the export database.

Starting in Oracle Database 10g, Oracle has built in a means of using the Transportable Tablespace feature of the database and allowing it to transfer tablespaces across platforms. This is discussed in Chapter 2, in the section "Transportable Tablespaces."

The Linux servers arrived late in the week, and were configured with the Oracle software image over the weekend. On Monday, the development lead needs to get the data moved from the production Woodscrew database to the Linux servers. So the development lead contacts the senior DBA for the database and asks that they transition the data to the new Linux servers.

The dilemma for the DBA is that getting a read-consistent view of the Woodscrew tables is nearly impossible for long enough to get an export to complete. The only time there is a large enough window for such an operation would be the following weekend. The backups cannot be used, because they are backups of Solaris datafiles. But if they wait for the weekend, the development team will sit idle all week on a project that has imminent deadlines. How can they get the data moved across platforms in an expedient way?

Cyclical Database Resource Requirements

User needs often cycle over the course of time, based on business needs, such that some users will not find the database to be inaccessible until there is a massive amount of activity in a certain area, and then suddenly there are not enough resources.

Accounts Receivable, at Horatio's Woodscrews, has this problem. As the end of each month comes to a close, they have to close out the previous month's accounts and run massive reports on the status of all opening and closing accounts. This month-end processing sends the database processing needs of the AR department through the roof—but only for a week or so, before it settles back into a more routine usage pattern.

> ## Use Services to Allocate Workloads to Higher Priority Applications
>
> The concept of using different services for different applications in Oracle Database 10g can allow the DBA to set up differing resource limits and thresholds for different applications. Those thresholds can be modified easily using the Resource Manager, allowing different limits to apply to applications at different times. So, at the start of each month, the reporting group can get more resources than at other times during the month, the paycheck group gets month-end, and the orders group gets an annual bump in resource allocation. By combining services and real application clusters, different applications can be allowed access to a differing number of nodes, so that higher priority applications can scale up faster when needed. Services are discussed in more detail in Chapter 6.

At the same time, Human Resources typically finds its peak at the lead-up to the end of the month, as it processes employee hours, salaries, and payments. They will need the most resources, then, at a different time than the AR department.

The reporting of these two groups always affects the Order Entry group, as they have a relatively steady database resource usage pattern over the entire course of the month. However, as the summer approaches, the hardware stores begin to increase the stock of woodscrews, and so orders will steadily increase as the summer approaches, and then steadily decrease as weather cools.

What Reports Were Those, Exactly?

The problem with attempting to allocate the correct resources to the correct applications at the correct time of month or year is that often it is nearly impossible to get trended data on usage over time.

The DBA at Horatio's Woodscrews is faced with this dilemma. The different application groups have been complaining about the performance of their reports at different times, but the DBA has not been able to get accurate data on which problem reports or application batch processes are truly in need of more resources. He's been reading up on his performance tuning techniques, but the month is coming to an end again, and he can already hear his pager beginning to beep.

> **Use AWR and ADDM to Quickly Identify
> and Resolve Bottlenecks**
> With Oracle Database 10g, the Automatic Workload Repository (AWR) collects
> performance information every hour, and stores it in the Workload Repository for
> a week so that the HA DBA can go back and review historical information and
> past performance issues. In addition, baselines can be maintained indefinitely, so
> that the HA DBA can compare problem periods to points in the past when things
> were running smoothly. The Automatic Database Diagnostic Monitor, or ADDM,
> runs at the end of every AWR report period and proactively reports on any
> discovered problems, as well as recommending solutions or running additional
> tuning advisors. We discuss this in more detail in Chapter 3.

Out of Space in the Woodscrew Tablespace

Availability can be significantly hampered by routine database management
tasks. Take something as straightforward as datafile management. Where
the files reside, how big they are, and on what disks, can lead to significant
availability problems.

Horatio's Woodscrew database recently ran out of disk space while
autoextending a datafile in the WS_APP_DATA tablespace. They had turned
autoextend on so that they would not have to be faced with disk management.
But business has been booming, and the orders and customer tables are
growing dramatically. In addition, new reports are being generated by upper
management looking to mine the data for more edge in the marketplace. In a
word, the single datafile on a single disk volume has begun to fall short of
their needs. They recently had disk problems, and the system administrator
is reporting excessive I/O on WS_APP_DATA datafiles. A disk burnout is
imminent.

However, reorganizing the datafiles across new disk volumes not only
means an explicit investigation into which tables, exactly, are getting hit the
hardest, but also the outage that would be required while the tablespace is
reorganized across new datafiles on new volumes. Such a massive undertaking
could take days.

Use ASM to Simplify Disk and File Management
In Oracle Database 10g, automatic storage management, or ASM, greatly
simplifies file management by removing the burden of laying out files to avoid
hot spots, and also by simplifying file creation and sizing. ASM is a volume
manager for Oracle files, which gives the ability to stripe and mirror files with
very little effort on the part of the DBA or the sysadmin. In addition, ASM is
constantly monitoring for I/O hot spots, and it will automatically direct reads
of allocation units or segments to disks that are least heavily used, to avoid
the occurrence of hot spots and maintain I/O performance. Aside from this,
if a disk fails, or if a new disk is added to an ASM disk group, ASM will
automatically rebalance the existing files, to maintain the distribution of I/O.
ASM will be discussed in more detail in Chapter 3.

Downtime for Hardware Fixes

Database availability can be taken out of the hands of the DBA when an outage is
related to a hardware problem on the database server. At Horatio's Woodscrews,
they have had users complaining about losing their connection to the database
intermittently. The DBA could find nothing wrong with their setup, but the system
administrator ran some diagnostics that pointed to a flaky network interface card.
The solution is to replace the network card as soon as possible. Doing so means
taking the database down, shutting down the entire server, and replacing the card.
With month-end reports running around the clock in order to complete on time,
shutting down the database will mean that the reports will have to wait until after
the database comes back up.

RAC Clusters Mask Problems Involving a Single Node
With Real Application Clusters, multiple nodes are accessing the database at the
same time. As such, if a node fails due to hardware or operating system problems,
that node can be taken offline and repaired while users are still accessing the
database through the remaining nodes in the cluster. Once repaired, the node can
be restarted and will rejoin the cluster automatically, making the instance again
available to users. We discuss the setup and configuration of a RAC cluster in
Chapter 4.

Transparent Application Failover (TAF) Allows Queries to Be Failed Over to Another Node and Restarted Automatically
With Real Application Clusters and transparent application failover, should an instance on one node crash, it is possible for users connected to that instance to automatically fail over to one of the remaining nodes in the cluster, and have queries be restarted—and then to continue on uninterrupted. This is discussed in Chapter 11.

Restarting Long-Running Transactions

In the event of some kind of instance outage, there will inevitably be transactions that will stop, and then have to be restarted manually. This can lead to significant shortcomings in time-sensitive reporting and processing.

At Horatio's Woodscrews, the developers that were sitting idle due to the Linux servers having no data decided to try and get a little work done by connecting to the production database to review some of the database structure. However, one of the developers had installed a beta version of the ODBC drivers. When this ODBC driver connected to the production database, it caused a heap corruption that resulted in an ORA-600. The ORA-600 caused the database to crash.

Just like that, all the long-running reports that had been generated by the Accounts Receivable teams began to receive the error ORA-3113 "End-of-File on Communication." The DBA's pager started to beep, and beep, and beep. He was able to restart the database, but all of the long-running transactions had to be restarted.

Slow Crash Recovery

Even after the DBA restarted the database, it seemed to be hung at the startup command. There were no errors, but when he checked the alert log, he noted that the last line indicated the database was performing instance recovery (also known as crash recovery). This recovery must be done to recover any changes in the redo logs that have not been committed to the datafiles. Depending on the size of the redo logs, and the frequency of checkpoints, this can take a considerable amount of time. When there is a lot of pressure to make a database available as quickly as possible, waiting on a poorly tuned crash recovery session can be excruciating.

RAC Handles Instance Recovery from Surviving Nodes
With Real Application Clusters, should an instance that is part of the cluster crash, the instance recovery is handled immediately by one of the surviving instances in the cluster. We discuss this in Chapter 5. In addition, Oracle10g has, through Enterprise Manager, a new feature called the Redo Log Advisor, which will allow you to automatically tune redo logs so that checkpoints occur at a rate that allows for faster instance recovery in the event of a crash. This is discussed in Chapter 3.

Dealing with Block Corruption (ORA 1578)

At Horatio's Woodscrews, the system administrators finally installed the new network card. With the system down, they took the opportunity to install new drivers for their storage area network (SAN) device. Then they contacted the DBA to let him know he could start the database.

The DBA starts the database, and begins to run through the system checks to make sure all the applications will start up correctly. Then he initiates all the reports that failed because of the shutdown. Everything seems to be going smoothly, until he notices that one of the reports has an error:

```
ORA-1578: ORACLE data block corrupted (file # 121, block # 68)
```

As the DBA began to investigate the problem, the system administrators called him back: the new SAN driver is causing problems, and he should shut down the database immediately. But the damage has already been done—database corruption.

But there is only one corrupt block, in the WS_APP_DATA01.DBF file. Just one block out of thousands of perfectly good blocks. With datablock corruption, the solution to the problem is to restore the entire datafile from backup, and then apply archivelogs to recover the file. Because the datafile contains parts of the Woodscrew, woodscrew_orders, and woodscrew_inventory tables, these objects will be offline until the file can be restored and recovered. The brief outage for the hardware fix now has been extended to include the restore of a file from backup, and then the application of the archivelogs to that file. The tablespace will not be available until recovery completes.

**Recovery Manager (RMAN) Provides
Media Recovery of Data Blocks**
When RMAN is utilized for backups, you can use those backups to restore a
single block from the last good backup, and then perform media recovery on
that block (apply archive log changes, if there are any). You can do it for a
single block or for a list of corrupt blocks, and the tablespace stays online
while you do recovery. In fact, the corrupt table stays online, too. We discuss
this in Chapter 8.

Waiting for the File to Restore from Tape

For our poor DBA at Horatio's Woodscrews, it only gets worse. He needs to restore
the file WS_APP_DATA01.DBF from backup and then perform media recovery
using archivelogs. He contacts the backup administrator and asks that the file be
restored from tape.

After some shuffling around, the backup administrator finds the last
backup and begins the tape restore. Because of the size of the file, this will
take a few hours to get the file queued over the network from the tape jukebox
to the database server. The DBA asks if there are any backups of the file on
disk, knowing that there is plenty of unused space on the new SAN that could
be used for disk backup of important files. The backup administrator just runs
the tape servers, though, and knows nothing about the SAN. That's a different
department.

Avoid Long Tape Restores with RMAN Flashback Recovery Area
Using new RMAN functionality, you can create backup jobs that always store
at least the last full copy of the database on a disk location called the flashback
recovery area. Then, when you take the next backup, RMAN will automatically
age out the last backup, or you can set it up to move the old backups to tape
from the disk area. When you go to initiate the restore from RMAN, it knows
where the last best copy is. The restore can be instantaneous, as we can switch
out the bad file with the new file and begin applying archivelogs immediately.
We discuss this in Chapter 8.

Protect Against Node Failure with a Robust Archive Strategy
While RAC does provide a higher degree of protection against outages, you have to be careful how you configure the database so that you don't invent single points of failure. In this case, the archivelogs from Node2 are required for recovery, but Node2 is off the network temporarily. For help with archive strategies with RAC, see Chapter 5, in the section "Redo Logs and Media Recovery." Also see Chapter 8, particularly Figure 8-8.

RAC and the Single Point of Failure

The DBA for Horatio's Woodscrews is no fool. He knows that he needs to transition the data to a RAC cluster. As part of the preparation, he has configured the Sales Department's smaller database on a RAC cluster with two nodes. He set it up quickly, with minimal configuration, and it's been running smoothly for a few weeks.

However, the network configuration issues that affected the production database had also affected the Sales system. One of the nodes in the cluster was not available on the network. The DBA wasn't worried, however, because the other node was still available.

But one of the files was asking for media recovery, so the DBA issued the recovery command and it asked for an archivelog that was required for recovery. The DBA pressed ENTER to accept the default archivelog. But the media recovery session failed. He looked a little closer, and noted that the requested archivelog was on the unavailable node. Suddenly, his RAC cluster was not operational as he waited for the other node to become available so he could perform recovery.

Rewinding the Database

Perhaps the most difficult outage situations are those tricky logical errors introduced by the users themselves—when a user updates the wrong table, or updates the wrong values. These types of errors are tough to overcome because they are not perceived by the database as errors, but just another transaction. Typically, user errors do not occur in a vacuum; an erroneous update can occur alongside hundreds of correct updates. Pretty soon, the bad data is buried by thousands of additional updates. How can you fish just one of those transactions out? Can you "rewind" the database back to a previous point in time?

Use Flashback Table to Restore a Table to a Previous State
In Oracle Database 10g, Oracle introduced the ability to rewind a table to a previous state without performing point-in-time recovery. This is called Flashback Table, and it's part of the Flashback Technologies discussed in Chapter 9.

You can also use LogMiner to review transactions in the archived redo logs in order to determine where exactly the bad data was entered, as well as to retrieve the good transactions entered after the bad transaction. LogMiner is discussed in Chapter 2.

At Horatio's Woodscrews, the problem was reported by the Accounting team. As they went through their month-end processing, they began to realize that the data seemed incorrect. All the roll-up values seemed to be impossibly high, even during a good month. They could not figure out what had happened, but the data had been incorrectly entered at some point in the morning. Now, in the afternoon, they came to the DBA and asked that he "start over" all of their tables as they had looked in the morning.

The options for restoring just a few tables are limited, without rolling the entire database back to a previous point-in-time. Oracle has provided for a tablespace point-in-time recovery (TSPITR), where just a single tablespace is restored to a previous point. But that is labor-intensive, and the smallest unit that can be restored is the entire tablespace. The Accounting group does not want to redo all their work for the day, just the work in a few tables.

The Dropped Table

Like an incorrect update to the table, an inadvertently dropped table can be catastrophic. Unlike an inadvertent DML statement (insert, update, or delete), a drop cannot be explored and fixed manually. Once dropped, the table must be restored from a backup of some sort.

The DBA at Horatio's Woodscrews did this one to himself: he was trying to clean up unused objects in the production database. There were some leftover tables that had been used for testing purposes in a now-abandoned user's schema. The DBA was reviewing the objects and then dropping them to free up the extents. However, for the Woodscrew table, he put the wrong username in the DROP statement by accident, and he knew it immediately: ws_app.woodscrew had just been dropped.

Use Flashback Drop to Restore Dropped Objects
In Oracle Database 10g, as part of the Flashback Technologies, Oracle introduced Flashback Drop. Now, when an object is dropped, it is placed in a Recycle Bin, where it is stored until there is space pressure in the tablespace. Until it ages out, the object can be "undropped" in only a few moments. For more information, see Chapter 9.

The Truncated Table

Another deadly user error can be the use of TRUNCATE to remove rows of an incorrect table. With no undo generated, a truncate is permanent in a way that even a Flashback Transaction or LogMiner operation cannot assist with. Once truncated, the data is missing, and nothing can be done except to restore from a backup and then cancel recovery prior to the truncate.

　　The DBA was still trying to figure out how to restore the Woodscrew table when he was interrupted by a page. Someone in the Sales group, impatient because their cluster was down, had logged into the production database with a borrowed password. The salesperson had been trying to delete rows from a small sales table, but it was taking too long so he used TRUNCATE. But the production table he truncated had more than just rows for his region, and suddenly the woodscrew_inventory table was empty:

```
select count(*) from WS_APP.WOODSCREW_INVENTORY;
no rows selected.
```

**When There Is an Unrecoverable Operation,
Use Flashback Database**
A TRUNCATE operation can be deadly to a database, as it is not a DML operation that gets a "before image" stored in the undo segments. A Flashback Table won't be of any use. Typically, a truncate done in error requires a point-in-time recovery. In Oracle Database 10g, we can use the Flashback Database, which quickly rewinds the database back in time in a manner that does not require a media restore operation—so no waiting for all the files to come from tape. Our flashback can occur in minutes, instead of hours. See Chapter 9 for more information.

Use Oracle Streams to Replicate Data to Unique Databases on Different Operating Systems
If you've researched Oracle Advanced Replication in the past, you may have discovered that it provides a good way to share data among multiple, independent databases. But the performance could slow data processing to some degree. With Oracle Streams, replication has improved its speed dramatically and provides a way to integrate a heterogeneous OS environment into a shared data/high-availability model. For more on Streams, see Chapter 10.

Connecting Online, Identical Databases

The DBA at Horatio's Woodscrews finally found the time to move the production data from the Solaris production database to the Linux servers run by the Test and Development team. The development lead was very excited about the performance they were getting from the Linux boxes, and the application code ported with very little trouble.

In a few weeks, however, the Solaris box was simply overworked. New orders were coming in faster than ever, and the new warehouses were coming online in four new distribution areas. With all the new data, the database began to bog down. The Chief Information Officer approached the DBA and asked a simple question: how can we leverage the Linux servers for our production system? Can we start connecting the Order Entry group to the Linux database, for instance, and just keep the internal groups running against the Solaris system?

Complete and Total Disaster

Disaster struck Horatio's Woodscrews on a particularly wet spring day. Rain had been falling steadily for weeks in the city. The DBA was sleeping soundly, dreaming of data protection systems, when his pager began to beep. He called the number groggily, looking at the clock. It was the middle of the night.

A water main had busted near the Woodscrew building, and the basement had flooded. The basement held all of the database systems—the production Solaris box, the Sales RAC cluster, the test and dev servers, everything. The utility company was marking the area as a disaster area, and not letting anyone near the building.

All the servers were lost. The DBA had to think fast. Did they move the tape backups off-site, as was proposed a few months back? He could not remember, so he called the backup administrator. Did they have those old Solaris boxes they'd retired last year someplace? The DBA dialed the system administrator.

A conference call was put together in the middle of the night. Where were the archived tape backups? Were they moved to a different building? When was the last time the tapes were moved to the other location? How much data would be lost in the flood?

The questions flew around to the system administrator—Where could they find new systems to install Oracle? Would there be enough disk space without the SAN device? Should they contact the vendors to get emergency hardware shipped in?

Then the questions came to the DBA: Could we rebuild the data once the drives were salvaged from the flood? Could we hobble along on one of the older servers at the other office? How fast could he get Oracle installed, patched, and ready to start the file restore from the archive tapes?

And, finally, the ultimate question: Who's going to call the CEO and tell him what happened?

Where to Go from Here

The downtime scenarios that we have tried to illustrate in this chapter are but the tip of the iceberg. We wanted to show you that there are common, everyday situations that can be fixed using new functionality in Oracle Database 10g. Often, this is functionality that you already have at your fingertips and can leverage right now, with just a few steps that we outline in the following chapters.

We also wanted to show you some of the more disruptive events that can immobilize a database: user errors, such as a truncated table, or a hardware failure. These types of events happen less frequently, but the outage can be extremely long without careful planning that accounts for the possibility. From RAC to Flashback, careful planning and forethought will guide you through these disruptions.

Protect Yourself Against Disaster with Data Guard
Oracle Data Guard offers the most effective protection against complete site failure, with real-time data push from the primary database to the standby database. Data Guard allows you to activate an exact copy of the primary database in just a few minutes (or seconds), so that the outage is almost unnoticeable. It can be configured in many different ways to meet the business demands you may have. The standby database can be used as a reporting database, for taking backups of the production database, or even as a failover site during massive system reconfiguration at the primary site. For a complete rundown of the flexibility and usability of Oracle Data Guard, see Chapter 7.

Even less predictable, and less frequent, is the complete loss of a system due to natural disaster or site network outage. In situations where the entire database is lost and cannot be quickly restored, there are important questions that begin to circulate, and some of them have to do with who's at fault for the lack of a disaster plan. Oracle Data Guard offers one of the most advanced disaster-proofing solutions on the market.

So, now that you've explored just a few of the situations that might cause an outage, its time to explore the technologies that can prevent (or significantly reduce) those disruptive downtimes.

CHAPTER
2

RDBMS Features
for Availability

elax and get comfortable; the geeked-out turbo-powered propeller-head stuff is waiting for you later in this book. You know the goods we speak of—the tech so heady we felt compelled to put it in the book title: RAC, Data Guard, Flashback. RMAN, streams, and transparent application failover—the stuff to take your database to the next level.

But we have to cover a few of the less buzzy-sounding items first. Fact of the matter is, availability starts a long time before you get your Data Guard–protected 16-node flashback-enabled Oracle database up and running. Availability starts in the guts of your data architecture, inside the tables and indices and constraints and packages. The skeleton on which the meat of your data hangs must be built to withstand a nonstop, round-the-clock barrage of DML and query.

This chapter is dedicated to those little features inside the Oracle RDBMS that provide the groundwork for a high-availability (HA) environment. These are the features that drive your HA on a day-to-day basis, from the first day you go live. These are the features that allow you to change and morph on the fly, instead of taking massive outages to compensate for growth and (let's just admit it) shrinkage. You should note that all the internal features of the database that allow for high availability cannot possibly be covered in one chapter. What we have attempted here is a cross between a highlight reel and the standard college survey course: we hit the sexy features and provide a little depth to get your feet wet with each of them. Then, you can take what features you need to explore further and use our bibliography to research each of them further.

Enterprise Manager

Before we go any further, we need to talk about Oracle's GUI interface for the database: Oracle Enterprise Manager (EM). Enterprise Manager has been around for a long time, and if you are like most DBAs in the world, you have steadfastly avoided it as though it carried disease—which it may have at some time; the reports vary. EM has always set out to be an interface built to simplify the overwhelming duties of the DBA by consolidating all database management into a single suite of utilities that could be configured to monitor the entire enterprise. As such, EM has made some excellent selling points for itself. If you manage 100 or more databases, chances are you use EM as a point of necessity. And the visual look at database information was always a blessed reprieve from V$VIEW hunting.

But, alas, EM was always hampered by a bulky, three-tier implementation. While effective for the large-enterprise user, this stood in the way of wide adoption among the experimenting and tinkering crowd, or anyone without massive free resources. In addition to having a huge footprint, EM never matched up well against third-party add-on products that had slick interfaces and fast (read: C instead of Java) loads.

We're here to tell you, though, that EM has turned the proverbial corner. The latest version, now written almost entirely in HTML, is fast, effective, and light-footed. It's not going to win any design awards, but EM now gets the job done with little preconfiguration. And EM now leverages the built-in functionality of the Oracle RDBMS in ways that make it requisite instead of optional.

If you are wary, we understand. EM has been hampered by problems in the past, when hours could quickly disappear as you attempted to get it up and running. But it's simply too good to pass up in Oracle Database 10*g*. So much so that we are basing most of our exercises in this book on Enterprise Manager interfacing. The bottom line is that the new functionality of Oracle Database 10*g* is simple and straightforward when you use EM; when you hit everything at the command line, you are usually just reinventing the wheel, or worse, missing out on some of the best reasons to upgrade.

Oracle Database Control

The easy-to-use, light-footed version of Enterprise Manager is now referred to as Oracle Database Control. This is to differentiate the database console from the three-tier, 400-pound gorilla known as Oracle Grid Control (discussed next). Database Control comes standard when you install Enterprise Edition, and if you use the Database Configuration Assistant, it is set up without any trouble. By default, with the first database created, you can immediately connect via your web browser to Database Control on port 5500:

```
http://lnx02.hadba.com:5500/em/console
```

After you do this, you need to log in as the sys user as sysdba, and then you have access to the Database Control console. The entire suite of control features now exists as HMTL, which may not be as pretty as the Java app version, but makes it far more effective for connecting remotely from other systems, as it can all be handled from within a web browser.

Database Control Console: Navigation

EM is divided into four pages: Home, Performance, Administration, and Maintenance—accounting for the primary uses for the GUI.

EM Home

The home page provides general information, such as the database status, host name, and listener. As shown in Figure 2-1, it gives a quick look at the CPU utilization and the active sessions, and then, by default, provides the latest Automatic Database Diagnostic Monitor (ADDM) advice and standard system alerts.

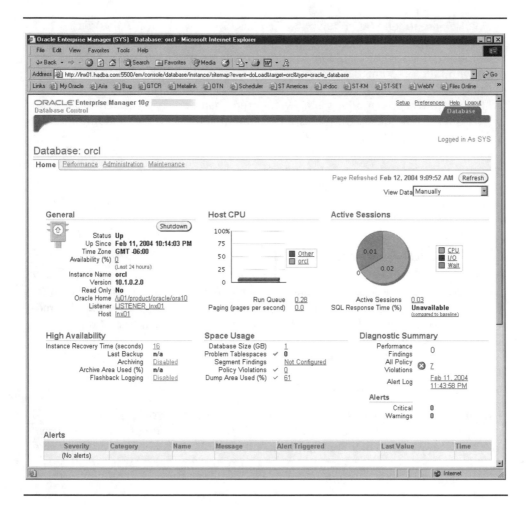

FIGURE 2-1. *EM Database Control home page*

Performance

The Performance page provides generalized performance indicators for the instance to which you are connected. It provides a look at host resources, instance service time, and instance throughput. For a closer look at current top usage sessions, for instance, you could click on the box for CPU Used in the Instance Service Time graph. This will load a Top Sessions chart that you can then review, as shown in Figure 2-2.

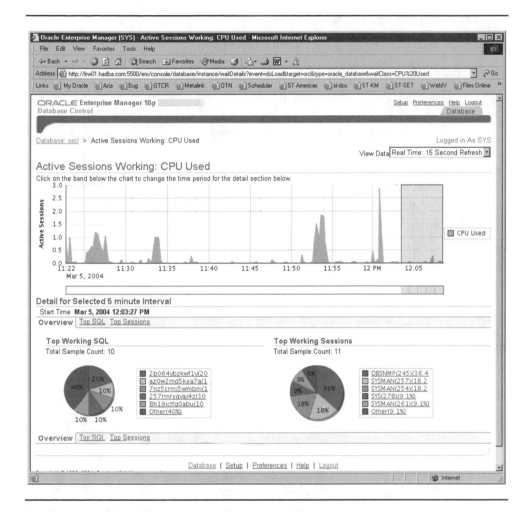

FIGURE 2-2. *Top Sessions from the Performance page*

The performance charts default to running a check every 15 seconds, but this can be altered from the View Data drop-down list in the upper-right corner of the page.

Administration

The Administration page is divided into sections that represent the different areas of administration that are typical of the DBA: schema, storage, security, and instance (see Figure 2-3). Here is where you can work with the Resource Manager and Scheduler, as well as materialized views (under Summary Management).

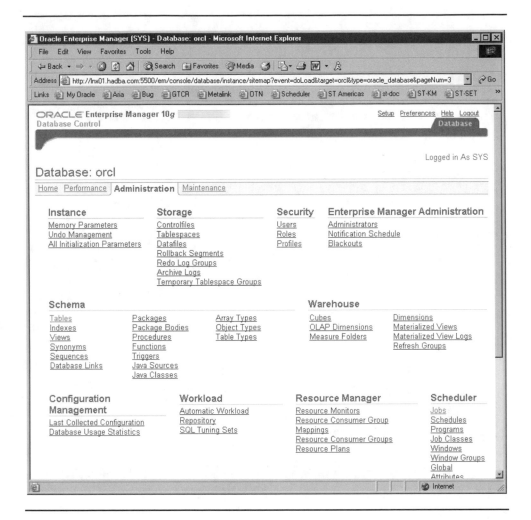

FIGURE 2-3. *The Administration page*

Maintenance

The Maintenance page provides access to three groupings of functions: utilities, backup/recovery, and software management. The utilities section provides access to export, import, and SQL*Loader; it also allows you to use the SQL Access Advisor (we talk about this in the section "Materialized Views") and also to reorganize objects. (See "Online Reorganization" later in the chapter.) The backup/recovery is discussed in Chapter 9. Finally, the software management allows you to review patching and upgrade information for the instance. See Figure 2-4 for an example of the Maintenance page.

FIGURE 2-4. *The Maintenance page*

Oracle Enterprise Manager Grid Control

The Grid Control EM is the fully loaded Enterprise Manager behemoth we
have come to love/hate. Grid Control provides a singular interface for managing
multiple databases across an enterprise, where Database Control is for control of
an individual database. In addition, Grid Control extends EM functionality out past
the database, to include application server and node management. Grid Control
requires a central repository (think Oracle Management Server, from previous EM
releases) to operate, and installs and requires the kind of management duties that

were common in the base EM release in 9*i*. EM Grid Control is a separate installation from the database, requires a repository database, has an enormous memory footprint, and (you guessed it) is separately priced and licensed. Grid Control is aimed squarely at users who need a consolidation client for monitoring and managing a large number of databases, application servers, and web servers. If you are not that person, EM Grid Control may not be necessary for you.

Oracle Grid Control in this Book

In this book, most of the EM functionality we discuss comes by way of the EM you get by default with any Oracle Database 10*g* Enterprise Edition installation, and by connecting to the host name 5500/em. However, EM Grid Control is required if you want to use the GUI for Real Application Clusters (RAC) management and Data Guard (DG) management. This is due to the fact that RAC and DG require access to more than a single instance of a database, and must consolidate information about systems across an enterprise. Thus, an enterprise utility is required.

For installation and configuration tips on EM Grid Control, your first stop should be *Oracle Enterprise Manager Grid Control Installation and Basic Configuration 10*g *Release 1 (10.1),* from the online documentation set. See the bibliography for more information. The installation and configuration specifics are beyond the scope of this book.

EM and Availability

Sometimes, one of the biggest snags in availability is our own scrambling to get a full picture of the situation, or our attempt to get at a functionality that requires a significant amount of SQL or PL/SQL coding. The bottom line is that EM allows an easy and manageable way to use new Oracle Database 10*g* functionality without getting lost in the step-by-step details. Granted, a knowledge of the details will always prove to be important. But with a utility such as EM, you can choose what details matter to you, and leave the rest to the GUI interface.

Database Configuration on the Fly

When it comes to availability, one of the most important advancements within the RDBMS has been the ability to reconfigure the database without shutting it down. This starts with the initialization parameters: forever bound to the realm of the init.ora, changes in the init parameters have traditionally meant a database bounce to reconfigure the instance. That is typically not the case anymore, with most parameters now dynamically changeable with a SQL ALTER command:

```
SQL> alter system set shared_pool_size=300000000;
SQL> alter session set nls_date_formate='MM-DD-YYYY';
```

spfile or init.ora?

The spfile was introduced in Oracle9*i* as an alternative to the ASCII text file init.ora for enabling or disabling system parameters for the database. It is a binary file that can only be modified via SQL commands in the database—you cannot edit this file manually, as you can the init.ora. This has led to an outpouring of grief and consternation on the part of the Oracle community, and rightly so, as the power to quickly review and update the init.ora has been a favorite of DBAs for years.

But the spfile was introduced for a very specific purpose: to be able to make a change dynamically in the database that was also permanently for the duration of the database. Until the spfile came along, if you issued an ALTER SYSTEM command, the change was made to your instance, but when you rebooted, the value reverted to whatever was in the init.ora. To combat this, you had to make sure that you issued the ALTER SYSTEM and then also updated the init.ora manually. The spfile, on the other hand, can take an ALTER SYSTEM command issued against the database and store it permanently for the next reboot. Of course, we could have had the best of both worlds, where the spfile was still just a human-readable text file that Oracle could also use… but alas, it is a binary file. To review the contents of the spfile, you can issue a command from SQL*Plus:

```
SQL> show parameter
```

You can limit this to a subset by naming a word string that Oracle will match against the parameter name list:

```
SQL> show parameter log_archive
```

You can also dump the spfile to an init file with a SQL command. Or, you can create an spfile from an init.ora file. This process can be used to manually modify a value—you first dump the spfile to an init.ora file, then make the change, and then rebuild the spfile from the init file.

```
SQL> create pfile='/u01/oracle/ora10/dbs/initORCL.ora' from spfile;
SQL> create spfile from pfile='/u01/oracle/ora10/dbs/initORCL.ora';
```

To change a parameter value in the spfile, you issue the ALTER SYSTEM command, then provide the scope. The scope refers to how you want the change applied—just for the duration of the currently open database (Scope=Memory), or permanently each time the database is started (Scope=spfile). You can also choose *both*, like this:

```
alter system set shared_pool_size=300000000 scope=spfile;
alter system set shared_pool_size=300000000 scope=both;
```

So which should you use? Init or spfile? We personally like the spfile, despite the added headaches of making certain changes and the added SQL complexity. Once utilized, the spfile can be backed up and restored using RMAN, so we don't have to consider it as part of the OS file system backup. It also means we don't have to bother with init.ora configuration to make a dynamic change. As an HADBA, these are compelling reasons for adoption. However, if you've been in the game a while, it may be that you cannot give up the init.ora. Stick with what you are comfortable with.

Nondynamic Parameters

Because nearly every configuration parameter is dynamic, it actually makes more sense to talk about those few that are static and require a reboot. These are the changes that will require you to bring the database down. Some of them require only that the particular instance be down, but the clustered database can still be up—you just take down one thread at a time. Others require that the entire database be down, as the change affects all clustered nodes. Those parameters that require the cluster to be down will be discussed in Chapter 4. In Table 2-1 we provide a reference list of those parameters that cannot be modified with an ALTER SYSTEM or ALTER SESSION command.

At this time, there are 218 published parameters for Oracle Database 10*g*, and inumerable unpublished parameters (starting with an underscore). We have not listed them all, but there are 82 static parameters in Table 2-1 that range from important to wildly obscure. We have listed in alphabetical order and then put in bold those parameters that typically you should be concerned with, as they will affect your database and its operations. Some of these have been deprecated in favor of new parameters. We have noted these, as well as the new parameters (if any), in Table 2-1.

Parameter Name	Notes
ACTIVE_INSTANCE_COUNT	RAC parameter
AUDIT_SYS_OPERATIONS	
AUDIT_TRAIL	
BACKGROUND_CORE_DUMP	
BITMAP_MERGE_AREA_SIZE	BITMAP_MERGE_AREA_SIZE has been deprecated in favor of PGA_AGGREGATE_TARGET

TABLE 2-1. *Static Database Parameters*

Parameter Name	Notes
BLANK_TRIMMING	
CLUSTER_DATABASE	RAC parameter
CLUSTER_DATABASE_INSTANCES	RAC parameter
CLUSTER_INTERCONNECTS	RAC parameter
COMMIT_POINT_STRENGTH	
COMPATIBLE	
CONTROL_FILES	
CPU_COUNT	
CREATE_BITMAP_AREA_SIZE	CREATE_BITMAP_AREA_SIZE has been deprecated in favor of PGA_AGGREGATE_TARGET.
CURSOR_SPACE_FOR_TIME	
DB_BLOCK_BUFFERS	DB_BLOCK_BUFFERS has been deprecated in favor of DB_CACHE_SIZE.
DB_BLOCK_SIZE	Can't change this one—ever
DB_DOMAIN	
DB_FILES	DB_FILES must be the same for all instances in RAC.
DB_NAME	
DB_UNIQUE_NAME	
DB_WRITER_PROCESSES	
DBWR_IO_SLAVES	
DISK_ASYNCH_IO	
DISTRIBUTED_LOCK_TIMEOUT	
DML_LOCKS	
ENQUEUE_RESOURCES	
EVENT	
FILEIO_NETWORK_ADAPTERS	
GC_FILES_TO_LOCKS	RAC parameter

TABLE 2-1. *Static Database Parameters* (continued)

Parameter Name	Notes
GCS_SERVER_PROCESSES	RAC parameter
GLOBAL_CONTEXT_POOL_SIZE	
HI_SHARED_MEMORY_ADDRESS	
IFILE	
INSTANCE_GROUPS	RAC parameter
INSTANCE_NAME	RAC parameter
INSTANCE_NUMBER	RAC parameter
INSTANCE_TYPE	RAC parameter
JAVA_MAX_SESSIONSPACE_SIZE	
JAVA_SOFT_SESSIONSPACE_LIMIT	
LOCK_NAME_SPACE	
LOCK_SGA	
LOG_ARCHIVE_FORMAT	
LOG_BUFFER	
LOGMNR_MAX_PERSISTENT_SESSIONS	
MAX_COMMIT_PROPAGATION_DELAY	
MAX_ENABLED_ROLES	
O7_DICTIONARY_ACCESSIBILITY	
OPEN_LINKS	
OPEN_LINKS_PER_INSTANCE	
OS_AUTHENT_PREFIX	
OS_ROLES	
PARALLEL_AUTOMATIC_TUNING	PARALLEL_AUTOMATIC_TUNING has been deprecated. See *Oracle Database 10*g *Reference Guide.*
PARALLEL_EXECUTION_MESSAGE_SIZE	
PRE_PAGE_SGA	
PROCESSES	
RDBMS_SERVER_DN	

TABLE 2-1. *Static Database Parameters* (continued)

Parameter Name	Notes
READ_ONLY_OPEN_DELAYED	
RECOVERY_PARALLELISM	
REMOTE_ARCHIVE_ENABLE	
REMOTE_LOGIN_PASSWORDFILE	
REMOTE_OS_AUTHENT	
REMOTE_OS_ROLES	
REPLICATION_DEPENDENCY_TRACKING	
ROLLBACK_SEGMENTS	ROLLBACK_SEGMENTS has been deprecated in favor of UNDO_MANAGEMENT.
SERIAL _REUSE	
SESSION_MAX_OPEN_FILES	
SESSIONS	
SGA_MAX_SIZE	
SHADOW_CORE_DUMP	
SHARED_MEMORY_ADDRESS	
SHARED_POOL_RESERVED_SIZE	
SMTP_OUT_SERVER	
SPFILE	
SQL92_SECURITY	
TAPE_ASYNCH_IO	
THREAD	RAC parameter
TRANSACTIONS	
TRANSACTIONS_PER_ROLLBACK_SEGMENT	
UNDO_MANAGEMENT	
USE_INDIRECT_DATA_BUFFERS	
UTL_FILE_DIR	Use DIRECTORIES instead of UTL_FILE_DIR for dynamic changes—i.e., create directory '/u02/out';.

TABLE 2-1. *Static Database Parameters* (continued)

Parameter Name	Parameter Name
DB_FILE_NAME_CONVERT	NLS_TERRITORY
HASH_AREA_SIZE	NLS_TIMESTAMP_FORMAT
NLS_CALENDAR	NLS_TIMESTAMP_TZ_FORMAT
NLS_COMP	OBJECT_CACHE_MAX_SIZE_PERCENT
NLS_CURRENCY	OBJECT_CACHE_OPTIMAL_SIZE
NLS_DATE_FORMAT	OLAP_PAGE_POOL_SIZE
NLS_DATE_LANGUAGE	PARALLEL_MIN_PERCENT
NLS_DUAL_CURRENCY	SESSION_CACHED_CURSORS
NLS_ISO_CURRENCY	SORT_AREA_RETAINED_SIZE
NLS_LANGUAGE	SORT_AREA_SIZE
NLS_NUMERIC_CHARACTERS	TRACEFILE_IDENTIFIER
NLS_SORT	

TABLE 2-2.   *Session-Only Dynamic Parameters*

In addition, there is an interesting subset of parameters that can be modified at the session level but not at the system level, meaning you can change them for a particular session but not for the entire system. In a sense, this makes them nondynamic because you cannot make a permanent change without bouncing the instance. The impact is small, as you can see from the type of parameters—they have to do more with session-level issues and typically do not affect the entire database. However, we felt it important to make the distinction here, as shown in Table 2-2.

Data Architecture and Availability

The architecture of your database objects has much to do with availability. There are multiple factors that play into the ultimate availability of your data: outage during recovery situations, performance across large tables or during heavy usage, and DDL operations that modify objects. Oracle provides specific types of database structures that help mediate the effect of these factors: table and index partitioning, index-organized tables, materialized views, and online reorganization of tables and indices.

It should be noted that we are not offering application availability solutions in this book. Creating applications that enhance availability based on proven execution plans, optimized SQL and PL/SQL, and application server management are all outside the scope of this tome—which is not to say they are not important. We just had to draw the line somewhere. Tom Kyte's books are great sources for building Oracle applications; for performance tuning, we recommend Richard Neimec's works. For application server management (from the Oracle perspective, of course), we suggest Garmany and Burleson's latest Oracle Database 10*g* tome. See the bibliography at the end of this book for more information.

Partitioned Tables and Indexes

Table and index partitioning refers to the ability within Oracle to organize a single table of data into multiple logical parts that can be maintained and treated independently. Each partition of a table can be housed in a separate tablespace, on different disks (or disk groups), and be dropped or reorganized independent of the other partitions. This provides a superb level of performance and, of course, availability. If a datafile associated with a partition goes belly up, all other partitions can remain available to users while you repair the bad file.

Tables can be partitioned, as can indices. From a performance standpoint, partitions are an excellent method for data searching: in parallel, each partition can be searched at the same time, whether they be index or table partitions. So, index range scans go faster, and even full table scans (heaven forbid) go faster. There are significant maintenance benefits from partitioned tables and indices, as well. Individual partitions can be dropped, moved, and loaded without affecting other partitions in the same table.

Partitioning is a huge topic to cover, and, frankly, we don't have the space here. We will, however, introduce the concepts and benefits, and provide a few simple examples. After that, please refer to the bibliography for where to learn more about all the nitty-gritty details.

What Tables and Indexes Are Partitioning Candidates?

Partitioning is usually a maintenance-to-performance trade-off: maintaining partitions requires more DBA footwork, but typically provides better performance. It is usually assumed that only really large tables benefit from partitioning, but even medium-sized objects can reap benefits if you feel like putting the grunt work in. So, if you are looking for performance gains on data lookup, give partitioning a try. In addition, partitioning is an excellent way to manage time-generated data. If you have data that rolls in every day, and you need a way to manage older data, partitioning can provide invaluable services. It provides for a way to archive or delete older data in a table without affecting performance for the rest of the table. In a nutshell, partitioning is worth a little exploration for your larger data tables, particularly those that grow over time.

Table Partitioning Types

There are three distinct types of partitions for tables: range, hash, and list. Each type of partition serves a slightly different purpose, based on the nature of the data and how it would be best divided into parts—for performance, as well as for logical grouping. Partitioning is determined by a *partition key* that is specified at table creation time. The partition key is the column (or columns) that you tell Oracle to use as the basis for data segmentation into partitions.

Range Partitioning   The most common form of partitioned tables is the range partition. The range partition divvies up data into segments that are separated by ranges of values, such as dates. Range partitioning is best implemented when the range values by which you partition result in the partitions having equally sized amounts of data. The following example uses the woodscrew_orders table discussed in Chapter 1, as part of the database for Horatio's Woodscrew company. In this example, we divide the table up by order date column. The DBA believes that his orders are steady enough over the months that he can partition by month, and each month will have roughly the same amount of data.

```
create table woodscrew_orders (
   ord_id              number not null,
   ord_date            date,
   cust_id             number not null,
   scr_id              number not null,
   ord_cnt             number,
   warehouse_id        number not null,
   region              varchar2(20),
   constraint pk_woodscrew_orders primary key (ord_id, ord_date)
   using index tablespace ws_app_idx)
   partition by range (ord_date)
   (partition values less than ( TO_DATE('1-OCT-2003','DD-MON-YYYY'))
       tablespace wdscrord_sep_2003,
    partition values less than ( TO_DATE('1-NOV-2003','DD-MON-YYYY'))
       tablespace wdscrord_oct_2003,
    partition values less than ( TO_DATE('1-DEC-2003','DD-MON-YYYY'))
       tablespace wdscrord_nov_2003,
    partition values less than ( TO_DATE('1-JAN-2004','DD-MON-YYYY'))
       tablespace wdscrord_dec_2003)
   enable row movement;
```

Hash Partitioning   There are times when you have large tables that would benefit from partitioning for performance and maintenance reasons, but the tables do not lend themselves to range partitioning. The Woodscrew table from Chapter 1 is a good example. There are no reliable range values for the table, but the table is growing larger and larger and performance is beginning to trail off. In this situation, a hash partition would be appropriate. Instead of segmenting the table based on a range of values, Oracle will hash the key column you specify and segment the incoming data based on the hash value. This provides a way to take a column such as SCR_ID and use it as the partitioning key, and Oracle will ensure that we get like-sized partitions.

```
create table woodscrew (
  scr_id          number not null,
  manufactr_id    varchar2(20) not null,
  scr_type        varchar2(20),
  thread_cnt      number,
  length          number,
  head_config     varchar2(20),
  constraint pk_woodscrew primary key (scr_id, manufactr_id)
using index tablespace ws_app_idx)
  partition by hash (scr_id)
  partitions 4
  store in (wdscr_part1, wdscr_part2);
```

List Partitioning   List partitioning provides a hybrid-looking table that stands somewhere between a range and a hash partition. List partitioning occurs by grouping specific values to be placed in each partition. Thus, you can group data logically that does not have a natural range grouping, and control which partition is used (unlike a hash, where the DBA has no control over the system hash function). List partitioning is excellent in situations where you need explicit control over partition placement for performance or maintenance reasons, and where the partition key does not lend itself to a range.

List partitioning has only one limitation that the other two types do not have: the partition key can only be a single column—you cannot list partition on two or more columns.

For the DBA at Horatio's Woodscrews Company, a good candidate for list partitioning is his woodscrew_inventory table, where he needs to be able to load data based on manufacturer, and he also has multiple data-mining operations that are manufacturer-centric. So he lists partitions based on MANUFACTR_ID, like this:

```
create table woodscrew_inventory (
  scr_id          number not null,
  manufactr_id    varchar2(20) not null,
  warehouse_id    number not null,
  region          varchar2(20),
  count           number,
  lot_price    number)
partition by list (manufactr_id)
  (partition east_suppliers values ( 'Tommy Hardware', '2Many Parts')
           tablespace wdscr_inv_part1,
   partition west_suppliers values ( 'Balaji Parts' )
```

```
              tablespace wdscr_inv_part2,
  partition other values (DEFAULT)
              tablespace ws_app_data)
enable row movement;
```

Subpartitioning

For the hierarchy enthralled, you can take partitioning to the next level and subpartition your partitions.

Hash Subpartitioning   The first type of subpartitioning introduced in Oracle was the composite range-hash partition. This methodology allows you to set a range partition key, and then for values in that range subdivide the data along a hash function. This provides better performance and more granularity.

This is, essentially, a way to organize hash-organized partitions into ranges. Using a range-hash partition table, you can organize data by a date range, and then within the date range further divide the data into manageable components that are equitably distributed and provide a higher level of parallelism during large data-mining operations.

In the range partition example in the preceding section, the Woodscrew DBA partitioned his woodscrew_orders table by ORD_DATE. To garner better performance, and to further distribute the load across tablespaces for recoverability, the DBA now subpartitions the same table by hash:

```
create table woodscrew_orders (
ord_id            number not null,
ord_date            date,
cust_id            number not null,
scr_id            number not null,
ord_cnt            number,
warehouse_id      number not null,
region            varchar2(20),
constraint pk_woodscrew_orders primary key (ord_id, ord_date)
using index tablespace ws_app_idx)
partition by range(ord_date) subpartition by hash(ord_id)
 subpartitions 2
(partition values less than ( TO_DATE('1-OCT-2003','DD-MON-YYYY'))
    store in (wdscrord_sep_2003_part1, wdscrord_sep_2003_part2),
 partition values less than ( TO_DATE('1-NOV-2003','DD-MON-YYYY'))
    store in (wdscrord_oct_2003_part1, wdscrord_oct_2003_part2),
 partition values less than ( TO_DATE('1-DEC-2003','DD-MON-YYYY'))
    store in (wdscrord_nov_2003_part1, wdscrord_nov_2003_part2),
 partition values less than ( TO_DATE('1-JAN-2004','DD-MON-YYYY'))
    store in (wdscrord_dec_2003_part1, wdscrord_dec_2003_part2))
enable row movement;
```

Range-List Partitioning   Oracle finally introduced this option in Oracle9*i*
Release 2—the ability to partition by range, and then subpartition by list. In
this way, you can very specifically control how the partitions shape up, so that
maintenance and mining operations can be targeted to the best granular level.
This is a very targeted approach to partitioning, and really should be undertaken
only if you have enough historical data to determine that a highly controlled
partitioning structure will provide the right benefits to your application without
hampering performance or skewing partitions to the point they are grossly
disproportionate to each other.

Our Woodscrew DBA has to rethink the range-hash partitioning of the woodscrew_
orders table, due to the search methodologies of his application. While the ORD_DATE
is an excellent way to organize historical data, the hash subpartitions don't provide
as much control as the DBA would like. So, he decides to use the REGION column
for a list subpartition. This allows him to monitor and organize data along regional
sales areas.

```
create table woodscrew_orders (
ord_id            number not null,
ord_date            date,
cust_id            number not null,
scr_id            number not null,
ord_cnt            number,
warehouse_id      number not null,
region            varchar2(20),
constraint pk_woodscrew_orders primary key (ord_id, ord_date)
using index tablespace ws_app_idx)
partition by range(ord_date)
subpartition by list(region)
(partition wdscrord_sep_2003
    values less than ( TO_DATE('1-OCT-2003','DD-MON-YYYY'))
   (
    subpartition wdscrord_sep_2003_west values ('SOUTHWEST', 'NORTHWEST')
        tablespace wdscrord_sep_2003_part1,
    subpartition wdscrord_sep_2003_east values ('SOUTHEAST', 'NORTHEAST')
        tablespace wdscrord_sep_2003_part2
    ),
partition wdscrord_oct_2003
    values less than ( TO_DATE('1-NOV-2003','DD-MON-YYYY'))
   (
    subpartition wdscrord_oct_2003_west values ('SOUTHWEST', 'NORTHWEST')
        tablespace wdscrord_oct_2003_part1,
    subpartition wdscrord_sep2003_east values ('SOUTHEAST', 'NORTHEAST')
        tablespace wdscrord_oct_2003_part2
    ),
```

```
partition wdscrord_nov_2003
    values less than ( TO_DATE('1-DEC-2003','DD-MON-YYYY'))
    (
    subpartition wdscrord_nov_2003_west values ('SOUTHWEST', 'NORTHWEST')
        tablespace wdscrord_nov_2003_part1,
    subpartition wdscrord_nov_2003_east values ('SOUTHEAST', 'NORTHEAST')
        tablespace wdscrord_nov_2003_part2
    ),
partition wdscrord_dec_2003
    values less than ( TO_DATE('1-JAN-2004','DD-MON-YYYY'))
    (
    subpartition wdscrord_dec_2003_west values ('SOUTHWEST', 'NORTHWEST')
        tablespace wdscrord_dec_2003_part1,
    subpartition wdscrord_dec_2003_east values ('SOUTHEAST', 'NORTHEAST')
        tablespace wdscrord_dec_2003_part2
    ))
enable row movement;
```

Index Partitioning

In addition to table partitions, Oracle allows indices to be partitioned. With index partitioning, range scans along the index can be greatly reduced because the cost-based optimizer can prune partitions that do not match the query parameters. In addition, index rebuilds, moves, and deletes can be isolated to subsets while the rest of the index remains unaffected. There are two types of index partitions: local and global.

Local Index Partition   A local index has its structure imprinted by the underlying partitioned table. Oracle calls this *equipartitioned*—the index has the same delimiters as the partitioned table, and will be maintained automatically along with the table that it is based on. That is, if you split a table partition into two new partitions, the local index on that partition will also be split into two new partitions. Local indices require less maintenance than global indices, because they can be automatically altered along with the underlying table.

Global Index Partition   A global index can be partitioned independent of the table on which it is based. In fact, a global index can be partitioned, while the underlying table is not partitioned. This provides a degree of independence, but it also may require more maintenance than a local index. Global partitions are superb when you have access paths that do not match the partitioning path. For instance, our Woodscrew DBA has noted that the application frequently performs batch updates to the woodscrew_orders table based on customer ID (CUST_ID), which is not part of the range partition key for the table. So the DBA can build a global hash-partitioned index on CUST_ID that allows for parallel range scanning.

Partition Maintenance

Partition maintenance provides for a high level of flexibility in how you go about removing old data, adding new partitions, splitting partitions, and other operations. Table 2-3 provides a quick look at maintenance operations at your fingertips.

Maintenance Operation: Tables	Type of Partition
Adding a partition	Range, hash, list, range-hash, range-list
Dropping a partition	Range, list, range-hash, range-list
Exchanging a partition	Range, hash, list, range-hash, range-list
Merging a partition	Range, list, range-hash, range-list
Moving partitions	Range, hash, list, range-hash, range-list
Renaming partitions	Range, hash, list, range-hash, range-list
Splitting partitions	Range, list, range-hash, range-list
Truncating partitions	Range, hash, list, range-hash, range-list
Coalesce a partition	Hash, range-hash
Modify default attributes for a partition table	Range, hash, list, range-hash, range-list
Modify real attributes for a partition	Range, hash, list, range-hash, range-list
List partition: add values	List, range-list
List partition: drop values	List, range-list
Maintenance operations—Indices	Type of Index
Rendering an index partition unusable	Global
Modifying a local index to use NOLOGGING option	Local
Rendering entire index unusable	Local, global
Rebuilding an index partition	Local, global
Dropping an index partition	Global
Coalescing an index partition	Global
Splitting a global index partition	Global
Renaming an index partition	Local, global
Modifying index default values	Local, global

TABLE 2-3. *Available Partition Maintenance Operations*

Partitioning and High Availability

So what does all this partitioning mean for availability? Partitioning is an excellent way to leverage functionality inside the database to maximize performance for the end users for heavily used tables. In OLTP and DSS environments, partitioning can make a difference in the usability of large tables, meaning that the end-user perceived availability goes up. In addition, by granulating a large table out across multiple tablespaces, you mitigate the downtime associated with a failure in a single partition—media recovery can be isolated to a single partition. You are also ensuring a higher level of availability during table and index maintenance.

Index-Organized Tables

Index-organized tables (IOTs) deserve brief mention, if for no other reason than they are really cool. IOTs allow you to organize tables into B-tree leaf blocks based on your defined primary key. So, instead of having a table with blocks that are simply piled on top of one another in no order, and then having an index that allows you to locate the rows in those blocks, now you can store the table rows in the index leaf blocks themselves. This means that once the index lookup is complete, the operation is done. No secondary block lookup to the table, because the row values are stored inline with the primary key value in the index.

Like we said, it's all very cool. The gains come from performance, where you are looking up fewer blocks and therefore decreasing disk IO. You also decrease maintenance demands on heavily used OLTP tables that need constant reorganization and defragmentation—with IOTs, the organization is built into the table, and reorgs can be done online (see the upcoming section "Online Reorganization"). You will also see a decrease in total space required, because you are no longer duplicating the primary key values in the table and in the index.

IOTs also allow for key compression, if the primary key is a composite of multiple columns. In such tables, if key compression is used, Oracle will divide the key into a prefix and a suffix. Then it will share the prefix column among multiple leaf blocks with the same prefix, so that the prefix key value does not need to be recorded as frequently.

IOTs also benefit from decreased sort operations, if the ORDER BY clause of a query names the key value of the IOT. In such a case, Oracle will skip the sort operation because the data will already be returned in key value order. With this in mind, you can maximize the return on queries if you have tables that are frequently ordered by the primary key.

Other than the organizational structure, the IOTs behave just as any normal table would: you can insert, update, delete, truncate, move, and partition them. They can be reorganized online and replicated, and can have materialized views created on them. You can even create secondary indices on them, so that alternate access paths can be used to access the data in the same way you would a heap-organized table (*heap* meaning you pile the data into the table randomly).

For an example of an IOT, remember our DBA's heavily hit woodscrew_orders table. Because of heavy demand for woodscrews, this table is very volatile and adds new rows constantly, but the access path is generally always the same, coming from a lookup on the order ID and the order date. So, the DBA could rebuild the table as an IOT so as to increase performance on these lookups. He has already partitioned the woodscrew_orders table, but that isn't a problem. An IOT can be partitioned just like a heap-organized table.

```
create table woodscrew_orders_new (
ord_id              number not null,
ord_date             date,
cust_id              number not null,
scr_id              number not null,
ord_cnt              number,
warehouse_id        number not null,
region              varchar2(20),
constraint pk_woodscrew_orders primary key (ord_id, ord_date))
organization index
including ord_date pctthreshold 20
overflow tablespace wd_scr_overflow
partition by range (ord_date) ...
```

Like we said before, IOTs are not inherently a high-availability feature of the RDBMS. But anything that helps with performance helps with the perception of availability—which is half the battle. Plus, IOTs are so *cool*.

Materialized Views

It is always worth repeating one of the HADBA mantras: availability is defined as much by end-user perceptions as by database realities. If the end user cannot access the data in a speedy, reliable way, then the data is not available, even if the problem is due to table size, execution path, or bad ad hoc queries. Essentially, this means that performance is as important to availability as database uptime.

Which is where materialized views (we shorten it to mview for everyone's sake) offer up the same type of availability as IOTs, in the sense that an mview does not stop outages—it just increases performance. A materialized view is an umbrella name for an Oracle object that serves different purposes in different arenas. For our purposes, an mview is just what its name implies. First, consider a *regular* view in Oracle. A regular view is nothing more than a stored query that can be used to mask a table's columns to users, or to simply provide a quick coding shortcut to a complex lookup task. But each time you perform a select from a view, you are accessing the underlying table and its indices, and causing whatever performance hit is required to do so. This can get very expensive for tables that are large because of the number of rows, or large because of the number of column values.

A materialized view, on the other hand, is an actual re-creation of a subset of the data from the master table (or tables). When you create an mview, you do not just create the query; you create a new table that stores rows from the master table based on your mview criteria. In this way, you can get faster results from queries against the mview, because there are fewer rows (or fewer columns) to navigate through. Granted, you need the storage space to hold copies of rows held elsewhere, but the performance gains are such that it often outweighs the storage expense. Materialized views can contain joins and aggregates, making them extremely useful for data summaries and roll-up value mining.

Materialized views are the logical growth of the object Oracle used to call a snapshot. Snapshots were used in distributed database systems to offer local copies of centralized data tables found at a master database. Mviews take this system and apply it to a local object, such that the same structure can be used for performance gains on the master database itself. Like snapshots, mviews can be refreshed from the base table, and all new rows and row changes are propagated from the base table to the mview. The refresh can be complete or fast. A *complete* refresh rebuilds the entire mview from scratch. A *fast* refresh only updates new or changed rows since the last refresh.

A fast refresh requires a materialized view log. This is a separate object that is created on the base table. Whenever a DML operation is performed against the base table, the mview log is updated with the same change. Then, you can periodically check the mview log for those changes, propagate them to the mview, and purge the records from the log.

Mviews can still be used for distributed database needs. You can create mviews on remote databases via database links and refresh them from the master table. However, such mviews have a subset of functionality compared to local mviews, and we will not cover them in this book. Instead, see Chapter 10 for the next generation of distributed database functionality for high availability.

Mviews can be created on tables, partitioned tables, index-organized tables, and partitioned index-organized tables. In addition, you can partition an mview, which provides benefits when refreshing the mview in parallel.

Creating mviews

To create an mview, you first need to determine what subset of data, or what joined data, or what aggregated data, you want to have in the mview. We will continue to look at Horatio's Woodscrew database for our examples. The DBA has noted that the CEO of Horatio's Woodscrews Company makes a weekly review of the yearly order trends of the largest customers, and in particular likes to see what kind of screws are being ordered. Once he sees the whole order list, he reviews how many slot-headed vs. Phillips orders are being placed. To get this data, the DBA had created an application button on the business intelligence screen that the CEO could use to compile the screw orders per customer, and this data includes the head configuration. But this report has been running slowly, and the CEO has requested that it be sped up considerably.

To get past this, the DBA implements a series of materialized views that echo the query pattern of the CEO. For example, he builds an mview for the customer identified by cust_id=2002, with a join from Woodscrew to include screw details. First, he builds the mview logs on the base tables:

```
create materialized view log on ws_app.woodscrew
tablespace ws_app_data;
create materialized view log on ws_app.woodscrew_orders
tablespace ws_app_data;

CREATE MATERIALIZED VIEW ws_app.cust_ws_order_mv
PCTFREE 0 TABLESPACE ws_app_data
STORAGE (INITIAL 16k NEXT 16k PCTINCREASE 0)
PARALLEL
BUILD IMMEDIATE
REFRESH on demand
ENABLE QUERY REWRITE AS
SELECT w.scr_type, w.head_config, wo.cust_id, wo.ord_cnt, wo.scr_id
FROM ws_app.woodscrew_orders wo, ws_app.woodscrew w
where w.scr_id=wo.scr_id
and wo.cust_id = 2002;
```

Query Rewrite

Perhaps the most compelling feature of mviews is the ability for the Oracle cost-based optimizer to automatically use an mview instead of the base table when a query against the base table matches the mview. This functionality is known as *query rewrite*, and it's yet another HA feature you can exploit—but not in the traditional sense. Query rewrite allows you to implement mviews on the fly, without having to rebuild application code or change user behavior. Once the queries are determined, you can build the mview based on the query, and then Oracle will automatically use the mview instead of the base table. This allows you to increase performance and change execution paths without taking the database out of the users' hands first, or integrating new functionality into existing applications.

Turning on query rewrite is simple. You can do it for a session or for the entire system:

```
SQL> alter session set query_rewrite_enabled=true;
SQL> alter system set query_rewrite_enabled=true;
```

You can also turn query rewrite on for specific mviews, based on an ALTER or CREATE command on the mview itself, as seen in the preceding section in the creation of the mview CUST_WS_ORDER_MV.

Summary Advisor

You might be asking yourself, how did the Woodscrew DBA know to create materialized views on the specific joins? Well, there is functionality in the Oracle database to provide advice for mview creation. In Oracle9*i*, this was called Summary Advisor, and was implemented through the DBMS_OLAP utility. In Oracle Database10*g*, DBMS_OLAP is still around for backward compatibility, but it has been deprecated in favor of the SQL Access Advisor, which can be run from EM. (It can also be run from DBMS_ADVISOR, but it's wicked slick from EM.)

The DBA simply went to the Maintenance page of the EM console, and then clicked on Advisor Central. From here, there is a link to SQLAccess Advisor. This takes you on a four-page wizard path where you specify what usage information to use in making its recommendations.

Online Reorganization

Thus far, we've talked about partitioning, index-organized tables, and materialized views as ways to increase performance and minimize possible downtime due to maintenance or recovery scenarios. But there remains an important question: how can these be implemented for tables and indices that are already in production? For that question, we give you online reorganization.

DBMS_REDEFINITION

Oracle provides the means of reorganizing tables through use of the wrapped procedures in DBMS_REDEFINITION. This bundle provides a series of procedures that allow you to build an interim table with the new structure you desire, and then move rows from the original table to the interim table. After the interim table is complete, the original table is locked briefly; then, the names are transposed on the tables so that the interim table gets the original table name.

DBMS_REDEFINITION uses materialized view logs on the original table to keep track of changes that have occurred since the start of the redefinition process. In this way, the original table is available for query and DML even as it is being rebuilt with new definitions. After the original build is complete, the new rows from the mview log are propagated to the interim table. There is a brief lock at the end of the process so that the final switchover can occur.

Online table reorganization can be used in the following situations:

- Change a table to an index-organized table (or vice versa)

- Change a table to a partitioned table (or vice versa)

- Add or drop a column

- Move a table to a different tablespace, or change storage parameters

HA Workshop: *Use DBMS_REDEFINITION to Change a Table to a Partitioned IOT*

Workshop Notes
This workshop will change the woodscrew_orders table into a partitioned, index-organized table while the woodscrew_orders table stays online for OLTP operations. Note that if you built a materialized view on woodscrew_orders, as shown in the section "Creating Mviews" earlier, you will need to drop the mview before proceeding—a table with mviews is not a candidate for online reorganization.

Step 1.   Get a row count of the table. This will help you determine when the first phase of the reorg is complete.

```
select count(*) from woodscrew_orders;
```

Step 2.   Confirm that the table is a candidate for reorganization.

```
BEGIN
DBMS_REDEFINITION.CAN_REDEF_TABLE('sales','woodscrew_orders',
 dbms_redefinition.cons_use_pk);|
END;
/
```

Step 3.   Build the interim table. In our situation, we need a partitioned, index-organized structure for the woodscrew_orders table.

```
create table woodscrew_orders_new (
ord_id            number not null,
ord_date           date,
cust_id            number not null,
scr_id            number not null,
ord_cnt            number,
warehouse_id      number not null,
region            varchar2(20),
constraint pk_woodscrew_orders primary key (ord_id, ord_date))
organization index
including ord_date pctthreshold 20
overflow tablespace wd_scr_overflow
partition by range (ord_date)
(partition values less than ( TO_DATE('1-OCT-2003','DD-MON-YYYY'))
    tablespace wdscrord_sep_2003,
 partition values less than ( TO_DATE('1-NOV-2003','DD-MON-YYYY'))
    tablespace wdscrord_oct_2003,
```

```
partition values less than ( TO_DATE('1-DEC-2003','DD-MON-YYYY'))
    tablespace wdscrord_nov_2003,
partition values less than ( TO_DATE('1-JAN-2004','DD-MON-YYYY'))
    tablespace wdscrord_dec_2003);
```

Step 4. Begin the reorganization process. Because we are not remapping any columns, we need only specify the schema, original table, and interim table.

```
BEGIN
DBMS_REDEFINITION.START_REDEF_TABLE('ws_app', 'woodscrew_orders',
'woodscrew_orders_new', dbms_redefinition.cons_use_pk);
END;
/
```

Step 5. Automatically rebuild all table dependencies (indices, triggers, and so forth).

```
BEGIN
DBMS_REDEFINITION.COPY_TABLE_DEPENDENTS('ws_app', 'woodscrew_orders',
'woodscrew_orders_new', TRUE, TRUE, TRUE, FALSE);
END;
/
```

Step 6. Depending on the amount of data that may accumulate while the dependent objects are built, you may want to perform a refresh of data from the mview logs that have been created in the background.

```
BEGIN
DBMS_REDEFINITION.SYNC_INTERIM_TABLE('ws_app', 'woodscrew_orders',
'woodscrew_orders_new');
END;
/
```

Step 7. Complete the reorganization by locking the original table, then finishing any last sync operations with the interim table, and then swapping table names between the two.

```
BEGIN
DBMS_REDEFINITION.FINISH_REDEF_TABLE('ws_app', 'woodscrew_orders',
'woodscrew_orders_new');
END;
/
```

Step 8. After you have completed the final step, you can now delete the interim table—in this case, woodscrew_orders_new. This is actually the original table renamed.

Resource Manager and Scheduler

Sometimes, availability is defined on a more limited scope than system-wide availability—perhaps the database is so available for one user that another user cannot get access to resources. Sure, you can always try to throw more resources at the problem, but let's face it, sometimes you have to make do with what you have. And that means that you have to mitigate the demands between different kinds of database users that compete for limited resources. For instance, if a long-running report is kicked off at night for end-of-month review, it could still be running come morning time when the OLTP users come in to begin transaction processing for the day. The users may find their updates running too slowly, or completely hung. To use modern buzzy words, you can think of the process of automatically controlling resource allocation as *provisioning*, albeit on a database scale only.

Oracle implemented the Resource Manager to assist with managing and mediating the pool of resources for the database between different classes of users and jobs. Then, to help expand the power of the Resource Manager, Oracle introduces in Oracle Database 10*g* the Scheduler.

Managing Limited Resources

The Resource Manager can be used to control database resource utilization to a high degree of granularity. It can be used to

- Allocate CPU percentages to user groups to better distribute processor time

- Guarantee a certain amount of processing power to specific users

- Based on optimizer estimates, prevent any transactions that would run longer than a specified time

- Limit session idle time, and allow for session-killing of blocking, idle sessions

- Limit the degree of parallelism allowed for user groups

As a DBA, you must determine which users or groups of users need which types of resource limitations or guarantees, and then you can use the DBMS_RESOURCE_MANAGER package. This package allows you to (most importantly) set up resource consumer groups. Consumer groups allow you to group users based on function or activity type, so that you can better control the group as a single entity.

To get started with the Resource Manager, you can set up a simple resource plan that does not require any complex associations, other than the creation of consumer groups and their CPU allotment.

```
BEGIN
DBMS_RESOURCE_MANAGER.CREATE_SIMPLE_PLAN(SIMPLE_PLAN => 'woodscrew_plan',
    CONSUMER_GROUP1 => 'order_placement', GROUP1_CPU => 70,
```

```
    CONSUMER_GROUP2 => 'order_review', GROUP2_CPU => 30);
END;
/
```

There is clearly a lot more to the Resource Manager than simple CPU mapping, but we wanted to at least introduce you to the concept before we move on. From an availability perspective, a good handle on resource provisioning can help you keep available resources for those that need them most, when they need them most, and put a stop to those users who may be overutilizing resources best allocated elsewhere.

Heir to the Job Throne: The Scheduler

Oracle has introduced in Database 10*g* a new job scheduling utility. In previous versions, database jobs were administrated using the DBMS_JOB package, and the jobs themselves were run by job queue processes that would check the job queue at regular intervals to see if jobs needed to be executed. In Oracle Database 10*g*, DBMS_JOB has been deprecated in favor of DBMS_SCHEDULER, a more robust and complex job scheduling and administrating utility.

The Scheduler is rooted in the power of object-oriented programming for its modularization of tasks and attributes. Whereas the DBMS_JOB package was a simplistic list of what to do, and when to do it, the Scheduler allows for more fine-tuned control of the entire job, including job grouping, scheduling, and resource allocation maintenance. In essence, the Scheduler allows for better programmatical structuring of job creation, execution, and maintenance so that jobs better reflect the needs of your applications and business.

The first thing worth noting is that the Scheduler now breaks up a job into its different components, so that you now create a schedule, a program, and a job.

Schedules

Schedules reflect the *when* of a job, as well as its *interval*. By freeing schedules from each individual job, and making them independent database objects, you can now use the same schedule for multiple jobs.

A schedule is comprised of its name, a start date, an end date, and the repeating interval for any jobs that are assigned this schedule. You build a schedule with DBMS_SCHEDULER:

```
begin
dbms_scheduler.create_schedule (
schedule_name     => 'nightly_review_schedule',
start_date        => '24-DEC-2003 01:00:00AM',
end_date          => '01-JAN-2005 01:00:00AM',
repeat_interval   => 'FREQ=DAILY; INTERVAL=1',
comments          => 'Schedule for Nightly Reviews');
end;
/
```

NOTE
The repeat_interval uses a new calendaring syntax. You first need to specify the type of interval unit—DAILY, WEEKLY, MONTHLY, YEARLY, even MINUTELY (no, we're not kidding); then you specify how many intervals of those units should pass before rerunning any jobs with this schedule.

Programs

Programs define the *how* of a job. More specifically, think of a program as the metadata about a job that is run by the Scheduler: the program name, the program action, the program type, and the number of input arguments for the program. The program action will refer to what the program will do—run an executable file, or name a PL/SQL procedure. The program type defines what type of program this is: an external executable, a PL/SQL block, a stored procedure, a Java stored procedure, and so forth.

For instance, you can create a program that runs an external shell script for monitoring the alert log for errors:

```
BEGIN
dbms_scheduler.create_program (
program_name      => 'alert_review_script',
program_action    => '/oracle/ora10/admin/PROD/scripts/alert_rev.sh',
program_type      => 'EXECUTABLE',
comments          => 'executes an alert review');
end;
/
```

Jobs

A job describes *what* it is you want to do. As in the past, you can schedule a free-standing job that has internalized its task and its schedule. However, if you have created a schedule and a program that you can use, the job is nothing more than a combination of the schedule and the program:

```
BEGIN
dbms_scheduler.create_job (
job_name          => 'daily_alert_review',
program_name      => 'alert_review_script',
schedule_name     => 'nightly_review_schedule');
end;
/
```

Thus, based on the start time and interval of the schedule, and the metadata from the program, our job will kick off an external shell script called alert_rev.sh every night at 1:00 A.M.

Job Classes

In situations where there are high numbers of jobs that need to be maintained, Oracle introduces the job class, which allows you to group jobs by purpose similarity, run times, or any other classification system you want to use. Job classes allow you to prioritize work within jobs of the same class, as well as set attributes for all jobs in a class. Classes provide a maintenance opportunity as well as the ability to manage resources.

Windows

Windows are essentially resource allocation definitions. You create a window of time, be it a day or a week or a quarter, and then you assign a resource plan to the window. Thus, you can change resource allocation among users and groups based on the time of day or the month of the year.

Windows are created using DBMS_SCHEDULER, but they have little to do with jobs, necessarily. Windows are more a way of scheduling resource plan changes to coincide with different resource needs at different times. Windows are defined by when they open, when they close, the window priority, and the resource plan associated with the window. The window priority is included so that Oracle will know what to do if two or more windows overlap.

```
Begin
dbms_scheduler.create_window (
window_name        => 'Year_end_reporting_window',
resource_plan      => 'woodscrew_plan',
start_date         => '01-JAN-2004 01:00:00AM',
repeat_interval    => 'FREQ=YEARLY',
end_date           => '31-JAN-2006 01:00:00AM',
duration           => interval '30' day,
window_priority    => 'HIGH',
comments           => 'end of year sales reporting for CEO');
end;
/
```

LogMiner: Transaction Extraction

The section on using LogMiner could very well be placed in Chapter 8, on backup and recovery, as the primary function of LogMiner is to undo a bad transaction, or to redo transactions that were lost due to a point-in-time recovery. However, the

LogMiner utility can be yet another useful tool for your HA toolbelt. LogMiner does just what its name implies: it mines the data in the online redo logs and archived redo logs for information about what changes have been recorded in the database.

There is a bit of setup and configuration involved, but you do not need to configure it before you need it. For example, if you need to look at archivelogs from last week, you can get LogMiner set up today to review the old archivelogs. However, reacting to situations is not the call of the HADBA. We are, in a single buzz-wordy kind of way, proactive. (Someone please explain the difference between active and proactive. Actually, that's okay. We embrace our inner buzz word.) In fact, we are *ultra*-proactive, as HADBAs, so let's take a close look at LogMiner usage.

You set up LogMiner to work from the SQL interface. The packages for doing so are DBMS_LOGMINER_D and DBMS_LOGMNR. Both packages are required for configuring and using LogMiner if you will be configuring LogMiner to review archivelogs for a noncurrent database. Otherwise, you will only need DBMS_LOGMNR.

HA Workshop: *Configuring and Using LogMiner from the SQL Interface*

Workshop Notes
This workshop will step you through the review of a delete transaction within an archivelog. Note that a system parameter change is required prior to generating the delete in order to get full transaction discovery.

Step 1. Turn on Supplemental Logging for the database.

```
SQL> ALTER DATABASE ADD SUPPLEMENTAL LOG DATA;
SQL> SELECT SUPPLEMENTAL_LOG_DATA_MIN FROM V$DATABASE;
```

Step 2. Switch the logfile, then generate a delete.

```
connect / as sysdba
alter system switch logfile;

connect ws_app/ws_app
delete from woodscrew;
commit;

connect / as sysdba
alter system switch logfile;
select name from v$archived_log;
```

Step 3.   Add the new logfile we just generated to the LogMiner list.

```
EXECUTE DBMS_LOGMNR.ADD_LOGFILE( -
      LOGFILENAME =>
'/u02/oradata/flash_recovery_area/ORCL/o1_mf_1_161_032xckmg_.arc', -
OPTIONS => DBMS_LOGMNR.NEW);
```

Step 4.   Specify the online catalog for LogMiner to use. This is available if the source database is open and available.

```
EXECUTE DBMS_LOGMNR.START_LOGMNR(-
      OPTIONS => DBMS_LOGMNR.DICT_FROM_ONLINE_CATALOG);
```

Step 5.   Query the V$LOGMNR_CONTENTS for information on the delete.

```
SQL> select username, sql_redo, sql_undo
      from v$logmnr_contents where username='WS_APP'
      and operation = 'DELETE';
```

With an eye for availability, it is best to see LogMiner as a companion in data extraction and data rebuilding operations that do not require a database outage. By reviewing SQL redo and SQL undo based on time or user (or both), you can overcome possible user errors that occurred outside of the window of review with Flashback Technologies (see Chapter 9). In addition, if you are forced to do a FLASHBACK DATABASE, and there is transaction loss that has occurred, the archivelogs that were generated after the flashback point-in-time can be mined for the lost transactions, and those transactions can be executed again. If you do need to mine the archivelogs of a database that is not in its current state, you will need to generate the LogMiner dictionary into a flat file instead of using the online catalog. This requires an additional step using the DBMS_LOGMINER_D package.

```
Execute dbms_logmnr_d.build ('dictionary.ora', -
      '/u02/oradata/', -
      dbms_logmnr_d.store_in_flat_file);
```

Transportable Tablespaces

Almost done with this crash course in RDBMS HA functionality, and we wanted to discuss one more tool for your consideration. Transportable Tablespaces (TTS) allows you to copy a set of datafiles for a tablespace on one database and plug that tablespace into a different database. The time it takes to transfer data is limited to how long it takes to move the datafiles to the target database via ftp, copy, and so forth.

The core functionality serves multiple purposes. The most obvious usage of Transportable Tablespaces is for warehousing data from an OLTP system to a DSS system. Another use would be to publish data from a central database to multiple smaller databases that need certain fact tables, or to publish data to customers that use Oracle for data storage. TTS can also be used for forms of point-in-time-recovery, to create test copies of data sets, or to migrate data to a new database without using export/import utilities.

The Overview

Transporting a tablespace from one database to another is relatively simple, although you will want to become familiar with the processes before integrating TTS into your production database environment.

Determine what the transport set will be. The transport set refers to the set of tablespaces that you will move together, such as a data tablespace and the index tablespace that corresponds to the data. You use the package DBMS_TTS to make sure that a tablespace set qualifies for transportation. After executing the procedure, you must check a view to see if there are any violations:

```
EXECUTE DBMS_TTS.TRANSPORT_SET_CHECK('WDSCRORD_SEP_2003,
WDSCRORD_OCT_2003, WDSCRORD_NOV_2003, WDSCRORD_DEC_2003', TRUE);

SELECT * FROM TRANSPORT_SET_VIOLATIONS;
```

After determining if there are any violations, you must turn the tablespaces into read-only tablespaces. This is required in order to confirm that no DML operations (inserts, updates, or deletes) are occurring while we copy the underlying datafiles.

After setting the tablespaces to read-only, you export the metadata for the tablespaces. You can use the new export data pump utility to do this export. The metadata that gets exported will be used to identify the tablespace and its contents to the target database.

After the export is taken, you can copy the datafiles to the new location, by whatever methodology best suits you. After the file copy has been completed, you can put the tablespace set back in read-write mode at the source database, and the work at the source is complete.

At the target database, after you move the copied datafiles into position, you just have to import the metadata from the export you created at the source. Then, if necessary, you convert the new tablespaces to read-write mode, and you are finished.

A Few Restrictions

There are a few restrictions on what tablespaces can qualify for transportability that you should be aware of, since they will determine whether you want to employ TTS in your environment.

- You cannot transport the SYSTEM tablespace or any of its contents. This means that you cannot use TTS for PL/SQL, triggers, or views. These would have to be moved with export.

- The source and target database must have the same character set and national language set.

- You cannot transport a table with a materialized view unless the mview is in the transport set you create.

- You cannot transport a partition of a table without transporting the entire table.

Cross-Platform Transportable Tablespaces

Transportable Tablespace functionality has existed since 8*i*, but there is a revolutionary upgrade that has occurred in Oracle Database 10*g*. Now, TTS can transport tablespaces across different platforms. In the past, TTS required that the source and target database both be the same operating system; now, TTS can pass the datafiles between different platforms without blinking (okay, sometimes, it requires a blink).

There are a limited number of operating systems that allow cross-platform transportation. You can view the list by querying any Oracle Database 10*g* database:

```
COLUMN PLATFORM_NAME FORMAT A30
SELECT * FROM V$TRANSPORTABLE_PLATFORM;
PLATFORM_ID PLATFORM_NAME                   ENDIAN_FORMAT
-----------------------------------------------------------
          1 Solaris[tm] OE (32-bit)         Big
          2 Solaris[tm] OE (64-bit)         Big
          7 Microsoft Windows NT            Little
         10 Linux IA (32-bit)               Little
          6 AIX-Based Systems (64-bit)      Big
          3 HP-UX (64-bit)                  Big
          5 HP Tru64 UNIX                   Little
          4 HP-UX IA (64-bit)               Big
         11 Linux IA (64-bit)               Little
```

Note the column ENDIAN_FORMAT. The *endianness* of the platform determines how many steps will be required during transportation to make the transition to a new platform. If the endianness is the same between the two platforms, then transporting a tablespace between platforms is the same as doing it on matching platforms. However, if the endian_format is different, you will have to convert the datafiles to the new endian_format before you can plug them into the new platform. The conversion steps require that you use RMAN to alter the datafiles.

Other than the endian format, the only other new restriction is that you can only transfer Oracle Database 10*g* datafiles between platforms. Otherwise, the restrictions for same-platform TTS apply.

HA Workshop: *Transport a Tablespace from Solaris to Linux*

Workshop Notes
This workshop will outline how to transport a single partitioned tablespace from the woodscrew_orders table from Oracle Database 10*g* on Solaris to Oracle Database 10*g* running on Linux. As we noted, you cannot transport a single partition of a table without transporting the entire table. Therefore, we will need to exchange the partition with a stand-alone table temporarily, so that the partition becomes its own table. Then, we can move forward with the TTS process.

Step 1. Create a temporary table for the partition exchange.

```
create tablespace ws_sep_trans datafile
   'u01/product/oracle/oradata/orcl/ws_sep_trans01.dbf' size 50m;
create table woodscrew_orders_sep (
ord_id          number not null,
ord_date        date,
cust_id         number not null,
scr_id          number not null,
ord_cnt         number,
warehouse_id    number not null,
region          varchar2(20),
constraint pk_woodscrew_orders_sep primary key (ord_id, ord_date)
using index tablespace ws_app_idx)
tablespace ws_sep_trans;
```

Step 2. Exchange the partition with the table.

```
alter table woodscrew_orders
exchange partition wdscrord_sep_2003 with table woodscrew_orders_sep;
```

Step 3. Confirm that the stand-alone table in the WDSCRORD_SEP_2003 tablespace qualifies for transportation. Note that Oracle does not actually move any data in the partition exchange—it simply swaps data dictionary information. Therefore, the partition is now in our new tablespace, WS_SEP_TRANS, but that is not the one being moved. The tablespace we will actually move is the original tablespace named WDSCRORD_SEP_2003 (which happens to be the same name as our original partition), because that tablespace now contains our stand-alone table.

```
connect / as sysdba;
EXECUTE DBMS_TTS.TRANSPORT_SET_CHECK('WDSCRORD_SEP_2003', TRUE);
SELECT * FROM TRANSPORT_SET_VIOLATIONS;
```

Note that with the way we have set up our examples, there is a constraint violation when we select from TRANSPORT_SET_VIOLATIONS, as our index is in a tablespace that is not in our transport set. We can overcome this by choosing not to export constraints when we do the actual export (as you will see in Step 5).

Step 4.   Set the tablespace to read-only.

```
alter tablespace wdscrord_sep_2003 read only;
```

Step 5.   Export the metadata. Note that we specify no constraints. We will have to rebuild the primary key on the table at the new database.

```
exp file=/u01/product/oracle/oradata/orcl/ws_sep_dat.dmp transport_tablespace=y
  constraints=n tablespaces= wdscrord_sep_2003
Export: Release 10.1.0.1.0 - Beta on Mon Dec 29 11:15:02 2003
Copyright (c) 1982, 2003, Oracle.  All rights reserved.
Username: / as sysdba
```

Step 6.   Use RMAN to convert the datafile to little endian for transfer to Linux.

```
convert tablespace wdscrord_sep_2003
to platform 'Linux IA (32-bit)'
FORMAT ='/u01/product/oracle/oradata/orcl/wscrord_sep_2003_for_LNX.dbf';
```

Step 7.   Move the datafile to the Linux system. You can use any type of file transfer that matches your needs for speed and ease of use. We used a binary ftp, renaming the datafile upon transfer (from wscrord_sep_2003_for_LNX.dbf to wscrord_sep_2003.dbf).

Step 8.   On the source, set the tablespace to read-write and then exchange the partition back into place. You will need to revalidate the indices for the table.

```
Connect / as sysdba
alter tablespace wdscrord_sep_2003 read write;
```

```
connect ws_app/ws_app
alter table woodscrew_orders
exchange partition wdscrord_sep_2003 with table woodscrew_orders_sep;
```

Step 9.   On the target Linux system, import the metadata for the datafile.

```
imp file=/u01/product/oracle/oradata/orcl/ws_sep_dat.dmp transport_
tablespace=y tablespaces=wdscrord_sep_2003
datafiles='/u01/product/oracle/oradata/orcl/wscrord_sep_2003.dbf' tts_
owners=(ws_app)
```

Step 10.   Set the new tablespace to read-write.

```
Connect / as sysdba
alter tablesapce wedscrord_sep_2003 read write;
```

CHAPTER
3

Tuning Your Database for Availability

hen we talk about high availability, we must take into account more than just the basic question of "is the database up?" Much more than just that simple question is at stake. What really matters is the perceptions of the users. If the database is up but responsiveness of the database is poor, then from the end user perspective, uptime is affected. This is not a revelation to anyone, but it bears repeating, as this is the premise of this chapter, and the reason for its existence within the covers of a high-availability book. Oracle Database 10*g* has added numerous tuning enhancements, as well as manageability enhancements that will make it easier to detect bottlenecks in the database, and to alleviate those bottlenecks, sometimes automatically.

In this chapter, we will discuss some of these key features, including a better understanding of what they are, and how to set them up to enable the HA DBA to take full advantage of them. Since manageability is a key component of this as well, we will also base many of our examples on the Oracle Database 10*g* Enterprise Manager. This latest version of EM is web-based, and is greatly enhanced to make identifying and fixing bottlenecks easier and more intuitive than ever before.

Intelligent Infrastructure

Oracle Database 10*g* has made great strides in utilizing the information that the database knows about its own inner workings, and turning that knowledge into an infrastructure that will allow the HA DBA to easily and automatically take advantage of that information. This *intelligent infrastructure*, as termed by Oracle, begins with the Automatic Workload Repository. The Workload Repository gathers information on activity in the database at regular intervals. Each run of the Workload Repository is followed by an automatic run of The Automatic Database Diagnostic Monitor (ADDM), which interprets the information supplied by AWR and makes recommendations. One can dig deeper into these recommendations by then manually running one of several advisors that Oracle has provided. In addition, an active session history, or ASH, is maintained to track all events that sessions are waiting for, to allow real-time information gathering. Altogether this is referred to as the intelligent infrastructure. Combined, these tools give the HA DBA more immediate access than ever before into the inner workings of the Oracle RDBMS.

MMON Background Process

The MMON background process is a new background process introduced in Oracle Database 10*g*, responsible for the automatic monitoring that goes on within the database. MMON is responsible for kicking off the Automatic Database Diagnostic Monitor at the end of each AWR run, to check for bottlenecks or problems identified within the report. In addition, MMON monitors the ALERT_QUE, a queue owned by sys, once a minute, for any new information/alerts. MMON can be used to either automatically take a corrective action or to send an alert via the ALERT_QUE. These alerts are then displayed on the database home page in Enterprise Manager. Additional subscribers (such as third-party or home-grown tools) can be added to the ALERT_ QUE using the DBMS_AQADM.ADD_SUBSCRIBER procedure, allowing alerts to be sent to multiple locations. If the ALERT_QUE is unavailable for some reason, alerts will go to the alert.log for the instance.

AWR: Automatic Workload Repository

We begin by looking at one of the key components of these enhancements in Oracle Database 10g—the Automatic Workload Repository, or AWR. For those of you who are familiar with StatsPack from previous releases, AWR will have a familiar look and feel to it. For those who are new to Oracle, or perhaps did not take advantage of StatsPack in previous releases, we will begin with an overview of how it works. Later in this section, we will talk about what is new between AWR and the older versions of StatsPack.

What Is AWR?

AWR is essentially a job-based scheduled collection of statistics, gathered and stored in the Oracle database, containing information about the database itself. This metadata repository by default is kept in a new tablespace in Oracle Database 10g, called SYSAUX. The script catawr.sql creates the Workload Repository, with objects owned by sys. Workload Repository object names are prefaced with WRH$, WRI$, or WRM$. When creating a new database in Oracle Database 10g, the Workload Repository schema and the job to gather statistics are automatically created as part of the database creation. By default, statistics collection will run every 60 minutes, gathering information from within the database on stats such as I/O waits and other wait events, CPU used per session, sorts, I/O rates on various datafiles, and so forth. In order for this to occur, the parameter STATISTICS_LEVEL must be set to ALL or TYPICAL (TYPICAL being the default). At the end of a run, the repository is updated with current information for that period. Reports can then be generated, using begin and end values corresponding to previous Workload Repository runs, to determine what was happening within the database during a given period of time.

Since AWR runs are scheduled by default when the database is created, nothing special need be done to enable this functionality. As mentioned above, AWR runs at 60-minute intervals, collecting stats and storing that information. However, as you can imagine, this can lead to a rather large repository over time, so by default, the data will be purged after seven days. Should you wish to change these defaults— either the frequency of the runs, or how soon the repository is purged—it is easy enough to do so using Enterprise Manager. Should you wish to disable AWR altogether, you may do that as well; however, we strongly recommend that you do *not* do this. The overhead for AWR is minimal, and the gains achieved by allowing the statistic gathering can come in handy at the most unexpected times.

Command-Line API for AWR

As mentioned in the previous section, the functionality of the Workload Repository can best be utilized within Enterprise Manager (EM). Thus, the majority of examples in this chapter will be EM-centric. However, for those of you who are command-line junkies, the API for the Workload Repository is a new one, aptly named DBMS_ WORKLOAD_REPOSITORY. This can be used to create snapshots, drop snapshots, build baselines, and so forth. We will not be delving into the details of the DBMS_ WORKLOAD_REPOSITORY package, but for those of you who are so inclined (or are desperately in need of some heavy reading), please refer to the Oracle Database 10*g* Release 1 Guide titled "PL/SQL Packages and Types Reference," which is part of the Oracle documentation set.

Viewing an AWR Report

OK, so the Workload Repository is populated every 60 minutes with statistics, and this happens automatically. That's nice. Now what? What do I do with this information? The answer is that you define times outlined by AWR runs, in which to turn this information into a report. When creating an AWR report, you define the beginning and ending interval for the reports using snapshot IDs from the Workload Repository. Your report will begin at one snapshot and end at a later snapshot.

An AWR report can be viewed in Enterprise Manager, using the administration page. From there, select Automatic Workload Repository, from under the Workload section, and then click on the underlined number next to Snapshots. Note that here you can also change the interval for AWR—we will cover these steps in more detail in an HA Workshop later in this section. As mentioned previously, you can determine the interval of the reports, with the beginning of the interval going back as far as the repository keeps the data. Reports can be viewed using a full report view in HTML format, or you can view the data with pertinent information summarized in the details view. If you prefer the old text look of the reports, as in the Oracle9*i* and Oracle8*i* StatsPack Reports, then a text report must be generated using the AWR_REPORT_ TEXT function of the DBMS_WORKLOAD_REPOSITORY command-line API.

Interpreting the Workload Repository Report Output

The report, when viewed in its full form, will begin with a heading, which provides the DB information such as DB_Name, DBID, instance_name, and so on. The begin and end snap times will also be shown, with the total elapsed time for the report displayed in minutes. This interval should not be too long, or else the results will be diluted. The default interval of 60 minutes is usually a good starting point, but when troubleshooting a specific issue, you may want to lower that interval to 30 minutes to get more granularity in your data. After the heading information, the report is then broken out into several sections, covering various different types of statistics of value.

When reviewing the report, the Report Summary section at the top will give a quick overview of the database performance. The ending cache sizes will be shown, as well as the load profile, instance efficiency percentages, shared pool statistics, and the top five wait events. This report summary gives a quick look at the system, allowing an immediate review of the most common sources of bottlenecks. The Instance Efficiency section gives a quick look at the buffer and library cache hit ratios, sorts, parsing information, and so on, and allows you to immediately see if these areas of memory need to be increased. The load profile gives you an overall picture of how much of certain types of activity is going on in the database, such as physical reads and writes, sorts, parses, logons, and so forth. The top five timed events tell us where we are spending most of our time waiting, and are also categorized now into wait classes, which we will discuss later in this chapter. The wait classes give the HA DBA another opportunity for a quick look at the situation. For example, if the top five wait events are all I/O related, it can be made readily apparent by showing that all five events are part of the same wait class.

RAC Statistics
If you are running in a RAC environment, the next section will contain a quick look at RAC statistics to give you an idea of the overall performance of your cluster. This section provides information on the workload characteristics of your cluster, and gives insight into how much traffic is going across the interconnect, how frequently instances need to read from the remote cache vs. the local cache, and what the average times are for these operations.

Main Report
After the top sections, the main report body will follow. Here you will have links to various other sections of the report that are of interest, including sections on SQL statements ordered by various stats such as buffer gets, reads, executions, file and tablespace I/O stats, SGA stats, and so forth. These sections will help pinpoint specific areas that are common bottlenecks, by highlighting poorly tuned or frequently executed SQL, and/or by bringing to light I/O hot spots where disk response time is not acceptable. Each report contains a virtual goldmine of information on what is happening within the database, and what may be causing slowdowns at various stages of operation. Our purpose here is not to discuss each individual section, but rather to provide an overview of how to gather and review the reports. Automating the interpretation of these reports via ADDM will be discussed later in this chapter.

Creating Baselines for Comparing the Workload

Evaluating the reports is also made easier if there is a comparison point. We may suspect, as we evaluate sections of the AWR report, that something does not look right—the top SQL may show SQL statements with an excessive number of buffer gets, as an example. It would be invaluable to be able to compare the report to a similar point in time in the past, when similar work was being done and performance was better. For example, perhaps the same SQL was run at points in the past, but the buffer gets for that same statement were much lower. This might indicate that an index has been dropped, or the data distribution of the tables queried has somehow changed.

A baseline (also called a Preserved Snapshot Set) is used to have a comparison point to refer back to if and when performance suffers. The basic idea is that on a Monday morning (or any other time), when out of the blue the HA DBA is barraged with users advising that the database performance is less than exemplary, the first thing that he or she can do is compare the current performance (or, say, the performance over the past hour) to a baseline that was previously set up for that time frame. This will give the HA DBA an immediate idea of what is different from last week (or whatever point in the past you are comparing to) and a head start on where to look for the solution to the problem.

Periods for Baseline Creation

As you can probably tell already, it is necessary to anticipate periods when you might expect to have performance problems. For this, you must have an understanding of the nuances of your particular business. For example, you may experience different peaks at different times of the day—a busy period may occur between 8:30 A.M. and 1:00 P.M., and another peak from 2:30 P.M. to 4:30 P.M. Fortunately, it is possible to create multiple baselines, each covering different points in time. Therefore, you may decide to create a different, separate baseline for each of those periods.

On the other hand, it is difficult to create a baseline for every possible period. If performance problems occur with no appropriate baseline having been created, don't fret. Depending on how long the retention time is for the Workload Repository, you can go back and create the baseline from a similar time frame in the past. For that reason, we recommend that you increase the workload retention time from the default of seven days. You may want to consider two weeks, or even a value of just over a month, depending on your storage capacity and the overall impact this has on your system. Keep in mind that this information will be stored in the SYSAUX tablespace, so size the SYSAUX tablespace accordingly.

Consider our scenario at the beginning of this section. Let's say the DBA did not have a baseline for the early Monday morning period when performance was bad. Let's assume that the problem began at 5:30 A.M. In this shop's line of work, Monday mornings are rather unique, but it is unusual for the system to be loaded this early. The DBA would like to compare this morning's workload to last week at the same time. However, with the default retention time of seven days, stats from last Monday at 5:30 A.M. would have already been purged from the database. If the retention time were set to eight days, or fourteen days, the DBA could go back in time in the Workload Repository, create a quick baseline covering last Monday morning, and then compare the current day's snapshot to last week at the same time.

Comparing Current Stats to Baseline   The advantage of creating baselines is twofold. First, the baseline data remains in the repository indefinitely, until it is explicitly deleted, so it is not subject to being aged out like the rest of the snapshots. This means that the data will still be there in a month to refer back to and compare. Hence the term "Preserved Snapshot Set." The second advantage is the ability to quickly run comparisons of a snapshot to a baseline.

It is easiest to do the comparison using EM. From the Workload Repository section, you can select the option to Compare Timelines. This will allow you to first select the time frame that you wish to compare (presumably a period of time with poor performance), and then you can select a preserved snapshot set (or any other period of time within your retention range) to compare that to. The output will give you such fodder as comparison of block change rates for each period, physical reads, parse time, user commits, and so on. The display will show the timelines side by side, in graphical format, allowing you to quickly see the differentiators between the two timelines for the given periods.

HA Workshop: *Exploring the Workload Repository*

Workshop Notes
The Workload Repository is best understood by using Enterprise Manager, giving a graphical view of the snapshots available and masking the complexity of the APIs used. This example walks through using EM to view reports, edit the retention policies, and create baselines for comparison.

Step 1.   Log in to EM using the following URL, substituting in the hostname of the database server for <server_name>:

    http://<server_name>:5500/em

If using Enterprise Manager Grid Control (discussed in Chapter 5), use the machine name for the management repository database, with port 7777, as such:

    http://<repository_server>:7777/em

Navigate to the Workload Repository by clicking on the Administration link for your particular database, and then, under Workload, click the Automatic Workload Repository link.

Step 2. Note the Snapshot Retention time (in days), the Snapshot Interval, and the Collection Level, under the General section. Click on Edit to change these. Set the Retention Period value to 30 days, and the System Snapshot Interval to 30 minutes, as shown in Figure 3-1, and then click OK.

Step 3. Back on the main Workload Repository page, in the Snapshots section, click on the underlined number next to Snapshots. This link will propel you into the Snapshots screen, where you can view the times of all AWR snapshots that currently reside in the repository.

Step 4. To view a report, navigate to the box titled Actions and change the selection to View Report. Click on the radio button next to an existing snap ID (not the last one) and then click Go. The next page will display all snapshots created

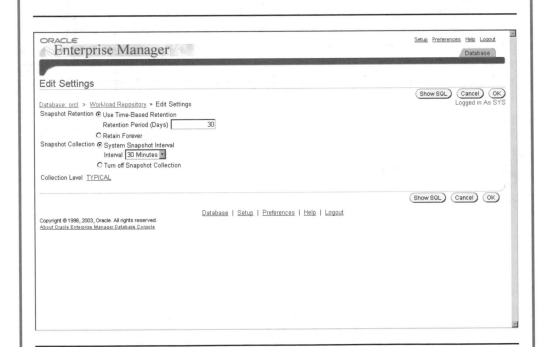

FIGURE 3-1. *Changing default snapshot retention time*

after the beginning snap ID that was previously selected. Select the one created directly after the beginning snap ID (this will give us a 30-minute interval), and then click OK. After a few seconds, you will see the Snapshot Details screen, with the ability to see in report format or details format. Save it by clicking on the Save to File button in the Report screen.

Step 5.   Next, to create a baseline, return to the Snapshots screen by clicking on the Snapshots link across the top. For this exercise, we will create a baseline for the time period of 9:00 A.M. to 12:00 P.M., on a weekday, so select the radio button next to an existing snapshot with a capture time as near as possible to 9:00 A.M. on a weekday. Ensure that Create Preserved Snapshot Set is selected in the Actions box, and choose Go.

Step 6.   On the Create Preserved Snapshot Set page, give the Snapshot Set a name of Weekday Morning and then select the Ending Snapshot to be the snapshot ID closest to 12 P.M. on the same day. Click OK to create the baseline (preserved snapshot set).

Step 7.   Now, to compare a report interval to the baseline you have just created, return to the Snapshots screen by clicking on the Workload Repository link and then the Snapshots link again (see Step 3). In the Actions box, select Compare Timelines and, for the beginning snap ID, choose a snapshot from 9:00 A.M. on a weekday *other* than the baseline you just created.

Step 8.   Choose the ending snapshot of 12:00 P.M. on that same day and choose Go.

Step 9.   On the Second Timeline Start screen, choose the Select a Preserved Snapshot Set option and then select the weekday morning baseline that was created in Step 6. Click Next, and then click Finish to get the Compare Timelines: Results screen. This screen will give you a graphical comparison between the baseline (second timeline) and the date that you had selected for comparison.

> **NOTE**
> *You do not have to have a preserved snapshot set to do the comparison—you can compare intervals between any two periods for which you still have snapshots in the repository, based on your snapshot retention period.*

ADDM (Automatic Database Diagnostic Monitor)

Well, after going through all of the information available in a Workload Repository report, it can seem a bit daunting to interpret. Further, you may ask yourself, geez— do I need to read through these reports every 60 minutes? Once a day? Once a week? The answer to that depends on your social life. However, the good news is that you do not *have* to read these reports on an hourly basis. The Automatic Database Diagnostic Monitor will do that for you.

ADDM is constantly running in the background, monitoring information that is collected in the Workload Repository. ADDM uses this data, as well as data from the active session history (ASH), and automatically analyzes this information to provide proactive recommendations on tuning and performance issues. The home screen in Enterprise Manager has an Advice section, with links to ADDM Findings, as well as an ADDM Analysis section where this information is displayed.

ADDM essentially can be used in two separate modes—what we would refer to as a *proactive* and a *reactive* mode. The proactive mode is defined by the automatic diagnosis mentioned above. Aside from these automatic ADDM checks, additional ADDM tasks can be created to look for specific problems, or to go back in time and look at a period in time when a problem was observed or reported. This is the reactive mode usage of ADDM.

Viewing the ADDM Reports

The ADDM runs are scheduled to run automatically at the end of each Workload Repository snapshot run—so each time a snapshot is gathered, ADDM runs automatically behind the scenes, gathering information on the last 60 minutes of activity (as defined by the system snapshot interval). From the command line, the DBMS_ADVISOR API can be run to get the stored advice from ADDM. For example, the last/most recent report can be viewed directly from SQL*Plus with the following query:

```
SQL> set long 1000000
SQL> set pagesize 50000
SQL> column get_clob format a80
SQL>select dbms_advisor.get_task_report(task_name) as ADDM_report
    from   dba_advisor_tasks
    where  task_id = (
       select max(t.task_id)
       from   dba_advisor_tasks t, dba_advisor_log l
       where  t.task_id = l.task_id
```

```
and   t.advisor_name = 'ADDM'
and   l.status = 'COMPLETED');
```

The output of this query will look something like this:

ADDM_REPORT

```
--------------------------------------------------------------------------
            DETAILED ADDM REPORT FOR TASK 'ADDM:1037082046_1_198' WITH ID 310
            -----------------------------------------------------------------

                  Analysis Period: 10-DEC-2003 from 20:30:51 to 21:00:36
              Database ID/Instance: 1037082046/1
                   Snapshot Range: from 197 to 198
                    Database Time: 1119 seconds
            Average Database Load: .6 active sessions


~~~~~~~~~~~~~~~~~~~~~~~~~~~~~~~~~~~~~~~~~~~~~~~~~~~~~~~~~~~~~~~~~~~~~~~~~~~~~~~~~


FINDING 1: 100% impact (7136 seconds)
-------------------------------------
SQL statements were found waiting for row lock waits.

   RECOMMENDATION 1: Application Analysis, 100% benefit (7136 seconds)
      ACTION: Trace the cause of row contention in the application logic. Use
         given blocked SQL to identify the database objects involved.
         Investigate application logic involving DML on these objects.
      RATIONALE: The SQL statement with SQL_ID 18n2c85u5p8zf was blocked on
         row locks.
         RELEVANT OBJECT: SQL statement with SQL_ID 18n2c85u5p8zf
         update emp set ename = ename
      RATIONALE: The SQL statement with SQL_ID 275zcmg41cx02 was blocked on
         row locks.
         RELEVANT OBJECT: SQL statement with SQL_ID 275zcmg41cx02

      RATIONALE: The SQL statement with SQL_ID 5dhfmtds8m5qs was blocked on
         row locks.
         RELEVANT OBJECT: SQL statement with SQL_ID 5dhfmtds8m5qs

      RATIONALE: The SQL statement with SQL_ID 872zuyfy72zs5 was blocked on
         row locks.
         RELEVANT OBJECT: SQL statement with SQL_ID 872zuyfy72zs5


   SYMPTOMS THAT LED TO THE FINDING:
      Wait class "Application" was consuming significant database time. (100%
      impact [7136 seconds])
```

```
FINDING 2: 100% impact (1790 seconds)
------------------------------------
PL/SQL execution consumed significant database time.

   RECOMMENDATION 1: SQL Tuning, 100% benefit (1790 seconds)
      ACTION: Tune the PL/SQL block with SQL_ID fjxa1vp3yhtmr. Refer to the
         "Tuning PL/SQL Applications" chapter of Oracle's "PL/SQL User's Guide
         and Reference"
      RELEVANT OBJECT: SQL statement with SQL_ID fjxa1vp3yhtmr
      BEGIN EMD_NOTIFICATION.QUEUE_READY(:1, :2, :3); END;
```

ADDM and Enterprise Manager

While you can do this from the command line, as we have noted previously, it is
far easier to view the latest run (and any past runs of ADDM) by using Enterprise
Manager. These findings can be viewed by clicking on the Advisor Central link from
the database or instance home page. This link will take you directly to the Advisors
page in EM, where you will see the task name associated with the last ADDM run (if
you follow the link from the database home page of a cluster database, you will see
the last ADDM run for *each* instance). To view the same output as the above query
showed, ensure that the radio button next to the task is selected, and then click
View Result. On the next screen, any findings will be summarized under the section
Information Findings. To view the actual report, click on the View Report button.

Viewing Past Advisor Runs   By default, the reports generated as we see above are
stored in the database for a period of 30 days. Therefore, if you need (or want) to
review this information reactively, you can simply go back in time to view a past
ADDM run, and see the advice that was dispensed along with this report. From the
command line, it is possible to get this information from the DBA_ADVISOR_TASKS
and DBA_ADVISOR_LOGS views, but it is a bit more difficult than the above query.
The above query simply used the max(task_id) to get the latest run. If you want to
get a specific ADDM run from the past, you need to know the specific task_id.
Therefore, we again recommend using Enterprise Manager for this.

   Again, from the EM database home page, choose Advisor Central from the
Related Links section at the bottom of the page. Under Advisory Type, choose All
Types, and under Advisor Runs, choose All, and then click Go. This will pull up a
summary page of all advisory runs still stored in the database, with a description,
the task name, and the start and end time of each run. You can now go back to a
specific point in time, and view the advice dispensed by ADDM for that time period
by simply clicking on the task's Name link, as shown in Figure 3-2.

FIGURE 3-2. *ADDM report as viewed in EM*

What Drives ADDM?

So, what is the force behind the Automatic Database Diagnostic Monitor? What is it that makes ADDM generate a finding? Is it based on the mood that ADDM happens to be in when awakened after a 60-minute slumber? Is a "finding" precipitated by a congressional investigation, or triggered by an unfounded report on a fringe web site? Fortunately, ADDM is a bit more structured than that.

ADDM uses a combination of sources for its findings and recommendations: wait events for individual sessions; the DB time model to determine how much DB time is spent in database calls, with a focus on reducing the overall database time spent on operations; wait classes, which are high-level groupings of the more fine-grained wait events; and operating system and database metrics. Using this information stored in the Workload Repository and the active session history (ASH) lays the groundwork for ADDM to make the call to report a finding, and then come up with a subsequent recommendation.

Wait Events and Active Session History

Wait events are essentially the lifeblood of diagnosing a performance problem. In past releases, if the DBA could capture a problem while it was occurring, they could go into the V$SESSION_WAIT view and determine what it was that sessions were waiting on. This would give him or her the impetus to then move forward in resolving the issue. If we missed the event, however, we would have to either rerun it (somehow) or rely on information from StatsPack (or AWR) on what the top wait events were for that period, and make the leap of faith that these waits were corresponding to what our particular problem was. With Oracle Database 10*g*, there is a new view introduced called V$ACTIVE_SESSION_HISTORY, which maintains data from active sessions, capturing the wait events and their wait times, the SQL_ID, and session information for the waiting session. This allows us to then go back to the past and view this detailed information as it existed in the past. ADDM can use this for proactive and reactive analysis purposes. In addition, the view V$SESSION_WAIT_HISTORY will provide the last 10 wait events for an active session.

Wait Classes   With Oracle Database 10*g*, there are now over 700 wait events, primarily due to the fact that many previous wait events have been broken down into more granular events to make diagnostics more precise. To make these wait events easier to interpret, they are categorized into wait classes, with each wait class pointing to a high-level category of problem for a particular wait event. Each wait event is assigned to a specific wait class, with the wait class pointing toward the problem and solution. The most common wait classes and their descriptions are listed here:

- **Administrative**   Commands issued by a privileged user (that is, DBA) that result in other users waiting—an index rebuild, for example.

- **Application**   Generally related to application design, this category includes lock waits caused by row-level locking and explicit or implicit lock commands (implicit lock commands such as those generated by a DDL statement).

- **Cluster**   Global cache, global enqueue, and global messaging–related wait events in a RAC environment.

- **Commit**   Currently only includes a wait event for redo log sync confirmation after a commit.

- **Concurrency** Generally, waits involving concurrent parsing and buffer cache latch and lock contention; indicative of many sessions going after the same resources.

- **Configuration** Wait events in this category can generally be resolved by tuning; includes undersized log buffer space, logfile sizes, buffer cache size, shared pool size, ITL allocation, HW enqueue contention, ST enqueue contention, and so on.

- **Idle** Session is inactive.

- **Other** Catchall for wait events not associated with one of the predefined classes.

- **Network** Waits for data to be sent over the network—specifically waits in the networking layer or on hardware.

- **Scheduler** Waits due to Resource Manager prioritization.

- **System I/O** Waits on I/O done by background processes (except for MMON and SMON).

- **User I/O** Wait for blocks to be read off disk by foreground process, SMON, or MMON.

The DB Time Model

The DB time model is a way of looking at performance based on the overall time spent in the database. Time-based statistics are kept in two new views in Oracle Database 10g—V$SYS_TIME_MODEL and V$SESS_TIME_MODEL. While these views contain various different time-related stats, the most significant of these is DB time. The goal of any tuning activity should be to reduce that overall time. If the overall time spent in the database, in database calls, is reduced, then the tuning has been effective. ADDM will use the DB time model as a basis for findings and recommendations. In addition, automatic tuning of the SGA (discussed later in this chapter, in "Memory Advisor and ASMM") will take DB time into consideration when deciding where to allocate SGA resources, with the goal being to reduce overall DB time.

Advisor Central

Now that we are on the topic of the advisors, let's go back and take a more detailed look at each of the advisors in the Advisor Central page. This page offers links to the following advisors, along with the ability to create a task for these advisors:

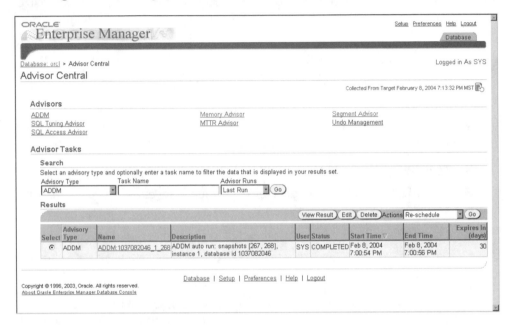

SQL Tuning Advisor

The SQL Tuning Advisor gives recommendations on changing SQL statements, to be rewritten so that they are more efficient. The SQL statements are referenced by a new column that is part of V$ACTIVE_SESSION_HISTORY, called SQL_ID. ADDM will detect statements that appear to be inefficient, and/or are leading to a disproportionate number of waits, and may suggest that you run the SQL Tuning Advisor against a given SQL statement. The SQL Tuning Advisor, when accessed from Advisor Central, will allow you to look at the top SQL for a specific period of time, create SQL tuning sets, or choose to view/create snapshots and/or baselines.

If a high-usage SQL statement shows up in an ADDM run, that statement will be displayed in the ADDM Analysis section of the EM database home page. Clicking on the statement will take you into a slightly different look, in the ADDM Finding Details view. From here, you will be able to run the SQL Tuning Advisor against the particular SQL statement.

Top SQL and Period SQL

The Top SQL link shows us by default the Spot SQL view, which shows five-minute intervals over the past hour. The highlighted section can be moved to display any five-minute interval over the past hour. The top SQL statements will be ordered by activity percentage, CPU percentage, and wait percentage, respectively, with the SQL_ID being the identifier for a given statement. The Period SQL link will allow a look at SQL statements over a longer period of time (a week), with the highlighted section giving you a look at a given 24-hour period within that week.

Clicking on the SQL_ID will give you an in-depth look at that particular statement, including the actual statement itself, the execution plan, current statistics, and execution history. The Current Statistics link has valuable information on the amount of space the statement takes in the shared_pool, as well as loads (parses) and invalidations, referring to the number of times this particular statement has been aged out of the shared_pool. A statement with a high number of loads and/or invalidations may be a candidate for pinning in the shared_pool.

Creating SQL Tuning Sets

SQL tuning sets can be created from within this page to allow a group of statements, either by type or by time period, to be analyzed. You may even want to create a tuning set based on just a single statement. Once the set is created, you can view the SQL statements by cost, buffer gets, disk reads, and so on. You can then choose to run either the SQL Tuning Advisor or the SQL Access Advisor against the tuning set. When choosing the criteria to create a tuning set, you might want to look at all of the statements in a given period of time, you may look at all SELECT statements within a period of time, or you may want to just grab the top one or two statements to create a tuning set.

SQL Access Advisor

The SQL Tuning Advisor will *not* give suggestions on adding or removing indexes, or making other physical changes. Changes like this would change the access method of a statement without changing the actual statement itself. For those types of recommendations, we refer you to the SQL Access Advisor. The SQL Access Advisor gives recommendations on either creating materialized views or creating indexes, or both, in order to give more efficient access for SQL statements. As input, you can use current and/or recent SQL activity that is still cached in memory. In addition, you can use a workload from the SQL Repository (requires that a SQL tuning set be created), or you can get a user-defined workload from a table. In addition, you can create a hypothetical workload, given certain inputs.

Memory Advisor and ASMM

In Oracle 9*i*, the concept of a dynamically resizable SGA was introduced, giving a DBA the ability to adjust one SGA parameter downward and then increase another value upward in its place. The Memory Advisor in Oracle Database 10*g* allows shared memory management to be enabled, which essentially automates this same process—hence the term automatic shared memory management, or ASMM. When shared memory management is enabled, a new parameter, SGA_TARGET, is set to a numeric value that becomes the ceiling on the total SGA size. Once shared memory management is enabled, you are essentially allowing Oracle to automatically adjust the values that define the total SGA size, on the fly, up to the total for SGA_TARGET.

ASMM Ceilings and Floors

As an oversimplified example, consider if your total SGA size is 1GB, divided equally between db_cache, large_pool, shared_pool, and java_pool. This would essentially give you values of around 250MB for each of these parameters. With shared memory management enabled, Oracle will monitor the stats associated with these SGA values, and may decide to reduce one parameter in favor of increasing another. For example, suppose Oracle detects that during a certain interval, the buffer cache hit ratio is lower than 80 percent, while at the same time the amount of free memory in the large_pool is relatively high. Oracle may decide to reduce the large_pool_size by 50 percent (to 125MB), and then dynamically increase the db_cache_size by 50 percent to 375MB. The overall memory used for the SGA is still the same, meaning that we have not exceeded our ceiling (as defined by SGA_TARGET). However, the distribution of that memory has been altered, with the overall effect of increasing performance by using that memory where it is most needed.

When ASMM is enabled (by setting the SGA_TARGET), you should explicitly set the automatically managed pieces of the SGA to 0. In Oracle Database 10*g* Release 1, this includes the four parameters mentioned above: shared_pool_size, large_pool_size, java_pool_size, and db_cache_size (only the default db_cache_size is automatically tuned). All other SGA-related parameters should still be manually set. If you set one of the above parameters, defined as auto-tunable, to an explicit value in the spfile or init file, that value will be used as the floor for that parameter—meaning that while Oracle may be allowed to increase the amount of memory allocated to that particular piece of the SGA, it will not be allowed to drop below the explicitly set value. So, continuing with our example, if we set SGA_TARGET to 1GB, and then set each of the above parameters to an explicit value of 250MB, no automatic tuning can be done because the floor for each parameter adds up to the total of SGA_TARGET, which is our ceiling. This leaves no room to increase or decrease anything. For this reason, when SGA_TARGET is set via the Memory Advisor in Enterprise Manager, Enterprise Manager will automatically *unset* all of the other SGA parameters (that is, set them to 0 values), thus giving Oracle the freedom to modify all parameters on the fly as it sees fit (whether to higher values or lower values). You can view the current settings that Oracle has arrived at for each of the SGA components by querying the view V$SGA_DYNAMIC_COMPONENTS, and these values can also be viewed in the Memory Advisor on EM.

Non-ASMM Tunable SGA Components   The above is an oversimplified example, as the SGA is, of course, comprised of more than just those four parameters. SGA_TARGET must actually account for the entire SGA, including a new parameter in Oracle Database 10*g*: STREAMS_POOL_SIZE. Aside from that, SGA_TARGET must account for values for the LOG_BUFFER, any KEEP pools, the RECYCLE pool, and any nondefault buffer caches. However, the KEEP pools, the RECYCLE pool, nondefault buffer caches and Streams_Pool values are not currently auto-managed, so these parameters must be set explicitly, even while the other main components of the SGA should be set to 0.

NOTE
Oracle cannot increase the total SGA beyond the value for SGA_MAX_SIZE, which by default is set exactly equal to the total SGA size. If you attempt to increase the total SGA size (using the Memory Advisor Wizard) to a value greater than SGA_MAX_SIZE, you will receive an error.

Memory Advice Parameters

If you choose not to enable shared memory management, the Memory Advisor will still be able to give advice on sizes for parameters within the SGA, such as DB_CACHE_SIZE and SHARED_POOL_SIZE, as well as provide advice on the setting of PGA_AGGREGATE_TARGET. This advice is enabled automatically if STATISTICS_LEVEL is set to either TYPICAL or ALL. For advice on the buffer cache, you must also have the parameter DB_CACHE_ADVICE=ON (this will default to ON if the STATISTICS_LEVEL parameter is set to TYPICAL or ALL).

The following views are populated when the above parameters are set to their default values:

```
v$db_cache_advice
v$shared_pool_advice
v$java_pool_advice
v$mttr_target_advice
v$pga_target_advice
```

This information is formatted and available in graphical format via the Memory Advisor on Enterprise Manager. By clicking on the Advice button next to the Buffer Cache values in the Memory Advisor, you will see calculations of what the difference would be in number of block reads for various values of DB_CACHE_SIZE. Similarly, the Advice button next to the Shared Pool value (see Figure 3-3) will give you estimates of parse times under different values of SHARED_POOL_SIZE.

By the same token, within the Memory Advisor, you can view estimates on the PGA workload by going to the PGA link (see Figure 3-3 again) and clicking on the Advice button there. This value, of course, depends on PGA_AGGREGATE_TARGET being set to a nonzero value in the init.ora (or spfile).

NOTE
Many of these parameters can be changed dynamically, both in memory and for future startups, if using an spfile. For example, SGA_TARGET, DB_ CACHE_ADVICE, and STATISTICS_LEVEL can all be changed on the fly, and SGA parameters such as DB_CACHE_SIZE and SHARED_POOL_SIZE can all be lowered (set to 0) dynamically via an ALTER SYSTEM command.

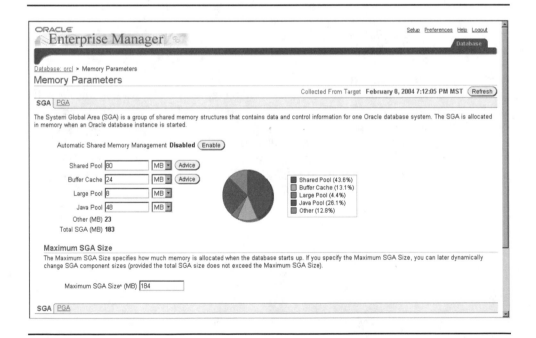

FIGURE 3-3. *Memory Advisor*

Additional Advisors

The previous advisors merited sections on their own due to the impact that they potentially have and the new features that they bring with them to Oracle Database 10*g*. In addition to the advisors mentioned, Advisor Central provides links to other new advisors that can offer useful insights into the performance and layout of your database.

MTTR Advisor

The MTTR Advisor allows making changes to fast_start_mttr_target, which essentially controls how long we want instance recovery to take, should we have a crash. Setting a target value here will cause Oracle to make internal changes to how frequently data is flushed to disk, or checkpointed, to ensure that *if* a crash recovery occurs, the time to roll forward will be close to the targeted value. This means the crash recovery will complete within *x* number of seconds, and the database will then be opened and made available. The view V$MTTR_TARGET_ADVICE is used to provide an idea of what additional I/O might be incurred if the MTTR is reduced. This advisor also allows for the setting up of a flash recovery area, and enabling database archivelog mode. This is not tuning related, but of course is intrinsic to high availability, so these topics are covered more appropriately in other chapters.

Segment Advisor

The Segment Advisor essentially looks at space usage and advises on whether you can free up space. It also checks for fragmentation, and determines whether reorganizing individual segments and/or making changes to entire tablespaces can gain efficiencies. If it finds segments that can be reorganized, it will highlight them and provide a recommendation to do a shrink of the segment, and offer the ability to schedule a job to do so immediately or schedule the run for some future time. In Oracle Database 10*g*, a table or index segment can be compacted via the alter <object> <object_name> shrink ... command. This command can be done while the table or index is online, without impacting user access to the segments and without the need to rebuild the indexes afterward. However, row movement must be enabled on the table in question first. Note in Figure 3-4 that the segment in question has generated advice, but the advice cannot be executed because row movement is not enabled. Thus, the selection is grayed out. In order to make any changes to this table, you will have to enable row movement (alter table PROD_EMP enable Row Movement) and then rerun the Segment Advisor. Then you will be able to select the option under the Recommendations section to shrink the segment.

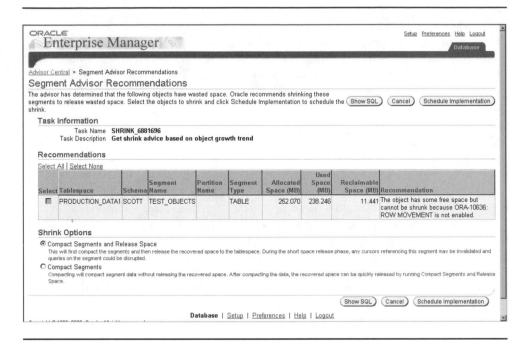

FIGURE 3-4. *Segment Advisor*

Undo Management Advisor

The Undo Management Advisor first takes you into a review of the undo management
parameters and allows you to make or change settings for enabling automatic undo
management, which will automatically tune the UNDO_RETENTION time for you
based on longest running queries and available space in the UNDO tablespace. In
addition, the Undo Management Advisor allows for making changes to the UNDO
tablespace, or actually changing the undo to a different tablespace altogether. From
here, you can actually launch into the Undo Advisor itself, and Oracle will give
advice on what the undo retention should be (in seconds) to avoid Snapshot Too
Old errors (ORA-1555). In addition, the Undo Advisor will estimate the size that the
UNDO tablespace needs to be in order to retain that amount of undo. Since Oracle
Database 10*g* provides you with the opportunity to *guarantee* the retention period,
the Undo Advisor will take data from the past seven days (by default), analyze that
data, and determine how much undo has been generated during that period. The
Undo Advisor will then provide a graph, showing you how large the UNDO
tablespace needs to be to achieve the desired UNDO_RETENTION time without
running out of space in the UNDO_TABLESPACE.

Automatic Storage Management (ASM)

Automatic Storage Management, or ASM, is another new Oracle Database 10*g*
feature that revolutionizes the way Oracle and the HA DBA manage database files.
ASM combines volume management with the concept of Oracle managed files to
allow the HA DBA to create a database comprised of datafiles that are not only
self-managed, but also the I/O is automatically balanced among available
disks. ASM combines the ability to simplify management of files with the ability to
automatically self-tune, while at the same time providing a level of redundancy
and availability that is absolutely imperative for the storage grid.

The implementation of ASM involves the creation of a normal Oracle instance
with the parameter INSTANCE_TYPE=ASM set to a value of ASM on a node where a
database or databases reside. This instance does not have an associated database,
but rather is used to manage the disks that are accessed by your database(s). As
such, an ASM instance is never opened—it is only mounted. Mounting an ASM
instance involves mounting the disk groups associated with the ASM instance, so
that the disk groups and files are then accessible from the other instances. We will
discuss ASM in various sections throughout the remainder of the book, but we will
take the time here to discuss the concepts behind ASM, how to implement ASM in
your environment, and how to manage an ASM environment once you are up and
running.

ASM Concepts

The underlying concept behind ASM is that it is a *file system* created specifically
for Oracle datafiles, on top of RAW or block devices. This file system is kept and
maintained by the Oracle kernel, so Oracle knows where file extents are and
automatically manages the placement of these extents for maximum performance
and availability of your database. You, as the HA DBA, will not know or care where
Oracle is placing extents on disk. Oracle will do all of that management for you
through ASM. No volume management software is needed, and no file system
is needed.

ASM Disk Group

At its highest level, within ASM you will create ASM disk groups, comprised of
one or more disks (usually RAW, but certified NFS storage will work as well).
Oracle will take that disk group as the location for creating files, and will lay down
files in 1MB extents across however many disks are available. The more disks that
are used within a disk group, the more flexibility you will give Oracle to spread the
I/O out among disks, resulting in better performance and improved redundancy.
ASM disk groups can be used for all Oracle files, including the spfile, the controlfile,
the online redo logs, and all datafiles. In addition, you can use an ASM disk group

for your flashback recovery area (discussed in Chapter 8), as a location for all RMAN backups, flashback logs, and archived logs. Bear in mind, however, that ASM was created specifically for Oracle, so it cannot be used as a general purpose file system. As such, files in an ASM disk group are not visible at the OS, and files such as Oracle binaries and Oracle trace files must be kept on a regular file system (such as UFS or NTFS).

NOTE
We mentioned that extents are written out in 1MB sizes, and this is true for all files except controlfiles and logfiles. Redo logs, controlfiles, and flashback logs use fine-grained striping, by default, which results in extents of 128K, rather than 1MB. This allows large I/Os to be split into smaller chunks and processed by more disks, resulting in better performance for these types of files.

Stripe and Mirror Everything (SAME)

ASM adheres to the *same* philosophy, which recommends to stripe and mirror everything. This is handled in ASM by allowing the setting of redundancy levels during the creation of a disk group. Normal redundancy implies that you have at least two disks, because every allocation unit (or extent) will be written twice, to two different disks within the disk group. High redundancy implies three-way mirroring, meaning every allocation unit (or extent) will be written to three separate disks within the disk group. This mirroring is not the traditional type of mirroring that you may be used to, however—this is done at the extent level. For example, let's assume that we are mirroring with normal redundancy (two-way mirroring), and that we have five disks in a disk group. If we then create a 10MB file on that disk group, the first 1MB extent may be mirrored across disks 3 and 5, the next 1MB extent may be mirrored across disks 2 and 4, the next extent across disks 1 and 3, and so on. When all is said and done, every extent has been mirrored, but no two disks will contain identical data. If you choose external redundancy when creating a disk group, this is perfectly acceptable, but it implies that all mirroring is handled at the hardware level.

By the same token, ASM achieves striping by spreading the extents, aka allocation units, for a given file across all available disks in a disk group. So, your TEMP tablespace may be 4GB in size, but if you have a disk group with 10 disks in it, you will not care how the tablespace is laid out—Oracle with ASM will automatically spread the extents for this file across the disks, seeking to balance out the I/O and avoid hot spots on disk. If Oracle detects that a particular disk is getting too much

I/O, it will attempt to read the mirrored copy of an extent from a different disk, if it is available. The same is true for all files, including redo logs.

NOTE
Mirroring is actually performed to what are known as "partner" disks. Within an ASM disk group, any given disk can have a maximum of eight partners. This means that the extents written to a disk can be mirrored to any one of the eight partners defined for that disk. In our simple example, where we have only five disks, any disk can be the partner of another disk because we have not exceeded this limit. However, in a disk group with more than eight disks (say, hundreds or even thousands of disks), it is important to realize that each disk will be limited in the number of partners that can participate in the mirroring for that disk. This is done intentionally, as limiting the number of partners minimizes the possibility that a double disk failure could lead to data loss—this could only happen if the two disks that fail also happen to be partners. Utilizing high redundancy (triple-mirroring) reduces this likelihood even further. An ASM disk group will theoretically support up to 10,000 disks with a single ASM instance, spread across as many as 63 disk groups. ASM also supports up to 1 million files in a disk group. In Oracle Database 10g Release 1, only one ASM instance is allowed per node.

Failure Groups   A failure group allows you to take the redundancy of disks to the next level, by creating a group containing disks from multiple controllers. As such, if a controller fails, and all of the disks associated with that controller are inaccessible, other disks within the disk group will still be accessible as long as they are connected to a different controller. By creating a failure group within the disk group, Oracle and ASM will mirror writes to different disks, but will also mirror writes to disks within different failure groups, so that the loss of a controller will not impact access to your data.

File Size Limits on ASM
As we have discussed, ASM disk groups support a variety of different file types, including online redo logs, controlfiles, datafiles, archived redo logs, RMAN backup

sets, and Flashback Logs. In Oracle Database 10*g* Release 1, ASM imposes a maximum file size on *any* file in an ASM disk group, regardless of the file type. That maximum size depends on the redundancy level of the disk group itself, as shown here:

Max File Size	Redundancy Level
300GB	External redundancy
150GB	Normal redundancy
100GB	High redundancy

These maximum values do not affect the maximum values imposed by other limitations, such as a maximum size for database files themselves. In Oracle Database 10*g* Release 1, for example, a database file is limited to approximately 4 million blocks. This limit applies irrespective of the underlying storage mechanism, file system, or platform. As you can see, for most block sizes this will not be an issue. However, some platforms (such as Tru64) support a db_block_size of up to 32k. As such, the normal maximum database file size with a 32K block would be 128GB. However, if you are on a high-redundancy ASM disk group (3-way mirroring), the maximum file size would actually be 100GB.

In addition, Oracle Database 10*g* includes a new feature: the ability to create a tablespace using the BIGFILE syntax. When creating a BIGFILE tablespace, you are only allowed a single datafile in that tablespace, but the limit on the number of blocks is increased to approximately 4 billion blocks (from 4 million). The theoretical maximum file size for a datafile in a BIGFILE tablespace would then be in the Terabytes—but as you can see, ASM will limit the datafile size to 300GB or lower, based on the Redundancy Level of the disk group. Expect this limitation to be removed in subsequent patches or releases. See Metalink Note 265659.1 for details.

Rebalancing Operations
Inherent to ASM is the ability to add and remove disks from a disk group on the fly without impacting the overall availability of the disk group itself, or of the database. This, again, is one of the precepts of grid computing. ASM handles this by initiating a rebalance operation any time a disk is added or removed. If a disk is removed from the disk group, either due to a failure or excess capacity in the group, the rebalance operation will remirror the extents that had been mirrored to that disk and redistribute the extents among the remaining disks in the group. If a new disk is added to the group, the rebalance will do the same, ensuring that each disk in the group has a relatively equal number of extents.

Because of the way the allocation units are striped, a rebalance operation only requires that a small percentage of extents be relocated, minimizing the impact of this operation. Nevertheless, you can control the rebalance operation by using the parameter ASM_POWER_LIMIT, which is a parameter specific to the ASM instance. By default, this is set to 1, meaning that any time a disk is added or removed, a rebalance operation will begin—using a single slave. By setting this value to 0 for a disk group, you can defer the operation until later (say overnight), at which time you can set the ASM_POWER_LIMIT to as high as 11. This will generate 11 slave processes to do the work of rebalancing. This can be accomplished via the alter system command:

```
alter system set asm_power_limit=0;
alter system set asm_power_limit=11;
```

Background Processes for ASM   An ASM instance introduces two new types of background processes—the RBAL process and the ARB*n* processes. The RBAL process within the ASM instance actually determines when a rebalance needs to be done and estimates how long it will take. RBAL then invokes the ARB processes to do the actual work. The number of ARB processes invoked depends on the ASM_ POWER_LIMIT setting. If this is set to the max of 11, then an ASM instance would have 11 ARB background processes, starting with ARB0 and ending with ARBA. In addition, a regular database instance will have an RBAL and an ASMB process, but the RBAL process in a database instance is used for making global calls to open the disks in a disk group. The ASMB process communicates with the CSS daemon on the node and receives file extent map information from the ASM instance. ASMB is also responsible for providing I/O stats to the ASM instance.

ASM and RAC
Because it is managed by Oracle, ASM environments are particularly well-suited for a RAC installation. Using a shared disk array with ASM disk groups for file locations can greatly simplify the storage of your datafiles. ASM eliminates the need to configure RAW devices for each file, simplifying the file layout and configuration. ASM also eliminates the need to use a cluster file system, as ASM takes over all file management duties for the database files. However, you can still use a cluster file system if you want to install your ORACLE_HOME on a shared drive (on those platforms that support the ORACLE_HOME on a cluster file system). We discuss ASM instance configuration in a RAC environment in the next section, as well as in Chapter 4.

Implementing ASM
Conceptually, as we mentioned, ASM requires a separate instance be created on each node/server where any Oracle instances reside. On the surface, this instance is just like any other Oracle instance, with an init file, init parameters, and so forth,

except that this instance never opens a database. The major difference between an ASM instance and a regular instance lies in a few parameters:

- INSTANCE_TYPE = ASM (mandatory for an ASM instance)
- ASM_DISKSTRING = /dev/raw/raw* (path to look for candidate disks)
- ASM_DISKGROUPS = ASM_DISK (defines disk groups to mount at startup)

Aside from these parameters, the ASM instance requires an SGA of around 100MB, leaving the total footprint for the ASM instance at around 130MB. Remember— no controlfiles, datafiles, or redo logs are needed for an ASM instance. The ASM instance is used strictly to mount disk groups. A single ASM instance can manage disk groups used by multiple Oracle databases on a single server. However, in a RAC environment, each separate node/server must have its own ASM instance (we will discuss this in more detail in Chapter 4).

Creating the ASM Instance

If you are going to create a database using ASM for the datafiles, you must first create the ASM instance and disk groups to be used. It is possible to do this via the command line by simply creating a separate init file, with INSTANCE_TYPE = ASM. Disk groups can be created or modified using SQL commands such as CREATE DISK GROUP, ALTER DISK GROUP, DROP DISK GROUP, and so on. The instance name for your ASM instance should be +ASM, with the + actually being part of the instance name. In a RAC environment, the instance_number will be appended, so ASM instances will be named +ASM1, +ASM2, +ASM3, and so forth.

However, as in the past, we recommend using the GUI tools such as DBCA. The simplest way to get an ASM instance up and running is to create your database by using the DBCA. If there is not currently an ASM instance on the machine, the DBCA will create an ASM instance for you, in addition to your database instance. If you are using the DBCA to create a RAC database, then an ASM instance will be created on each node selected as part of your cluster. After creation of the ASM instance, you will be able to create the disk groups directly from within the DBCA, which is created by providing disks in the form of RAW slices. The ASM instance will then *mount* the disk groups before proceeding with the rest of the database creation. Figure 3-5 shows the option you will have when creating the database, to choose the type of storage on the Storage Options screen. After selecting this option, you will be presented with the ASM Disk Groups screen, which will show you the available disk groups. On a new installation, this screen will be blank, as there will be no disk groups. So, at this point, on a new installation, you would choose the Create New option.

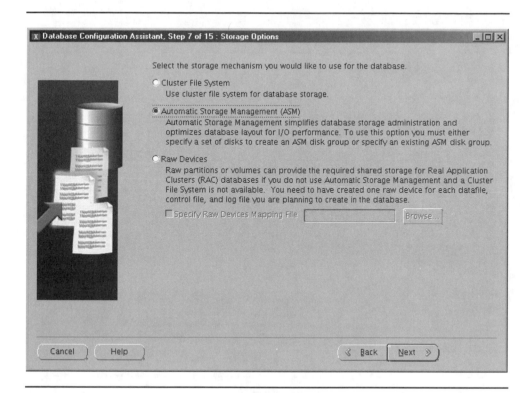

FIGURE 3-5. *Choosing ASM on the DBCA Storage Options screen*

Creating ASM Disk Groups Using the DBCA

In the Create Disk Group screen (see Figure 3-6), ASM searches for disks based on the disk discovery string defined in the ASM_DISKSTRING parameter. Different platforms have different default values for the disk string. On Linux, the default will be /dev/raw/*, and on Solaris, the default will be /dev/rdsk/*. This value can be modified from within the DBCA, as shown in Figure 3-6, by clicking the Change Disk Discovery Path button. Once you have the correct path, you should end up with a list of possible candidate disks. Note in Figure 3-6 that the Show Candidates radio button is selected. This will only display disks in the discovery string that are not already part of another disk group. Note also that two of the disks have FORMER under the Header Status. This is because these two disks were at one time part of a different disk group, but that group was dropped. This status might also show up if a disk is removed from an existing disk group—nevertheless, these disks are available to be added to this group, and are considered valid candidates. In Figure 3-6, you can see that we have selected these two disks to make up our new disk group.

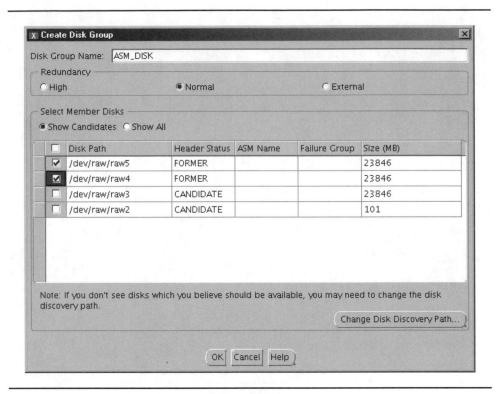

FIGURE 3-6. *Creating the ASM disk group*

NOTE
On most Linux platforms, Oracle provides a special ASM library to simplify the ASM integration with the operating system, and to ease the disk discovery process. At this time, the library is not available for all platforms, but you can check OTN periodically for the availability of a library for your platform at http://otn.oracle.com/software/tech/linux/asmlib/ index.html

At this point, the ASM instance has already been created by the DBCA, and the disk group will be mounted by the ASM instance. If this is a RAC environment, the ASM instance will have been created on all nodes selected as participating in the database creation. (ASM mounts the disk groups in a manner similar to how it mounts the database, but rather than via an ALTER DATABASE MOUNT; command, the ALTER DISKGROUPS MOUNT; command is used instead.) Once the disk group is mounted, you can proceed to select the group for your database files and continue on with the creation of the actual database. You will be asked if you want to use Oracle managed files, and you will also be prompted to set up a flashback recovery area. If you choose to set up a flashback recovery area, we recommend that you set up a separate ASM disk group for the flashback recovery area. You will be given an opportunity by the DBCA to create that separate disk group. If you choose not to do so during creation time, you can create additional disk groups later on, either manually or using Enterprise Manager.

NOTE
ASM requires that the ocssd daemon be running (cluster synchronization service) even in a single instance. (On Windows, ocssd manifests itself as a service called OracleCSService.) For this reason, Oracle will install/create the ocssd daemon (or OracleCSService) automatically on a new Oracle Database 10g install, even in a single-instance environment.

Managing ASM Environments with EM

Using Enterprise Manager to help you manage your ASM environment is most likely the simplest way to keep on top of the situation. In order to do so, we recommend that you configure Enterprise Manager Grid Control (as described in Chapter 5). This is a particular necessity when running in a RAC environment, as Grid Control allows you to manage all instances in the cluster, as well as all ASM instances from one central location.

Navigating Through EM

Enterprise Manager provides a graphical interface for such ASM operations as adding or removing disks from a disk group, dropping and creating new disk groups, mounting and dismounting disk groups, and rebalancing within a disk group. While you cannot create the instance itself through EM, you can modify parameters such as ASM_DISKSTRING or ASM_POWER_LIMT. Additionally, while we mentioned that files in an ASM disk group are not visible at the OS, Enterprise Manager will allow you to look at the file and directory structure used by ASM to manage these files. To end this section, we will go through a HA Workshop that will walk you through the steps needed to navigate ASM through Enterprise Manager.

HA Workshop: *Managing ASM Through Enterprise Manager*

Workshop Notes

This workshop assumes that Enterprise Manager Grid Control has already been configured in your environment, and also assumes that an ASM instance is running. If EM Grid Control has not been configured, please refer to Chapter 5 for an overview of Grid Control configuration, or refer to the Oracle Database 10*g* Release 1 *Oracle Enterprise Manager Advanced Configuration* guide.

Step 1.   Log on as SYSMAN to the Enterprise Manager Grid Control screen using the host name of the management repository machine, and port 7777. In this example, rmsclnxclu1 is a node in our cluster, but it also happens to be the host for the EM management repository:

   http://rmsclnxclu1:7777/em

Step 2.   Click on the Targets tab across the top, and then choose All Targets from the blue bar. This will list all instances, including ASM instances.

Step 3.   Find the ASM instance from the list of targets. The name will be something along the lines of +ASM1_rmsclnxclu1.us .oracle.com, where rmsclnxclu1.us .oracle.com is the host name where the ASM instance is running. Click on the link to the ASM instance. This will bring you to the home page for the ASM instance. Here, you can see a list of disk groups, the databases serviced by the disk groups, and a graphical depiction of the amount of disk space each database is using. In addition, you will see any alerts related to
your ASM instance.

Step 4.   Click on the Performance link for the ASM instance. (You may be prompted to log in—if so, provide the sysdba password for the ASM instance.) Here you will see a graphical depiction of the throughput, disk I/O per second, and disk I/O response times for all disk groups managed by ASM. Clicking on the Expand All option at the bottom of the page will allow you to see the cumulative statistics for each disk in the disk group.

Step 5.   Next click on the Configuration link across the top. Here you can modify
the values for the ASM_DISKSTRING, ASM_DISKGROUPS, and ASM_POWER_
LIMITS parameters.

Step 6.   Now click on the Administration link. This will provide you a link to
each ASM disk group managed by the ASM instance, as shown in Figure 3-7. If
there are no disk groups, you can create them from here, or create additional groups
by clicking on the Create button. Disk groups can also be mounted or dismounted
from here—if you are in a RAC environment, you will be prompted to select which
instances you want to dismount the group from. By selecting the options from the
drop-down list, you can initiate an immediate rebalance operation as well, as shown
in Figure 3-7.

Step 7.   Click on the disk group itself now, to again see the disks in the
group. This will take you into the General description page for that disk group.

FIGURE 3-7.   *ASM disk groups in Enterprise Manager*

Here you can check the disks' integrity, add disks to the disk group, or delete disks from the group. You can also drill down further to see performance stats for the individual disks.

Step 8. Next click on the Files link to view the files on the ASM disk group. Choose the Expand All option to view all the files within all of the ASM directories. In Figure 3-8, we have displayed a partial expansion of the directory list. As you can see, Oracle creates a directory structure within the ASM disk group, which it maintains internally. In this example, Oracle managed files are in use, meaning that the parameter DB_CREATE_FILE_DEST is set to +ASM_DISK. Oracle automatically created an ASM directory with the database name, and then within that directory

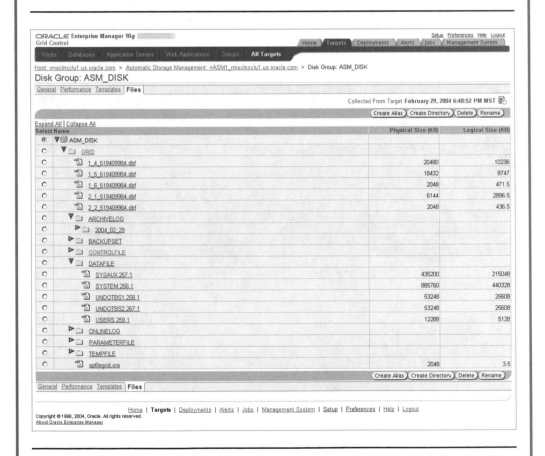

FIGURE 3-8. *Viewing ASM files from within Enterprise Manager*

created additional subdirectories for controlfiles, logfiles, datafiles, and so forth. When using Oracle managed files, it is not necessary to specify either the name or the location of the file. Oracle will determine the location based on the ASM file type, and will then assign a filename based on the type of file, the file number, and the version number.

Step 9.   Lastly, click on a single file to get a description of how the file is mirrored, the block size and number of blocks in the file, the file type, the creation date, and the striping (either coarse or fine). The output should look something like this:

```
SYSAUX.270.3: Properties
Name SYSAUX.270.3
Type DATAFILE
Redundancy MIRROR
Block Size (bytes) 8192
Blocks 64001
Logical Size (KB) 512008 KB
Striped COARSE
Creation Date 15-FEB-2004 02:43:32
```

ASM Metadata

As we have discussed, an ASM instance has no physical storage component associated with it—the ASM instance is purely a logical incarnation, in memory. However, there are physical components to an ASM disk group, essentially stored on disk on each ASM disk. When a disk is made part of an ASM disk group, the header of each disk is updated to reflect information, including the disk group name, the physical size of all disks in the group, the allocation unit size, and so on. The header also contains information relating specifically to that disk, including the size, the failure group, the disk name, and so forth. In addition, metadata is stored in ASM files on the disks themselves, using file numbers below 256. For this reason, when creating a new database on an ASM disk group, the system datafile will generally be file 256, and the rest of the files in the database are numbered upward from there—because file 255 and below are reserved for ASM metadata. The ASM metadata is always mirrored across three disks (if available), even when the external redundancy option is chosen.

PART
II

Real Application
Clusters

CHAPTER
4

RAC Setup and Configuration

o what does grid computing mean to the database? The underpinnings of the "database grid" is Real Application Clusters, or RAC for short. RAC came into its own in Oracle9*i*, realizing the potential of Oracle Parallel Server (OPS) by making applications truly scalable, without modifications. The central idea behind RAC is the same as the central idea behind grid computing—plug in nodes as needed to handle the additional workload, or remove nodes and move them elsewhere when the situation warrants.

Oracle Database 10*g* has taken that to the next level by both simplifying the process of adding and removing nodes, and by increasing the number of nodes one can have in a RAC cluster. Aside from this, Oracle has gone to the next level by providing end-to-end clustering solutions on all supported platforms, as well as providing its own cluster file system on some platforms and (as discussed in Chapter 3) a volume management solution with Automatic Storage Management (ASM). This chapter will explain the concepts behind RAC in Oracle Database 10*g*, as well as provide configuration steps for installing your own cluster. As before, in keeping with the philosophy of commodity hardware and OS, our focus will be on the Linux platform, but these principles will apply to all supported platforms. When appropriate, we will try to point out where certain steps are specific to the Linux platform.

Cluster-Ready Services (CRS)

Historically, Oracle has relied on operating system vendors to provide the clusterware layer needed at the OS to enable Oracle Parallel Server (OPS), and later on, RAC, to function. The normal process for the HA DBA would be to defer to the sysadmin and/or the hardware/OS vendor to configure the operating system, and then create a cluster using the OS vendor's software or clustering software from a third party. Once the OS and cluster were configured, the installation and configuration of Oracle (either OPS or RAC) would be undertaken by the DBA. This scenario could oftentimes lead to confusion and possibly fingerpointing between hardware vendors, software vendors, the sysadmin, and the DBA.

Starting with version 7.3.3.0.1 on the Windows platform, this began to change. Out of necessity, due to the lack of viable clustering software for Windows, Oracle began to provide a clustering layer on the Windows platform to enable the use of OPS on Windows. Eventually, with the rising popularity of Linux, Oracle was compelled to also provide clusterware for the Linux platform. Prior to Oracle9*i*, the clusterware on Windows was distributed through hardware vendors, coming indirectly from Oracle. Starting with Oracle9*i*, the clusterware became an integrated part of the Oracle9*i* Enterprise Edition offerings for both Windows and Linux.

Now, with Oracle Database10*g*, Oracle has introduced CRS, which is the logical next step in the evolution of the clusterware provided by Oracle. CRS is clusterware provided by Oracle to cluster together nodes on any supported operating system, including Sun, HP, Tru64, AIX, Windows, Linux, and so forth (all nodes in a cluster must be on the same operating system). It is possible to use CRS instead of the OS vendor clusterware, or third-party clusterware on any of these platforms. It is also possible to use CRS alongside third-party or operating system clusterware: if the HA DBA chooses to stick with the vendor-provided or third-party-provided clusterware, then CRS can be used to integrate Oracle clustering with the existing third-party clusterware, allowing the Oracle RDBMS to communicate and work correctly with the existing cluster vendor. When using Oracle's CRS, it is now supported to run RAC with the Standard Edition of Oracle.

CRS Architecture

CRS consists of three major components, which manifest themselves as daemons, run out of inittab on Unix operating systems, or as services on Windows. The three daemons are ocssd, or the cluster synchronization services daemon; crsd, which is the main engine for maintaining availability of resources; and evmd, which is an event logger daemon. Of these components, ocssd and evmd run as user oracle, while crsd runs as root. The crsd and evmd daemons are set to start with the respawn option, so that in the event of a failure they will be restarted. When running as part of CRS, the ocssd daemon is started up with the fatal option, meaning a failure of the daemon will lead to a node restart. This is required to prevent data corruption, should nodes lose contact with each other. Note, however, that the ocssd daemon is also used in single-instance environments, in order to enable the usage of ASM, as we mentioned in Chapter 3. If ocssd is running in a single-instance environment, independent of CRS, then failure of the daemon is not fatal to the node. We will go into a bit more detail on the two main components you need to be familiar with—namely, ocssd and crsd.

CSS: Cluster Synchronization Services

CSS is the foundation for interprocess communications in a cluster environment. As such, CSS is also used to handle the interaction between ASM instances and regular RDBMS instances in a single-instance environment. In a cluster environment, CSS also provides group services—dynamic information on which nodes and instances are part of the cluster at any given time, and static information, such as the names and node numbers of nodes (can be modified when nodes are added or removed). Also, CSS handles rudimentary locking functionality within the cluster (though most locking is handled by the Integrated Distributed Lock Manager within the RDBMS itself). In addition to other jobs performed, CSS is responsible for maintaining a heartbeat between the nodes in the cluster and monitoring the voting disk for split-brain failures.

CRSD

The crsd daemon is primarily responsible for maintaining the availability of application resources, aka services, as we will discuss in Chapter 6. The crsd daemon is responsible for starting and stopping these services, relocating them to another node in the event of failure, and maintaining the service profiles in the Oracle Cluster Registry (OCR). In addition, crsd is responsible for overseeing the caching of the OCR for faster access, and also backing up the OCR. Chapter 6 will be devoted to these operations, all of which fall under the realm of the crsd daemon.

Virtual IP Addresses, or VIPs

Oracle CRS takes advantage of the concept of virtual IP addresses, or VIPs, in order to enable a faster failover in the event of a failure of a node. Thus, each node will have not only its own statically assigned IP address, but also a virtual IP address that is assigned to the node. The listener on each node will actually be listening on the virtual IP (VIP), and client connections are meant to come in on the VIP. Should the node fail, the virtual IP will actually fail over and come online on one of the other nodes in the cluster.

Note that the purpose in doing so is *not* so that clients can continue to connect to the database using that VIP on the other node. The purpose of the IP address failover is to reduce the time it takes for the client to recognize that a node is down. If the IP has failed over and is actually responding from the other node, the client will immediately get a response back when making a connection on that VIP. However, the response will not be a successful connection, but rather a logon failure, indicating that while the IP is active there is no instance available at that address. The client can then immediately retry the connection to another address in the address list, and successfully connect to the VIP that is actually assigned to one of the existing/ functioning nodes in the cluster. This is referred to as *rapid connect-time failover*, and will be discussed in more detail in Chapter 11.

CRS Installation

CRS is provided on a separate CD-ROM from the RDBMS install. CRS needs to be installed before the Oracle RDBMS and it must go into its own home, separate from the home for the Oracle RDBMS (this is generally referred to as the CRS_HOME). Ideally, CRS should be the first Oracle product that you install. For this reason (among others), if you are planning an Oracle Database 10g single-instance install but think you may use CRS/RAC in the future, you may want to consider installing CRS first, in its own home. You can then run the Oracle install as Local Only (that is, no RAC option), but you will have the opportunity later on to install with the RAC option, with CRS already in place. By doing this, you will enable the ocssd daemon running out of the CRS home, and this daemon can then be used for ASM by all other Oracle Database 10*g* installations, whether they are local only installs or RAC installs.

Operating System Configuration for CRS

As mentioned previously, our focus here is primarily on commodity clusters, so this section will be focused on configuring the Linux operating system in preparation for a CRS and RAC install. We will also go into some of the specific tasks needed for operating system configuration—tasks normally handled by an experienced systems administrator, but that more and more must be undertaken by the DBA. We will discuss the various storage and file configurations available, the preparation needed for the different types of storage, and other requirements such as networking pieces, kernel requirements and memory requirements.

Storage Requirements for CRS/RAC

On most platforms, CRS gives you three possible configurations to be used for storage—the two basic configurations available on all platforms are to use either RAW devices or Automatic Storage Management (ASM) for the shared files required by CRS and RAC. In addition, Oracle offers its own cluster file system (OCFS) on both the Linux and Windows platforms. Other vendors also offer cluster file systems on other platforms. A fourth option on the Linux platform is to use NFS mounts via a certified network attached storage device (such as Network Appliance) for storage of the shared database and CRS files. We will attempt to describe the basics of these options in the "Shared Storage Configuration" section, later in this chapter.

Shared Everything Disk Storage

The one thing all storage options listed above share in common is that they all involve disks that are accessible from multiple nodes, simultaneously. This is often referred to as a *shared everything* architecture, referring to all disks as being shared. Some cluster vendors and DBMS utilize a different architecture—that is, a shared nothing architecture, in which a disk can only be accessed by one node at a time. If a node accessing a disk goes down, that disk must be failed over to another, surviving node. The advantage that Oracle has with the shared everything architecture is that any node can access the data needed on any disk at any given time. It is not necessary to go through one specific node to get to the disks.

Oracle requires that all controlfiles, all online redo logs, and all database files be stored on the shared drives, and these files are therefore accessible from all nodes in the cluster. In addition, certain files such as archived redo logs, the system parameter file, and flashback logs can be stored on the shared drives, depending on the type of storage.

Straight RAW Devices

If using straight RAW devices for all files, you are essentially forgoing a file system altogether. Since there is no file system, you must create a separate partition for every single file that you will be using for the database. Soft links are then created to the RAW devices, and Oracle writes files out to the RAW devices via the link names. As such, it is not practical or possible to store archived logs on RAW devices. The advantage of RAW devices is that they generally allow for faster I/O. However, disadvantages include the complexity of managing these files without the use of a file system. Also, on platforms such as Linux, there is a limit to the number of partitions you can create, thus a limit to the number of files you can have.

Automatic Storage Management

As we discussed in Chapter 3, Automatic Storage Management allows the use of block devices (or RAW devices), which are managed completely by Oracle. In many ways, this removes the complexity of RAW devices, while still giving the advantage of speed that block devices provide. When using ASM, all file management (including taking of backups) must be done from within the database. While archived logs and flashback logs *can* be stored on ASM disk groups, the Oracle binaries cannot, so it is still required to have either a cluster file system for the Oracle install (supportability depends on the platform and version of the cluster file system) or install to the private drives of each node. Since ASM is volume management that is specific to the Oracle database, it is designed with RAC in mind, so it is an ideal choice as a shared storage mechanism for database files in a RAC environment.

Cluster File System

As mentioned previously, Oracle provides a cluster file system for both Windows and Linux platforms, which can be used for all required database files. The obvious advantage of the cluster file system is that it simplifies the management of the shared files by allowing a directory structure, and by allowing multiple files to be stored on a single shared disk/partition. In addition, on some platforms, the cluster file system can also be used as a shared location for the installation of the Oracle binaries for the ORACLE_HOME. The cluster file system Oracle provides for Windows has supported the ORACLE_HOME since the beginning. The cluster file system for Linux will support installation of the ORACLE_HOME, starting with version 2.*x* of OCFS for Linux.

NFS Mounts

On the Linux platform, it is also possible to have the shared device for the datafiles be on an NFS mount, using a certified network attached storage vendor. This requires that all nodes have network access to the device and have the same NFS mount point. The advantage is that it does also allow file system management, easing the complexity. The disadvantage is that network latency introduced into the file I/O equation can slow down performance, depending on the speed of your network and the cards. While NFS mount points should not be used for the ORACLE_HOME, you may use NFS mounts as a location for archived logs and flashback logs (via the flashback recovery area).

Networking Requirements for CRS and RAC

In order to configure a RAC environment, you must have two network cards in each node at a minimum: one network card to be used for client communication on the public network, and the other network card to be used for private cluster communication. With this configuration in mind, you must first configure the /etc/ hosts file on *each* node to have a unique name for both the public and private nodes, ideally with easily identifiable host names for public and private—that is, node1, node1_private, node2, node2_private, and so on. While it is possible in a two-node cluster to have the private network consist of a simple crossover cable, that is not recommended, and on some platforms it is not supported because of the media sensing behavior of the operating system. On Windows, for example, if one node is powered down, the card for the interconnect on the surviving node is disabled because there is no more activity being sensed across the interconnect. This can lead to errors on the surviving node.

The best solution is to have a dedicated switch between the nodes, which means there is constant activity on the card (coming from the switch), even when the other node is down. Of course, this also allows for expansion of your cluster to more than two nodes. The other consideration for production environments is that the switch and the cards for the interconnect should be capable of handling all of the cache fusion traffic and other messaging traffic across the interconnect—therefore, you want this network to be a high-speed network (1GB Ethernet or faster).

Kernel Parameters

The detailed kernel parameter requirements for each platform are discussed in the specific chapter of the installation and configuration guide for that particular operating system. In this section, we will touch briefly on the specific requirements for Red Hat Linux 3.0. With Red Hat 3.0, kernel changes can be made by making modifications to the /etc/sysctl.conf file. In our case, we simply added the following lines to the end of the file:

```
kernel.shmall = 2097152
kernel.shmmax = 536870912
kernel.shmmni = 4096
kernel.sem = 250 32000 100 128
fs.file-max = 65536
net.ipv4.ip_local_port_range = 1024 65000
```

For the case of kernel.shmmax, the value of 536870912 is equal to half of the physical RAM installed on each node.

OCR and Voting Disk Requirements

In our previous section on shared storage and the types of files stored on the shared disks, we intentionally left out two specific files. As part of the CRS install, you will be prompted to provide a separate location for the Oracle Cluster Registry (OCR) and the voting disk used by CRS. We did not mention these files previously because they are not associated with any database in particular, but rather, these are files used by your cluster itself. They are required to be stored on the shared disk, as all nodes must have access to the files. The OCR is essentially the metadata database for your cluster, keeping track of resources within the cluster, where they are running, and where they can (or should) be running. The voting disk will be used for resolving split-brain scenarios: should any cluster nodes lose network contact via the interconnect with the other nodes in the cluster, those conflicts will be resolved via the information in the voting disk.

Location of the OCR and Voting Disk

How you define the location of these files/disks depends on what medium you have decided to use for the shared storage. If you are using straight RAW devices, you must set aside two slices (partitions)—one for the OCR and one for the voting disk—*before* CRS is installed. The same is true if using ASM—while all of the database files can exist in ASM disk groups, the OCR and voting disk must be on RAW slices of their own. However, if you are using OCFS as the storage medium for the database, the OCR and voting disk can be just another file on the OCFS volume. The volumes must be configured and mounted using OCFS prior to the CRS install, and appropriate directories should be created for the files if that is the case. Lastly, in the case of NFS mounts, you can also use these mount points as the bastion for these files, similar to the case of OCFS.

NOTE
Use caution when placing the OCR and voting disk on an OCFS drive on Linux. At this point, we recommend, even in the case where OCFS is used for the database files, that the OCR and voting disk be placed on RAW devices. If using OCFS for the location of the voting disk and OCR on Linux, be sure that you are on OCFS version 1.0.11 or higher.

Preparing for the CRS Install

To ensure that your CRS install goes as smoothly as possible, you want to be certain that you have done the necessary preparation. If so, the actual install itself will take only a few minutes, but the preparation is the key. This can be broken down into two major categories: first, configuring the shared storage, and second, configuring the networking components. In an upcoming section, we will go through a workshop that walks you through the steps for configuring the shared storage.

HA Workshop: *Configure a Linux/RAC Cluster*

Workshop Notes

This HA Workshop is geared toward setting up a test environment with a two-node RAC cluster running Red Hat Linux 3.0 Advanced Server. While you have several options to choose from for setting up a test environment, including shared SCSI devices, NFS, and so forth, we have chosen to use Firewire drives for this workshop. The primary reasons for this are the cost and the simplicity. We caution you that Firewire is not an officially supported environment for RAC, and there are some gotchas. However, there is a concerted effort underway to support the IEEE 1394 standard on Linux (see http://www.linux1394.org), and as such, later versions of the kernel are increasingly improving support for Firewire. We demonstrate it here because it does afford a low-cost means of testing the functionality and concepts of RAC, using hardware that is readily affordable and accessible for just about anyone. We believe in a chicken in every pot, two cars in every garage, and a test cluster under the desk of every DBA. In the vein of a very low-cost test system, we were able to configure a two-node RAC cluster using hardware that cost around $1,500.00 (less than the cost of the laptop I am currently using to write this chapter). While you do not have to do it so cheaply, this also demonstrates how RAC can be used to turn low-cost commodity hardware into a highly available system.

Step 1.   Procure/beg/borrow the necessary hardware. The hardware specs on our cluster are as follows:

```
Two Refurbished Single CPU Pentium 4 machines -   $825.00
Single CPU - 2.6 GHz Processor
512 MB RAM
40 GB Internal Hard Drive
CD-ROM Drive
On-Board 100 MB Ethernet
Memory upgrade to 1GB on each node -              $300.00
```

```
80GB IDE Drive        -                      $117.00
Firewire Enclosure and Firewire cables -     $95.00
2 Firewire Cards -                           $95.00
2 Additional Ethernet Network Cards -        $40.00
10/100 Ethernet Switch -                     $50.00
```

> **NOTE**
> *The Firewire enclosure must support the*
> *OXFORD911 chipset standard, to allow*
> *simultaneous multinode access. For more*
> *information, see http://oss.oracle.com/projects/*
> *firewire/.*

Step 2.   Install Red Hat 3.0 on each node—use the Install Everything option, to ensure that you have all of the necessary components. During the install, ensure that both network cards are in place to simplify the assignment of IP addresses to the cards. See the upcoming section on network configuration for information on IP addresses for the private cards.

Step 3.   Install kernel-unsupported-2.4.21-4.EL.i686.rpm from Red Hat Disk3 on each node. This kernel has device support for many nonstandard devices, including the Firewire cards and drive:

```
cd /mnt/cdrom/RedHat/RPMS
rpm -iv kernel-unsupported-2.4.21-4.EL.i686.rpm
```

Step 4.   Add the following lines to the /etc/modules.conf on each node:

```
options sbp2 sbp2_exclusive_login=0
post-install sbp2 insmod sd_mod
post-remove sbp2 rmmod sd_mod
```

The sbp2_exlcusive_login=0 essentially disables exclusive access to the device from one node—by default, this value is set to 1, meaning exclusive_login is true, or enabled, and only one node will be able to access the disk. Setting this to 0, or disabled, will allow both nodes in the cluster to access the disk simultaneously. In theory, this should allow up to four machines to access the drive at once.

Step 5.   Reboot each node. During the reboot, you should be in front of the console during the boot process, as Red Hat should detect your disk during startup. The Add Hardware Wizard will pop up and prompt you to configure the disk, but if you do not respond within 30 seconds, the boot process will continue without configuring the disk. If the reboot does not detect your disk, proceed to Step 6 regardless. You may need to reboot again, after running the commands in Step 6.

Step 6.   After the reboot, run the following commands to detect the cards and drive:

```
modprobe sd_mod
modprobe scsi_mod
modprobe ohci1394
modprobe sbp2
echo "scsi add-single-device 0 0 0 0" > /proc/scsi/scsi
```

As an alternative to the ECHO command, you can also run the rescan-scsi-bus.sh shell script, available for download from many sites, including the following:

http://www.garloff.de/kurt/linux/rescan-scsi-bus.sh

Step 7.   After running these commands, you should be able to see the drive. You can confirm this by running the dmesg command:

```
dmesg | more
```

Look through the dmesg output for lines such as

```
Attached scsi disk sda at scsi0, channel 0, id 0, lun 0
SCSI device sda: 156301488 512-byte hdwr sectors (80026 MB)
 sda: sda1 < sda5 sda6 sda7 sda8 sda9 >
```

In this case, you can see that the scsi device is named sda. You can now begin to prepare the drive by running commands such as fdisk, by using /dev/sda as the target:

```
fdisk /dev/sda
```

Step 8.   Once you are in fdisk, type **m** to see the full menu of commands. To create a new partition, choose n. You should first create an extended partition, equal to the size of the entire shared disk. The first partition will be created as /dev/sda1. After this, the remaining partitions can be created as logical partitions. The number of partitions you create will depend on what type of file system you intend to use. For OCFS, we recommend a 100MB RAW partition for the OCR and a 50MB RAW partition for the voting disk, and then the rest can be used for the CFS disk. For ASM, we recommend the same, where the remainder is used for ASM. However, for ASM, if you want to test the functionality of having multiple disks, you can partition the remaining space into multiple logical partitions. This will allow you to simulate the behavior of adding and removing disks from a disk group, where the disks are actually just partitions on the same drive—but of course, it will not give you any true redundancy, should the actual disk fail. Once finished with the partitioning, type **w** to save and exit. The command fdisk –l will allow you to see all of the partitions created and confirm their configuration.

Step 9.   In order to ensure that the disk is visible automatically on reboot from each node, you can add the commands listed in Step 6 to the /etc/rc.local file, which is executed at startup each time the machine is restarted. The /etc/rc.local script will then look like this:

```
touch /var/lock/subsys/local
modprobe sd_mod
modprobe scsi_mod
modprobe ohci1394
modprobe sbp2
echo "scsi add-single-device 0 0 0 0" > /proc/scsi/scsi
```

You can also confirm that the disk is discovered by checking the /var/log/ messages file:

```
# cat messages | grep sda
Jan 10 14:57:37 rmsclnxclu2 kernel: Attached scsi disk sda at scsi0, channel
0, id 0, lun 0
Jan 10 14:57:37 rmsclnxclu2 kernel: SCSI device sda: 156301488 512-byte hdwr
sectors (80026 MB)
Jan 10 14:57:37 rmsclnxclu2 kernel:  sda: sda1 < sda5 sda6 sda7 sda8 sda9 >
```

> **NOTE**
> *As we mentioned, Firewire drives do have their quirks. If, after running through the previous steps, the drive is still not recognized, try powering off all nodes and the drive. Then power each piece on one at a time, starting with the drive first. Wait for each node to boot completely before attempting to start the next node.*

Network Configuration

For networking configurations, as we mentioned above, you should absolutely have a minimum of two network cards, meaning that at least one of these is dedicated solely to the private interconnect—this will be used for cluster communication as well as cache fusion traffic between the instances, once you have your database created. It is imperative that these networks be correctly configured before the installation of CRS.

The Interconnect

The card that is used for the public network should, of course, be assigned an IP address that is accessible on the network, and most likely that IP address will be registered in your DNS server. The IP assigned to the card for the private network will depend on how you configure that network. While you may be able to successfully configure a two-node cluster using only a crossover cable, it is strongly recommended that a switch (not a hub) be used for the private network. This will allow for more than two nodes on the interconnect, should the need arise, and will also allow for constant activity to the private card, even if or when the other node is down, preventing the card from being shut off or disabled by the OS.

In addition, it is strongly recommended that the network speed for the interconnect be as fast as you can afford. While 100MB Ethernet cards and switches are adequate for testing purposes (certainly for our simple test environment that we have demonstrated), in a production environment you should plan for a Gigabit Ethernet network for the interconnect, at a minimum. The advantages of cache fusion in a RAC environment can be quickly lost if the interconnect is not robust enough to handle the amount of traffic required to ship high numbers of blocks between instances.

Configuring the Hosts File

The first step in the configuration of the network piece, after having installed multiple NICs in the machine, is to configure the public and private names in the /etc/hosts file. Even if the public names are registered in your network's DNS server, we recommend defining them in the hosts file as well. If the network for your interconnect is dedicated for use only by nodes of the cluster (as we have recommended), you may assign any IP address that you wish to these cards, provided each machine knows about it by having an entry in the hosts file:

```
127.0.0.1        localhost.localdomain     localhost
138.1.144.100    rmsclnxclu1.us.oracle.com        rmsclnxclu1
138.1.144.124    rmsclnxclu2.us.oracle.com        rmsclnxclu2
138.1.144.128    rmscvip2.us.oracle.com   rmscvip2
138.1.144.125    rmscvip1.us.oracle.com   rmscvip1
10.1.1.2         private2
10.1.1.1         private1
```

In this example, the IP addresses and node names of private1 and private2 are defined in the hosts file on each node, and in the networking properties of the network card itself. Verify this by running the ifconfig –a command. The output should look similar to this:

```
$ ifconfig -a
eth0      Link encap:Ethernet  HWaddr 00:01:03:2C:69:BB
          inet addr:138.1.144.100  Bcast:138.1.147.255  Mask:255.255.252.0
...
eth1      Link encap:Ethernet  HWaddr 00:0B:DB:C0:2E:C4
          inet addr:10.1.1.1  Bcast:10.1.3.255  Mask:255.255.252.0
...
```

So interface eth0 is the public NIC, while eth1 is the private NIC. You will also notice in the sample hosts file above that there are two additional entries—rmscvip1 and rmscvip2. These entries are not currently used, and won't be used by the CRS install, but these are the virtual IPs that will be needed for the installation and creation of the database. Note that these IP addresses are on the same subnet as the public card—this is required, as these host names/IP addresses will be used for the actual client connections once the database is configured. Therefore, the VIPs must be valid, unused IP addresses on your public network, and *must* be on the same subnet as the public cards. For more information on the VIPs, refer to Chapter 11.

Ping Everything, from Everywhere

Once the network cards and the hosts file are configured, check your work by issuing a ping command of each host name, both public and private, from each node, including pinging yourself. For example, from Node1, which is rmsclnxclu1, make sure that you can first ping your own public name, followed by your own private name, and then ping the remote node's public and private name:

```
[root@rmsclnxclu1 etc]# ping rmsclnxclu1
PING rmsclnxclu1.us.oracle.com (138.1.144.100) 56(84) bytes of data.
64 bytes from rmsclnxclu1.us.oracle.com (138.1.144.100): icmp_seq=0 ttl=0 time=0.045 ms
[root@rmsclnxclu1 etc]# ping private1
PING private1 (10.1.1.1) 56(84) bytes of data.
64 bytes from private1 (10.1.1.1): icmp_seq=0 ttl=0 time=0.032 ms
[root@rmsclnxclu1 etc]# ping rmsclnxclu2
PING rmsclnxclu2.us.oracle.com (138.1.144.124) 56(84) bytes of data.
64 bytes from rmsclnxclu2.us.oracle.com (138.1.144.124): icmp_seq=0 ttl=64 time=0.456 ms
[root@rmsclnxclu1 etc]# ping private2
PING private2 (10.1.1.2) 56(84) bytes of data.
64 bytes from private2 (10.1.1.2): icmp_seq=0 ttl=64 time=0.199 ms
```

You can also ping the VIPs, even though you will not get a response—however, you *will* be able to check that the names are resolving to the correct IP addresses:

```
[root@rmsclnxclu1 etc]# ping rmscvip1
PING rmscvip1.us.oracle.com (138.1.144.125) 56(84) bytes of data.
From rmsclnxclu1.us.oracle.com (138.1.144.100) icmp_seq=0 Destination Host Unreachable
```

Repeat these steps from each node in the cluster, being sure to ping *all* nodes and all IP addresses. Remember that the VIPs will be unreachable at this stage of the install, but all of the other IP addresses (public and private) should respond successfully from each node. If not, then revisit the networking setup and make sure that there are no typos in the hosts file or in the network card definition. You may need to add both the public and private node names into the /etc/hosts.allow file.

Configure User Equivalence

As part of the networking setup, you must also set up user equivalence between the nodes in the cluster. Starting with Oracle Database 10*g*, the Oracle Universal Installer will first test user equivalence using ssh and scp. If this works, the secure shell and secure copies will be used. Otherwise, the OUI will revert back to rsh/rcp for the install. Since rsh and rcp are the most commonly used from past versions, we will begin by describing the configuration of user equivalence using rsh. You can do this by setting up entries in either /etc/hosts.equiv or in the .rhosts file in the Oracle user's home directory. You will want to add entries for both the public and private node names under the oracle account as follows:

```
rmsclnxclu1 oracle
rmsclnxclu2 oracle
rmsclnxclu1.us.oracle.com oracle
rmsclnxclu2.us.oracle.com oracle
private1 oracle
private2 oracle
rmscvip1 oracle
rmscvip2 oracle
rmscvip1.us.oracle.com oracle
rmscvip2.us.oracle.com oracle
```

In order for rsh to work on Linux, you must also enable it by setting disable=no in the /etc/xinetd.d/rsh file. The same can be accomplished by running ntsysv as root (command-line menu interface), or by running the GUI serviceconf utility and checking the box next to rsh so that it is set to start automatically at reboot. The serviceconf utility will allow you to click a restart button and start rsh right away. Test that rsh works by running a command similar to the following from each node (the following command was run from node rmsclnxclu1):

```
# rsh rmsclnxclu2 hostname
rmsclnxclu2
```

Using SSH for User Equivalence In some instances, users may prefer to use ssh and scp, rather than rsh and rcp for user equivalence. Starting with version 2.3.0.4.0 of the Oracle Universal Installer, the installer will first try to use ssh if it is present, and will revert back to rsh if not. Thus, if you prefer, you may use ssh. A basic ssh configuration can be achieved by using the ssh-keygen utility and the DSA Protocol 2, which is part of the Red Hat 3.0 install. For example, on our two-node cluster, run the following from Node1 (rmsclnxclu1):

```
oracle@/home/oracle>: ssh-keygen -t dsa
Generating public/private dsa key pair.
Enter file in which to save the key (/home/oracle/.ssh/id_dsa):
Enter passphrase (empty for no passphrase):
Enter same passphrase again:
Your identification has been saved in /home/oracle/.ssh/id_dsa.
Your public key has been saved in /home/oracle/.ssh/id_dsa.pub.
```

On the above command, we took all defaults. Once the public key is created, write out the contents of id_dsa.pub to the authorized_keys file:

```
oracle@/home/oracle>: cd .ssh
oracle@/home/oracle/.ssh>: cat id_dsa.pub > authorized_keys
```

Next, do a binary ftp of the file authorized_keys to Node2. Repeat the process of generating the key on Node2 by running ssh-keygen -t dsa as user oracle on Node2, again just pressing ENTER to accept the defaults:

```
Generating public/private dsa key pair.
Enter file in which to save the key (/home/oracle/.ssh/id_dsa):
Enter passphrase (empty for no passphrase):
Enter same passphrase again:
Your identification has been saved in /home/oracle/.ssh/id_dsa.
Your public key has been saved in /home/oracle/.ssh/id_dsa.pub.
```

Now, append the information from id_dsa.pub into the authorized_keys file as follows, on Node2:

```
oracle@/home/oracle/.ssh>: cat id_dsa.pub >> authorized_keys
```

Node rmsclnxclu2 now has an authorized_keys file that will allow the oracle user from either node to do an ssh to Node2. Copy this file back over to Node1 now, replacing the original authorized_keys file on that node. Test the user equivalence setup from each node via a command such as

```
oracle@/home/oracle/.ssh>: hostname
rmsclnxclu1
oracle@/home/oracle/.ssh>: ssh rmsclnxclu2 hostname
rmsclnxclu2
```

Shared Storage Configuration

In the "Configure a Linux/RAC Cluster" HA Workshop, we described how to configure a Firewire disk for shared access. Whether you are using a test Firewire cluster or a SAN with SCSI/Fiber connections, the disk configuration is the same. Once both nodes can see the disk, we must still create the partitions on those disks that CRS will need for the install. If you decide to use OCFS, the preparatory work will involve making sure that the OCFS drive is formatted and mounted on each node prior to the install, and directories are created so that the necessary CRS files can be created. If you plan to use either RAW devices or ASM, you must ensure that, at a minimum, you create two partitions for the CRS install to use (as previously mentioned, for the OCR and voting disk). Of course, you will need more partitions later on, for the database, particularly if using straight RAW devices, as you will need one partition for each datafile. However, for purposes of the CRS install, we will initially focus on the two that we need at the moment.

RAW Devices or ASM

If using RAW devices or ASM, the device needed by the CRS install for the OCR disk should be a minimum of 100MB. This should be kept in mind when creating the partitions using fdisk. We recommend the same minimum size for the voting disk. The actual space used by the OCR will depend on the number of nodes, databases, and services in your cluster—100MB should be large enough to accommodate the current supported maximum number of nodes and services. To bind a RAW device to a partition, you need to add an entry for each partition to the /etc/sysconfig/ rawdevices file. If using RAW devices, you will be creating the two devices for the OCR and voting disk, and then several other partitions for all of the datafiles. If using ASM, you should only create the partitions for the OCR and voting disk, and then one partition on each disk (unless you simply want to test the functionality by having multiple partitions on a single disk).

Use the output from the fdisk –l command to add entries into the /etc/sysconfig/ rawdevices file. An example of the fdisk –l output is seen here:

```
Disk /dev/sda: 80.0 GB, 80026361856 bytes
255 heads, 63 sectors/track, 9729 cylinders
Units = cylinders of 16065 * 512 = 8225280 bytes

   Device Boot    Start      End    Blocks   Id  System
/dev/sda1             1     9729  78148161    5  Extended
/dev/sda5             1       13    104359+  83  Linux
/dev/sda6            14       26    104391   83  Linux
/dev/sda7            27     3066  24418768+  83  Linux
```

```
/dev/sda8          3067      6106   24418768+   83   Linux
/dev/sda9          6107      9146   24418768+   83   Linux
```

Taking that information, we see that /dev/sda5 and /dev/sda6 are each 100MB. These will be used for the OCR and voting disk. The remaining partitions are 25GB apiece, and will be used for ASM disk groups. So, the rawdevices file on *each* node looks like this:

```
# raw device bindings
# format:   <rawdev> <major> <minor>
#           <rawdev> <blockdev>
/dev/raw/raw1   /dev/sda5
/dev/raw/raw2   /dev/sda6
/dev/raw/raw3   /dev/sda7
/dev/raw/raw4   /dev/sda8
/dev/raw/raw5   /dev/sda9
```

After saving the rawdevices file, run ntsysv and make sure that the box next to the rawdevices service is checked. Run SERVICE RAWDEVICES RESTART to restart the service immediately without the need to reboot. The modifications to /etc/syconfog/rawdevices and the restart of the rawdevices service has to be done on each node. The location for our OCR will now be /dev/raw/raw1, with the location for the voting disk being /dev/raw/raw2. Ownership of all of the devices needs to be changed to oracle, and permissions set to 755.

Preparing Disks Using OCFS

If you are using OCFS, you could simply create a single partition on each disk via fdisk, and there is no need to add anything to the rawdevices file. With OCFS, we have already pointed out that the voting disk and the OCR can be files rather than partitions, but this requires you to have formatted and mounted the shared drive before starting the CRS install. To do this, you must first download the OCFS driver and OCFS tools from Oracle's web site at http://oss.oracle.com. The files that you need will, of course, depend on the operating system version, and also the number of CPUs on the system—either single CPU of SMP system. Specifically, for Red Hat 3.0, the location for download is http://oss.oracle.com/projects/ocfs/files/RedHat/RHEL3/i386/.

For systems with multiple processors, be sure to download the SMP versions of the files.

NOTE
The OCFS versions are subject to change as updates are put out. Note also, as we mentioned previously on Linux, that if you are putting the OCR and voting disk on an OCFS drive, ensure that you have the latest version of OCFS, containing the fix for Patch 3467544. In addition, at the time of printing, OCFS Version 2, which will support the ORACLE_HOME as well as additional enhancements, is a beta release. Information on OCFS Version 2 can be found at http://oss.oracle.com/projects/ocfs2/.

Using ocfstool Once the kernel is installed, ocfstool, part of the ocfs-tools rpm, is used to format and mount the drive. We will go through an HA Workshop in the next section that walks you through the steps of formatting and mounting an OCFS drive. The drive needs to be mounted from each node, and then you must determine what directory structure you want to use for the OCR and voting disk. Create the necessary subdirectories, changing the ownership of the subdirectories to the oracle user and setting the permissions as appropriate on those directories.

Combinations of RAW/ASM/OCFS
As we have alluded to previously, it is possible to use a combination of RAW/ASM and/or OCFS for the shared partitions. This likely makes the most sense if you are using OCFS for the ORACLE_HOME and ASM for the disks. In this case, you would need at least one shared OCFS formatted partition to be used for the ORACLE_ HOME (you would be able to put the OCR and voting disks on this partition). You would then create RAW partitions, defined in the /etc/sysconfig/rawdevices file, which would be used later on as components of the ASM disk groups. ASM and OCFS will work together in this manner without any conflicts, provided you keep track of which partition is used for what.

HA Workshop: *Install OCFS and Configure OCFS Drives*

Workshop Notes
This workshop focuses on installing and configuring the Oracle Cluster File System on Linux. While Oracle may support third-party cluster file systems (or global file

systems, as referred to in some cases), Oracle actually provides the OCFS drivers
for both Windows and Linux. This workshop will walk you through the process of
installing and configuring OCFS on Red Hat Linux 3.0.

Step 1. Download the latest OCFS rpms from http://oss.oracle.com, making them
available to each cluster node (either locally or via an NFS mount point).

Step 2. Install the rpms on each node of the cluster in the following order, using
this syntax:

```
[root@rmsclnxclu1 RPMS]# rpm -iv ocfs-support-1.0.9-12.i686.rpm
Preparing packages for installation...
ocfs-support-1.0.9-12
[root@rmsclnxclu1 RPMS]# rpm -iv ocfs-2.4.21-EL-1.0.9-12.i686.rpm
Preparing packages for installation...
ocfs-2.4.21-EL-1.0.9-12
Linking OCFS module into the module path [  OK  ]
[root@rmsclnxclu1 RPMS]# rpm -iv ocfs-tools-1.0.9-12.i686.rpm
Preparing packages for installation...
ocfs-tools-1.0.9-12
```

Step 3. ocfstool requires an X-Term; so to configure your *display* so that an
X-Window connection can be made, first run xhost +:

```
[root@rmsclnxclu1 root]# xhost +
access control disabled, clients can connect from any host
[root@rmsclnxclu1 root]# DISPLAY=localhost:1
[root@rmsclnxclu1 root]# export DISPLAY
```

In this example, we used localhost:1 because we were connecting using the
VNC client to a VNC server for root, which was listening on port 1. Your display
setting may be different.

Step 4. ocfstool is loaded into the /usr/bin directory by default, which should
be part of your path, so simply run ocfstool to open the X-Window:

```
[root@rmsclnxclu1 root]# ocfstool
```

Step 5. In order to prepare OCFS, we must first generate a configuration file by
selecting the Generate Config option from the Tasks menu in the OCFS Tool screen.
This will open up the OCFS Generate Config window, as seen in Figure 4-1. Change
the interface to the private interface. In our example, we are using eth1 as the private
network. Leave the port to its default value of 7000, and then put the private name
in the Node Name box. Repeat the same steps on all cluster nodes, and then close
out of OCFS tool.

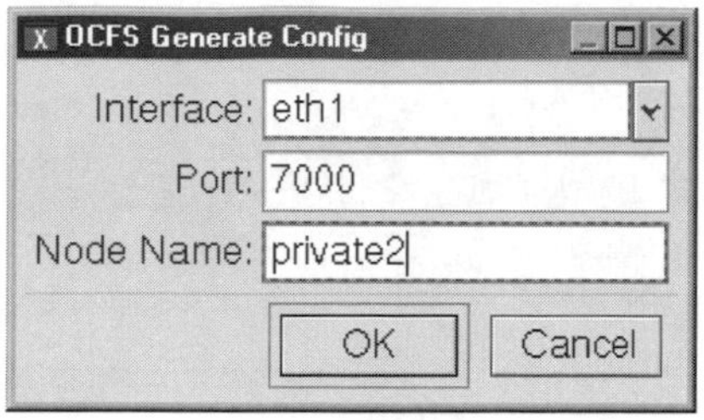

FIGURE 4-1. *Generate Config Window in ocfstool*

Step 6. On *each* cluster node, create a mount point for the OCFS drive(s). This mount point must be the same on each node, and should preferably be created directly off of the root. In this example, we are using /ocfs as the mount point:

```
[root@rmsclnxclu1 root]# cd /
[root@rmsclnxclu1 /]# mkdir ocfs
```

Step 7. Determine which partition(s) on the shared drive you want to use for OCFS. In our case, the partition is going to be /dev/sda7. Start ocfstool back up on *one* of the nodes, and this time choose Format from the Tasks menu. The OCFS Format window will open up, as seen in Figure 4-2. In the Device box, select the device you have determined will be the OCFS drive (/dev/sda7). Select the appropriate mount point, leaving the rest of the values as their defaults, and then click OK.

Step 8. After a few moments, the format operation should complete and you will be returned to the OCFS Tool window. Your device (/dev/sda7) should now be listed and highlighted (see Figure 4-3). Click on Mount to mount it to your directory. You should now be able to start ocfstool on the other nodes and mount the device on those nodes as well.

Step 9. One way to set up the drive such that it mounts automatically each time the node is rebooted is to add the following line to the /etc/rc.local script, using ocfs as the file system type:

```
mount -t ocfs /dev/sda7 /ocfs
```

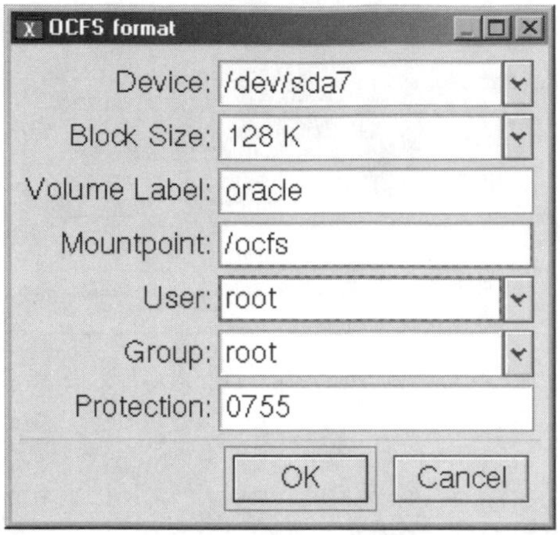

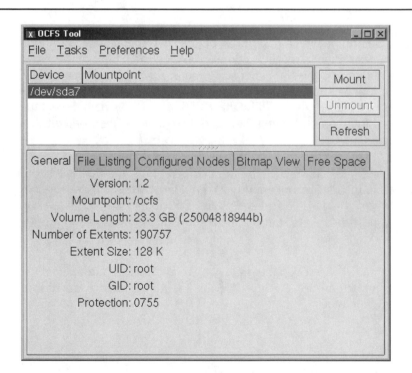

FIGURE 4-2. *OCFS Format window*

FIGURE 4-3. *Mounting the drive via ocfstool*

Step 10.   The mount point (/ocfs) should remain owned by root. As root, you can now cd into the /ocfs directory and create additional subdirectories, whose ownership can then be changed to the oracle:oinstall group:

```
[root@rmsclnxclu1 /]# mkdir /ocfs/ocr
[root@rmsclnxclu1 /]# mkdir /ocfs/vote
[root@rmsclnxclu1 /]# mkdir /ocfs/oradata
[root@rmsclnxclu1 /]# chown oracle:oinstall /ocfs/*
```

The Actual CRS Install Itself

Now that we have configured the shared storage and networking components properly, we can move on to the actual install of CRS. Assuming that all of the above configuration steps have been followed correctly, the actual CRS install itself is pretty straightforward. Get the CRS disk, mount the CD-ROM, and run ./runInstaller. Follow the prompts, and within a few minutes, voila!—you have a cluster.

However, there are still a couple of caveats—the biggest being an existing Oracle Database 10*g* single-instance install. If you have a need or desire to run a separate ORACLE_HOME, which supports only a single instance on one or all of the nodes, you may do so, but you should still install CRS first. The reason for this is the ocssd daemon. This daemon is needed, even in a single-instance environment, for the purpose of possibly using ASM for your storage (recall that ASM can be used for single-instance or RAC installs). However, you should only have one CSS daemon, and if you also have a RAC environment, the CSS daemon *must* be running out of the CRS home. If you install CRS first, and then later install the Oracle RDBMS, this should work fine. During the RDBMS installation, the installer will give you the option to do a single-instance install (referred to as *local only*), whereby you can check a box on the Cluster Node Selection screen. You can therefore install Oracle into multiple homes—with one or more home(s) being a RAC home, and one or more home(s) being a single-instance (or local only) home, as long as CRS is installed first.

Coexistence of CRS and Local Only Installs

How about the case, then, where there is already an existing Oracle Database 10*g* single-instance install in place? This existing single-instance home will already have the CSS daemon running out of it, but we want that daemon to be running out of the CRS home, *not* out of the existing single-instance home. In that situation, there is a solution. Oracle provides a shell script in the ORACLE_HOME\bin directory called localconfig.sh (on Windows, it is localconfig.bat). This script can be run (as root) from the existing single-instance ORACLE_HOME with the delete flag, like so:

```
/u01/app/oracle/10g/bin]$ ./localconfig delete
```

Running LOCALCONFIG DELETE will stop the ocssd daemon and remove its entries from /etc/inittab. It will also remove the existing OCR. Thus, during the CRS install, the entries for ocssd will be added back into /etc/inittab, but will be created to run out of the CRS_HOME instead of the existing ORACLE_HOME. The localconfig script must be run on each node that will be part of the cluster, if there is an existing Oracle Database 10*g* single-instance install on that node.

NOTE
Since ASM relies on CSS, you must not run localconfig while any ASM instances are running. Since any other databases using ASM rely on the ASM instances, they should also be stopped before running localconfig.

Installing CRS

The main pieces that you need are now in place. All that is left is to decide the location of the CRS install. It is worth reiterating that CRS should be installed into its own home, separate from any RDBMS installs. To have an OFA-compliant install, you should create an ORACLE_BASE directory, followed by a subdirectory within the ORACLE_BASE for the CRS_HOME itself. In the examples we are using for this chapter, the path to the ORACLE_BASE is /u01/app/oracle. Within there, we have created a directory called CRS, making the full path of the CRS_HOME /u01/app/ oracle/CRS. Within the ORACLE_BASE directory is another subdirectory called 10G, which will be used later as the ORACLE_HOME. The directories from /u01 on down should be owned by the oracle user, and permissions are 775 on all directories and subdirectories.

Installation Walkthrough

Before starting the installer, make sure that you are logged on as the oracle user, and ensure that you have the ORACLE_BASE environment variable set appropriately in your environment. Kick off the installer by running ./runInstaller as the oracle user. The first screen you will see will be a Language Selection screen, after which you will see the File Locations screen. In the File Locations screen, fill in the location for the CRS_HOME in the target page, and ensure that you assign this home a unique name. The first time you install, you will also be prompted to define the inventory location and then run the orainstRoot.sh to set up the inventory directories. The orainstRoot.sh script will create the oraInst.loc file, which defines the location for the Oracle inventory and the install group, which should be oinstall.

Next, you will see the Cluster Configuration screen (see Figure 4-4), where you will be prompted to enter the public and private names of each node. This is where

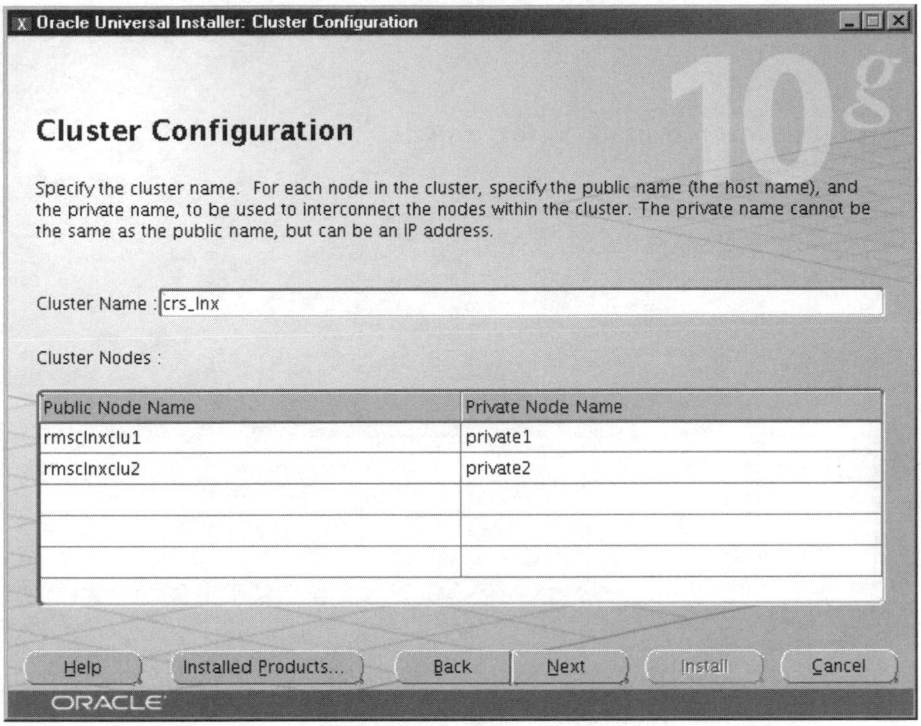

FIGURE 4-4. *Defining cluster name, and public and private node names*

your previous assignments come into play—here is where we define the private and public names for the nodes, previously set up and defined only in the hosts file. Note here that you can also give the cluster a name—this name can be anything you like and will be stored in the Oracle Cluster Registry, in the SYSTEM.css .clustername section.

The next screen is the Private Interconnect Enforcement screen (see Figure 4-5). This screen allows you to do two things. First, we can ensure that the correct network is being used for IPC traffic (that is, the interconnect) by choosing that network as Private and the other as Public. The other advantage that this screen provides, however, is the ability to choose *multiple* networks for private traffic. Thus, if you have three or more network cards and want to use two networks for private/IPC traffic (thus providing extra bandwidth on the interconnect), you can define it as such on this screen. Simply click on the box under the Interface Type and select Private next to each network you wish to use for IPC traffic. If you have additional

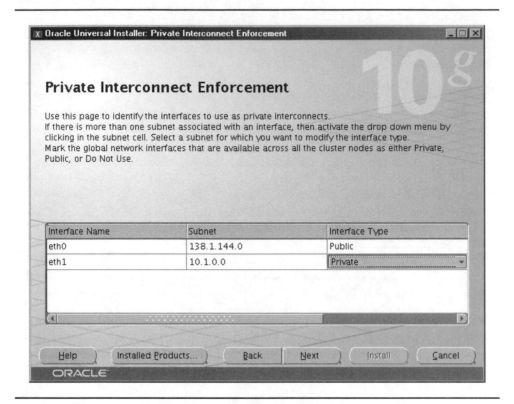

FIGURE 4-5. *Private Interconnect Enforcement screen*

network cards that you do not want to be used for the RAC configuration, simply leave the default of Do Not Use for those particular subnets.

NOTE
Private interconnect enforcement can also be achieved by using the init.ora parameter CLUSTER_ INTERCONNECTS. On Linux, this parameter will be necessary until Patch 3385409 has been applied. See Chapter 5 for more information on setting CLUSTER_INTERCONNECTS in the spfile.

Next, you will be prompted for the location of the OCR, followed by the location of the voting disk. Recall that if using RAW devices or ASM, you must have two separate partitions—you will enter paths such as /dev/raw/raw1and /dev/raw/raw2.

In Figure 4-6, you see that we are actually using an OCFS drive for the OCR. The permissions should be 755, with oracle as the owner (this will be changed for the OCR at the end of the install, such that root is the owner—but prior to the install, oracle must be the owner). One thing to note during the CRS install is that during the running of root.sh, a file in /etc/oracle will be created called ocr.loc, which will point to the location of the OCR. If this is an upgrade, or if the CRS install has been run previously, you will *not* be prompted for this location, meaning this screen will not display, but rather the location defined in the ocr.loc file will be used. You will see the screen for the voting disk location, regardless of any previous installs.

At the end of the install, you will be prompted to pause and run the root.sh script, found in the ORA_CRS_HOME/bin directory. This must be done on each node, one node at a time. This script will change the ownership of the OCR, as well as the ownership of the ORA_CRS_HOME directory to the root user, but will give execute

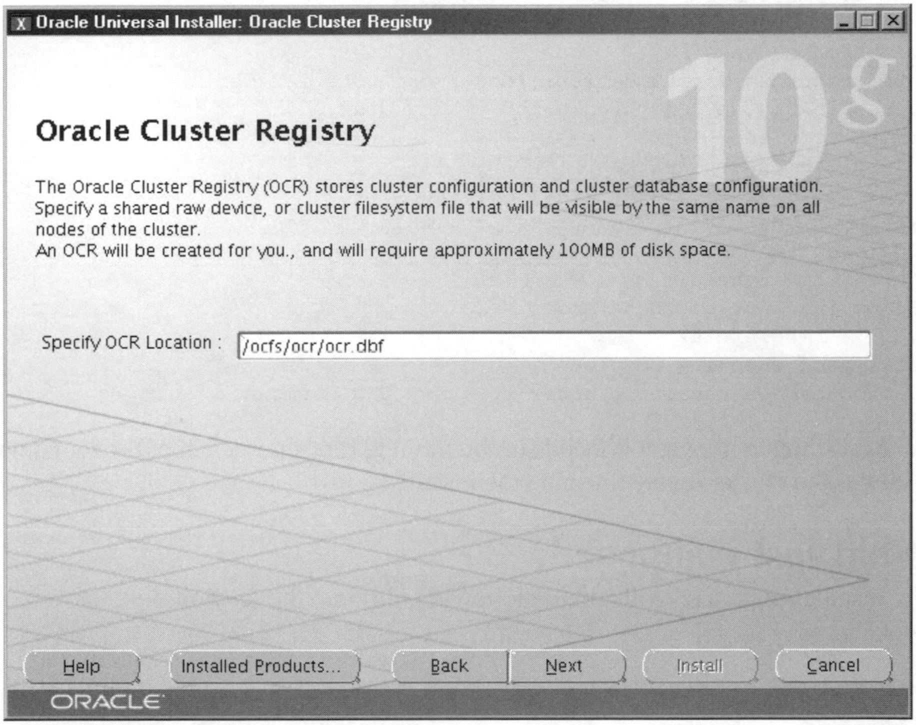

FIGURE 4-6. *OCR location*

permissions to all users on the CRS_HOME. root.sh is where the CRS stack is first started. Successful output from root.sh should look something like this:

```
root@/u01/app/oracle/CRS>: ./root.sh
Checking to see if Oracle CRS stack is already up...
/etc/oracle does not exist. Creating it now.
Setting the permissions on OCR backup directory
Oracle Cluster Registry configuration upgraded successfully
WARNING: directory '/u01/app/oracle' is not owned by root
WARNING: directory '/u01/app' is not owned by root
WARNING: directory '/u01' is not owned by root
assigning default hostname rmsclnxclu1 for node 1.
assigning default hostname rmsclnxclu2 for node 2.
Successfully accumulated necessary OCR keys.
Using ports: CSS=49895 CRS=49896 EVMC=49898 and EVMR=49897.
node <nodenumber>: <nodename> <private interconnect name> <hostname>
node 1: rmsclnxclu1 private1 rmsclnxclu1
node 2: rmsclnxclu2 private2 rmsclnxclu2
Creating OCR keys for user 'root', privgrp 'root'..
Operation successful.
Now formatting voting device: /ocfs/vote/vote_lnx.dbf
Successful in setting block0 for voting disk.
Format complete.
Adding daemons to inittab
Preparing Oracle Cluster Ready Services (CRS):
Expecting the CRS daemons to be up within 600 seconds.
CSS is active on these nodes.
        rmsclnxclu1
CSS is inactive on these nodes.
        rmsclnxclu2
Local node checking complete.
Run root.sh on remaining nodes to start CRS daemons.
```

As instructed above, follow this up by running root.sh on each of the remaining nodes in the cluster before finishing the install.

What Just Happened?

The installation of CRS will add the following files into the /etc/init.d directory (on Linux):

```
-rwxr-xr-x    1 root      root            763 Jan 16 18:02 init.crs
-rwxr-xr-x    1 root      root           2250 Jan 16 18:02 init.crsd
-rwxr-xr-x    1 root      root           5939 Jan 16 18:02 init.cssd
-rwxr-xr-x    1 root      root           2269 Jan 16 18:02 init.evmd
```

Soft links S96init.crs and K96init.crs are created in /etc/rc2.d, /etc/rc3.d, and /etc/rc5.d pointing to the init.crs in /etc/init.d, along with the following entries in the /etc/inittab file:

```
h1:35:respawn:/etc/init.d/init.evmd run >/dev/null 2>&1 </dev/null
h2:35:respawn:/etc/init.d/init.cssd fatal >/dev/null 2>&1 </dev/null
h3:35:respawn:/etc/init.d/init.crsd run >/dev/null 2>&1 </dev/null
```

This will spawn the crs, css, and evm daemons at startup of the cluster node. The respawn option tells init to restart the daemon should it fail, whereas the fatal option advises that should cssd fail, the entire node will be rebooted. This is necessary to avoid the possibility of data corruption, should the node become unstable.

Troubleshooting the CRS Install

Should errors occur during the CRS install, they will most likely be during the running of the root.sh script at the end. This is where the modifications are made to the inittab and the CRS daemons are started up for the first time. Failure of these daemons to start will be reported at the end of the root.sh run. Should you get an error here, the first place to check is the logfiles for each of the associated daemons. These logfiles are found in the CRS_HOME under the appropriate directory—that is, <CRS_HOME>/css/log, <CRS_HOME>/crs/log, or <CRS_HOME>/evm/log.

Installing the RDBMS

Once CRS is installed, you are now ready for the RDBMS install itself. Again, one of the first considerations to take into account before beginning the RDBMS install is the storage that will be used, both for the ORACLE_HOME and for the database itself. As we have said, in most environments, you have a couple of options, and you can mix and match between them.

ORACLE_HOME on Local or Shared?

Probably the most basic option is to simply do the install to a private (or local) drive for each node. The CRS install will do the push for you, allowing you to do the install just once from a single node. You will have the option of selecting the nodes to be pushed to during the install. If you choose this route, you may still choose to use OCFS for the datafiles, or you may choose either RAW devices or ASM as the storage medium.

ORACLE_HOME on Cluster File System

If you prefer, you may decide to use a shared ORACLE_HOME, by using OCFS as the file system for the shared ORACLE_HOME. On Linux, this requires that you be running OCFS version 2.0 or higher. OCFS version 1.*x* on Linux does *not* support installing the ORACLE_HOME—this version of OCFS can only be used for the database files. On the Windows platform, Oracle also provides a cluster file system that can be used for both the ORACLE_HOME and the RDBMS. This functionality has been available from Oracle on the Windows platform since the initial release of OCFS, shortly after 9.2.0.1 was released.

ASM Considerations

Using OCFS for the ORACLE_HOME will not necessarily tie you into using OCFS for the datafiles themselves, though that is an option. In fact, Oracle envisions environments with OCFS as the file system for a shared ORACLE_HOME, with the database files themselves being stored using ASM. Since ASM will not support regular files (only database files and database backups), OCFS is a logical alternative for the ORACLE_HOME on those platforms that support it. In addition, you can still choose to install to the private drive on each node, and use ASM for the datafiles.

Confirm CRS Configuration

Prior to beginning the RDBMS installation, you must ensure that the CRS stack is running on all nodes in the cluster. To make this determination, run the olsnodes command from the bin directory in the CRS_HOME. Usage of olsnodes can be found by using the –help switch:

```
[root@rmsclnxclu1 bin]# ./olsnodes -help
Usage: olsnodes [-l] [-n] [-v] [-g]
        where
                -l print the name of the local node
                -n print node number with the node name
                -v run in verbose mode
                -g turn on logging
```

For example, olsnodes -n should return the node name of each node, as well as its node number:

```
[root@rmsclnxclu1 bin]# ./olsnodes -n
rmsclnxclu1     0
rmsclnxclu2     1
```

After verifying the correct feedback from the olsnodes command, you can begin with the RDBMS install. Ensure that the ORACLE_HOME and ORACLE_BASE environment variables are properly set. (Recall in our examples that ORACLE_BASE is set to /u01/app/oracle, and ORACLE_HOME is /u01/app/oracle/10G.) You will also want to append the ORACLE_HOME/bin directory to the path. An example of the environment variables we have set is shown here:

```
ORACLE_BASE=/u01/app/oracle
ORACLE_HOME=$ORACLE_BASE/10g
ORACLE_SID=grid1
PATH=$ORACLE_HOME/bin:/usr/local/bin:$PATH
LD_ASSUME_KERNEL=2.4.19
export ORACLE_BASE ORACLE_HOME ORACLE_SID PATH LD_ASSUME_KERNEL
```

Note the value for LD_ASSUME_KERNEL. This environment variable is required if installing on Red Hat 3.0 (not needed for Red Hat 2.1, or other Linux variants). However, if running Red Hat 3.0, this variable should not only be set for the oracle user, but it also must be set for root. This is required for running the Virtual IP Configuration Assistant (VIPCA) at the end of the installation; otherwise, you may encounter a failure of VIPCA. To be sure that it is set, we recommend that you also add the above lines for LD_ASSUME_KERNEL to the .bash_profile in /root, and ensure that you reconnect as root prior to running root.sh at the end of the install. This will ensure that the environment variable is in effect for VIPCA.

Installing the Product

When running the installer for the RDBMS, with the CRS stack running on all nodes, you should then see the Specify Hardware Cluster Installation Mode screen directly after the File Locations page of the installer. This screen is depicted in Figure 4-7. As alluded to earlier in this chapter, this is where you will have the choice, if you prefer, to check the box for a Local Installation, which will allow you to install into a home without the RAC option. However, for our purposes here, that is not what we want. Instead, you will want to ensure that all nodes in your cluster are listed in the Cluster Installation window. If you wish to do individual installations to each node in the cluster, you may do so by checking only the box next to the local node. Our recommendation is that in this window, you check the box for all nodes in the cluster, so that the install can be done only once and pushed to all nodes. This will also ensure consistency in the installations on all nodes. It will also simplify the process of patching later on down the road.

Prerequisite Checks

After choosing Enterprise Edition, Standard Edition, or Custom for the installation type, you will then be placed into the Product-Specific Prerequisite Checks screen. Here, the OUI will go through various checks, depending on which options you have chosen to install. These checks include confirmation of the required operating system version, any OS patches or packages needed, kernel parameters, and so on. If a particular portion of the checks does not pass—for example, kernel parameters—but you know that the parameters are adequate for your needs, you can manually check the box next to that particular check, and the status will switch to User Verified and then allow you to proceed.

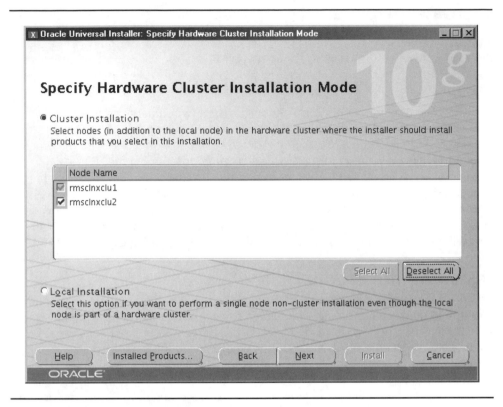

FIGURE 4-7. *Cluster Installation screen—select nodes for install*

Database Creation

The next big decision you must make is to decide whether or not you want to create a database at the end of the installation. We recommend that you do not create a starter database during the installation—you can manually run the Database Creation Assistant afterward, creating the database once the installation is completed. Therefore, our advice is to select the option next to "Do not create a starter database" and just get the binaries laid down. We will cover the creation of the database in the next section.

Install Progress and Pushing to Remote Nodes

For those of you who are experienced with Oracle installations, one of the pleasant surprises you will find with Oracle Database 10*g* is that the speed of the install is much faster. Many extraneous items have been moved off of the installation CD to a Companion CD, so that the install itself can all fit onto a single CD. This alleviates the need to swap disks and/or to have to stage the CDs to get a smooth install. In addition, the process for pushing to the other nodes in the cluster is now smoother. In previous releases, most of the work on the other nodes was put off until the end, so the HA DBA would be stuck watching an installer that was sitting at 100 percent, wondering if the installation was hung or if there actually was work being done on another node. With Oracle Database 10g, operations on remote nodes are spread out across various stages of the install, so as the status bar crawls across the screen, it is a more accurate indicator of the overall progress. The bottom line is that you no longer have to let the install run overnight to ensure that it completes.

Configuration Assistants

At the end of the installation, several assistants will be kicked off to finish out the configuration of your installation. Previously we have mentioned the VIPCA, or Virtual IP Address Configuration Assistant. This assistant is actually run as root, kicked off by running a root.sh script toward the end of the installation. VIPCA must be run successfully before you can use the DBCA to create a database. The NETCA will automatically configure your tnsnames.ora and listener.ora files. In addition to the Database Configuration Assistant (DBCA), the OC4J Assistant will be run. This is necessary for Enterprise Manager and Grid Control functionality. In the following sections we will provide an overview of what is needed for the two most critical assistants, the VIPCA and DBCA.

VIPCA   As we mentioned, at the end of the installation, you will be prompted to run the root.sh script out of the ORACLE_HOME directory on each node. Prior to doing so, you should ensure that the display is set appropriately for an X-Term, because this root.sh script will fire up the VIPCA. Remember, it is critical on Red Hat 3.0 that root has the LD_ASSUME_KERNEL env variable set to 2.4.19. The other critical component to the success of the VIPCA is that the virtual IPs to be used have been previously configured in the hosts file on each node, as we demonstrated earlier in this chapter.

While root.sh must be run on each node of the cluster, VIPCA will only be fired off on the first node. The first screen is simply a Welcome screen, while the second screen will display all of the network interfaces found on the cluster. Select all of the *public* interfaces you will be using (do not select the private interfaces), and then proceed to the next screen, where you will actually put in the aliases and IP addresses used as virtual IPs. Refer to Figure 4-8, as well as the example hosts file that we provided earlier in this chapter in the section "Configuring the Hosts File," for specifics on what you will provide on this screen.

After root.sh and VIPCA are run on the first node, run root.sh on all other nodes in the cluster. As noted, the VIPCA should not have to be run on the other cluster

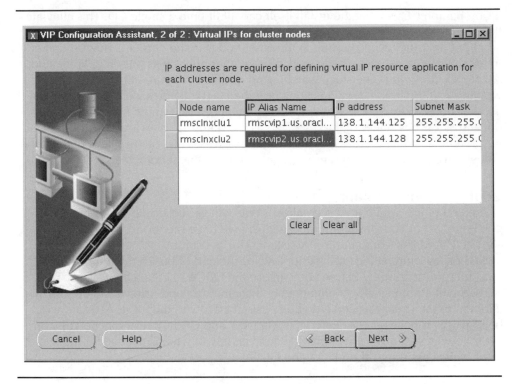

FIGURE 4-8. *Specification of virtual IP addresses*

nodes. Instead, what you should see at the end of the root.sh script on the remaining nodes is feedback such as this:

```
Now product-specific root actions will be performed.
CRS resources are already configured
```

Once root.sh has been run on all nodes, return to the Installation screen and click on OK to finish out the installation.

DBCA   The DBCA will be run at the end of the install automatically, if you chose the option to configure a database. If you did so, you would have been prompted for various pieces of the RDBMS configuration prior to the installation actually having started. This would include options such as the type of database, the database name, and storage options (that is, RAW, ASM, or file system). We recommend that you run the DBCA independently after the installation, as you will have more flexibility in specifying parameters and other options. In addition, if you are using

ASM, you have more flexibility in defining disks and disk group names to be used by the database.

What we do *not* recommend is attempting to manually create the database without using the DBCA at all. The DBCA automates many functions, particularly those necessary for a smooth operation in a RAC environment. Examples include configuration of networking files using the VIPs, running of srvctl commands (which we will discuss in Chapter 6), and the automatic creation of ASM instances if you decide to use ASM for your storage, as we discussed in Chapter 3.

The DBCA can be run on its own, as the oracle user, by changing to the ORACLE_HOME/bin directory and simply running ./dbca. Again, make sure that the display is set properly for an X-Term session. Ensure that the CRS stack is properly configured (see the olsnodes command previously mentioned) so that we can be sure that when DBCA is run, we will see the Node Selection screen. The very first screen in the DBCA should give you the option to choose between an "Oracle Real Application Clusters database," and an "Oracle single instance database." If you do not get the choice for the Real Application Clusters database, that is an indication that the CRS stack is not running or has experienced a problem (see the section on the ocrcheck utility at the end of Chapter 6 for instructions on checking the integrity of the Oracle Cluster Registry). The next two screens should then allow you to select the option to create a database and then choose the nodes on which instances for that database will be created. Subsequent screens will allow you to choose a predefined database template or create your own custom database. You will then be prompted for the DB name, passwords for various accounts, and the all-important Storage Options screen (see Figure 4-9).

Using RAW Devices for Database Files   Storage Options, as shown in Figure 4-9, allows you to choose between a cluster file system (CFS), ASM, or RAW for the location of your database files. For details on using ASM, please refer to the "Automatic Storage Management (ASM)" section of Chapter 3, which has details on how the DBCA creates the ASM instance and disk groups for use with your database. If choosing a cluster file system, the database creation is very straightforward. We would simply recommend that you ensure that a base directory such as /ocfs/oradata is created ahead of time on the appropriate OCFS drive(s), and owned by oracle. So far, we have not made much mention of using RAW devices, so we will devote the rest of this section to that very topic.

For RAW device configuration, you should ensure that you have created all of the necessary RAW slices, as defined in the appropriate preinstallation chapter. For Linux, refer to the section earlier in this chapter, in the "Shared Storage Configuration" section, and to the HA Workshop at the beginning of the chapter, where we discussed using the fdisk command to create the partitions. Keep in mind that you must create one partition for *each* file. This includes every datafile, logfile and controlfile, as well as the system parameter file (discussed more in Chapter 5).

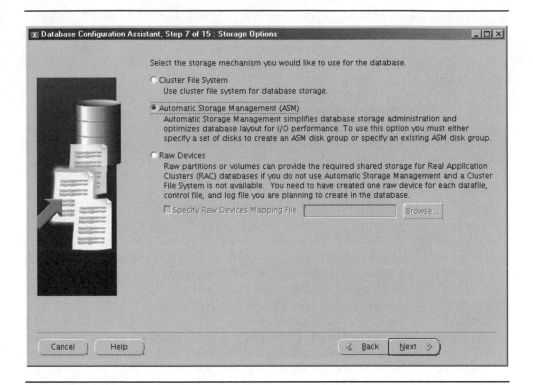

FIGURE 4-9. *Database Storage Options screen in DBCA*

In addition, we recommend that you create a RAW device mapping file, mapping predefined link names for each file associated with the database to a specific RAW slice in the /etc/sysconfig/rawdevices file. In our example, the db_name is grid, so you would create a mapping file called grid_raw.conf. Within that file, each link should be defined, pointing to a RAW slice of the appropriate size for that file. The following table gives you an idea of how to lay these files out:

Link Name	Disk Slice	Size
System	/dev/raw/raw5	600MB
Sysaux	/dev/raw/raw6	600MB
Users	/dev/raw/raw7	100MB
Temp	/dev/raw/raw8	500MB

Link Name	Disk Slice	Size
redo1_1	/dev/raw/raw9	250MB
redo1_2	/dev/raw/raw10	250MB
redo2_1	/dev/raw/raw11	250MB
redo2_2	/dev/raw/raw12	250MB
control1	/dev/raw/raw13	100MB
control2	/dev/raw/raw14	100MB
undotbs1	/dev/raw/raw15	650MB
undotbs2	/dev/raw/raw16	650MB
Spfile	/dev/raw/raw17	25MB
Pwdfile	/dev/raw/raw18	25MB

The sizes listed are recommended minimum values. You may decide you need larger sizes, specifically for certain tablespaces and/or the redo logs. Adjust the values in the above table as you deem appropriate. Also keep in mind, as we mentioned in the "Shared Storage Configuration" section, that these mappings must be created in the /etc/sysconfig/rawdevices file, pointing to the actual partitions (as shown via the fdisk –l command).

Combine this information with the information in your rawdevices file to lay the files out so that they are evenly distributed across multiple disks to balance out I/O operations. Use the Size column to verify that the partitions are adequately sized for the appropriate file. Then, create the grid_raw.conf file by mapping each filename to the appropriate RAW device—for example:

```
system=/dev/raw/raw5
sysaux=/dev/raw/raw6
users=/dev/raw/raw7
etc.
```

After choosing the appropriate storage options, continue on, setting initialization parameters as needed for the SGA size, choosing the desired character set, and so on. At the end of the database creation, you should see a screen pop up like that seen in Figure 4-10, signifying that you are done. (That example used ASM as the storage medium.) Voila! You are done—you now have a RAC-enabled database. In the next two chapters, we will go into more detail on managing your RAC environment, as well as configuring resources for high availability.

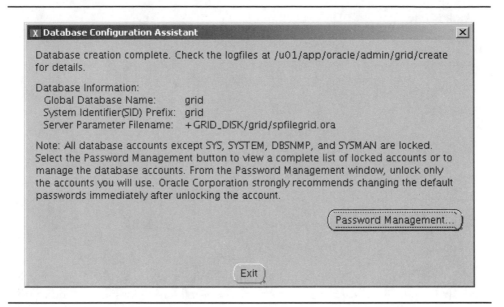

FIGURE 4-10. *Database Creation Complete*

CHAPTER
5

Database
Administration in a
RAC Environment

o, now that you have configured your RAC cluster and have a running RAC environment, what is needed to keep it that way? How is a RAC database different from a regular database, and how are they the same? What special knowledge is needed in the Brave New World of RAC to maintain your system as a highly available system? The reality and beauty of a RAC environment is that there really is *not* that big of a difference between a single-instance configuration and a RAC environment. However, there are enough differences that we can afford to devote a chapter to that discussion, as well as some of the other administrative needs you will have with regard to maintaining a RAC system.

RAC Essentials

In this section, we will discuss some of the underlying concepts of how RAC implements multiple instances for a single database, and give you the essentials for being able to determine how the database is set up and works. This includes points such as special parameters for RAC, how parameters differ for different instances, how redo and undo are managed, and differences in data dictionary views. This section will provide the most value to those who are new to the world of RAC with Oracle.

Instance Naming

This is just a short blurb on instance naming conventions in a RAC environment. We must first distinguish between the instance name and the database name. As noted in Chapter 4, the DBCA will prompt you for the database name—this will always be the same regardless of the node that you are on, as it is associated with the physical database itself. The instance name, on the other hand, is associated with the memory on each node, so the instance name must be unique to each node. As a general rule, you want the instance name to be the same as the database name, with the instance number appended to it—that is, <db_name>1, <db_name>2, and so on. This is how the DBCA will name the instances (note that sid and instance are synonymous). While you could deviate from this standard, it is strongly recommended that you do not do so.

spfile in the RAC World

This brings us next to the topic of the spfile, as that is the first file read as your RAC instance starts up. The spfile, or system parameter file, contains all of the parameters read by each instance. The spfile itself was first introduced in Oracle9*i*, as an alternative to the regular parameter file or pfile. The advantage of an spfile is that it gives you the ability to know for certain the file that was used by a given instance to start up—this is done via the following command:

```
SQL> show parameter spfile
```

With a regular parameter file, once the instance is started, there is no record of what file was used for startup. You can view the parameters used at startup by checking the alert log, but there is no record of what file was read for those parameters.

Viewing the spfile

While the spfile can be viewed using a CAT or MORE command or a text editor such as WordPad (on Windows), it is actually a binary file. As such, the only way to edit or change it is from within the database itself, via an ALTER SYSTEM command. This is a double-edged sword, as it can sometimes complicate the simple task of changing a parameter. However, it also has the advantage of allowing the HA DBA to make dynamic parameter changes, which take effect immediately and at the same time have permanence. This is due to the fact that the same command can have the changes written to the spfile, for use on subsequent startups. This is not possible using a regular parameter file.

In a RAC environment, all instances should share the same system parameter file. For parameters that are required to be unique for a given instance, that parameter must be prefaced with the instance name, in the form of

<sid_name>.<parameter_name>

For parameters that apply to all instances (the majority of parameters), the instance name is replaced by an asterisk (*). As an example, view these parameters:

```
grid2.instance_number=2
grid1.instance_number=1
*.java_pool_size=50331648
*.job_queue_processes=2
```

In this example, the instance_number applies only to either the grid1 or grid2 instance, while the values for the java_pool_size and job_queue_processes parameters will apply to all instances in the cluster.

Modifying the Parameters in the spfile

Should you need to change a parameter, you will need to do so via the ALTER SYSTEM SET XXX command. This section will briefly discuss how to modify the parameters in the spfile. The first thing to be aware of is that some parameters can be modified dynamically to take effect immediately, while others require a restart of the instance before they take effect. In either case, you must still modify the parameters via an ALTER SYSTEM command, but the SCOPE argument is used to determine how or when the parameter will be implemented.

By default, SCOPE is set to BOTH, meaning that if it is not specified, the ALTER SYSTEM command will assume that you want to write the new value out to the parameter file *and* also have it take effect immediately in memory. If you try to modify a parameter in memory that cannot be changed dynamically, you will get an ORA-02095 or an ORA-32018 error message. If this occurs, you must specify the SCOPE=SPFILE option, indicating that the parameter should be written only to the spfile and will take effect at the next startup of the instance.

Specifying the SID when Modifying Parameters

In a RAC environment, a key component of the ALTER SYSTEM command is the sid option. This tells Oracle which sid the change should apply to. If you leave the sid clause out, the default will be sid='*', meaning that the change is meant to apply to all instances. If you wish a change to apply to only one instance, you must specify sid='<sid_name>'. For example, the following command will set the parameter in the spfile for sid grid1:

```
SQL> alter system set db_cache_size=500m scope=spfile sid='grid1';

System altered.
```

This means that when the instance is restarted, grid1 will have a db_cache_size of 500MB, but this will not take effect until restart, since SCOPE=SPFILE was specified. In addition, the change will only impact the grid1 instance—not any other instances in the cluster.

RAC-Specific Parameters

The parameters instance_number and thread are examples of parameters that have specific purposes in a RAC environment. Each instance must have a unique value associated with it. It is not that these parameters do not exist in a regular instance—it is just that in a single-instance environment, the value of each defaults to 1. In a RAC environment, these take on a special meaning—the thread number defines which redo logs are associated with a given instance and the instance number will map to the inst_id column for many data dictionary views beginning with GV$ (as opposed to V$ views). These topics are discussed later in this chapter, in the sections "Cache Coherency in a RAC Environment" and "Managing REDO and UNDO in a RAC Environment." The instance number is also used in other areas such as job scheduling. To avoid confusion, the thread number and instance number should be the same for a given instance.

Aside from the instance and thread parameters, there are a few other parameters that take on a special significance in a RAC environment. These parameters include (but are not limited to) CLUSTER_DATABASE, CLUSTER_INTERCONNECTS, ACTIVE_ INSTANCE_COUNT, and MAX_COMMIT_PROPAGATION_DELAY. We will cover these parameters briefly, and what they mean to the HA DBA, in this next section.

CLUSTER_DATABASE

CLUSTER_DATABASE essentially defines the instance as being part of a cluster. It determines if the controlfile will be mounted in a shared mode, meaning other instances can also mount it. In most cases, all instances must have this value set to TRUE. However, there are some unique situations where all instances but one will need to be shut down, and a single instance will be open with CLUSTER_DATABASE set to FALSE. One example of this is when upgrading or applying a patch. The upgrade scripts are generally run after a STARTUP MIGRATE command, which must be done from one instance with CLUSTER_DATABASE set to FALSE. Another example is when putting the database into archivelog mode, or flashback mode.

CLUSTER_INTERCONNECTS

CLUSTER_INTERCONNECTS allows you to specify the network that is used for the IPC traffic for the cluster. As we have demonstrated, this is specified during the cluster install, so you generally will not need to set this. However, as we noted in Chapter 4, you may need to set this parameter if you do not have Patch 3385409, to ensure that the correct network is used for the interconnect. You also may find it helpful to set this parameter if you have multiple networks for the interconnect, and/ or if you add network cards after the CRS install. When modifying the parameter CLUSTER_INTERCONNECTS, you must do it for each sid, specifying the sid as such:

```
alter system set cluster_interconnects = '10.1.1.1' scope=spfile sid='grid1';

alter system set cluster_interconnects = '10.1.1.2' scope=spfile sid='grid2';
```

Note, however, that you do not have to connect individually to each instance— you can issue the above commands all from the same session. If you wish to specify multiple networks for the interconnect, you would specify both IP addresses in the same command, separated by a colon. For example:

```
alter system set cluster_interconnects = '10.1.1.1:192.168.0.1' scope=spfile sid='grid1';
alter system set cluster_interconnects = '10.1.1.2:192.168.0.2' scope=spfile sid='grid2';
```

There are two ways to confirm that the correct network is being used for the interconnect traffic. The first, and simplest, is to check the alert log immediately after the startup parameters are listed. You should see an entry in the alert log similar to the following:

```
Cluster communication is configured to use the following interface(s)
for this instance  10.1.1.2
```

If your database has been up and running so long that you no longer have the alert log from the startup (it is a highly available database, after all), then you can check the interconnect via the ORADEBUG IPC command in SQL*Plus. You must first attach to a pid, as such:

```
SQL> oradebug setmypid
Statement processed.
SQL> oradebug ipc
Information written to trace file.
```

The trace file this information is written to will be in the udump directory—look for the last file created there—the command LS –LTR will sort the files by creation date. The trace file will have an entry such as this toward the end, showing the IP that is used:

```
SSKGXPT 0xbf8cd8c flags SSKGXPT_READPENDING    info for network 0
        socket no 8      IP 10.1.1.2      UDP 52804
        sflags SSKGXPT_WRITESSKGXPT_UP
```

ACTIVE_INSTANCE_COUNT

ACTIVE_INSTANCE_COUNT applies only in a two-node cluster. If set to a value of 1, in a two-node cluster, it will determine that the first instance to start up will be considered the *primary* instance. The second instance will be considered a secondary instance, and will only accept connections if the primary goes down for some reason. In a grid computing environment, you will generally want all instances active and accepting connections, so this parameter will most likely be set to the total number of instances in the cluster.

MAX_COMMIT_PROPAGATION_DELAY

MAX_COMMIT_PROPAGATION_DELAY defines the maximum amount of time that the system change number (SCN) is held in the SGA of the local instance before it is refreshed by the LGWR process. By default, the value of 700 (or 7 seconds) is generally adequate. However, in some extreme cases, where committed DML statements (that is, inserts, updates, or deletes) are taking place on one node, followed by the immediate need to query the new data from another node, this value may need to be changed to 0. Setting this parameter to 0 causes commits to be broadcast immediately to all other nodes, ensuring that the SGA has the current SCN on all nodes. When this parameter is set to 0, you will see an entry in the alert log like this:

```
This instance was first to open
Picked broadcast on commit scheme to generate SCNs
```

Otherwise, if this parameter is set to a value greater than 0, you will see the Lamport scheme is chosen:

```
This instance was first to open
Picked Lamport scheme to generate SCNs
```

The downside to setting this parameter to 0 is that it will have a slight performance impact, as it increases the messaging traffic on the interconnect and causes LGWR to do more work to keep the SCNs in sync. In general, we recommend leaving this value set to its default, allowing messages to update the SCN across instances to be combined with other cluster communications, and thereby working more efficiently. If you have the need to change this value, it must be set to the same value on all cluster nodes.

Additional Background Processes in a RAC Instance

Aside from additional parameters in a RAC environment, you will also find that there are additional background processes associated with each RAC instance. The purpose of these processes is to work together in a coordinated fashion to maintain the locks necessary for multiple instances to access resources simultaneously, and to ensure that these resources are made available to the instances where they are most needed, in a timely fashion.

A simple query like the following will give you an idea of the background processes involved in a RAC environment:

```
SQL> select name, description from v$bgprocess where PADDR <> '00';
NAME   DESCRIPTION
-----  ----------------------------------------------------------------
PMON   process cleanup
DIAG   diagnosibility process
LMON   global enqueue service monitor
LMD0   global enqueue service daemon 0
LMS0   global cache service process 0
LMS1   global cache service process 1
MMAN   Memory Manager
DBW0   db writer process 0
LGWR   Redo etc.
LCK0   Lock Process 0
CKPT   checkpoint
SMON   System Monitor Process
RECO   distributed recovery
CJQ0   Job Queue Coordinator
QMNC   AQ Coordinator
MMON   Manageability Monitor Process
MMNL   Manageability Monitor Process 2
17 rows selected.
```

Of these processes, the ones specific to a RAC instance are the DIAG, LCK, LMON, LMDn, and LMSn processes. We will give a brief description of each and how they interact in a RAC environment next.

DIAG: Diagnosability Daemon
The diagnosability daemon is responsible for capturing information on process failures in a RAC environment, and writing out trace information for failure analysis. The information produced by DIAG is most useful when working in conjunction with Oracle Support to troubleshoot causes for a failure. Only a single DIAG process is needed for each instance.

LCK: Lock Process
The lock process (LCK) manages requests that are *not* cache-fusion requests, such as row cache requests and library cache requests. Only a single LCK process is allowed for each instance. LCK maintains a list of lock elements and uses this list to validate locks during instance recovery.

LMD: Lock Manager Daemon Process
The lock manager daemon is also known as the global enqueue service daemon, as it manages global enqueue and global resource access. From within each instance, the LMD process manages incoming remote resource requests (that is, requests for locks that come from other instances in the cluster). It is also responsible for deadlock detection and monitoring for lock conversion timeouts.

LMON: Lock Monitor Process
LMON is the global enqueue service monitor. It is responsible for the reconfiguration of lock resources when an instance joins the cluster or leaves the cluster, and also is responsible for the dynamic lock remastering (discussed later on in this section). LMON will generate a trace file whenever a reconfiguration occurs (as opposed to remastering of a subset of locks). It is the responsibility of LMON to check for the death of instances clusterwide, and to initiate reconfiguration as quickly as possible.

LMS: Lock Manager Server Process
The LMS process (or global cache service process) is in charge of shipping the blocks between instances for cache-fusion requests. In the event of a consistent-read request, the LMS process will first roll the block back, creating the consistent read (CR) image of the block, and will then ship that version of the block across the interconnect to the foreground process making the request at the remote instance. In addition, LMS must interact with the LMD process to retrieve lock requests placed by LMD. An instance may dynamically generate up to 10 LMS processes, depending on the load.

Cache Fusion: A Brief Intro

To understand further what these background processes are doing, let's take a moment to discuss the basics of how RAC works in terms of managing access to shared datafiles from multiple nodes. The centerpiece of this is what is known as cache fusion. Cache fusion essentially enables the shipping of blocks between the SGAs of nodes in a cluster, via the interconnect. This avoids having to push the block down to disk, to be reread into the buffer cache of another instance. When a block is read into the buffer cache of an instance in a RAC environment, a lock resource is assigned to that block (different from a row-level lock) in order to ensure that other instances are aware that the block is in use. Then, if another instance requests a copy of that block, which is already in the buffer cache of the first instance, that block can be shipped across the interconnect directly to the SGA of the other instance. If the block in memory has been changed, but that change has not been committed, a CR copy is shipped instead. This essentially means that, whenever possible, data blocks move between each instance's buffer cache without needing to be written to disk, with the key being to avoid any additional I/O being necessary to synchronize the buffer caches of multiple instances. This is why it is critical to have a high-speed interconnect for your cluster—because the assumption is that the interconnect will always be faster than going to disk.

Dynamic Resource Mastering

In addition, a new feature in Oracle Database 10*g* is the concept of dynamic resource remastering. Locks are resources that are held in the SGA of each instance, and they are used to control access to database blocks. Each instance generally holds, or masters, a certain amount of locks, which are associated with a range of blocks. When an instance requests a block, a lock must be obtained for that block, and it must be obtained from the instance that is currently mastering those locks. This may or may not be the same instance that is requesting it. In Oracle Database 10*g*, the concept of dynamic remastering is introduced, which essentially means that if a certain instance is requesting locks for certain blocks more often than any of the other instances, that lock will eventually be moved into the SGA of the requesting instance, making future lock requests more efficient.

Reconfiguration

In the case of a node's death, the process of remastering that node's locks across the remaining instances is referred to as a *reconfiguration*. When a node or an instance dies or is taken offline, the locks (resources) that were previously mastered in that instance's SGA are distributed among the remaining instances. In the case of an instance rejoining the cluster, a reconfiguration will again take place, and the new instance will end up mastering a portion of the locks previously held by the other instances in the cluster. As mentioned above, this is known as a reconfiguration, and is different from dynamic remastering.

A reconfiguration can be seen in the alert log, prefaced with the line

```
Reconfiguration started (old inc 1, new inc 2)
```

and ending with the line

```
Reconfiguration complete
```

In addition, you can view the allocation of resources between instances by querying the view GV$RESOURCE_LIMIT.

Cache Coherency in a RAC Environment

Aside from the normal performance metrics monitored in a single-instance environment, a RAC environment requires some additional metrics be monitored. Primarily, we recommend that the HA DBA focus on metrics related to messages across the interconnect, to gauge the amount of traffic across the interconnect and also the response time. This traffic essentially falls into two categories when it comes to your RAC database—global cache services (GCS) and global enqueue services (GES).

Global Cache Service

The global cache service relates to the idea of the global buffer cache, which is integral to the cache-fusion concepts. As such, *global cache* is referring to database blocks. The global cache service is responsible for maintaining cache coherency in this global buffer cache by ensuring that any time an instance attempts to modify a database block, a global lock resource is acquired, avoiding the possibility that another instance modifies the same block at the same time. The instance making the change will have the current version of the block (with both committed and uncommitted transactions) as well as a past image of the block. Should another instance request that block, it is the duty of the global cache service to track who has the block, what version of the block they have, and what mode the block is held in. The LMS process is the key component of the global cache service.

Global Enqueue Service

Aside from the maintenance and management of database blocks themselves, it is also incumbent in a RAC environment that certain other resources be coordinated between nodes. Enter the global enqueue service. The global enqueue service, or GES, is responsible primarily for maintaining coherency in the dictionary cache and the library cache. The dictionary cache is essentially a cache of data dictionary information stored in the SGA of an instance for fast access. Since this dictionary information is stored in memory, changes on one node that result in dictionary changes (such as DDL statements) must be immediately propagated to the dictionary cache on all nodes. The GES is responsible for handling this and avoiding any discrepancies between instances. By the same token, library cache locks are taken out on objects within the database for parsing of SQL statements that affect those objects. These locks must be maintained among instances, and the global enqueue service must ensure that deadlocks do not occur between multiple instances requesting access to the same objects. The LMON, LCK, and LMD processes work together to perform the functions of the global enqueue service.

GV$ Views

With all of this globalization we have discussed, it is only natural that we point out the addition of *global* views in a RAC environment. These are views that are the same as the more commonly used V$ views, except that they will have a column added called INST_ID, which will map to the instance_number of each instance in the cluster. As such, in a three-node cluster, queries against a GV$ view will give you three times as many rows, because each instance will have its own set of data to display. Knowing this, you can query stats for a specific instance or all instances without needing to connect specifically to each node. An example of some of the information you can gather is shown in the following query:

```
SQL> select * from gv$sysstat where name like '%gcs %';

INST_ID STATISTIC# NAME                                      CLASS      VALUE
------- ---------- ------------------------------- ---------- -----------
      1         38 gcs messages sent                            32        716
      2         38 gcs messages sent                            32      57325
```

This allows you to see, with one query, that instance number 1 has sent 716 gcs messages, whereas instance number 2 has sent 57325 messages, a disparity that may warrant further investigation.

Monitoring RAC Metrics Using AWR

As discussed in Chapter 3, the reports generated from the Automatic Workload Repository in a RAC environment will contain a section titled "RAC Statistics," where you can easily gather information on operations related to the global cache and global enqueues. You can get a quick look at the frequency of reads from the local cache, vs. the remote cache, and how frequently you need to go to disk for a read, as well as viewing average get times for various operations. Generally, these average values should not be higher than 30 ms, as the top range, but normally are lower. For example, the average current block receive time may be as high as 30 ms, but the average CR block receive time should not be much higher than 15 ms. The sum of the current block pin, and send and receive time altogether account for the total average time to process a current block request, and this total should not exceed 30 ms.

Interconnect Performance   If you find that the performance of the interconnect is sub-par, you should likely begin with looking at the interconnect hardware. The first thing, of course, is the speed itself. As we have mentioned several times, you want the fastest possible network to be used for the interconnect. In addition, you should ensure that the UDP buffers are set as high as possible. On Linux, you can check this via the following command:

```
sysctl net.core.rmem_max net.core.wmem_max net.core.rmem_default net.core.wmem_default
net.core.rmem_max = 65535
net.core.wmem_max = 131071
net.core.rmem_default = 65535
net.core.wmem_default = 65535
```

Alternatively, you can read the associated values directly from the respective files in the directory /proc/sys/net/core. These values can be increased to a max of 256K apiece, via the following SYSCTL commands:

```
sysctl -w net.core.rmem_max=262144
sysctl -w net.core.wmem_max=262144
sysctl -w net.core.rmem_default=262144
sysctl -w net.core.wmem_default=262144
```

Managing REDO and UNDO in a RAC Environment

One of the keys to administration in a RAC environment is understanding how redo and rollback are managed. The key here is realizing that each individual instance requires its own, independent set of redo logs, and second, its own undo tablespace. Generally speaking, redo and undo are handled on a per-instance basis. Therefore, if a RAC database is comprised of three instances, each instance must have two sets of redo logs, one set for each instance, for a minimum of six online redo log groups. Each instance can, of course, have more, but just as with a regular instance, two is the minimum. In the case of the undo tablespace, each instance also must have its own undo tablespace. These files still must be on the shared drive.

Redo Logs and Instance Recovery

Instance recovery occurs when an instance goes down abruptly, either via a SHUTDOWN ABORT, a killing of a background process, or a crash of a node or the instance itself. After an ungraceful shutdown, it is necessary for the database to go through the process of rolling forward all information in the redo logs, and the rolling back of any transactions that had not yet been committed. This process is known as instance recovery and happens automatically, because the information that is required for recovering the instance should be available in the online redo loges.

In a RAC environment, the redo logs must be accessible from all instances for the purpose of doing instance recovery of a single instance, or of multiple instances. Should instance recovery be required because a node goes down ungracefully (whatever the reason), one of the remaining instances must have access to the online redo logs in order to perform the instance recovery. Thus, even though the instance is down, the data in the redo logs is accessible and can be rolled forward by a surviving instance, with any uncommitted transactions being rolled back. This happens immediately in a RAC environment, without the need to wait for the downed instance to come back online. Here is an example of what you may see in the alert log of the instance performing instance recovery:

```
Post SMON to start 1st pass IR
Sun Feb 01 12:01:47 2004
Instance recovery: looking for dead threads
Sun Feb 01 12:01:47 2004
Beginning instance recovery of 1 threads
Sun Feb 01 12:01:47 2004
Started first pass scan
Sun Feb 01 12:01:50 2004
Completed first pass scan
 3941 redo blocks read, 165 data blocks need recovery
Sun Feb 01 12:01:51 2004
Started recovery at
 Thread 1: logseq 12, block 33210, scn 0.0
Recovery of Online Redo Log: Thread 1 Group 2 Seq 12 Reading mem 0
  Mem# 0 errs 0: /ocfs/oradata/grid/redo02.log
Sun Feb 01 12:01:53 2004
Completed redo application
```

The fact that instance recovery is done by a remaining node in the cluster means that when the crashed instance is restarted, no instance recovery is needed on that instance, because it will have already been done. If multiple instances go down, online instance recovery can still be done as long as there is a surviving instance. If all instances go down, then crash recovery is performed by the first instance to start up.

Redo Logs and Media Recovery

Media recovery differs from instance recovery in that it cannot be done automatically—it requires manual intervention, and may also require the application of archived redo logs. If it is necessary to perform media recovery on some or all of the database files, you must do this from a single node/instance. If you are recovering the entire database, all other instances must be shut down, and then you can mount the database on the node you have chosen to do recovery from. If you are recovering a single file (or set of files) that does not impact the entire database, then all instances can be open, but the file(s) that needs to be recovered must be offline, and will therefore be inaccessible.

Redo Threads

As we discussed previously, each instance is assigned a thread number, starting at 1, and the thread number for that instance should not change. The thread number is defined by the spfile parameter <sid>.THREAD=*n*, where *n* is the thread number for that instance. Thus, when a redo log group is created, it is assigned to a given instance using the thread number like so:

```
alter database add logfile thread 2 group 5
'/ocfs/oradata/grid/grid/redo02_05.log' size 100m;
```

The above example is a database on an OCFS drive.

A query similar to the following can be used to easily view the online redo logs, their groups, and their threads. This example is on a cluster using ASM:

```
set linesize 120
col inst_id for 99
col group# for 99
col thread# for 99
col sequence# for 9999999
col status for a10
col member for a40
col bytes for 9999999999
select a.group#, a.thread#, a.sequence#, b.member
  from v$log a, v$logfile b where a.group#=b.group# order by 1,2,3;

GROUP# THREAD# SEQUENCE# MEMBER
------ ------- --------- ----------------------------------------
     1       1        14 +ASM_DISK/grid/onlinelog/group_1.265.3
     1       1        14 +ASM_DISK/grid/onlinelog/group_1.264.3
     2       1        15 +ASM_DISK/grid/onlinelog/group_2.263.3
     2       1        15 +ASM_DISK/grid/onlinelog/group_2.262.3
     3       2        11 +ASM_DISK/grid/onlinelog/group_3.258.3
     3       2        11 +ASM_DISK/grid/onlinelog/group_3.256.3
     4       2        12 +ASM_DISK/grid/onlinelog/group_4.257.3
     4       2        12 +ASM_DISK/grid/onlinelog/group_4.261.5
```

Multiple Threads and Media Recovery

If you need to recover a datafile, or multiple datafiles, whether you are doing it with the database open or mounted from a single instance, you will need the archived redo logs from *all* threads of redo, and these will need to be made available in the archive destination of the instance doing the recovery. (This assumes, of course, that you are running in archivelog mode, as any good HA DBA will.) How you accomplish this recovery depends greatly on the type of file system that you are using for your datafiles. Recall that you have three options for storing files on the shared disk—

OCFS, ASM, or RAW devices. We will discuss each option, and how it affects the archival process, in the sections to follow. (Note that in Chapter 8 we will discuss these options more in conjunction with the use of RMAN for backing up the database and archivelog.)

Archiving with RAW Devices as the File System   Recall that if your shared files are on RAW devices, you must have a separate RAW slice (with a link name) for *every* file. Therefore, in this situation, it is not practical (or possible) to have the archived logs created on RAW slices themselves. Therefore, if you are using RAW devices, the most common solution to archiving would be to have the archive destination set to the private drive on each node. In the event that media recovery is necessary, it would then be required that all archived redo logs from all instances be copied to the archive destination from which recovery is being initiated. To speed the recovery process up, this can be avoided by setting up nfs mounts on each node, similar to the following:

```
mount -t nfs rmsclnxclu2:/u01/app/oracle/oradata/test/archive /archive
```

Here we have mounted the archive destination from Node2 (rmsclnxclu2) to a directory called /archive on Node1 (rmsclnxclu1). Assuming that node rmsclnxclu1 has the same path for archiving, you can then have two archive destinations, as such:

```
LOG_ARCHIVE_DEST_1=location='/u01/app/oracle/oradata/test/archive/'
LOG_ARCHIVE_DEST_2=location='/archive/'
```

By doing this, Node1 is now archiving to two separate destinations—the first destination is its own local archive directory. The second destination, the /archive directory, is actually the nfs mounted archive destination used by Node2. If you reverse the process on Node2, issuing an nfs mount from Node2 back to the archive destination on Node1, what you will have is both instances archiving to their own local archive destination as well as the archive destination of the other node. What this means, in the event that media recovery is needed, is that no matter which node you do the media recovery from, you should have access to the archived logs from all threads. As you can see, this can get rather complicated if you have many more than two nodes, but in a two-node cluster this is a workable solution.

NOTE
If you make both archive destinations mandatory, you may cause a hang of the instance if the nfs mount point for LOG_ARCHIVE_DEST_2 is inaccessible. Therefore, we recommend that you make the second destination optional in this configuration, to lessen the impact if one of the nodes is down.

Archiving in a Cluster File System Environment   If you are using OCFS for your datafiles, you can take advantage of this to greatly simplify the archival process. Simply specify the same directory on the OCFS drive as your LOG_ARCHIVE_DEST on each node. Each instance will then be writing archivelogs directly to the same directory. If you are using this option, we also strongly recommend that you specify a second archive destination on a private drive of each node. This will protect you in the event of a catastrophic failure of the disk subsystem where your OCFS drive(s) are.

One word of caution here: If archiving to the same directory on OCFS, a directory lock is taken out when a new archived log file is generated. This directory lock will be held until the file is created, preventing another instance from being able to archive at the same time. This will manifest itself as a short delay on the second instance, until the directory lock is released. As such, it may be advisable to create separate directories on the OCFS drive for each instance. This sacrifices convenience somewhat, as in the event a recovery is needed, you will need to move or copy files into the same directory. However, it avoids a possible performance hit during normal day-to-day operations.

Archiving in an ASM Environment   Lastly, if you are using ASM as the storage medium for your datafiles, you can also use an ASM disk group as a location for your flashback recovery area. Doing so will allow each instance to write out the archived logs to the location that is specified by the DB_RECOVERY_FILE_DEST for each instance, allowing you to store the archived logs in an area accessible by all nodes for recovery. RMAN can use this location to restore and recover whatever files are necessary, with access to archived logs from all instances. Note also that by default, the value for LOG_ARCHIVE_DEST_10 is automatically set to be equal to the location for DB_RECOVERY_FILE_DEST, and will be used if *no* other values are set for LOG_ARCHIVE_DEST_*n* parameters. You can explicitly set one of the LOG_ ARCHIVE_DESTINATION parameters to use the flashback recovery area by setting it equal to the string LOCATION=USE_DB_RECOVERY_FILE_DEST. For example:

```
*.LOG_ARCHIVE_DEST_1='LOCATION=/u01/app/oracle/oradata/grid/archive/'
*.LOG_ARCHIVE_DEST_2='LOCATION=USE_DB_RECOVERY_FILE_DEST'
*.db_recovery_file_dest='+ASM_TEST'
*.db_recovery_file_dest_size=2147483648
```

We discuss this in more detail in Chapters 8 and 9. When archiving to an ASM disk group, Oracle will create a directory within the disk group for each day archived logs are generated. The directories containing the archived logs will stick around and cannot be deleted, even after they have been emptied (when the flashback recovery area and/or the archived logs are backed up via RMAN). Once a directory has been empty for seven days, it is deleted automatically when the controlfile is backed up using RMAN (either manually or via a controlfile autobackup).

NOTE
A flashback recovery area can also be used with OCFS. If using RAW devices, however, you will need to set up an ASM disk group if you want to define a flashback recovery area in a RAC environment or use an OCFS mount point.

Additional Notes on Archiving in a RAC Environment   During normal operations, it is highly likely that the rate of log switches may not be the same between all instances. Therefore, if one instance is having a large amount of redo and another instance is relatively idle, the gap between SCNs and logs may grow. In order to keep this gap from becoming too large, Oracle will periodically kick in and force a log switch on instances that are not seeing as much activity. In addition, redo threads that are closed but enabled are also subject to this redo log *kick*, meaning that if an instance is shut down for a long period of time but you do not disable the redo thread, you may very well find that it is still generating archive logs, which will be needed in the event of a recovery. If you find archived logs being generated for an instance that has been down for a while, the thread can be disabled via the command

```
Alter database disable public thread 3;
```

where 3 is the thread number to be disabled. To reenable it, replace DISABLE with ENABLE.

HA Workshop: *Enable Archiving and Flashback in a RAC Database*

Workshop Notes
This workshop will go through the step-by-step process of putting a RAC database in archivelog mode and then enabling the Flashback Database option. A database must first be in archivelog mode before flashback can be enabled, so that will be done first. Our example will be centered around a two-node cluster using ASM for the datafiles and for the DB_FILE_RECOVERY_DEST. Note that for the purposes of illustration here, the same ASM disk group is used for both the datafiles and the DB_FILE_RECOVERY_DEST. However, best practices would require that these normally be separated onto different disk groups. In this example, we will also use multiple archive destinations, with one destination pointing to the private drive of each node. We will also use the default value of 1440 (minutes) for the DB_FLASHBACK_RETENTION_TARGET. In this workshop, the database name is test, and the instance names are test1 and test2.

Step 1. Create the local directories on each node needed for the nonshared (private) archive destination. In this example, ORACLE_BASE is set to /u01/app/ oracle. Run these commands on each node:

```
[oracle@rmsclnxclu1 oracle]$ mkdir -p $ORACLE_BASE/test/archive
```

Step 2. Set the LOG_ARCHIVE_DEST_1 and LOG_ARCHIVE_DEST_2 parameters. Since these parameters will be identical for all nodes, we will use sid='*'. However, you may need to modify this for your situation if the directories are different on each node.

```
alter system set log_archive_dest_1='LOCATION=USE_DB_RECOVERY_FILE_DEST'
SCOPE=SPFILE SID='*'
System altered.
alter system set log_archive_dest_2='LOCATION=/u01/app/oracle/oradata/test/archive'
SCOPE=SPFILE SID='*' ;
System altered.
```

Step 3. Set LOG_ARCHIVE_START to TRUE for all instances to enable automatic archiving.

```
SQL> alter system set log_archive_start=true scope=spfile sid='*';
System altered.
```

Note that we illustrate the command for backward compatibility purposes, but in Oracle Database 10*g*, the parameter is actually deprecated. Automatic archiving will be enabled by default whenever an Oracle Database 10*g* database is placed in archivelog mode.

Step 4. Set CLUSTER_DATABASE to FALSE for the local instance, which you will then mount to put the database into archivelog mode. By having CLUSTER_ DATABASE=FALSE, the subsequent shutdown and startup mount will actually do a Mount Exclusive by default, which is necessary to put the database in archivelog mode, and also to enable the flashback database feature:

```
SQL> alter system set cluster_database=false scope=spfile sid='test1';
System altered.
```

Step 5. Shut down all instances. Ensure that all instances are shut down cleanly:

```
SQL> shutdown immediate
Database closed.
Database dismounted.
ORACLE instance shut down.
```

Step 6.   Mount the database from instance test1 (where CLUSTER_DATABASE was set to FALSE) and then put the database into archivelog mode.

```
SQL> startup mount
ORACLE instance started.
Total System Global Area  655434464 bytes
Fixed Size                   455392 bytes
Variable Size             125829120 bytes
Database Buffers          528482304 bytes
Redo Buffers                 667648 bytes
Database mounted.
SQL> alter database archivelog;
Database altered.
```

> **NOTE**
> *If you did not shut down all instances cleanly in*
> *Step 5, putting the database in archivelog mode*
> *will fail with an ORA-265 error:*

```
alter database archivelog
*
ERROR at line 1:
ORA-00265: instance recovery required, cannot set ARCHIVELOG mode
```

Step 7.   Confirm that the database is in archivelog mode, with the appropriate parameters, by issuing the ARCHIVE LOG LIST command:

```
SQL> archive log list
Database log mode              Archive Mode
Automatic archival             Enabled
Archive destination            USE_DB_RECOVERY_FILE_DEST
Oldest online log sequence     1281
Next log sequence to archive   1282
Current log sequence           1282
```

Step 8.   Confirm the location of the RECOVERY_FILE_DEST via a SHOW PARAMETER:

```
SQL> show parameter recovery_file
NAME                                 TYPE        VALUE
------------------------------------ ----------- ---------------------------
db_recovery_file_dest                string      +ASM_DISK
db_recovery_file_dest_size           big integer 8G
```

Step 9. Once the database is in archivelog mode, you can enable flashback while the database is still mounted in exclusive mode (CLUSTER_DATABASE = FALSE):

```
SQL> alter database flashback on;
Database altered.
```

Step 10. Confirm that Flashback is enabled and verify the retention target:

```
SQL>select flashback_on, current_scn from v$database;
FLASHBACK_ON     CURRENT_SCN
-------------    --------------
YES                         0
SQL> show parameter flash
NAME                                   TYPE        VALUE
------------------------------------   ----------- ---------
db_flashback_retention_target          integer     1440
```

Step 11. Reset the CLUSTER_DATABASE parameter back to true for all instances:

```
SQL> alter system set cluster_database=true scope=spfile sid='*';
System altered.
```

Step 12. Shut down this instance and then restart all cluster database instances. All instances will now be archiving their redo threads. We will discuss Flashback Database in more detail in Chapter 9.

NOTE
The archived logs will be written out based on the init parameter LOG_ARCHIVE_FORMAT. By default, the LOG_ARCHIVE_FORMAT parameter includes the %T option, which means the thread number for each thread is included. Therefore, even if two instances have the same sequence number and end up being archived to the same location, the Thread# component of the archivelog will guarantee uniqueness. However, when archived logs are placed on an ASM disk group, these archived logs will not be named in accordance with the LOG_ ARCHIVE_FORMAT, but rather will have system-generated names determined by Oracle, such as thread_2_seq_9.270.2, which still guarantees uniqueness across instances.

UNDO in RAC

Just as with the redo logs, each instance needs its own separate undo. In this case, each instance needs its own undo tablespace, again located on a shared drive. The undo tablespace will be defined by the parameter <instance_name>.UNDO_ TABLESPACE. Again, the undo will be needed during instance recovery, if required, by the instance that is doing the recovery. In addition, however, it is very likely that the undo tablespace will need to be read from other nodes during the course of normal activities. For example, assume that a user on Node1 issues an update statement, updating a row on a table. The before picture of that row will go into the undo tablespace associated with that instance. Next, assume a second user on Node2 is querying the same record that has been updated on Node1, but not yet committed—this user must read the undo record that is in the undo tablespace assigned to Node1.

An undo tablespace can be dynamically altered while the instance is up via the ALTER SYSTEM command; however, it can only be changed to a tablespace that is specifically created as a tablespace of type UNDO, and that tablespace must not already be in use by another instance. For example, assume that we have just created a new undo tablespace called UNDOTBS_MYTEST, and we want to set that new tablespace as the undo tablespace for our third instance (called test3). The following SQL will make that change dynamically:

```
alter system set undo_tablespace=undotbs_mytest scope=both sid='test3';
```

Since scope=both was used, this change will persist even after a restart of the test3 instance, unless another statement is issued to change it later on.

Adding and Removing Cluster Nodes

One of the central tenets of grid computing revolves around the ability to move resources from one area of need to another, adding additional capacity where it is needed most, and/or removing excess or unused capacity so that it can be better utilized elsewhere. In terms of the database grid (aka RAC), this means the ability to add and remove nodes from a cluster with relative ease and swiftness. There are other situations where this need is applicable—for example, aside from the need to move resources around to where they are needed most, if a node in a cluster fails completely, the HA DBA will want to remove all vestiges of that node from the memories of the remaining nodes. Later on, the HA DBA may want to add another node, or the same node, back into the cluster. Regardless of the circumstances, the ability to do this has been enhanced in Oracle Database 10*g*. This next section discusses how this is accomplished.

Adding a Cluster Node

We will begin with the scenario of adding a node into your existing cluster. As mentioned, you may have the need to do this as your capacity needs grow over time—these needs may be permanent or they may be temporary. Or you may have a situation where a cluster node suffered a catastrophic hardware failure, and therefore a new node needs to be brought online. We can essentially boil the adding of a new node down to a four-step process:

1. Configure the new hardware.

2. Configure the new operating system.

3. Add the node to the cluster at the cluster layer.

4. Add the new instance at the database layer.

Step 1: Configuring the Hardware

This step merely consists of ensuring that the new node is hooked up to the shared components of your cluster. Make sure that the shared disks are hooked up and visible to the new node. Ensure that all network cards are correctly connected— make sure that the private card(s) are going to the switch(es) used for the interconnect, and the public card is hooked up to your public network.

Step 2: Configuring the Operating System

Make sure that the operating system level on the new node is the same as that on existing nodes, including patch levels, kernel settings, oracle user and group settings, and so on. Configure user equivalence between all the nodes. For the complete list of steps required, please refer to the preinstall steps that were described in Chapter 4, applying those same steps to the new node that you intend to add to the cluster. In addition to configuring the hosts file on the new node, make sure that the hosts files on all existing nodes are updated to include references to the new node. Follow this up by verifying that you can ping the new node from all existing nodes in the cluster, and vice versa (using both the public and private node names).

CAUTION
You must also be sure that you have secured a VIP (virtual IP) for the node to be added, and that the VIP is also defined in the hosts file of each node, whether new or existing.

Disk Configuration on the New Node   If using RAW devices or ASM, configure the /etc/sysconfig/rawdevices file to match the RAW device bindings on the other nodes (or install the ASMLib provided by Oracle, if available for your platform). If using OCFS, install the matching version of the OCFS driver on the new node, and verify that you can mount the OCFS drive from the new node. Again, refer to Chapter 4 for details on configuring these pieces. Another important point to keep in mind if you are using RAW devices is that you will need to configure RAW partitions for your new instance's online redo logs and undo tablespace. If using OCFS or ASM, this is not necessary.

Step 3: Adding the Node to the Cluster Layer

Once the preaddition steps just listed have been completed, you are now ready to add the node into the CRS layer, or clusterware layer, making the other nodes aware of its existence. To do this, you must go to one of the *existing* nodes in the cluster, change into the <CRS_HOME>/oui/bin directory, and run the addNode.sh script as the oracle user. This will start up the Oracle Universal Installer in Add Node mode. Be sure that the display is set correctly. The Welcome screen will look the same as it always does.

Click Next on the Welcome screen, and you will see the screen to Specify Cluster Nodes for Node Addition, as shown in Figure 5-1. The upper table will show the existing nodes in the cluster, while you will be able to add in the information for the new node in the lower table. Specify the public and private node info for the new node, and then proceed to the next step. In the following screen, you will be prompted to run the oraInstroot.sh script as root on the new node (unless there is an inventory location there already).

Click Next from here, and you will see the Cluster Node Addition Progress page. At this point, the OUI begins copying the binaries from the CRS HOME on the local node to the CRS_HOME on the new node. It is important to note that you are copying the home from one node to the other (unless the home is a shared CRS_HOME on a cluster file system drive). This has two advantages—first, you do not have to provide the install media for CRS, as it is not needed. Second, if the CRS_HOME on the existing node(s) has been patched already, the patch level is propagated to the new node in one swell foop, foregoing the need to do multiple runs—that is, installing the base release and then patching on top of that. The same is true of the inventory— this is also updated on the remote node to reflect the version and patch level of what has been copied over.

After the copy of the CRS_HOME has completed, you will be prompted to run the rootaddnode.sh script, followed by a prompt to run the root.sh script. The rootaddnode.sh script should be run on the local node from which you are running

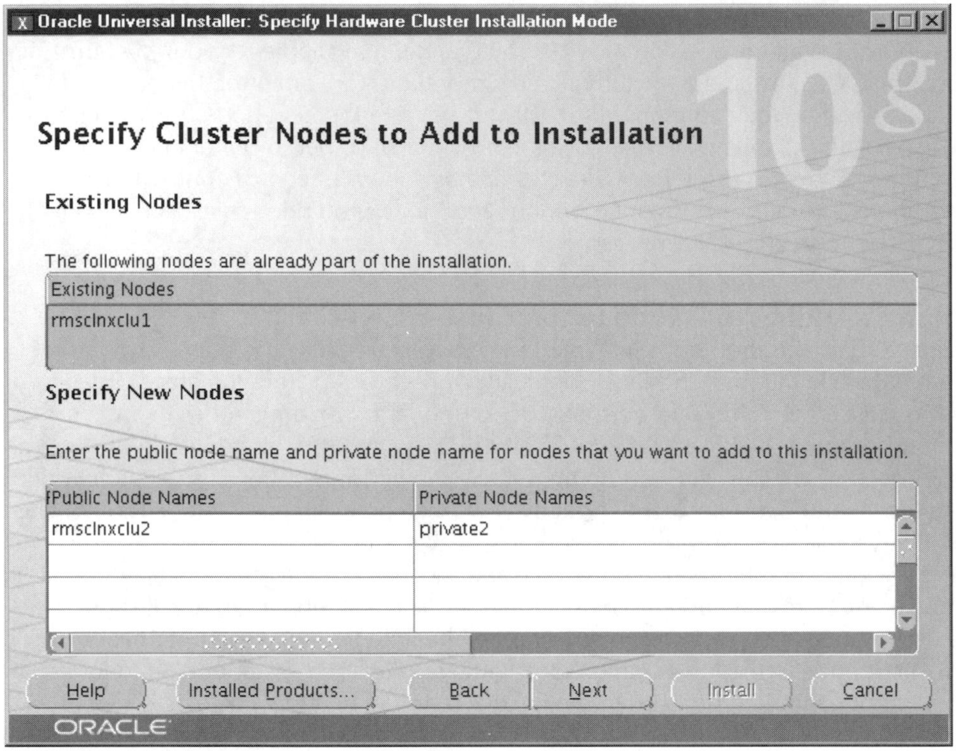

FIGURE 5-1. *Adding a node at the cluster layer*

the OUI, as root. In our case, we ran the addNode operation from node rmsclnxlcu1, so on that node we run rootaddnode.sh:

```
root@/u01/app/oracle/CRS>: ./rootaddnode.sh
clscfg: EXISTING configuration version 2 detected.
clscfg: version 2 is 10G Release 1.
Attempting to add 1 new nodes to the configuration
Using ports: CSS=49895 CRS=49896 EVMC=49898 and EVMR=49897.
node <nodenumber>: <nodename> <private interconnect name> <hostname>
node 2: rmsclnxclu2 private2 rmsclnxclu2
Creating OCR keys for user 'root', privgrp 'root'..
Operation successful.
```

Next you will be prompted to run root.sh on the new node(s) (in our case, the new node is rmsclnxclu2). This will start the CRS stack on the new node. A successful run of root.sh should have the following configuration information at the end:

```
...
...
Preparing Oracle Cluster Ready Services (CRS):
Expecting the CRS daemons to be up within 600 seconds.
CSS is active on these nodes.
        rmsclnxclu1
        rmsclnxclu2
CSS is active on all nodes.
Oracle CRS stack installed and running under init(1M)
```

The last step to complete the install is to connect as user oracle, on either node, and run the RACGONS command from the CRS_HOME/bin directory to add the Oracle Notification Services component. The command should be

```
./racgons add_config rmsclnxclu2:4948
```

where rmsclnxclu2 is the new node. The port used should be port 4948.

Step 4: Adding the Node at the RDBMS Layer

Once the new node is up and running as a member of the cluster, the next step is to proceed with adding the RDBMS layer onto the new node. To do this, again go to an *existing* node in the cluster and this time change to the ORACLE_HOME/oui/bin directory. Again run the addNode.sh script as user oracle (note that we are now in ORACLE_HOME/oui/bin as opposed to CRS_HOME/oui/bin). Again, the OUI will start up in Add Node mode, and clicking next on the Welcome screen will take you to the Specify Cluster Nodes to Add to Installation page. At this point, since we have successfully added the new node at the cluster layer, the new node should be listed in the Specify New Nodes section on the lower half of the screen. If the node is not listed, as shown in Figure 5-2, you must recheck the steps above in the section on adding the node to the cluster layer. From the Node Selection window at the bottom of the page, select the node you wish to add to the cluster and proceed.

Again, the add node process will copy the binaries from the ORACLE_HOME on the existing node directly to the ORACLE_HOME on the new node (unless OCFS is used for the ORACLE_HOME), precluding the need to provide the install media, and also precluding the need to reapply patches on the new node. At the end of the install, run root.sh as prompted.

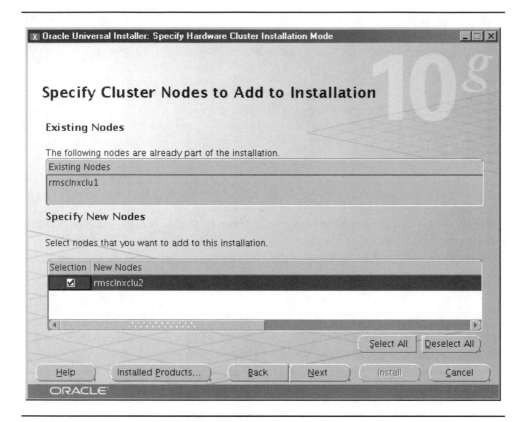

FIGURE 5-2. *Adding a node at the RDBMS layer*

Run VIPCA to Complete the RDBMS Install   After you have exited the installer, you must run the VIPCA from the command line on either node to ensure that all nodes that are part of the RAC install are included in the node list. Recall that VIPCA has to be run as root. Since this command will start up the GUI Configuration Assistant, make sure that your display is set properly before running the command:

```
vipca -nodelist rmsclnxclu1,rmsclnxclu2
```

The GUI Virtual IP Configuration Assistant will show the virtual IP information for the existing node(s) grayed out, allowing you only to specify the VIPs for the node(s) being added, as shown in Figure 5-3.

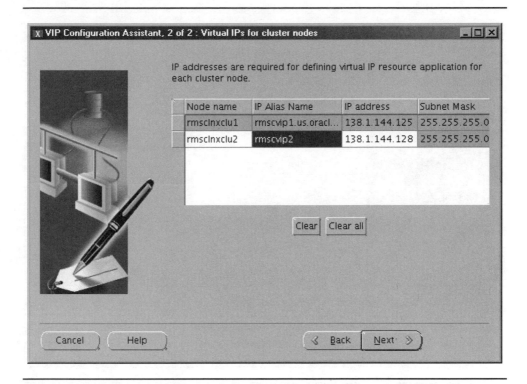

FIGURE 5-3. *Adding virtual IPs for new nodes*

Adding the Instance

Finally, you are ready to run the DBCA to configure the instance on the new node. Running DBCA from an *existing* node in the cluster, choose Real Application Clusters Database and then Instance Management. From there, select the Add Instance option, where you will be able to select the existing RAC database. You will need to authenticate yourself before you can add the new instance in. After typing in the password, be sure to tab out of the password field; otherwise, the password will not be recognized. Next, assuming that the new node is a visible member of the cluster, you will be given the opportunity to select that node and choose an instance name for it. The DBCA will assume that you want to call the instance <dbname>#, with the number being the next available instance number, as shown in Figure 5-4.

On the Database Services page, you will have the opportunity to make the new instance either an Available or Preferred instance for the existing services (see Chapter 6). Follow the prompts until you reach the Instance Storage page. If you are

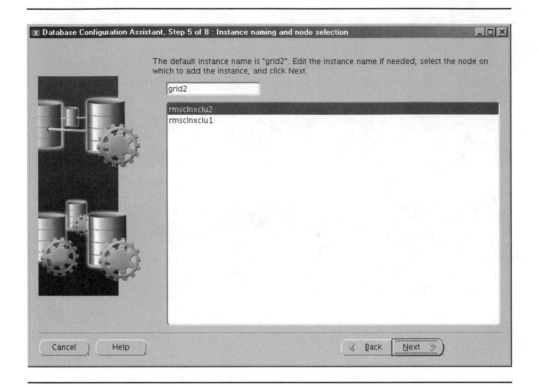

The default instance name is "grid2". Edit the instance name if needed, select the node on which to add the instance, and click Next.

grid2

rmsclnxclu2
rmsclnxclu1

Cancel   Help   Back   Next

FIGURE 5-4. *Naming and node assignment for the new instance*

using RAW devices, you will need to expand the storage options page for the undo tablespace and the redo logs to point to links for the RAW slices that you created in Step 2 earlier. If using OCFS or ASM for the existing database, you can simply click past this at the end of the configuration, allowing the DBCA to pick the file locations. Once the instance is added, your new node is fully functional and participating in your database grid.

Removing a Cluster Node

As discussed previously, though it is probably not as common, you may have the need to remove a cluster node from your RAC cluster for various reasons. It may be that you need to shift the hardware resources elsewhere, or it may be due to a complete failure of the node itself. In the event of a failure of the node itself, the node to be removed will no longer be accessible to do any cleanup. Therefore, depending on the circumstances, the next steps may not all apply. Even so, we need to make the other nodes aware of their cohort's demise—therefore, many of the node removal steps must still be run from one of the existing/remaining nodes in the cluster. The following steps are in essence the inverse of the steps previously listed:

1. Remove the database instance using DBCA.

2. Remove the node from the cluster.

3. Reconfigure the OS and remaining hardware.

Removing an Instance Using DBCA

To remove an instance from the database, you must run the DBCA from one of the existing/remaining nodes in the cluster. If the node is accessible, leave it up and running, as well as the instance that you are removing. This will enable the DBCA to get information regarding the instance, such as bdump/udump locations, and also to archive any unarchived redo logs. As before, select the Instance Management option in the DBCA. This time, choose Delete Instance from the Instance Management page. You will be prompted to select the database from which you intend to delete the instance, and you will also be prompted to supply the sys password. Again, after typing in the password, tab out of the Password field before clicking Next; otherwise, the password will not be recognized.

At this time, the List of Cluster Database Instances page will appear, as shown in Figure 5-5, presenting you the option to choose which instance should be deleted. Highlight the appropriate instance and click Next. If there have been services assigned specifically to the deleted instance, you will be given the opportunity to reassign those services via the Database Services page. We discuss services in more detail in Chapter 6. Modify the services so that each service can run on one of the remaining instances, and set Not Used for each service regarding the instance that is to be deleted. Once the services are reassigned, choose Finish. You will be prompted to confirm your choice.

Some Manual Cleanup Steps

Once complete, the DBCA should remove references to the instance from all listeners in the cluster, as well as deleting the instance's password file and init file, and removing the udump/bdump/cdump directories for that instance if the node is accessible. It will also disable the redo thread for that instance and modify the spfile, removing specific parameters for the removed instance. In addition, the undo tablespace for the defunct instance will be dropped.

If the instance is unavailable, however, or if the DBCA fails to remove all components, you may need to use SRVCTL commands to remove the instance from the OCR manually. For example:

```
srvctl remove instance -d grid -i grid2
```

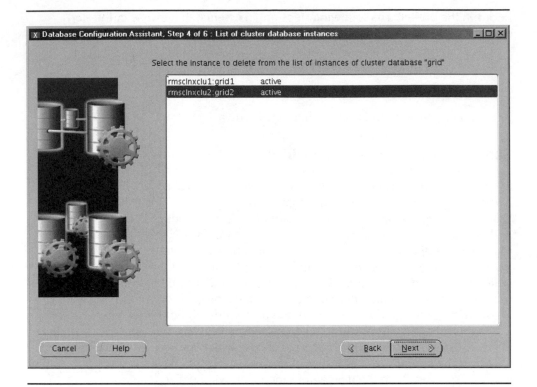

FIGURE 5-5. *Deleting an instance*

If for any reason the redo thread is not disabled, we discussed disabling redo threads in the section on redo logs earlier in this chapter. In addition, we discuss SRVCTL more in Chapter 6. To check for possible problems, a log of the DBCA's actions can be found in the $ORACLE_HOME/assistants/dbca/logs directory on the node where DBCA was run.

Dropping Red Logs May Fail in Archivelog Mode   If you are in archivelog mode, you may also find that the DBCA cannot drop the current log, as it needs archiving. If this happens, you will get an ORA-350 and ORA-312 error in a pop-up window. Click Ignore and the DBCA will continue, and should remove everything but the current redo log group on the instance you are deleting. After the DBCA completes, you will need to manually archive the logs for the instance to be deleted, and then drop that log group afterward via these commands:

```
alter system archive log all;
alter database drop logfile group 3;
```

Manually Remove the ASM Instance   If this node had an ASM instance, and this node will no longer be used as part of this cluster, you will need to manually remove the ASM instance before proceeding to remove the node from the cluster. Do so with the following command:

```
srvctl remove asm -n rmsclnxclu2
```

Removing the Node from the Cluster

After the instance has been deleted, the process of removing the node from the cluster is still essentially a manual process. This process is accomplished by running manual scripts on the deleted node (if available) to remove the CRS install, as well as scripts on the remaining nodes to update the node list and inform the remaining nodes of who is left. While we expect that this process will be simplified in forthcoming releases, we will go through the steps as they currently exist in the form of an HA Workshop.

HA Workshop: *Removing a Node from a Cluster*

Workshop Notes

This workshop will walk you step by step through the process of removing a node from a two-node cluster. The same principles can be applied to a cluster of however many nodes you have. We assume that the node to be removed is still functioning—that is, this is a resource shift, and this node is needed elsewhere. However, most commands can be done from any node in the cluster so, again, these concepts will apply even if the node is defunct. At the end of the workshop, we will point out steps that would be different if the node targeted for removal is unavailable. Pay heed, as well, to the user that you need to run each command as.

Step 1.   Start out as the root user. We first want to determine the node name and node number of each node, as stored in the Cluster Registry, so run the OLSNODES command first from the CRS_HOME/bin directory and make note of this information for your cluster:

```
oracle@/u01/app/oracle/CRS/bin>: ./olsnodes -n
rmsclnxclu1     1
rmsclnxclu2     2
```

Step 2.   In this case, we want to delete node number 2, which is rmsclnxclu2, but we first must stop the node apps (see Chapter 6). So, still as root, run the following command (be sure that the ASM instance—if it exists—has been removed, as we noted in the previous section):

```
srvctl stop nodeapps -n rmsclnxclu2
```

Step 3. Still as root, follow this up by running the rootdeletenode.sh script, passing in the node name to be removed:

```
$ORACLE_HOME/install/rootdeletenode.sh rmsclnxclu2
```

Note that this script is run from the ORACLE_HOME/install directory. Even though you are running this as root, the ORACLE_HOME environment variable should be set to the appropriate ORACLE_HOME. This script will remove the CRS node apps (discussed in Chapter 6).

In some cases, we have seen this command fail with the following error:

```
PRKO-2112 : Some or all node applications are not removed successfully
on node: rmsclnxclu2
```

Most likely this is due to not removing the ASM instance (as noted in the previous section). However, we have found that this is not a critical error, so if you see this error, you can still proceed to the next step.

Step 4. Now switch over to the oracle user account, and then follow up running the installer with the updateNodeList option (do this from the same node as previous steps):

```
$ORACLE_HOME/oui/bin/runInstaller -updateNodeList ORACLE_HOME=/u01/app/
oracle/10G CLUSTER_NODES=rmsclnxclu1
```

Note that this is all one command and should be entered on a single line. In this example, we have a two-node cluster and we are removing node RMSCLNXCLU2, so RMSCLNXCLU1 is the only remaining node. Therefore, we specified CLUSTER_NODES=rmsclnxclu1. If you have multiple nodes remaining, this should be a comma-separated list of the remaining nodes. Note also that even though the GUI installer window will not open, the display environment variable should still be set to a terminal with an X-Term.

Step 5. Next we switch back to root to finish up the removal. This command *must* be run from the node that we intend to remove. As root, run the following command to stop the CRS stack and delete the ocr.loc file on the node to be removed. The nosharedvar option assumes that the ocr.loc is *not* on a shared file system with any other nodes. (If it were, for example, on an HP Tru64 cluster, where the entire operating system exists on a shared cluster file system, you should specify sharedvar instead of nosharedvar.) Again, this command should be run on the node that you intend to remove, and this step is only necessary if that node is still operational.

```
root@/root>: /u01/app/oracle/CRS/install/rootdelete.sh remote nosharedvar
Shutting down Oracle Cluster Ready Services (CRS):
```

```
2004-03-08 17:54:00    : No CRSD seems to be running to shutdown resources.
bash: /root/.bashrc: Permission denied
Shutting down CRS daemon.
Shutting down EVM daemon.
Shutting down CSS daemon.
Shutdown request successfully issued.
Checking to see if Oracle CRS stack is down...
Oracle CRS stack is not running.
Oracle CRS stack is down now.
Removing script for Oracle Cluster Ready services
Removing OCR location file '/etc/oracle/ocr.loc'
Cleaning up SCR settings in '/etc/oracle/scls_scr/rmsclnxclu2'
```

Aside from stopping the CRS stack, this command will remove the inittab entries for CRS, and also remove the init files from /etc/init.d.

Step 6.   Next, switch back to the node where the previous steps have been executed. Still as root, run the rootdeletenode.sh script from the CRS_HOME/install directory. Here, rootdeletenode.sh, as run from the CRS home, *must* specify both the node name *and* the node number. Refer back to Step 1, where we ran the OLSNODES command to determine the node number of the node to be deleted. Do not put a space after the comma:

```
root@/u01/app/oracle/CRS/install>: ./rootdeletenode.sh rmsclnxclu2,2
clscfg: EXISTING configuration version 2 detected.
clscfg: version 2 is 10G Release 1.
Successfully deleted 13 values from OCR.
Key SYSTEM.css.interfaces.nodermsclnxclu2 marked for deletion is not there. Ignoring.
Successfully deleted 5 keys from OCR.
Node deletion operation successful.
'rmsclnxclu2,2' deleted successfully
```

Step 7.   Confirm the success by again running the OLSNODES command to confirm that the node is no longer listed—in our example, the only remaining node is the first node:

```
root@/u01/app/oracle/CRS/bin>: ./olsnodes -n
rmsclnxclu1     1
```

Step 8.   We are finally near completion. Switch back now to the oracle user, and run the same RUNINSTALLER command as before, but this time you are running it from the CRS_HOME instead of the ORACLE_HOME. Again, do this on an existing node, be sure that the display is set, and specify all remaining nodes for the CLUSTER_ NODES argument, just as we did in Step 4:

```
$CRS_HOME/oui/bin/runInstaller -updateNodeList ORACLE_HOME=/u01/app/
oracle/10G CLUSTER_NODES=rmsclnxclu1
```

Step 9. Once the node updates are done, you will need to manually delete the ORACLE_HOME and CRS_HOME from the node to be expunged (unless, of course, either of these is on a shared OCFS drive). In addition, while the inittab file will be cleaned up, and the init files will be removed from /etc/init.d, you may still want to remove the soft links from /etc/rc2.d, /etc/rc3.d, and /etc/rc5.d. The links are named K96init.crs and S96init.crs in each directory. Also, you can remove the /etc/oracle directory and the oratab file from /etc, if you wish. The node is now ready to be plugged into another cluster.

Removing a Node When the Node Is Fried   As noted previously, the above workshop assumes that the node to be removed is still fully functional. Obviously, there will be some cases where this is not so. In the above workshop, all of the commands/steps can be run from any node in the cluster, with the exception of Step 5. In the case where the node is no longer accessible, you can simply skip Step 5 altogether, as there is no need to bring down the CRS stack, nor is there a need to modify the inittab if the node is gone.

Additional RAC Considerations

In this section, we will discuss some of the other miscellaneous key differences between a RAC instance and a single Oracle instance. This includes a discussion on how ASM works in a RAC environment and how you can apply patches to the RDBMS in a RAC environment. We will finish with a discussion of how Enterprise Manager Grid Control fits into a RAC environment.

Managing ASM Environments

ASM instances in a RAC environment behave similarly to regular instances in a RAC environment. When using ASM, each node must have an ASM instance, and that instance should be part of its own database, so to speak, with the CLUSTER_DATABASE parameter set to TRUE and instance_number set to a unique value for each instance. There is no db_name parameter in an ASM environment, because there is not really a database. By the same token, the thread parameter has no meaning, as an ASM instance generates no redo. However, there are other similarities. Each instance must have a unique instance name, and will generally be in the form of +ASM1, +ASM2, +ASM3, and so on. When you create a RAC database using the DBCA, the DBCA will automatically create the RAC-enabled ASM instances on each node.

The format of the parameter file is the same as what we have discussed previously for a RAC instance—parameters specific to an instance will be prefaced with the sid name (that is, +ASM1.instance_number=1). Note that the parameter file will be a regular pfile, by default, and will *not* be on the shared disk. This is because the parameter file must be read by the ASM instance when it starts up, but the disk groups managed by ASM are not mounted and accessible until after the ASM instance starts.

ASM Disk Groups in a RAC Environment

If the database files for any RAC instance are on ASM disk groups, then each ASM instance *must* define and mount those disk groups. As discussed in Chapter 3, this is determined by the parameter ASM_DISKGROUPS. The disk group(s) must be mounted by all instances in order for the RAC instances for your database to be able to see the disks. It is possible that a given ASM instance can mount other disk groups that are not used by cluster databases. This may be desired if there are stand-alone databases on one or more of the nodes, and/or if there is additional storage that is attached to one of the nodes but not accessed by all nodes in the cluster. This storage would not be available for use by the cluster database, but could be used by individual stand-alone instances.

Patching in a RAC Environment

In releases prior to Oracle Database 10*g*, patching in a RAC environment was done to each node and instance at the same time, requiring that all instances be shut down during the maintenance window when patches were being applied. Oracle Database 10*g* allows, for certain patches, the ability to do rolling patch upgrades, meaning that you may apply a patch to a given node and instance while that instance is down and other instances in the cluster are up and running. Once the patch has been applied to the first node, the first instance can be brought back online and subsequent instances can then be brought down and patched. The ability to do this will depend on the patch itself, and will likely be for interim patches at first, rather than full patchsets.

For patches that do not qualify for the rolling upgrade option, it is still possible to maintain uptime during the patch application by combining your real application clusters environment with a logical standby database. By switching over to the logical standby database, you can have the user community up and running as usual while patches are being applied to the nodes and instances in the RAC environment. At the end of the patch installation, the users can then be switched back from the logical standby environment back over to the primary cluster environment with relatively little downtime. While this setup is beyond the scope of this chapter, we do discuss the setup and configuration of logical standby and RAC environments in Chapter 7.

Enterprise Manager Grid Control and RAC

We discuss Grid Control in this chapter and this section because we feel that Grid Control is a necessary ingredient in managing your RAC environment. We have discussed the *grid* concept on a couple of different levels—namely, the storage grid, with ASM and other storage components providing the redundancy and ability to add/remove and relocate components. We have discussed (or will discuss) the database grid with RAC and other components such as logical and physical standby, again providing redundancy and the ability to add and remove capacity as needed.

A core component of grid computing is also the ease of use and manageability. Enterprise Manager Grid Control is the tool that sits atop these various grids, making the integration and management of these components simpler and more flexible. (What we do not discuss in this book is the *application grid*, where mid-tier machines are clustered together to provide redundancy at the application server level, though that can be managed using Grid Control as well.)

Grid Control vs. Database Control

Database Control is the simplest form of Enterprise Manager, which comes installed by default with every Oracle Database 10*g* install. Nothing special is required to configure the DB Control piece—you simply start it at the operating system via the command

```
emctl start dbconsole
```

after the database has been installed. At that point, you will be able to connect to that instance using any standard browser, connecting to <http://<hostname>:5500/ em>. This allows you to manage that database on that machine, and not much more.

This is all well and good if that is all that is needed. However, in a real application clusters environment, you will have many machines, many instances, and many nodes to manage—having access to a single database at a time via the basic DB Control is just not adequate. This is where Grid Control comes in. Grid Control will allow you to manage multiple targets from one central console, including multiple instances on a single machine and multiple machines. Different types of targets are available for management as well, including a cluster_database, individual instances in a cluster database, and the cluster itself (not to mention application servers and other targets such as the hosts themselves).

Grid Control Installation Overview

Enterprise Manager Grid Control comes on a separate CD set from the Oracle Database 10*g* set. The initial Grid Control install creates a Management Server repository in its own Oracle database. The most straightforward option during the install is to do a complete install—simply allowing it to create its own repository database during the install. The option to create a repository database will actually create a 9.0.1.5 database, using the sid name of emrep by default. The Grid Control install will also install the Oracle Application Server. As such, this option requires that you have a minimum of 1GB of RAM on the machine where Grid Control is being installed, and the Grid Control install should be done to its own separate home. The complete install will also install the Oracle Database 10*g* Management Agent into its own separate home on that machine.

At the end of the Grid Control install, several configuration assistants will be kicked off. Most of these assistants have a status of Recommended to be completed. Should any of these assistants fail, we recommend that you choose the Retry option, as there is often a time lag in completing one or two of these assistants. Our experience has been that the retry will generally allow the failed assistant to complete successfully the second time around.

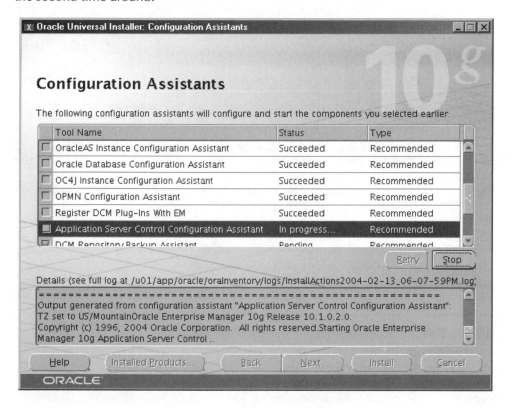

Management Agent

Once the Grid Control install has completed on the machine you have decided will be the management server machine, you must then determine which target machines you want to have managed via your Grid Control setup. On each of these target machines, you must install the Additional Management Agent option, again using the Grid Control installation media, as shown in Figure 5-6. During the install of the agent on each target, you will be prompted to register back to the management server. When prompted for the management service location, give the host name of the management server machine and port: 4889. Provide the same information on each target machine.

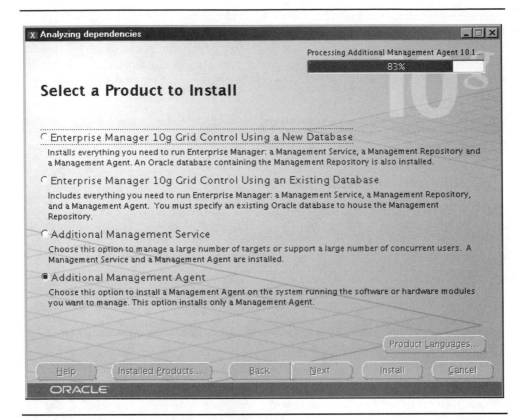

FIGURE 5-6. *Management Agent install*

Navigating Enterprise Manager Grid Control

Once the Grid Control Management Server install has completed, and targets have been registered, you can begin to manage them using a browser from any machine, just as with the Database Control. However, you will be connecting using the host name of the management server machine, rather than any of the targets, and using Port:7777. When prompted for login, you will actually be logging in to the OMS using the SYSMAN account, whose password was specified during the Grid Control installation. You will be placed into the home screen for Oracle Enterprise Manager 10*g* Grid Control, as shown in Figure 5-7, showing you the number of targets monitored and their availability. The Critical Patch Advisories section will be populated if you configured metalink login info during the installation. If not, you can configure it at any time by clicking on the link.

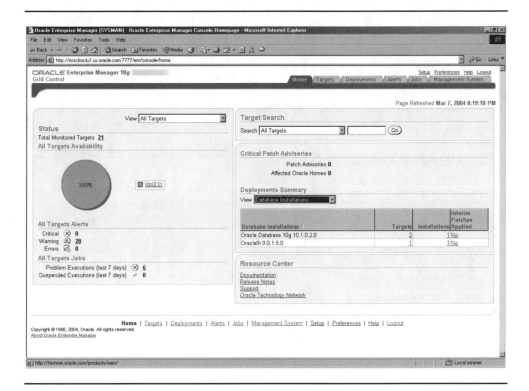

FIGURE 5-7. *Enterprise Manager Grid Control Home screen*

As you can see in Figure 5-7, in this case a total of 21 targets are being monitored, and currently all of them are available. To see the full list of targets, click on the Targets tab. This will initially show you each node/machine with a management agent, but clicking on the All Targets link will allow you to see all 21 targets being monitored. Note in Figure 5-8 that our cluster named crs_lnx is listed as a separate target, as are the Cluster Database itself (grid) and each instance in the cluster (grid1 and grid2). In addition, we can manage the ASM instances on each node (as mentioned in Chapter 3) and the listeners, as well as viewing/monitoring operating system configuration information for each individual node. To view each individual target, simply click on the target itself and supply the required login information, if prompted.

Unfortunately, the constraints of time and space prevent us from going in-depth on all of the various aspects of Enterprise Manager Grid Control. However, we encourage you to familiarize yourself with the resources and monitoring functionality available, as this tool will become more and more valuable in simplifying the management of complex environments. For additional information on Grid Control usage and configuration, please refer to the *Oracle® Enterprise Manager Advanced Configuration* guide.

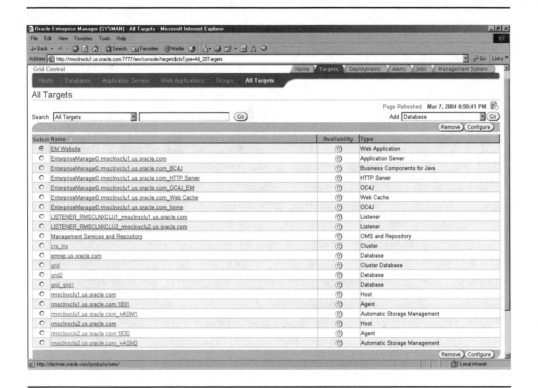

FIGURE 5-8. *Grid Control targets*

CHAPTER
6

Utility Computing:
Applications as
Services

ervices is a term that you will hear used quite often in Oracle Database 10*g*, and in the realm of high availability. While the concept of service, or a service, is nothing new to the computing world, the concept of services in Oracle Database 10*g* has been completely redefined. So, what exactly are services?

Services Concepts

Services can best be thought of as being associated with an application on the front end that needs to connect to the database on the back end. In the grid computing world, customers (end users) do not care where the application is going when they run it. They do not think in terms of the database at the back end, behind it all. Customers think of computing in terms of services, or applications at the front end—e-mail, calendaring applications, order entry, accounting, reporting, and so on. To the customer at the front end, it matters not where the power behind the scenes comes from. Just as a utility customer who plugs in an appliance does not care where or how the electricity comes in, an application user does not care where or how the data gets there. Utility customers do not think of appliances in terms of the power source; they think of appliances in terms of appliances—a hair dryer and a Nintendo are completely different in the mind of the consumer, regardless of the fact that they both get plugged into the same grid. From the grid perspective, all that matters is that the electricity is there when it is asked for.

Services as a Workload

By the same token, the application user cares not where the data that they need comes from. All that matters is that when the application gets "plugged in" to the database, it gets what it requires—service, in the form of data. Services, therefore, are a way for the DBA to think in terms of who is plugging into the database. In a general sense, services are essentially associated with an application that a customer may be using in your environment—connecting to, or plugging in to, a database in a grid at the back end. In a more specific sense, however, services are defined as an abstract way to group logical workloads. Services should be representative of a workload generated by a group of consumers that have something in common— primarily they are using the same functionality within the database, and they have the same needs in regard to availability and priority within the database. In addition, they generally use a similar amount of resources. You might also think of services in terms of a grouping of clients accessing the same or similar database objects, perhaps within the same schema.

Services as Applications

By this definition, it is probably the simplest and most helpful to think of a service in terms of the application itself, as opposed to thinking of a service in terms of the database. The application connects to a service, which is defined within the database grid. A service gives the HA DBA the ability to isolate workloads and manage them independently. This is more important than ever, in an era of consolidation and centralized computing. More and more, applications are being consolidated to run against a single back-end database that is part of a highly available, clustered environment. Services are a crucial part of this architecture, as they enable this isolation within the database, and allow for individual prioritization and monitoring. A service can be enabled or disabled based on the needs of the consumers of the service and the need to do maintenance on all or a portion of the database. For example, by isolating services from each other, it is possible to do application-specific maintenance on a schema associated with the service without affecting other services/applications. Simply disable the service for which the maintenance is scheduled, and then reenable it once the maintenance is completed.

Aside from isolating different applications and workloads from one another, the service definition within the database grid determines which nodes and/or instances the service (client application) can run on. In the event of a failure, Oracle relocates services (client applications) based again on the service definition, which defines which nodes the service is allowed to run on if the primary service has failed. All of this is irrelevant and transparent to the user/consumer of the service. The HA DBA, on the other hand, has the power to determine where these services run, their priority, and how they are handled in the event of a failure.

Services from the Database Perspective

So, how is this managed on the back end? We see now that a service is viewed by the user as a front-end application. But how does the HA DBA make sense out of this? How is this controlled from the database perspective? Well—the answer is that there are several pieces to that puzzle. At the most basic level, services are defined at the database level via the parameter SERVICE_NAMES = *My comma delimited list of service names*. With this parameter, the HA DBA can define various connection types into the database, at the instance level, that are associated at the client end with various different applications. For example, a given instance in a database cluster may have the following SERVICE_NAMES parameter defined,

```
SERVICE_NAMES=payroll, accounting, reporting, oltp
```

while another instance in the same database cluster may have a different value for SERVICE_NAMES defined:

```
SERVICE_NAMES=payroll, oltp
```

Thus, clients connecting via the payroll or OLTP service will be able to connect to either node, depending on its availability, while the accounting and reporting clients will only be able to connect to the first instance. This gives the HA DBA the flexibility to segment different portions of the user population across different instances. In addition, we are prioritizing services by saying that the payroll and OLTP services are more critical and less tolerant of failure, so these services need to be able to run on either node in the cluster. Obviously, the more instances existing in the cluster, the more flexibility you will have.

Prioritizing Services for Availability

As you can see, one way of prioritizing services is to define which services get the most/best service by granting certain applications the ability to run on more than one node at any given time. For example, suppose you have a three-node cluster. Based on your business needs and the resources at your disposal, you may decide that the payroll and OLTP services can run on any of the three nodes, the accounting service can run on Node1 or Node2, and the reporting service can only run on Node3. When all three nodes are functioning correctly, all of these applications are running correctly and will have access to their defined node. However, in the event of a failure of one of the nodes, it is only the OLTP and payroll services that are still guaranteed to have access to both remaining instances. The accounting service will have access to at least one remaining instance, but there is no guarantee that the reporting service would still have access.

By defining it this way, the HA DBA is essentially saying that OLTP and payroll have higher priority than the other services. Should Node1, Node2, or Node3 go down, the OLTP and payroll services would still have access to the two remaining nodes, but we will not necessarily want *all* applications running against these remaining two nodes. Instead, we only want our highest priority applications running—that is, the applications that have the greatest requirements in our business environment for high availability. By giving the reporting service access to only one of the nodes, we are saying that the priority for that service is not as high. In the event of a failure of Node3, we do not want that service running on the other nodes, as the remaining two nodes are going to be more heavily loaded than they would be otherwise. If Node1 or Node2 fails, the reporting service could easily be disabled on Node3. This helps to ensure not only that these applications are running, but also that there is enough capacity to handle the load until such time as the failed node can be repaired or a new node brought back online.

Resource Manager and Services

In the preceding example, it is easy enough to see that, should a node fail, the OLTP and payroll services are guaranteed to have access to one of the remaining nodes. However, as we explained, there may be an undue load placed on those remaining nodes. Suppose that the surviving nodes are Node1 and Node3. These are nodes that we have also defined as being available for the reports and accounting services. Now, all of the services are still accessible, which is a good thing. However, all services are running on two nodes now instead of three. Ideally, this will have been planned out such that the nodes with the highest number of services assigned are also the nodes that are the most robust—that is, have the greatest capacity. However, this may not always be the case. Therefore, this could impact our most important services—namely, the payroll and OLTP services. As we mentioned, we could easily disable the reporting service for a period of time, but that is a manual operation.

In this regard, Resource Manager can be used at the service level to define priorities for a given service. In prior releases, Resource Manager was used primarily at the session level, but with Oracle Database 10g, consumer groups can be defined for a given service so that services such as OLTP and payroll can be given a higher priority than services such as accounting and reporting. This can be done via Enterprise Manager, as we will discuss later in this chapter.

Resource Manager can intelligently manage resources such that when a machine is at full utilization of a given resource, certain groups/services are limited in how much of that resource they can utilize, based on the consumer group definition to which they are mapped. However, when the machine is not fully utilized, the database (knowing that there is excess capacity available) intelligently allows groups to consume more than their quota, because the capacity is there. In our earlier example, assume that the reporting service was mapped to a consumer group that allots it 10 percent of the total CPU. Thus, if the machine is 100-percent utilized, clients connecting to the reporting service will only be allotted 10 percent of the CPU, overall, while the remaining services are allowed to use 90 percent of the CPU. However, at times when the machine is *not* fully utilized (meaning the remaining services are not using their allotted 90 percent), the reporting service is allowed more than 10 percent of CPU, if needed, since the excess capacity is there. Therefore, at times when all three instances in our three-node cluster are running, the reporting service will most likely be able to run unfettered. However, if a node fails, leaving the remaining nodes running at higher loads than normal, the limits applied through Resource Manager will kick in automatically.

Creating Services

Now that we have a basic understanding of the concepts of services, and why and how they are used, we will walk through some examples of creating services. To begin with, there are two basic ways to create services. The most common is by using the Database Configuration Assistant (DBCA). The second way is to create services via the command line using the SRVCTL utility. In addition, the Net Configuration Assistant (NETCA) can be used to configure clients to connect to a service. However, by and large, we recommend that the DBCA be used to create the services, as the DBCA will automate the process and do all of the necessary work for you. In addition, once the services are created, Enterprise Manager Grid Control can be used to monitor and manage services—starting, stopping, and relocating services between nodes.

HA Workshop: *Using the DBCA to Create Services*

Workshop Notes
This workshop will walk you through the creation and definition of services using the DBCA. During the workshop, we will discuss at various stages what is being done via the DBCA.

Step 1. Execute DBCA from one of the existing nodes in the cluster. On the Welcome screen, select Oracle Real Application Clusters database and choose Next.

Step 2. Select Services Management from the next screen, as shown in Figure 6-1.

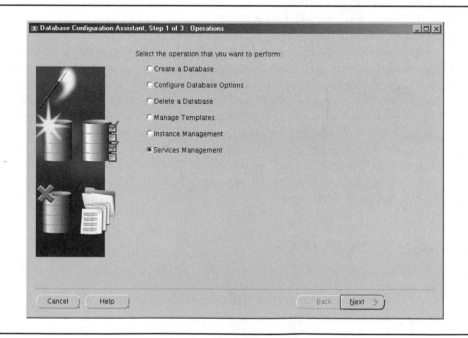

FIGURE 6-1. *Services Management screen in DBCA*

Step 3. Select the database that you want to add services for. In most cases, you will likely only have one cluster database to choose from, though it is possible to have more.

Step 4. On the page titled Step 3 of 3, choose Add to add the service name. Choose a name that has a meaning with it associated with your application— for example, a convention such as dbname_appname. In our example, we will choose a name of grid_callcenter, which we intend to be used by our callcenter application. After clicking OK, we will see the grid_callcenter service displayed in the DBCA on the left, under Database Services (see Figure 6-2).

Step 5. Now we define where this service can run. As you can see, by default, the service can run on all nodes as Preferred, meaning that the application can connect to any given node as long as it is running. Since the callcenter app in our example is a critical app, we will leave it as is, with both nodes as Preferred. Under TAF policy, we will set the policy by checking the radio button next to the Basic option.

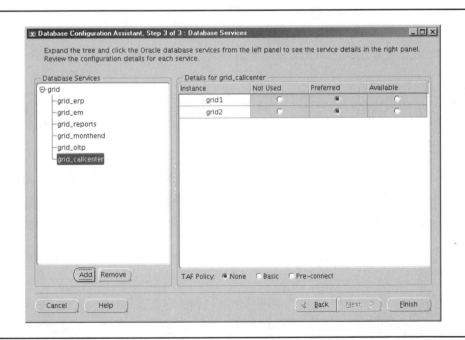

FIGURE 6-2. *Adding database services in DBCA*

Step 6. Finish the service creation by clicking Finish, and then click OK in the confirmation box that pops up. The DBCA will open up the Configuring Services window and give you a status bar indicating the progress.

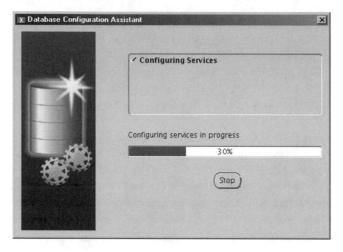

Step 7. Once completed, choose No when prompted to perform another operation.

Step 8. Now that the services are configured, we can see what has been done by connecting to the instances in SQL*Plus. From each instance, issue the following command:

```
Show parameter service_names
```

You should see that the service_name of grid_callcenter is listed under each node. Note that the spfile is not actually updated with the new service_names value; however, you should be able to see an update in the alert log via an ALTER SYSTEM command as follows:

```
ALTER SYSTEM SET service_names='grid','grid_callcenter' SCOPE=MEMORY
SID='grid1';
```

A similar command will be executed on each preferred instance that you have selected for the service to be run on.

Step 9. Next open up the tnsnames.ora file on each node (located in the $ORACLE_HOME/network/admin directory). You should see a definition for the new service that looks similar to the following:

```
GRID_CALLCENTER =
  (DESCRIPTION =
    (ADDRESS = (PROTOCOL = TCP)(HOST = rmscvip1.us.oracle.com)(PORT = 1521))
    (ADDRESS = (PROTOCOL = TCP)(HOST = rmscvip2.us.oracle.com)(PORT = 1521))
    (LOAD_BALANCE = yes)
    (CONNECT_DATA =
      (SERVER = DEDICATED)
      (SERVICE_NAME = grid_callcenter)
      (FAILOVER_MODE =
        (TYPE = SELECT)
        (METHOD = BASIC)
        (RETRIES = 180)
        (DELAY = 5)
      )
    )
  )
```

NOTE
*The host name is actually defined as the virtual IP.
We will discuss this in more detail later in this
chapter, in "Node Applications." In addition, we
cover the Virtual IP in Chapter 11.*

Step 10. Finally, test the connection using the new alias in the tnsnames.ora, and then run a quick query to verify the connection type:

```
connect scott/tiger@grid_callcenter
```

From another session with DBA privileges, you can check the connection type via a query like the following:

```
 select inst_id, username, failover_type, failover_method from
gv$session where username = 'SCOTT';
   INST_ID USERNAME   FAILOVER_TYPE   FAILOVER_METHOD
---------- ---------- --------------- -------------------------
         2 SCOTT      SELECT          BASIC
```

Viewing Services from Within the Database

Once the services have been created, information about them can be retrieved in various different ways. As noted in the preceding HA Workshop, the SHOW PARAMETER command can be used to view the service names. Aside from that, however, several additional views have been added in Oracle Database 10*g* to give the DBA the ability to view and monitor services and service activity from within the database. Some of the most useful of these views include the following:

- DBA_SERVICES

- V$SERVICES

- V$ACTIVE_SERVICES

- V$SERVICE_STATS

- V$SERV_MOD_ACT_STATS

Of course, all of the V$ views have their GV$ equivalents in a RAC environment. A query such as the following will allow you to view the services by instance (for instance, 1):

```
SQL> col inst_id for 99
SQL> col service_id for 99
SQL> col name for a15
SQL> col network_name for a15
SQL> select inst_id, service_id, name, network_name from gv$services
SQL> where inst_id = 1;
INST_ID SERVICE_ID NAME            NETWORK_NAME
------- ---------- --------------- ---------------
      1         10 grid_monthend   grid_monthend
      1         13 grid_payroll    grid_payroll
      1         12 grid_callcenter grid_callcenter
      1         11 grid_oltp       grid_oltp
      1          9 grid_reports    grid_reports
      1          8 grid_em         grid_em
      1          7 grid_erp        grid_erp
      1          5 grid           grid
      1          6 gridXDB         gridXDB
      1          1 SYS$BACKGROUND
      1          2 SYS$USERS
```

Using Enterprise Manager to View and Manage Services

To view and manage services from within EM, you should first log in to the Grid Control console. Recall that by default this will be

http://<hostname_for_mgmt_server>:7777/em

You will first need to log in to the Grid Control console using the sysman account. From there, choose Targets | Databases and select the cluster database where your services have been configured. From the cluster database home page, choose the Administration tab. On the right-hand side, under High Availability, click on the link for Cluster Managed Database Services as shown in Figure 6-3. At this point, you will be prompted for an operating system login in order to retrieve the information about the services from the Oracle Cluster Registry (which we will discuss later in this chapter). Specify the operating system account with the proper privileges and continue on from there.

Once logged in, you will be able to see all of the services defined cluster-wide, and their statuses. Note in Figure 6-4 that our service grid_callcenter is listed, and it shows that the status is up and that it is available for connection on both instances—grid1 and grid2. Note also in Figure 6-4 that there are additional services in various states of running. Like the grid_callcenter service, grid_erp, grid_em, and grid_payroll are all set up to run on either node. Note that grid_reports is set up to run only on grid2, whereas grid_monthend is set up to run on node1. The grid_monthend service has a warning, because it is not running on its preferred node. It can be relocated back to its preferred node by selecting the service and clicking on the Manage Service button. By the same token, the grid_oltp service can be started by selecting that service and choosing the Start Service option.

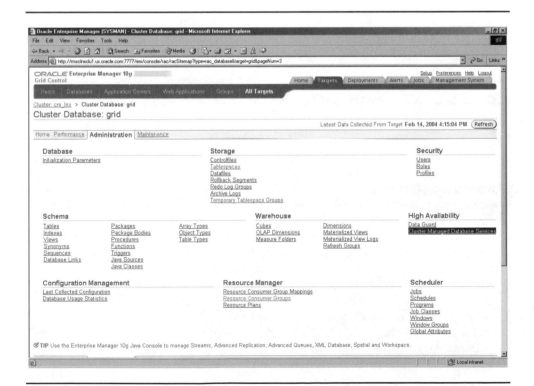

FIGURE 6-3. *Cluster-managed services in Enterprise Manager*

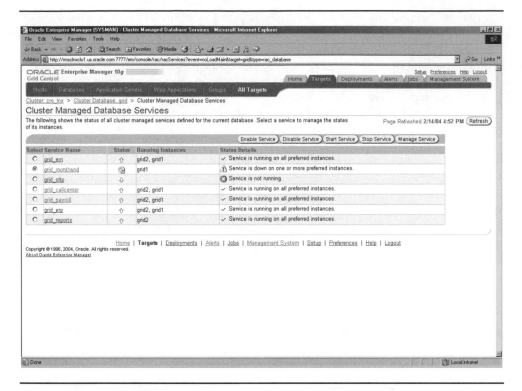

FIGURE 6-4. *Cluster Managed Database Services screen*

Modifying Services

Relocating a service can only be done to an instance that has been defined as Available for that service, when it was created via the DBCA (see Figure 6-2). If you wish to redefine a service so that it can run on additional nodes that were not part of the original service definition, you cannot currently do that through EM. Instead, you can run the DBCA again, and go through the service management steps. On the last screen, select the service that you wish to modify and change the definition. You can make multiple changes here, including adding and removing services. Once you have made the modifications, click on the Finish button in the DBCA and the services will be reconfigured. At that point, you can return to EM and refresh the page, and the modified services will now be available for relocation.

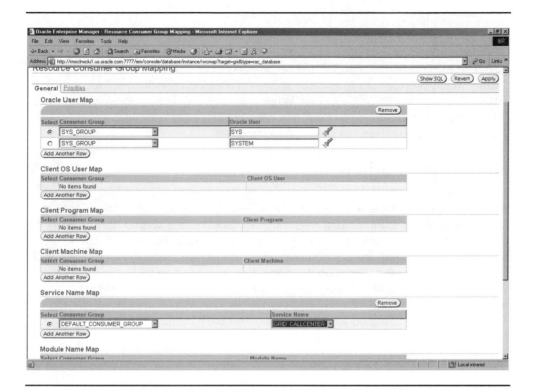

FIGURE 6-5.   *Mapping a service to a consumer group*

Resource Manager and Service Mappings in EM   As we mentioned, services
can be mapped to a resource group in Enterprise Manager, allowing you to assign
priorities at the service level for different types of services. To view or configure this
information in EM, go to the Targets tab in the Grid Control console and choose All
Targets. From there, select your cluster database, and then choose Administration.
Under Resource Manager, select the link for Resource Consumer Group Mappings.
You will then have the opportunity to map a service name to a consumer group, as
shown in Figure 6-5. For additional information on configuring consumer groups
in Resource Manager, refer to Chapter 24 of the *Oracle10g Release 1 Database
Administrator's Guide.*

Using SRVCTL to Manage Services
Aside from using the DBCA, Oracle provides the ability to manage services from the
command line using the SRVCTL utility. DBCA makes calls to SRVCTL behind the
scenes to execute the operations involved in creating the database, stopping and starting

instances, creating services, and so forth. The SRVCTL utility can be used to take a database or an instance offline, add or remove services, modify services, or stop and start services, particularly built-in services that are not user-defined. This is of particular use when maintenance operations need to be performed, where it is desirable that CRS (Cluster Ready Services) not monitor or attempt to bring online certain services while maintenance work is being performed. When using SRVCTL to add or remove services, databases and instances, and so forth, this information is written to the Oracle Cluster Registry, which we will discuss later in this chapter.

Node Applications

Node applications on a cluster consist of components at the cluster layer, sitting between the operating system and your RAC instances. Node applications are also known as *nodeapps*, and consist of components such as the Virtual IP Address (VIP) used by the node, the listener running on the node (which should be listening on the Virtual IP Address), the GSD (Group Services Daemon), and the ONS (Oracle Notification Services) daemon on the node. You might use srvctl in conjunction with the nodeapps option if you want to add any or all of these components to a node—for example, adding a virtual IP to a new node. When using srvctl to add a VIP to a node, you log on as root and then execute a command such as

```
srvctl add nodeapps -n rmsclnxclu3 -o /u01/app/oracle/10g -A
'138.1.144.129/255.255.255.0'
```

After the nodeapps have been added, you can start them via a START command such as

```
srvctl start nodeapps -n rmsclnxclu3
```

Another area where you may need to use the nodeapps configuration is if you need to change the virtual IP for an existing node. In order to do this, you must first stop the nodeapps, and then remove them, using the following syntax:

```
srvctl stop nodeapps -n rmsclnxclu3
srvctl remove nodeapps -n rmsclnxclu3
```

After removing the nodeapps, run the ADD NODEAPPS command as before, specifying the new/corrected IP address. Again, these commands must be run as root. All other srvctl operations should be done as the oracle user. Of course, prior to attempting to add a virtual IP, it should be defined in the hosts file. A listener entry would also need to be created for the new VIP, which will need to be done via the NETCA, or via a manual modification of the listener.ora.

Note also that generally the nodeapps are added when the addnode operation is run—when adding a new node—as we discussed in Chapter 5. As a general rule, you should not need to add nodeapps to a node if it has been configured properly via the OUI and DBCA. The VIPCA should add the nodeapps at the time the first instance is added to a new node. We simply illustrate the command here to give you an understanding of what nodeapps are, and how they are created—or in the rare case where you may need to change the VIP.

The srvctl utility can also be used to get the status of the nodeapps running on a particular node:

```
oracle@/home/oracle>: srvctl status nodeapps -n rmsclnxclu1
VIP is running on node: rmsclnxclu1
GSD is running on node: rmsclnxclu1
Listener is running on node: rmsclnxclu1
ONS daemon is running on node: rmsclnxclu1
```

This information is handy to check the status of these services in a node, and also to confirm the configuration after an install or after adding of a node.

Managing Databases and Instances via SRVCTL

The information stored in the OCR can be retrieved using SRVCTL commands. In addition, SRVCTL commands can be used to write information out to the OCR. An example of this is getting information about cluster databases that are part of the OCR. For example, the command SRVCTL CONFIG will show the name of any databases that exist in the Oracle Cluster Registry. Knowing the database name, you can use that information to retrieve additional information, such as the instances and nodes associated with the database. For example, we have a database with a db_name of grid. The following command will give us information about the grid database, as stored in the OCR:

```
oracle@/home/oracle>: srvctl config database -d grid
rmsclnxclu1 grid1 /u01/app/oracle/10g
rmsclnxclu2 grid2 /u01/app/oracle/10g
```

This tells us that node rmsclnxclu1 has an instance called grid1, and node rmsclnxclu2 has an instance called grid2. We can get the status of these instances using the STATUS command:

```
oracle@/home/oracle>: srvctl status database -d grid
Instance grid1 is running on node rmsclnxclu1
Instance grid2 is running on node rmsclnxclu2
```

A database can be added or removed from the configuration (OCR) using the SRVCTL ADD DATABASE or SRVCTL REMOVE DATABASE options, as well. The remove operation may be necessary if a database has been deleted, but the deletion was not done through the DBCA. This would leave information about the database in the OCR, meaning that you would not be able to re-create the database using the DBCA until that information was removed. A command such as the following can be used to remove the database from the OCR, thus allowing a new database with the same name as the original to be re-created:

```
srvctl remove database -d grid
```

A database can be manually added using the ADD DATABASE command. In our example with the grid database, and grid1 and grid2 instances, we could re-create the basic configuration with a couple of simple commands such as

```
srvctl add database -d grid -o /u01/app/oracle/10g
srvctl add instance -d grid -i grid1 -n rmsclnxclu1
srvctl add instance -d grid -i grid2 -n rmsclnxclu2
```

Where –d signifies the database name (DB_NAME), –o the ORACLE_HOME, –i the instance name, and –n the node name. These basic commands will define a database in the Oracle Cluster Registry, as well as the instances and nodes associated with that database.

SRVCTL and ASM Instances

Since an ASM instance is a special type of instance, with no real database associated with it, there is a separate command switch associated with the ASM instances—the asm switch. The SRVCTL CONFIG command that we mentioned in the preceding section will not show the ASM instances—only a regular cluster database. You can use the asm switch to get the status and names of the ASM instances on each node by using the following syntax:

```
oracle@/home/oracle>: srvctl status asm -n rmsclnxclu1
ASM instance +ASM1 is running on node rmsclnxclu1.
oracle@/home/oracle>: srvctl status asm -n rmsclnxclu2
ASM instance +ASM2 is running on node rmsclnxclu2.
```

To add an ASM instance into the OCR, the ADD ASM option would be used as shown in Example 1. To create a dependency between your database and the ASM instance (that the OCR is aware of), you can use the syntax as noted in Example 2:

- Example 1:
```
srvctl add asm -n rmsclnxclu1 -i +ASM1 -o /u01/app/oracle/10g
srvctl add asm -n rmsclnxclu2 -i +ASM2 -o /u01/app/oracle/10g
```
- Example 2:
```
srvctl modify instance -d grid -i grid1 -s +ASM1
srvctl modify instance -d grid -i grid2 -s +ASM2
```

In the preceding, the –s signifies the ASM instance dependency between the database instances grid1 and grid2 and the asm instances +ASM1 and +ASM2, respectively.

Again, note that these commands that we have walked through are done for you automatically when creating the database using the DBCA. The information provided here is meant to simply assist in understanding the configuration operations done by the DBCA, and how they relate to CRS. Should you decide to create a database manually, you would need to run these commands in order to ensure that the database and ASM instances are properly registered with CRS via the Oracle Cluster Registry. However, it is strongly recommended that the DBCA be used to create the databases, to avoid any issues with possible misconfiguration of the database.

Disabling Objects via SRVCTL

As we mentioned at the beginning of this section, where SRVCTL will come in handy is to disable the monitoring of these resources by CRS so that maintenance operations can be done. Disabling an object with SRVCTL will prevent the cluster from attempting to restart the object (a service or an instance, for example) when it is brought down, thus allowing for repair or other maintenance operations. The Disabled status persists through reboots, avoiding automatic restarts of an instance, the database, or a service— these targets will remain as Disabled until a corresponding ENABLE command is run.

For example, suppose that you need to do some maintenance such as adding or replacing memory on a node. This maintenance will require that you reboot the machine a couple of times, to confirm that the machine comes back up and to allow configuration changes such as kernel parameter modifications. If you shut down the instance through SQL*Plus, CRS will leave it alone—but on a reboot, CRS will try to start the instance back up, even though you do not want this until you are completely finished with your maintenance. To avoid this, you must first shut the instance down. You could do this via SQL*Plus, or you could use SRVCTL to stop the instance—after stopping the instance, simply disable it with SRVCTL, as in the following example:

```
srvctl stop instance -d grid -i grid1 -o immediate
srvctl disable instance -d grid -i grid1
srvctl stop asm -n rmsclnxclu1 -i +ASM1 -o immediate
srvctl disable asm -n rmsclnxclu1 -i +ASM1
```

Note that in this case, we have also stopped and disabled the ASM instance, as we also do not want that instance to start during our subsequent reboots. You can view the status of these targets by choosing the Targets tab | All Targets from within the EM Grid Control screen. As you can see in Figure 6-6, there is no special status to indicate that these instances (grid1 and +ASM1) are disabled—the targets are simply noted as being down or unavailable. Attempting to start the instances would be allowed—the disabled status simply indicates that CRS is not currently monitoring them.

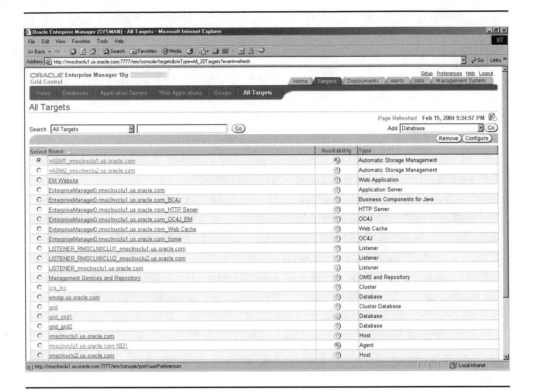

FIGURE 6-6. *Target availability in EM Grid Control*

After the subsequent reboots, and confirmations that the maintenance or repair has been completed to your satisfaction on this node, any instances can be reenabled using SRVCTL in the reverse order:

```
srvctl enable asm -n rmsclnxclu1 -i +ASM1
srvctl start asm -n rmsclnxclu1 -i +ASM1
srvctl enable instance -d grid -i grid1
srvctl start instance -d grid -i grid1 -o open
```

After a few moments, you should be able to refresh the screen in the Targets option of EM Grid Control and see that the database is back online.

In addition to taking a single instance offline and disabling it, it is also possible to stop and disable the entire database using the SRVCTL STOP DATABASE and SVRCTL DISABLE DATABASE commands:

```
srvctl stop database -d grid
srvctl disable database -d grid
```

This is particularly useful when you need to do maintenance or repairs that involve the entire cluster, especially if there are many instances/nodes involved, as the preceding commands will stop or disable *all* instances in the cluster. Enterprise Manager Grid Control uses the STOP command if you choose the Shutdown All option when shutting down the database from the Cluster Database screen.

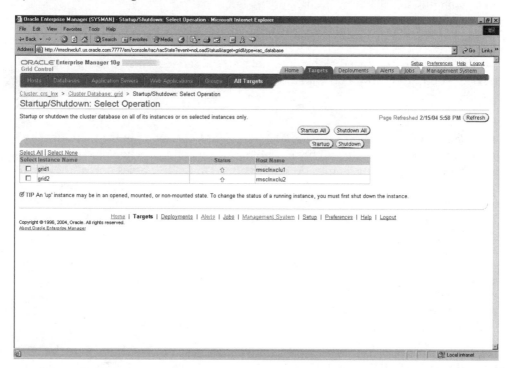

Managing Services via SRVCTL

Service creation, deletion, and management are also possible via the command line using the SRVCTL utility. The syntax is similar to what we have seen so far, with some additional switches. As we have seen through the DBCA, we can define services to run on a subset of nodes, or on every node in the cluster, and we can also define certain nodes as being preferred nodes or simply available. In addition, we have seen through EM that we can relocate services between nodes—the same is also possible using SRVCTL.

Creating Services with SRVCTL

Services are created from the command line using the ADD SERVICE option. The switches for defining the nodes and the failover policy are –r for the list of preferred instances, –a for the list of available instances, and –P for the failover policy, where the failover policy will be either NONE, BASIC, or PRECONNECT—the same options as seen in the DBCA. The following example will create a service within the grid database called grid_ap, with a failover policy of BASIC and node rmsclnxclu2 as the preferred node, with rmsclnxclu1 being available:

```
srvctl add service -d grid -s grid_ap -r grid2 -a grid1 -P NONE
```

Note that this command alone does not start the service. After creating the service, you must follow it up with a START SERVICE command:

```
srvctl start service -d grid -s grid_ap
```

At that point, you should see the ALTER SYSTEM command in the alert log from grid2, and the service will be available for connections. A key piece to note here, however, is that the entries do *not* get added to the tnsnames.ora, as they do when a service is created using the DBCA. However, you can still connect using the Easy*Connection syntax (which we will discuss more in Chapter 11). The Easy*Connection syntax is simply using //VIPname/servicename as the connect string. So, the following connections will now work, even though there is no entry in the tnsnames.ora:

```
SQL> connect scott/tiger@//rmscvip2/grid_ap
Connected.
SQL> connect scott/tiger@//rmscvip1/grid_ap
Connected.
```

Additional operations that can be done on services via SRVCTL include the DISABLE and ENABLE options, START and STOP, MODIFY, and RELOCATE. As with EM, the relocate operation will only relocate the service to an instance that has been defined initially as being available for that service. However, the command-line operations provide a bit more flexibility with the ADD and MODIFY options, which will allow you to change the list of preferred or available instances for a service. For example, let's say that a third node is added to the cluster, with an instance of grid3. In this case, the following command could be used to change our existing grid_ap service as an available instance:

```
srvctl add service -d grid -s grid_ap -u -a grid3
```

The following command should then show us the status of that service:

```
srvctl config service -d grid -s grid_ap
grid_ap PREF: grid2 AVAIL: grid3
```

A node can be upgraded from available to preferred using the MODIFY syntax as follows:

```
srvctl modify service -d grid -s grid_ap -i grid3 -r
```

This command will upgrade instance grid3 from an available instance to a preferred instance, so the SRVCTL CONFIG command should now show as follows:

```
srvctl config service -d grid -s grid_ap
grid_ap PREF: grid2 grid3 AVAIL:
```

So now, both grid2 and grid3 show as being preferred instances for this service. This change will not take full effect until the service is stopped and restarted.

Additional Notes on Services

To wrap up our discussion on services, we will discuss a couple of outstanding items that the HA DBA should be aware of. To begin with, in past releases, it was often necessary to configure and manually stop and restart the gsd service or daemon using commands such as GSDCTL STOP and START. While gsd is still required for the service operations that we have discussed, gsd is now part of the nodeapps, and as such is automatically stopped and started by CRS. Also, as we mentioned previously, running the VIPCA for the first time on a node will create and start the nodeapps, which in turn will start the gsd for you.

In addition, services should be configured to use the virtual IP address, and the listeners should be configured to be listening on the virtual IP address in order for the services and service recovery to work properly. Along those lines, the REMOTE_ LISTENERS parameter should be set in all instances, so that the listeners are cross-registered and are aware of all services across the database. We will discuss this configuration and client-side connection configurations in more depth in Chapter 11.

Limitations on the Number of Services

In Oracle Database 10g Release 1, you are limited to a total of 62 services defined for applications. This is on a per-database basis. In addition to the application services defined, there are two predefined internal services, which you may have noticed if you looked at the Resource Consumer Group Mappings in Enterprise Manager. The first is SYS$BACKGROUND, which is used by the background processes, and the second is SYS$USERS, which is used as the default service for any users connected outside of a regular service defined in the database. These internal services cannot be stopped or disabled. This brings the total maximum number of services for a database to 64.

The Oracle Cluster Registry

As you can see from the HA Workshop earlier in this chapter, and the discussion of services in the following section, much information is kept and maintained in the Oracle Cluster Registry, or OCR. Whether using the DBCA to create the services or using SRVCTL to create and/or display information, the OCR is used heavily by these operations, and also by CRS to manage the availability and accessibility of the database (the instances and services defined within it). In this section, we will spend some time discussing how the information in the OCR can be maintained, backed up, and/or reviewed

Information in the OCR

As we have seen, the OCR contains information on our services, our database itself (all databases that are part of the cluster), and the instances that are part of the databases. In addition to this application information, the clusterware itself (primarily CSS) uses the OCR when starting up. In addition, information on dependencies between applications (such as a database instance being dependent on an ASM instance) and the states of individual applications are stored in the OCR. This information must be maintained cluster-wide, so that all nodes have access to the same information when needed. No specific user configuration is needed. This is all handled by the CRS install and by the various applications that we have already discussed, such as the DBCA and SRVCTL utilities. We have also seen that the OCR can exist on either a cluster file system (where supported) or on RAW devices. Aside from the ability to work on multiple storage subsystems, the information maintained in the OCR is, for the most part, the same regardless of platform.

Physically Backing Up the OCR

Given the importance of the OCR to your cluster, it is obviously essential that the information there be backed up frequently. In fact, automatic backups of the OCR disk are taken every four hours—these backups are stored by default in the CRS_ HOME directory, under the cdata/<clustername> directory. By default, the last three backups are stored in that directory, though not always on the same node, as well as a day-old backup and a week-old backup. To view the backups, and which node is keeping them, you can run the following command:

```
ocrconfig -showbackup
private1    2004/02/15 18:24:15    /u01/app/oracle/CRS/cdata/crs_lnx
private2    2004/02/15 11:30:04    /u01/app/oracle/CRS/cdata/crs_lnx
private2    2004/02/15 07:30:03    /u01/app/oracle/CRS/cdata/crs_lnx
private2    2004/02/14 03:29:55    /u01/app/oracle/CRS/cdata/crs_lnx
private2    2004/02/13 19:29:53    /u01/app/oracle/CRS/cdata/crs_lnx
```

Note that the SHOWBACKUP command lists the times that each backup was taken, as well as the directory in which the backup is stored. In our case, the directory name is crs_lnx, as that is the name of the cluster. The other key piece of information is the node_name where that particular backup exists—using the private node name. In this case, you can see that the majority of the backups exist on Node2. A directory listing will show what type of backup each one is:

```
ls -al
total 45900
drwxrwxr-x    2 oracle    oinstall      4096 Feb 15 11:30 .
drwxrwxr-x    3 oracle    oinstall      4096 Feb 13 15:16 ..
-rw-r-----    1 root      root       9170944 Feb 15 11:30 backup00.ocr
-rw-r-----    1 root      root       9170944 Feb 15 07:30 backup01.ocr
-rw-r-----    1 root      root       9170944 Feb 15 03:30 backup02.ocr
-rw-r-----    1 root      root       9170944 Feb 15 03:30 day_.ocr
-rw-r-----    1 root      root       5500928 Feb 14 03:29 day.ocr
-rw-r-----    1 root      root       4718592 Feb 13 19:29 week.ocr
```

This directory listing was taken on Node2, where you can see a backup for each of the preceding two days, as well as the weekly backup taken on the 13th of February. What you do not see is the most recent backup—we know from the SHOWBACKUP command that a backup was taken at 18:24 on the 15th. We also know from that output that the particular backup in question exists on Node1.

If you do not like this default location for the automatic backups, you can modify the location using the OCRCONFIG command. The switch needed is the –backuploc option, followed by the new directory:

```
ocrconfig -backuploc /u02/backups
```

It is also prudent to occasionally move these backups to another machine or off-site location that is not part of the cluster.

Restoring the OCR   If you think you need to restore the OCR because of a suspected corruption problem, you should first run the OCRCHECK utility (as discussed in the next section) to confirm if the OCR is in good shape. If the OCR integrity check fails, you will need to determine which of the preceding backups to restore from. You will first want to identify which node has the most recent backup, or which node has the backup taken at a known good time in the past (for example, check the CRS_HOME/crs/log/<nodename.log> to determine a time when the cluster was functioning normally). Once you have determined which node to restore from, all other nodes in the cluster will need to be shut down. On the remaining node (the node with the desired OCR backup), boot up in single-user mode. This will bypass the inittab, meaning that the CSS and CRS daemons will not start up. Alternatively, you can simply back up the current inittab, and then copy over the original inittab

(inittab.orig) prior to rebooting. Once booted without the CRS daemons, do the restore using OCRCONFIG with the –restore option as root:

 `ocrconfig -restore /u01/app/oracle/CRS/cdata/crs_lnx/backup00.ocr`

You should be sure that this is done as root and that you are using the OCRCONFIG in the CRS_HOME/bin directory. Once the restore completes, run OCRCHECK again to confirm that the OCR passes the integrity checks. Then copy back the inittab with the CRS entries (inittab.crs), shut back down, and reboot in normal mode. Finally, bring up the remaining nodes in the cluster.

> **NOTE**
> *If you wish to change the location to which the OCR is restored, the ocrconfig_loc setting can be modified to control that. This pointer will be found in the ocr.loc file. Depending on the platform, this file may be found in /var/opt/oracle, or /etc/oracle. On Windows, the location for the file will be found in the registry under HKLM\Software\Oracle\OCR, in a registry value called ocrconfig_loc.*

Logical Backups and Restores of the OCR

In addition to the automatic physical backups, you can take a logical backup at any time by using an export switch for OCRCONFIG. The syntax of the export is, again, very straightforward:

`ocrconfig -export /tmp/ocr_logical_export`

Should you wish to restore from that export, it is recommended that you again follow the preceding steps of shutting down all nodes, and then booting up one node in single-user mode. Import with OCRCONFIG and the import switch:

`ocrconfig -import /tmp/ocr_logical_export`

After the import, restart the nodes in normal mode.

Dumping the Oracle Cluster Registry

Aside from taking backups, it is possible to dump all of the information in the Oracle Cluster Registry to an ASCII file. While the information therein cannot be used to rebuild the OCR, it has value for debugging purposes, and can be used by Oracle

Support or Oracle Development to help troubleshoot problems. To dump out the OCR information, use the OCRDUMP command. Again, the syntax is quite simple:

```
ocrdump <filename>
ocrdump /tmp/ocrdump.txt
```

If no filename is specified, the default name is OCRDUMPFILE, and it will be placed in the current directory where the command was issued from.

OCRCHECK   The last OCR utility that we will discuss is the OCRCHECK utility. It is run stand-alone, with no switches, and performs two basic operations. First, it will check the integrity of the OCR blocks, looking for any possible problems. Second, it checks the used and available space within the ocr file. The output should look similar to this:

```
oracle@/tmp>: ocrcheck
Status of Oracle Cluster Registry is as follows :
        Version                  :          2
        Total space (kbytes)     :     262144
        Used space (kbytes)      :       9252
        Available space (kbytes) :     252892

        Cluster registry integrity check succeeded
```

This is particularly handy if your ocr file is on a RAW device, and you are concerned that you are running out of space (which may happen if you have many nodes, many instances, many services, and a relatively small slice allocated for the OCR). If the used space is approaching the total space available on the RAW slice, you may want to consider relocating the OCR by changing the ocrconfig_loc and then restoring or reimporting the ocr file.

PART
III

Disaster Planning

CHAPTER
7

Oracle Data Guard:
Surviving the Disaster

p to this point we have learned how a correct Real Application Clusters (RAC) implementation can make a highly available database system. We learned how to configure a system so that most failures that occur at the instance level will be nearly transparent to the end-user community. With RAC, our database will scale out while simultaneously providing us with a maximized availability solution. Once we have our clustered database up and running, we can sit back in our chair and smile, basking in the glow of our own cleverness. Surely upper management is noticing. Surely the raise will be big this year!

And then it happens. Just ask Horatio's DBA.

Let's just suppose that the building that houses our RAC cluster burns to the ground in a fiery death. Or better yet, let's suppose that an earthquake knocks out the entire city where our data center resides. How long will it take for us to buy a new cluster and have it installed and configured? How long will it take for us to install all of the software and restore the database (you did keep the tapes at a different location, right?)? Days? Weeks? A month? Thoughts of big fat raises turn quickly to thoughts of updated resumes.

Relax. RAC can't save you from everything, but there is a solution. Oracle Data Guard has been designed from the ground up to provide an efficient disaster recovery solution that will save you from the fiery death or the crippling earthquake. Data Guard gives you the ability to failover in the event of a disaster so that your users have access to your data in minutes instead of days or weeks. Data Guard can be configured to guarantee no data loss, to minimize downtime of the production database, and to reduce the workload of the production database by offloading reports and backups. In this chapter we will learn how to take advantage of Data Guard's rich feature set and how to build a configuration that will give us safety and security while making efficient use of the additional resources.

Making the Right Choice

Data Guard is able to provide an efficient disaster recovery solution by maintaining transactionally consistent copies of the production database at a remote site. These copies, or *standbys*, can be one of two types: physical or logical. Which one you choose to include in your Data Guard configuration depends on what business needs you are trying to satisfy.

Physical Standby Databases

A physical standby database is kept in sync with the primary database by using media recovery to apply redo that was generated on the primary database. Because media recovery is used, we can be assured that a physical standby is a block-for-block identical copy of the primary database. Because of its nature, a physical standby is an excellent choice for disaster recovery. In the event of a failure, we can rest assured that our data will be intact and consistent with data that existed on the primary. A few of the primary benefits of a physical standby are

- Protection from user and logical errors

- Fast and efficient failover

- Ability to perform planned switchover for maintenance

- Ability to offload backups from the primary database

- Ability to open the standby database in read-only mode to perform reporting

Logical Standby Databases

A logical standby database is kept in sync with the primary by transforming redo data received from the primary into logical SQL statements and then executing those SQL statements against the standby database. Because we are applying SQL statements instead of performing media recovery, it is possible for the logical standby to contain the same logical information but at the same time have a different physical structure. As a logical standby is open for user access while applying changes, it is an ideal solution for a reporting database while maintaining its disaster recovery attributes. A few of the primary benefits for a logical standby are

- Ability to offload reporting from the primary database

- Ability to create additional objects to support better reporting

- Enables rolling upgrades of the primary database

Choosing which standby to implement is a very important yet straightforward process. As logical standby does not support all Oracle datatypes, the first step is to determine if your application makes use of any of the unsupported datatypes. To determine objects within your primary database that are using unsupported datatypes, run the following query:

```
select distinct owner, table_name
from dba_logstdby_unsupported
order by owner;
```

If your application is making use of the unsupported datatypes and you cannot transition to supported datatypes, a physical standby is your best choice.

Next you should consider if you have a need for the standby database to be open read-only or open read/write while changes are being applied. If you do have to have the standby open read-only, and your application does not make use of unsupported datatypes, you should evaluate logical standby as your option. If access to the standby while changes are being applied is not required or you have datatypes not supported by logical standby, you should implement a physical standby.

In some cases you should consider implementing both a physical and a logical standby. This type of configuration gives us the best of both worlds and provides the highest degree of data protection and use of system resources.

Creating a Physical Standby

In this section we will perform our first Data Guard HA Workshop, which outlines the procedure to create a physical standby. If we strip it down to the bare essentials, we see exactly how easy it is: create a backup of the primary, create a standby controlfile, transfer the files to the standby host, and mount the standby. Although it is really that simple, we will go into great detail so that we can make the right choices up front and thus save ourselves heartache later.

HA Workshop: *Creating a Physical Standby*

Workshop Notes
The following names will be used when building our configuration:

Host	Database Type	DB_UNIQUE_NAME	TNS Alias
hasun1	Primary	Orlando	Orlando_hasun1
hasun2	Physical Standby	Nashville	Nashville_hasun2

Properly configuring the primary database prior to creating the standby will ensure easier maintance and will smooth the road to later role transitions. While some steps are not mandatory, we will explain the benefits to illustrate how those choices can result in a more sound disaster recovery solution. Also, as several steps involve bouncing the primary, you should attempt to consolidate those steps to reduce the number of bounces.

Step 1.   Enable archiving.
As Data Guard is dependant on redo to maintain the standby, we must assure that the primary database is in archivelog mode. To place the primary into archivelog, perform the following steps:

```
shutdown immediate;
startup mount;
alter database archivelog;
alter database open;
```

The LOG_ARCHIVE_START parameter is no longer necessary in Oracle Database 10*g*. Automatic archiving is enabled by default when the database is placed into archivelog mode.

Step 2.   Create a password file.

Due to new log transport security and authentication features, it is mandatory that every database in a Data Guard configuration utilize a password file. In addition, the password for the sys user must be identical on every system for log transport services to function. If the primary database does not currently have a password file, create one with the following steps:

```
$cd $ORACLE_HOME/dbs
$orapwd file=orapwOrlando password=Not4U
```

Once the password file is created, you must set the following parameter in the spfile while the database is in the nomount state:

```
alter system set remote_login_passwordfile=exclusive scope=spfile;
```

Step 3.   Enable force logging (optional).

Any nologging operations performed on the primary are not fully logged within the redo stream. As Data Guard depends on the redo stream to maintain the standby, this can cause a lot of additional work for the DBA. In addition, it is difficult to know when nologging operations are occurring. One solution is to place the primary database into force logging mode. In this mode, nologging operations are permitted to run, but the changes are placed into the redo stream anyway. This assures that a sound disaster recovery solution is maintained.

To place the primary database in forced logging mode, enter the following as sys:

```
alter database force logging;
```

Step 4.   Create standby redo logs (optional).

Certain protection modes, such as maximum protection and maximum availability, mandate that standby redo logs be present. Standby redo logs are highly recommended regardless of your protection mode, as generally more data can be recovered during a failover than without them. A best practice is to create the standby redo logs on both the primary and the standby so as to make role transitions smoother.

By creating standby redo logs at this stage, we can assure that they exist on both the primary and newly created standby. When creating the standby redo log groups, we should have one more standby redo log file group than the number of online redo log file groups on the primary database. In addition, the size of the standby redo logs must match exactly with the size of online redo logs.

The following syntax is used to create the standby redo logs:

```
alter database add standby logfile thread 1
('/database/10gDR/srl1a.dbf') SIZE 500M;
```

Step 5.   Configure the primary initialization parameters.

When configuring the initialization parameters on the primary database, it is important to consider future role transitions. We must configure the parameters to control log transport services and log apply services so that the database will seamlessly operate in either role with no parameter modification. While the database is mounted on a primary controlfile, the standby parameters are not read and are not put into effect, so they will not affect the operation of the database while in the primary role.

The parameters shown here are to be placed into the primary init.ora:

```
## Primary Role Parameters ##
DB_UNIQUE_NAME=Orlando
SERVICE_NAMES=Orlando
LOG_ARCHIVE_CONFIG='DG_CONFIG=(Orlando,Nashville)'
LOG_ARCHIVE_DEST_1=
  'LOCATION=/database/10gDR/Orlando/arch/
   VALID_FOR=(ALL_LOGFILES,ALL_ROLES)
   DB_UNIQUE_NAME=Orlando'
LOG_ARCHIVE_DEST_2=
  'SERVICE=Nashville_hasun1
   VALID_FOR=(ONLINE_LOGFILES,PRIMARY_ROLE)
   DB_UNIQUE_NAME=Nashville'
LOG_ARCHIVE_DEST_STATE_1=ENABLE
LOG_ARCHIVE_DEST_STATE_2=DEFER
## Standby Role Parameters ##
DB_FILE_NAME_CONVERT=
  ('/database/10gDR/Orlando/','/database/10gDR/Nashville/')
LOG_FILE_NAME_CONVERT=
  ('/database/10gDR/Orlando/','/database/10gDR/Nashville/')
STANDBY_FILE_MANAGEMENT=AUTO
FAL_SERVER=Nashville_hasun1
FAL_CLIENT=Orlando_hasun1
```

NOTE
We initially defer LOG_ARCHIVE_DEST_2 until the
standby has been created and brought to the mount
state. Also note that the DB_FILE_NAME_CONVERT
and the LOG_FILE_NAME_CONVERT parameters
are only needed if the paths are not identical
between the primary and standby host.

Step 6.   Create a backup of the primary database.
   A physical standby can be created using either a hot or cold backup as long as
all of the necessary archivelogs are available to bring the database to a consistent
state. See Chapter 8 for information on using RMAN to back up the primary database.

Step 7.   Create a standby controlfile.
   With the primary database in either a mount or open state, create a standby
controlfile with the following syntax:

```
alter database create standby controlfile as '/database/10gDR/backup/
control_Nashville.ctl';
```

   You can also use RMAN to create a standby controlfile:

```
rman> backup current controlfile for standby;
```

Step 8.   Create an initialization parameter file for the standby.
   If your primary database is using an spfile, you will need to create a pfile for
use by the standby. Enter the following command on the primary database:

```
create pfile= '/database/10gDR/backup/initNashville.ora' from spfile;
```

   Once you have a pfile created for your standby, you will need to adjust several
parameters. Below are parameters that needed to be modified in our configuration:

```
control_files=("/database/10gDR/data/control_Nashville.ctl")
DB_UNIQUE_NAME=Nashville
SERVICE_NAMES=Nashville
LOG_ARCHIVE_CONFIG='DG_CONFIG=(Orlando,Nashville)'
LOG_ARCHIVE_DEST_1=
 'LOCATION=/database/10gDR/Orlando/arch/
  VALID_FOR=(ALL_LOGFILES,ALL_ROLES)
  DB_UNIQUE_NAME=Nashville'
LOG_ARCHIVE_DEST_2=
 'SERVICE=Orlando_hasun1
```

```
   VALID_FOR=(ONLINE_LOGFILES,PRIMARY_ROLE)
   DB_UNIQUE_NAME=Orlando'
LOG_ARCHIVE_DEST_STATE_1=ENABLE
LOG_ARCHIVE_DEST_STATE_2=ENABLE

## Standby Role Parameters ##

DB_FILE_NAME_CONVERT=
  ('/database/10gDR/Nashville/','/database/10gDR/Orlando/')
LOG_FILE_NAME_CONVERT=
  ('/database/10gDR/Nashville/','/database/10gDR/Orlando/')
STANDBY_FILE_MANAGEMENT=AUTO
FAL_SERVER=Orlando_hasun1
FAL_CLIENT=Nashville_hasun1
```

Please note that other parameters, such as dump destinations, may need to be modified depending on your environment.

Step 9.   Transfer files to the standby host.

Using an operating system utility, transfer the backup of the primary database, standby controlfile, and standby initialization parameter file to the standby host. If you are using RMAN, you can use the 'duplicate... for standby' operation to create a physical standby database with RMAN backups. See Chapter 8 for more information on RMAN and Data Guard.

Step 10.   Prepare the standby host.

If you are on the Windows operating system, we must create a service for the standby database on the standby host. To create the service, perform the following command:

```
oradim -NEW -SID Nashville -INTPWD Not4U -STARTMODE manual
```

If you are running in a Unix environment, you should create the appropriate environment variables.

Step 11.   Create the standby password file.

Due to new log transport security and authentication features, we must create a password file for the standby database, and its password for the sys user must be the same as specified for the primary database. To create the standby password file, enter the following commands:

```
$cd $ORACLE_HOME/dbs
$orapwd file=orapwNashville password=Not4U
```

Step 12.   Configure Oracle Net components.

Data Guard relies on Oracle Net as the transport mechanism to get changes made on the primary to the standby. We must configure Oracle Net listeners and Oracle Net aliases on both the primary and standby host in order to support Data Guards communication needs. Specifically we should configure the following:

■ A listener running on the primary host

■ A listener running on the standby host

■ An Oracle Net alias on the primary that points to the standby listener

■ An Oracle Net alias on the standby that points to the primary listener

Step 13.   Create an spfile for the standby instance.

If so desired, convert the initialization parameter file copied from the primary into an spfile by entering the following command on the standby instance:

```
create spfile from pfile;
```

The above command assumes that you placed the initialization file copied from the primary into the $ORACLE_HOME/dbs directory.

Step 14.   Start the standby database.

Finally, we are ready to start the standby database. To do so, enter the following command SQL*Plus prompt:

```
startup mount
```

Those that are used to mounting a standby prior to Oracle Database 10g will be asking "Don't I have to use the MOUNT STANDBY command?" Starting in Oracle Database 10g, when we mount a database we perform a check to determine if the controlfile is a primary or standby controlfile. If the controlfile is found to be a standby controlfile, the database is mounted as a standby automatically.

Step 15.   Begin shipping redo to the standby database.

If you remember, earlier we deferred LOG_ARCHIVE_DEST_2 on the primary database until we had the standby mounted. Now it is time to enable that destination and begin shipping redo to the standby. On the primary database, enter the following command:

```
alter system set log_archive_dest_state_2=enable scope=both;
```

> Next, perform a log switch on the primary and verify that the transmission of that log was successful:
>
> ```
> alter system switch logfile;
> select status,error from v$archive_dest where dest_id=2;
> ```
>
> If the transmission was successful, the status of the destination should be valid. If the status is invalid, investigate the error listed in the error column to correct any issues.
> In the "Managing a Physical Standby" section, we will cover starting managed recovery in depth. However, if you just can't help yourself, the following statement will instruct the standby to begin applying changes from archived redo logs:
>
> ```
> alter database recover managed standby database disconnect;
> ```

Creating a Logical Standby

In versions of Oracle prior to Oracle Database 10*g*, the creation of a logical standby required either a cold backup of the primary database or a period of time in which the primary was quiesce restricted. With the ever-growing demands for constant and consistent availability of databases, this restriction presented some challenges. With Oracle Database 10*g*, it is now possible to create a logical standby without having to shut down or quiesce the primary database. As you will see while creating the logical standby, we start with a working physical standby (which can be created using a hot backup) and convert it into a logical standby. This new creation procedure greatly reduces the impact that creating a logical standby has on the primary database and allows us to experiment without having to wait for maintenance windows to open up.

Is Logical Standby Right for Your Application?

The first step in creating a logical standby is to examine the applications on the primary and make sure that logical standby has support for all of the datatypes and tables. Determining support for your application database objects on the primary database before you create a logical standby database is very important. Changes made on the primary database to any objects that are not supported will not be propagated to the logical standby. When the log apply services on the logical standby encounters any unsupported objects, it will silently exclude all changes made to those objects— with no warning given to the user.

Determining Unsupported Objects

Fortunately, Oracle makes it very easy to determine exactly which objects are supported and which are not. To obtain a list of unsupported tables, use the following query on the primary database:

```
select distinct owner,table_name from dba_logstdby_unsupported
order by owner,table_name;
```

Tables that are returned from the above query are unsupported for one of several reasons—unsupported datatypes, use of compression, or belonging to a default Oracle schema that is not maintained. In most cases, the tables are unsupported due to datatype restrictions. To see exactly which column/datatype is unsupported, we can modify the above query to include column information for any tables returned:

```
select column_name,data_type from dba_logstdby_unsupported
where table_name = 'foo';
```

In Oracle Database 10*g*, the number of supported datatypes increased greatly— so much so that it's easier to list datatypes that are *not* supported:

BFILE	ROWID
UROWID	user-defined types
object types REFs	Varrays
nested tables	XMLType

Uniquely Identifying Rows on the Primary

When you update a row on the primary database, a redo record is created that can uniquely identify the exact row that was changed. In the absence of a primary key or unique key index, we will utilize the ROWID to locate the row. While this is a fast and efficient method for uniquely locating rows on the primary, it does not work in the case of a logical standby. A logical standby can have a drastically different physical layout, which makes the use of ROWID impossible. Without getting into a deep discussion of the architecture of SQL Apply, this can cause performance issues. To resolve the issue, Oracle recommends that you add a primary key or unique key index to as many of your application tables as possible. Doing so will allow SQL Apply to efficiently apply updates to those tables on the logical standby.

To identify tables on the primary that do not have a primary key or do not have a unique index, run the following query:

```
select owner, table_name,bad_column from dba_logstdby_not_unique
where table_name not in
(select table_name from dba_logstdby_unsupported);
```

It's important to note that tables returned in the above query can still be supported by SQL Apply, because supplemental logging will add information into the redo stream that will enable the rows to be uniquely identified. However, performance might be impacted. If your application ensures uniqueness, you should consider adding a RELY constraint onto that table on the primary along with an index of the unique columns on the logical standby.

HA Workshop: *Creating a Logical Standby*

Workshop Notes
Once you have confirmed that logical standby will support your application, it is time to perform the actual task of the creation process.

Step 1.   Create a physical standby.

Many of you might be scratching your head and thinking "Is that first step a typo?" It's not a typo. The first step in creating a logical standby is to create a physical standby using the same steps outlined in the preceding section. Once the physical standby has been created, we need to start the apply process and allow recovery to bring the standby up to a consistent state with the primary database.

Step 2.   Enable supplemental logging on the primary.

Supplemental logging must be enabled on the primary and standby databases in order for a logical standby to function and support role transitions. When supplemental logging is enabled, additional information is placed into the redo stream that is then used by SQL Apply to help uniquely identify rows and properly maintain tables in the logical standby. To determine if your primary or standby database currently has supplemental logging enabled, run the following query:

```
select supplemental_log_data_pk as pk_log,
supplemental_log_data_ui as ui_log
from v$database;
```

If either column reports NO, you must enable supplemental logging by issuing the following statement on both the primary and standby database:

```
alter database add supplemental log data (primary key, unique index) columns;
```

Once the above command completes, you should once again query V$DATABASE to assure that both the SUPPLEMENTAL_LOG_DATA_PK and SUPPLEMENTAL_LOG_DATA_UI return the value YES.

Step 3.   Prepare initiation parameters for both primary and logical standby.

As part of our physical standby creation process, we configured several parameters in both the primary and standby initialization. If the logical standby that we are creating in this example is to be in addition to the existing physical standby, we would need to configure several new parameters and modify a few existing ones. In the following example, we are maintaining support for the existing physical standby and adding support for the new logical standby. This example also supports both the primary and standby role so that role transitions will be seamless.

```
## Primary Role Parameters ##
DB_UNIQUE_NAME=Orlando
SERVICE_NAMES=Orlando
LOG_ARCHIVE_CONFIG='DG_CONFIG=(Orlando,Nashville,Nahsville_Reports)'
LOG_ARCHIVE_DEST_1=
 'LOCATION=/database/10gDR/Orlando/arch/
  VALID_FOR=(ALL_LOGFILES,ALL_ROLES)
  DB_UNIQUE_NAME=Orlando'
LOG_ARCHIVE_DEST_2=
 'SERVICE=Nashville_hasun1
  VALID_FOR=(ONLINE_LOGFILES,PRIMARY_ROLE)
  DB_UNIQUE_NAME=Nashville'
LOG_ARCHIVE_DEST_3=
 'SERVICE=Nashville_Reports_hasun1
  VALID_FOR=(ONLINE_LOGFILES,PRIMARY_ROLE)
  DB_UNIQUE_NAME=Nashville_Reports'
LOG_ARCHIVE_DEST_STATE_1=ENABLE
LOG_ARCHIVE_DEST_STATE_2=ENABLE
LOG_ARCHIVE_DEST_STATE_3=DEFER

## Standby Role Parameters ##

DB_FILE_NAME_CONVERT=
 ('/database/10gDR/Nashville/','/database/10gDR/Orlando/')
LOG_FILE_NAME_CONVERT=
 ('/database/10gDR/Nashville/','/database/10gDR/Orlando/')
STANDBY_FILE_MANAGEMENT=AUTO
FAL_SERVER=Nashville_hasun1
FAL_CLIENT=Orlando_hasun1
```

At this point, we should also create the initialization parameter file for the logical standby. If needed, convert the standby database spfile to a text initialization file by issuing the following command:

```
create pfile from spfile;
```

Now that we have the text initialization file, we can modify the file to contain the parameters needed to support a logical standby. What follows is an example initialization parameter file for the logical standby that supports both primary and standby roles:

```
## Primary Role Parameters ##
DB_UNIQUE_NAME=Nashville_Reports
SERVICE_NAMES=Nashville_Reports
```

```
LOG_ARCHIVE_CONFIG='DG_CONFIG=(Orlando,Nashville,Nahsville_Reports)'
LOG_ARCHIVE_DEST_1=
 'LOCATION=/database/10gDR/Orlando/arch/
  VALID_FOR=(ONLINE_LOGFILES,ALL_ROLES)
  DB_UNIQUE_NAME=Nashville_Reports'
LOG_ARCHIVE_DEST_2=
 'SERVICE=Orlando
  VALID_FOR=(ONLINE_LOGFILES,PRIMARY_ROLE)
  DB_UNIQUE_NAME=Orlando'
LOG_ARCHIVE_DEST_3=
 'LOCATION=/database/10gDR/Nashville_Reports/stby_arch/
  VALID_FOR=(STANDBY_LOGFILES,STANDBY_ROLE)
  DB_UNIQUE_NAME=Nashville_Reports'
LOG_ARCHIVE_DEST_STATE_1=ENABLE
LOG_ARCHIVE_DEST_STATE_2=ENABLE
LOG_ARCHIVE_DEST_STATE_3=ENABLE
## Standby Role Parameters ##
STANDBY_FILE_MANAGEMENT=AUTO
FAL_SERVER=Orlando_hasun1
FAL_CLIENT=Nashville_Reports_hasun1
```

Step 4.   Shut down the standby to be transitioned.

Shut down the physical standby that we are going to transition to a logical standby by issuing the following command:

```
shutdown immediate;
```

Step 5.   Create the new logical standby controlfile.

Issue the following statement on the primary database to create the logical standby controlfile:

```
alter database create logical standby controlfile as '/database/backup/control.ctl';
```

The above command can take some time to complete, depending on the current work load of your primary database. The above statement will not complete until any transactions that were running prior to the command being issued have completed. This is so that we can assure a consistent starting point for the logical standby.

Once the controlfile has been created, transfer the file to the standby host and place in the directory specified by the CONTROL_FILES initialization parameter.

Step 6.   Activate the standby database.

Now we must finish a bit of media recovery and activate the standby, thereby allowing it to be opened in read/write mode. We start this by bringing the standby to the mount state and starting managed recovery:

```
startup mount;
alter database recover managed standby database disconnect;
```

We must wait for media recovery to complete prior to continuing. We know that media recovery is complete when the following messages are printed to the alert log:

```
MRP0: Media Recovery Complete
MRP0: Background Media Recovery process shutdown
```

Once media recovery is complete, we must then activate the standby database with the following command:

```
alter database activate standby database;
```

Step 7. Reset the database name using nid.

It is a good practice to rename your database name to something other than the value of the primary database. This prevents confusion and inadvertently connecting to the wrong database. To perform this action, we must first shut down the standby and bring it back to the mount state:

```
shutdown immediate;
startup mount;
```

Next, we use the nid utility to change the database ID and name to a distinct value. In the following example, which is run as an OS command, assume we are on the standby host and the ORACLE_SID environment variable is set to Nashville:

```
nid TARGET=SYS/Not4U DBNAME=Nashville_Reports
```

The nid utility will prompt you for verification that you want to proceed. Once the utility has completed the database name and ID conversion, you will need to change the DB_NAME value in your standby initialization parameter file as well as the ORACLE_SID environment variable to the new database name. You will also need to generate a new password file for the new database name. As this should be it for major parameter changes, you can create an spfile from the text initialization parameter file at this point.

Step 8. Create tempfiles for the temporary tablespace.

If a locally managed temporary tablespace existed in the primary when you created the standby, the tablespace will also exist in the standby. All that is necessary now is to add the tempfiles to that locally managed temporary tablespace on the standby. To do this, use the following SQL to add the files:

```
alter tablespace temp
add tempfile '/database/10gDR/temp.dbf'
size 100m reuse;
```

Step 9.   Create a database link to primary database.

A database link that points to the primary will be necessary for use of the DBMS_LOGSTDBY.INSTANTIATE_TABLE procedure. You will need to reset the GLOBAL_DBNAME for your logical standby so that it is not the same as that of your primary database.

Step 10.   Start the SQL Apply engine.

Finally we are ready to start the SQL Apply engine and begin applying transactions from the primary. To do this, we issue the following statement on the logical standby as sys:

```
alter database start logical standby apply;
```

Step 11.   Verify that the SQL Apply engine is working.

When starting the SQL Apply engine for the first time, certain actions are taken to prepare the LogMiner dictionary that will be used for all future work. The time taken for this one-time work to complete will vary depending on the size of the dictionary and the capacity of the standby host. To view the SQL Apply engine, and the status of each process associated with the SQL Apply engine, you can use the V$LOGSTDBY view. The following query will show the name of the process, the SCN that it is currently working on, and its current status:

```
select type, high_scn, status from v$logstdby;
```

When all of the processes state that no work is available, they are considered to be idle—waiting on additional information to arrive from the primary.

Another good view to determine the progress of the SQL Apply engine is the DBA_LOGSTDBY_PROGRESS view. The APPLIED_SCN column lists the highest SCN that has been applied to the standby database. The NEWEST_SCN column lists the highest SCN that has been received from the primary. When the two values are equal, we know that all available redo that has arrived from the primary has been applied.

Log Transport Services

At the heart of Data Guard lies log transport services. The very basis of Data Guard is the fact that we are able to effectively ship changes generated on the primary database to a secondary site. Once those changes exist on the secondary site, we are protected from the dreaded disaster. But log transport services does more than simply ship redo from one site to another site. It also gives us the ability to determine the level of data protection for our database. Log transport services configuration can be performed in such a manner as to balance data protection and availability against any performance impact. In this section we will examine how to configure log transport services, as well as discuss items that should be considered when designing your disaster recovery solution.

Defining Log Transport Services Destinations

We define where and how log transport services will transmit redo using the LOG_ARCHIVE_DEST_*n* initialization parameter. Using this parameter, we can define up to 10 destinations, each of which can send redo to distinct destinations. We use the LOCATION and SERVICE attributes to determine if the redo is to be sent locally on disk or remotely to an off-site location. To send redo data to a remote standby, we must set the SERVICE attribute to an Oracle Net service name that points to the listener running on the remote host.

The example given below will ship redo to the Oracle Net service name using the default for all nonspecified attributes:

```
alter system set LOG_ARCHIVE_DEST_2='SERVICE=Nashville_hasun1' scope=both;
```

Once the parameter is set, Data Guard will send a copy of the archivelog to the Net service name at every log switch. To stop the shipment of archivelogs to the remote site, we simply defer the remote destination as in the following:

```
alter system set LOG_ARCHIVE_DEST_STATE_2=defer scope=both;
```

While the parameter in even its simplest form is very effective, we have many more attributes that allow us to control how and when data is sent. As covering all attributes in not practical for this chapter, we will describe some of the more frequently used below.

ARC Attribute (Default)

If neither the ARC nor LGWR attributes are specified, or if the ARC attribute is specified, archiving to the local or remote destination will be performed by the ARC process at the log switch boundary. The ARC process can be configured to perform the archiving in two different methods:

1. By default, an ARC process will first archive the online redo log to the local destination. After the ARC process writes the archive to the local destination, a second ARC process will spawn and begin transmitting data from the local archived redo log to the remote destination. Since the online redo logs are archived locally first, there is no chance that remote archiving across a slow network can impact the availability of the primary database, making this the optimal choice if you have a slow network between your primary and standby sites.

2. If the LOG_ARCHIVE_LOCAL_FIRST parameter is set to False, the ARC process follows the same method that was the default in previous versions. When a log switch occurs, the ARC process builds a list of archive destinations that need to be serviced. Once this list is complete, the ARC process will read a 1MB chunk of data from the online log that is to be archived. This 1MB chunk is then sent to the first destination in the list. When the write has completed, the same 1MB chunk is written to the second destination. This continues until all of the data from the online log being archived has been written to all destinations. So, it can be said that archiving is only as fast as the slowest destination. This method is optimal if you have a fast, reliable network between your primary and standby sites.

LGWR Attribute

In contrast to using the ARC attribute, which only transmits redo data to the standby site at log switch time, the LGWR attribute instructs the LGWR process to transmit redo data to the remote destinations at the same time the redo is writing to the online redo logs. The LGWR can transmit redo data to the remote destinations in either synchronous or asynchronous mode, depending on how the attribute is defined in the LOG_ARCHIVE_DEST_n parameter.

By default, the LGWR process will archive remotely in synchronous mode. If you wish to specify this at the parameter level, you would structure the LOG_ARCHIVE_DEST_n as such:

```
alter system set LOG_ARCHIVE_DEST_2='SERVICE=Nashville_hasun1 LGWR SYNC' scope=both;
```

The SYNC attribute with the LGWR process specifies that network I/O is to be performed synchronously for the destination, which means that once the I/O is initiated, the archiving process waits for the I/O to complete before continuing. If you specify the SYNC attribute, all network I/O operations are performed synchronously, in conjunction with each write operation to the online redo log. The transaction is not committed on the primary database until the redo data necessary to recover that transaction is received by the destination.

To have the LGWR process archive remotely in the asynchronous mode, you define your LOG_ARCHIVE_DEST_n as such:

```
alter system set LOG_ARCHIVE_DEST_2='SERVICE=Nashville_hasun1 LGWR ASYNC=20480' scope=both;
```

When using LGWR to remotely archive in ASYNC mode, the LGWR process does not wait for each network I/O to complete before proceeding. This behavior is made possible by the use of an intermediate process, known as an LGWR network server process (LNS), which performs the actual network I/O and waits for each network I/O to complete. Each LNS has a user-configurable buffer that is used to accept outbound redo data from the LGWR process. This is configured by specifying the size in 512-byte blocks on the ASYNC attribute in the archivelog destination parameter. For example, ASYNC=20480 indicates a 10MB buffer. The maximum size of the buffer in Oracle Database 10*g* is 50MB.

AFFIRM Attribute
The AFFIRM attribute ensures that all disk I/O at the standby site is performed synchronously and completed successfully prior to returning control back to the user on the primary.

NET_TIMEOUT Attribute
The NET_TIMEOUT attribute is used only when the LGWR process transmits redo data using a LGWR Network Server (LNS) process. During normal Data Guard operations, the LNS process establishes a network connection to the standby. The primary and standby then use this network connection to send data back and forth. If for some reason the network between the two hosts is lost, or if either side is unable to contact the other host, the network connection will go through normal TCP processing before determining that the connection no longer exists. In some cases, these TCP retries can take up to two hours. During the time that TCP is attempting to determine if the connection is still valid, the LNS process will be halted. This could affect processing on the primary database. Oracle developed the NET_TIMEOUT attribute so that the user could specify how many seconds the LNS process on the primary is to wait before giving up on a network connection.

REOPEN Attribute
If an archive destination receives an error, the destination will close and will not be retried until the period of time (in seconds) specified by the REOPEN attribute. Once REOPEN has expired, the destination is once again valid and will be attempted at the next log switch.

MAX_FAILURE Attribute
The MAX_FAILURE attribute defines the number of times we will retry a destination that has been closed due to a failure.

VALID_FOR Attribute
Both the primary and standby initialization parameters should be configured to support either the primary or standby role so that role reversals via switchover are seamless. In order to prevent the DBA from having to enable or defer archive destination, depending on when that destination should be utilized, Oracle developed the VALID_FOR attribute. The VALID_FOR attribute is used to specify exactly when an archive destination is to be used and what types of redo logs are to be archived.

The VALID_FOR attribute is comprised of two keywords, archival_source and database_role. The archival_source keywords are as follows:

- **ONLINE_LOGFILE**   Archive online redo logs only for this destination.

- **STANDBY_LOGFILE**   Archive standby redo logs only for this destination.

- **ALL_LOGFILES**   Archive both online and standby redo logs for this destination.

The database_role keywords are as follows:

- **PRIMARY_ROLE**   Archive to this destination only when in the primary role.

- **STANDBY_ROLE**   Archive to this destination only when in the standby role.

- **ALL_ROLES**   Archive to this destination when in either primary or standby role.

Let's consider two examples to see further how the VALID_FOR attribute works. In the previous section, when creating our physical standby, we set the following parameters:
Orlando Database:

```
LOG_ARCHIVE_DEST_1=
  'LOCATION=/database/10gDR/Orlando/arch/
   VALID_FOR=(ALL_LOGFILES,ALL_ROLES)
   DB_UNIQUE_NAME=Orlando'
LOG_ARCHIVE_DEST_2=
  'SERVICE=Orlando_hasun1
   VALID_FOR=(ONLINE_LOGFILES,PRIMARY_ROLE)
   DB_UNIQUE_NAME=Nashville'
```

Nashville Database:

```
LOG_ARCHIVE_DEST_1=
  'LOCATION=/database/10gDR/Orlando/arch/
   VALID_FOR=(ALL_LOGFILES,ALL_ROLES)
   DB_UNIQUE_NAME=Nashville'
LOG_ARCHIVE_DEST_2=
  'SERVICE=Orlando_hasun1
   VALID_FOR=(ONLINE_LOGFILES,PRIMARY_ROLE)
   DB_UNIQUE_NAME=Orlando'
```

In the above example, when the Orlando database is in the primary role, we will archive only the online redo logs to destination 1, as the standby redo logs are not active in the primary role. We will also archive the online redo logs to destination 2 while we are in the primary role. In the Nashville database, we will archive the standby redo logs to destination 1, as the online redo logs are not active in the standby role. We will not archive to destination number 2, as the Nashville database is not in the primary role. When a role reversal occurs, no change to the parameters is necessary to achieve the desired effect. The VALID_FOR attribute makes enabling or deferring destinations during role reversals unnecessary.

Log Transport Services and Security

In today's IT environment, security and availability cannot be separated. To ensure availability, we must be able to guarantee that the data is from an authorized agent and that the data is intact and unmodified. In Oracle Database 10*g*, Data Guard provides a disaster recovery solution that includes authentication and can provide encryption and data integrity checks by integrating Oracle Advanced Security Option.

By default Data Guard provides for authenticated network sessions between the primary and the standby when transferring redo. We do this by comparing the sys password from the password file to both sides to verify that they are the same. Since this authentication is now required, this means that your primary database and all standby databases within a Data Guard configuration must use a password file—and the password stored in the password file for the sys user must be the same for both the primary and standby databases.

Standby Redo Logs

Up to this point we have learned how to configure the transport services on the primary to assure that the redo data is getting transmitted to the standby according to our wishes. What we haven't discussed is what is happening on the standby, where the redo is being received. In this section we will come to understand the process flow that occurs on the standby once the primary's redo data has arrived.

When the LGWR or ARC process on the primary initiates a connection with the standby, the standby listener responds by spawning a process called the remote file server (RFS). The RFS process will create a network connection with the processes on the primary and will sit waiting for data to arrive. Once data begins arriving from the primary, the RFS process will place it into either standby redo logs or archive redo logs. You should think of standby redo logs as exact twins to online redo logs, except for the fact that they are only active when a database is in the standby role. In essence, they are just a separate pool of redo logs. The RFS process will pick the first available standby redo log and begin placing changes into that log. When a log switch occurs on the primary, we switch standby redo logs and the RFS process will go to the next available standby redo log. The standby redo log that we were into prior to the log switch will be archived by the standby database and that archive will be applied by log apply services. Standby redo logs are wonderful things, and

Oracle highly recommends that you use them. If you plan on setting one of the higher-level protection modes or plan on using real-time apply (covered in the "Starting Managed Recovery" section), the use of standby redo logs is mandatory. Some guidelines to follow when creating standby redo logs are

- The number of standby redo logs should be the same number as online redo logs plus one.

- The standby redo logs should be exactly the same size as your online redo logs.

- You should create standby redo logs on both the primary and standby to facilitate seamless role changes.

- In a RAC environment, all standby redo logs should be on a shared disk and may be thread-specific if desired.

Protection Modes

Determining the protection mode in which you operate your Data Guard configuration is one of the most important decisions you will make while configuring your disaster recovery solution. At the heart of this decision lies the answer to one question—how much data are you willing to lose? Naturally, everyone answers none. But as we well know from everyday life, there is no such thing as a free lunch. Data Guard can provide you with guaranteed no data loss but your management chain must be willing to spend the money necessary to provide the resources to support this protection mode. If management is unwilling to part with the funds, we must reconsider our first question—how much data are you willing to lose? Thankfully, Data Guard provides us with three options when it comes to protection modes, each offering a different level of protection to suit our business needs and abilities. First let's examine what each protection mode offers, and then we will ask some questions that will help you decide which is best for you.

Maximum Protection

To provide this level of protection, the redo data needed to recover each transaction must be written to both the local redo log and to a standby redo log on at least one standby database before the transaction commits. To ensure that data loss cannot occur, the primary database will shut down if a fault prevents it from writing its redo stream to at least one remote standby redo log.

To participate in maximum protection, the following requirements must be met:

- The primary must use the LGWR SYNC AFFIRM attributes in the archive destination used to archive to the standby.

- The standby must be configured with standby redo logs.

- At least one standby must be available.

By using the LGWR SYNC AFFIRM attributes in the archive destination going to the standby, we are stating that a commit complete message will not be returned to the user until we have successfully written the redo change into the standby redo logs on the standby host. Only after that write has been confirmed can the user continue with other transactions. As you can see, the speed of the network will have a great impact on the speed at which commits on the primary database can complete. You would not want to have your standby participating in maximum protection mode over a WAN or over a high latency network. A good recommendation for maximum protection mode is to have at least two standby databases available to satisfy the primary's requirements for maximum protection with one of the standby databases available on a high-speed low-latency network.

Maximum Availability

Maximum availability offers the next highest level of data protection while minimizing the impact on availability of the primary database. In the same manner as maximum protection mode, we do not return a commit complete message to the user until we have guaranteed that the redo has been completely written locally and into the standby redo log of at least one standby database. If for some reason the standby becomes unavailable and the primary is unable to write into the standby redo log, the primary database is not shut down. Instead, the primary database will temporarily drop its protection mode to maximum performance (using the ARC process) and continue. Once the standby becomes available, gap resolution with the primary will occur—in which any archivelog gaps will be filled. At the next log switch on the primary, the protection mode will once again be raised to maximum availability.

To participate in maximum availability, the following requirements must be met:

- The primary must use the LGWR SYNC AFFIRM attributes in the archive destination used to archive to the standby.

- The standby must be configured with standby redo logs.

- At least one standby must be available.

We can see by the above requirement to utilize LGWR SYNC AFFIRM attributes in the remote destination that maximum availability will also be impacted by a slow network. While slow networks will affect the time to return commits to the primary, an error condition will cause the protection mode to temporarily drop, thereby avoiding impact on the primary.

Maximum Performance

The maximum performance protection mode is the default protection mode for any Oracle database. It offers the highest level of database protection without affecting the availability or the performance of the primary database. User transactions on the primary are allowed to commit as soon as the transaction is written to the local online redo logs.

　　With maximum performance, no specific rules or requirements are enforced. The primary typically uses either the ARCH or LGWR ASYNC attributes in the remote destination going to the standby. The standby does not have to have standby redo logs, although their use is recommended. The primary database is allowed to open even if the standby is not available, unlike maximum availability and maximum protection.

HA Workshop: *Changing the Protection Mode*

Workshop Notes

When you first create an Oracle database, its protection mode is set to maximum performance by default. Once you have decided which protection mode is best for your business needs/objectives, you will need to change the default mode. Changing the mode involves setting the destination so as to meet the requirements as well as placing the database into the correct mode.

　　The following example shows how to change the protection mode from the default maximum performance to maximum availability.

Step 1.　Change the initialization parameters for the remote destination.

```
alter system set log_archive_dest_2=
'SERVICE=Orlando_hasun1
  LGWR SYNC AFFIRM
  VALID_FOR=(ONLINE_LOGFILES,PRIMARY_ROLE)
  DB_UNIQUE_NAME=Orlando'
scope=both;
```

Step 2.　Shut down all instances of the primary database and start up in exclusive mode.

```
shutdown immediate;
startup mount exclusive;
```

Step 3.　Change the protection mode via the ALTER DATABASE command.

```
alter database set standby to maximize availability;
```

Step 4.   Open all instances.

How Data Guard Handles Network Disconnects

As we learned in the "Protection Modes" section, the speed and latency of the network can have a considerable effect on how Data Guard operates. An equally important issue to understand is how network disconnects or dead connections affect Data Guard. In order to understand their importance, let's consider what occurs during a simple network disconnect between the primary and standby systems.

When the network between two host is disconnected or when one host within a TCP session is no longer available, the session is known as a *dead connection*. A dead connection indicates that there is no physical connection, but the connection appears to still be there to the processes on each system. If the LGWR and RFS processes are involved in a dead connection, when the LGWR process attempts to send a new message to the RFS process, it will notice that the connection appears to be broken. At this point, LGWR will wait on the TCP layer to timeout on the network session between the primary and standby before establishing that network connectivity has indeed been lost.

The TCP timeout, as defined by TCP kernel parameter settings, is key to how long either LGWR or ARCH will remain in a wait state before abandoning the network connection. On some platforms, the default for TCP timeout can be as high as two hours. In order to better control LGWR timeouts for network connections, the MAX_FAILURE, REOPEN, and NET_TIMEOUT attributes were developed.

On the standby side, the RFS process is always synchronously waiting for new information to arrive from the LGWR or ARCH process on the primary. The RFS process that is doing the network read operation is blocked until more data arrives or until the operating system's network software determines that the connection is dead.

Once the RFS process receives notification of the dead network connection, it will terminate itself. However, until the RFS process terminates itself, it will retain lock information on the archivelog on the standby site, or the standby redo log, whose redo information was being received from the primary database. Any attempt to perform a failover using the RECOVER MANAGED STANDBY DATABASE FINISH command will fail while the RFS process maintains a lock on the standby redo log. The RECOVER command will fail with the following errors:

```
ORA-00283: recovery session canceled due to errors
ORA-00261: log 4 of thread 1 is being archived or modified
ORA-00312: online log 4 thread 1:    '/database/10gDR/srl1.dbf'
```

At this point, we must wait for either the operating system network software to clean up the dead connection or kill the RFS process before the failover attempt will succeed. One method to decrease the time for the operating system network software to clean up the dead connection is the use of Oracle's Dead Connection Detection feature.

With Oracle's Dead Connection Detection feature, Oracle Net periodically sends a network probe to verify that a client/server connection is still active. This ensures that connections are not left open indefinitely due to an abnormal client termination. If the probe finds a dead connection or a connection that is no longer in use, it returns an error that causes the RFS process to exit. However, as we are still dependent on the operating system network software for timeouts and retries, it can take Dead Connection Detection up to 9 minutes to terminate the RFS network connection.

Once the network problem is resolved, and the primary database processes are again able to establish network connections to the standby database, a new RFS process will automatically be spawned on the standby database for each new network connection. These new RFS processes will resume the reception of redo data from the primary database.

Gap Detection and Resolution

When we see network glitches like those discussed in the previous section, it is possible to see gaps in the archivelog sequences on the standby host. Essentially, an archive gap is any number of missing archived redo logs that were created on the primary while the standby was unavailable. For example, an archive gap occurs when the network becomes unavailable, and while unavailable the primary database cycles through several online redo logs. When the network is available again, transmission of redo to the remote standby resumes and thus creates a gap.

Methods of Gap Resolution

Data Guard provides two methods for gap resolution, automatic and FAL (fetch archivelog). The automatic method requires no configuration, while FAL requires configuration via init.ora parameters. Both methods are discussed here.

Automatic Gap Resolution

Automatic gap resolution is implemented during log transport processing. As the LGWR or ARC process begins to send redo over to the standby, the sequence number of the log being archived is compared to the last sequence received by the RFS process on the standby. If the RFS process detects that the archivelog being received is greater than the last sequence received plus one, the RFS will piggyback a request to the primary to send the missing archivelogs. Since the standby destination requesting the gap resolution is already defined by the LOG_ARCHIVE_DEST_n parameter on the primary, the ARC process on the primary sends the logs to the standby and notifies the LGWR that the gaps have been resolved.

In addition to the above, the ARC process on the primary database polls all standby databases every minute to see if there is a gap in the sequence of archived redo logs. If a gap is detected, the ARC process sends the missing archived redo log files to the standby databases that reported the gap. Once the gap is resolved, the LGWR process is notified that the site is up-to-date.

FAL Gap Resolution

As the RFS process on the standby receives an archived log, it updates the standby controlfile with the name and location of the file. Once the media recovery process sees the update to the controlfile, it attempts to recover that file. If the MRP process finds that the archived log is missing or is corrupt, FAL is called to resolve the gap or obtain a new copy. Since MRP has no direct communications link with the primary, it must use the FAL_SERVER and FAL_CLIENT initialization parameters to resolve the gap.

Both of these parameters must be set in at least the standby parameter file. The two parameters are defined as the following:

Parameter	Description
FAL_SERVER	An Oracle Net service name that exists in the standby tnsnames.ora file and points to the primary database listener. The FAL_SERVER parameter can contain a comma-delimited list of locations that should be attempted during gap resolution.
FAL_CLIENT	An Oracle Net service name that exists in the primary tnsnames.ora files and points to the standby database listener. The value of FAL_CLIENT should also be listed as the service in a remote archive destination pointing to the standby.

Once log apply services needs to resolve a gap, it uses the value from FAL_SERVER to call the primary database. Once communication with the primary has been established, the FAL_CLIENT value is passed to the primary ARC process. The primary ARC process locates the remote archive destination with the corresponding service name and ships the missing archived redo logs. If the first destination listed in FAL_SERVER is unable to resolve the gap, the next destination is attempted until either the gap is resolved or all FAL_SERVER destinations have been tried.

Managing a Physical Standby

Up to this point, much of our discussion has been primarily (no pun intended) centered on the primary database and how to properly configure it. Finally, it's time to start discussing how to manage day-to-day operations on the standby. In this section we will examine how to start the standby, start managed recovery, open the standby in read-only, and perform general maintenance.

Starting a Physical Standby

For those of you who are familiar with a physical standby in a previous version, we have some very good news—and for those starting in this release, it's still good news. In the past, when starting a physical standby, we had to first bring the standby instance up to a nomount state. From there we would issue the command that would mount the standby database on a standby controlfile. After doing this over a thousand times, it can get a little monotonous; however, you will be able to type ALTER DATABASE MOUNT STANDBY DATABASE faster than anyone else in the world. This is where the good news comes in.

To start the standby and place it into the mount state, you simply enter the following command:

```
startup mount;
```

The startup process will determine the type of controlfile that is being mounted and implicitly issue the correct command to mount the standby. Similarly, to start the standby in read-only from the down state, you simply need to enter the following command:

```
startup;
```

To shut down a standby, you should cancel any managed recovery sessions currently active, disconnect any active sessions if open in read-only mode, and then issue the SHUTDOWN IMMEDIATE command.

Starting Managed Recovery

Once the standby database is up and running, it is constantly receiving changes from the primary in the form of redo. These changes will simply stack up until we instruct the standby to begin taking the redo and applying it to the standby. For a physical standby, the redo application is done via the managed recovery process

(MRP). The MRP will, depending on how it's started, automatically take the changes from the primary and apply them without any user intervention.

To start the MRP process as a foreground process, issue the following SQL statement:

```
alter database recover managed standby database;
```

The command will appear to hang because the MRP process is a part of the session in which it was started. If you exit the session, the MRP is also exited. If you wish to start the MRP as a background process, thus giving you your session back, you must use the DISCONNECT keyword. For example:

```
alter database recover managed standby database disconnect;
```

When the MRP is started with the above two commands, changes are applied to the standby database when either a) a complete archivelog is received from the primary or b) when one of the standby redo logs are completely archived. So, it's important to note that changes are only applied at an archivelog boundary.

If your physical standby has standby redo logs configured, it is possible to have the MRP begin applying changes as soon as they arrive to the standby instead of waiting for a log switch boundary and for the standby redo log to be archived. This new functionality is called *real-time apply*. To start real-time apply, you initiate the MRP by issuing the following command:

```
alter database recover managed standby database using current logfile;
```

If you want to verify that real-time apply is indeed running, you can examine the RECOVERY_MODE column from the V$ARCHIVE_DEST_STATUS view.

In the ideal world, you would have two physical standby databases running at the same time. One standby would remain in real-time apply so that it would be as close to the primary as possible. The other standby would lag behind the primary a certain distance in time so that we could easily catch user corruptions and logical errors. If someone dropped a table on the primary, we would allow the standby that's running on a time lag to recover to the point just prior to the error, open in read-only mode, export the table, and then import the table into the primary. To achieve this time lag, we start the MRP with a delay interval expressed in minutes. The redo is still shipped immediately from the primary, but the MRP does not apply the changes until the interval has passed. For example, to start the MRP with a delay interval of one hour, run the following command:

```
recover managed standby database delay 60;
```

To cancel delay and have the MRP complete applying all available archivelogs, issue the following command:

```
alter database recover managed standby database nodelay;
```

HA Workshop: *Monitoring a Physical Standby Progress*

Workshop Notes

Often you will want to verify that the physical standby's MRP is able to keep up with the rate at which redo is being sent from the primary. In this workshop we will examine several queries that will allow us to see the status of the Data Guard configuration.

The following procedure can be used to determine the number of archivelogs that have been received by the standby, but not applied, and calculate the number of archivelogs that exist on the primary that have not been received by the standby.

Step 1. Connect to the standby and get the sequence number of the last applied archivelog. Call the value retrieved laseq:

```
SELECT max(sequence#) from v$archived_log where applied='YES';
```

Step 2. Get the sequence number of the last complete archivelog on the standby. This is the last log the standby can apply without receiving additional archivelogs from the primary. Call the value retrieved lrseq:

```
SELECT min(sequence#) FROM v$archived_log WHERE ( (sequence#+1) NOT IN
(SELECT sequence# FROM v$archived_log) ) AND (sequence# > laseq)
```

If we subtract laseq from lrseq, we have the number of archived logs that have not been applied on the standby, but could be applied if the primary host becomes unavailable.

Next, we will view the potential data loss window for the physical standby.

Step 3. Connect to the standby and get the sequence number of the last applied log. Call the value retrieved laseq:

```
select max(sequence#) from v$archived_log where applied='YES';
```

Step 4. Get the sequence number of the last complete archivelog on the standby. This is the last log the standby can apply without receiving additional archivelogs from the primary. Call the value retrieved lrseq:

```
SELECT min(sequence#) FROM v$archived_log WHERE ( (sequence#+1) NOT IN
(SELECT sequence# FROM v$archived_log) ) AND (sequence# > laseq);
```

Step 5.   Connect to the primary database and obtain the sequence number of the
current online log. Call the value retrieved curseq.

```
select sequence# from v$log where status='CURRENT';
```

If we subtract curseq – lrseq, we have the number of archivelogs that the
standby database would not be able to recover should the primary host become
unavailable.

Using the Standby in Read-Only Mode

Not only can a standby protect your primary from disasters, it can also relieve some
of the user workload by allowing users to perform reporting. We accomplish this
by opening the standby in read-only mode. Once the standby is open in read-only
mode, reporting applications or user queries that do not perform any type of updates
can be performed on the standby, but you should be aware of a few consequences.

Read-Only Considerations

Before deciding to open the standby in read-only mode for use in reporting, you
should be aware that while open in read-only, redo changes generated from the
primary are not being applied. The managed recovery process mandates that the
standby be in the mount state in order for changes to be applied. For this reason,
reporting applications that are run against the standby will only see data that has
been applied just prior to opening in read-only. While the redo from the primary is
not being applied while open, the changes are still being received and stored until
such time as managed recovery is once again started. While the standby is out of
sync from the primary, you should be aware that switchover and failover times will
be greater as the standby must first apply all outstanding redo from the primary.

A good solution to avoid this negative impact on failover times is to implement
multiple standbys. One standby would remain in managed recovery and be as
close to transactionally consistent with the primary as possible. Another standby
could be open read-only and allow reports to run against a snapshot of the primary's
databases. In the event of switchover or failover, the standby that is most consistent
with the primary would be chosen for the role reversal.

Sorting for Read-Only Queries

When we are open in read-only, no updates to the database can occur. So how
do we handle user queries that need sorting space? First the queries will make use
of memory sorting using SORT_AREA_SIZE. If the sort space needed exceeds that

space, we must go to disk. By making use of tempfiles in locally managed temporary tablespaces, we can provide disk-based sorting space to the users without directly updating the dictionary.

If a locally managed temporary tablespace existed in the primary when you created the standby, the tablespace will also exist in the standby. All that is necessary now is to add the tempfiles to that locally managed temporary tablespace on the standby. To do this, we must first open the standby in read-only and use the following SQL to add the files:

```
alter tablespace temp
add tempfile '/database/10gDR/temp.dbf'
size 100m reuse;
```

If you did not have a locally managed temporary tablespace on the primary prior to creating the standby, we must first create the tablespace on the primary:

```
create temporary tablespace temp
tempfile '/database/10gDR/temp.dbf'
size 100m reuse
extent management local uniform size 25m;
```

Once the tablespace has been created, you simply need to switch logs on the primary and allow managed recovery on the standby to create the tablespace in the standby controlfile. Once the CREATE TABLESPACE command has been recovered, you will open the standby in read-only and add the tempfile to the tablespace with the same ALTER TABLESPACE command listed earlier.

Accommodating Physical Changes Made on the Primary

It is important to make sure that any physical database changes performed on the primary, such as adding datafiles or tablespaces, are also performed on the standby. Nobody wants to perform a failover during a disaster and realize that the new tablespace added last week didn't make it across to the standby. It's also important to have as many of these changes as possible performed on the standby without user intervention, so as to reduce undue work on the DBA. To accommodate these needs, the standby parameter STANDBY_FILE_MANAGEMENT was created. When this parameter is set to AUTO, actions from the following types of commands will automatically be performed on the standby:

- CREATE TABLESPACE
- ALTER TABLESPACE commands that add datafiles

- ALTER TABLESPACE commands that change the status of a tablespace
- ALTER DATABASE command that enables or disables threads
- DROP TABLESPACE commands that include the INCLUDING CONTENTS AND DATAFILES clause

NOTE
You must physically remove the file on the standby if the INCLUDING CONTENTS AND DATAFILES clause was not specified.

HA Workshop: *Handling Physical Changes*

Workshop Notes
Certain commands performed on the primary will require user intervention on the standby. One such example is renaming a datafile on the primary. In this workshop we will examine how to manually address the actions of a renamed datafile.

Step 1.   Assure that all archivelogs have been applied to the standby by using the V$ARCHIVED_LOG view on the standby.

Step 2.   Stop managed recovery on the standby.

```
alter database recover managed standby database cancel;
```

Step 3.   Rename the file to the correct path and name at the operating system level using an operating system command.

Step 4.   Bring the standby to the mount state.

```
startup mount;
```

Step 5.   Rename the datafile in the standby controlfile by using the following command on the standby:

```
alter database rename file
'/database/10gDR/old_name.dbf'
to '/database/10gDR/new_name.dbf';
```

Step 6.   Restart managed recovery with the original options.

```
alter database recover managed standby database disconnect from session;
```

Another example of a change on the primary that requires user intervention on the standby is any command that adds or alters online redo logs. While is it technically not necessary to keep the online redo logs the same between the primary and standby site, it is a good practice. Once you have added or dropped the online redo log on the primary, perform the following on the standby to bring it back into sync with the primary:

Step 1. Stop managed recovery.

```
alter database recover managed standby database cancel;
```

Step 2. Set the STANDBY_FILE_MANAGEMENT parameter to MANUAL.

```
alter system set standby_file_management=manual;
```

Step 3. Issue the SQL to drop or add the online redo log on the standby database.

Step 4. Set standby_file_management to AUTO.

```
alter system set standby_file_management=auto;
```

Step 5. Restart managed recovery with the original options.

Be aware that if you add an online redo log on the primary, you should also add a standby redo log on the standby and primary to maintain the correct number to ensure their use.

Managing a Logical Standby Database

While the log transport or the method of delivering changes to a physical and logical standby are the same, the method for applying changes is very different. Logical standbys applies changes by reading redo from either archivelogs or standby redo logs and converting this redo into SQL statements. These SQL statements are then applied to the database tables while the database is open read/write. Understanding these processes can greatly help in managing the configuration.

First let's look at the processes involved in SQL Apply. The SQL Apply engine is made up of several processes that, as a whole, read the redo, transform the redo, construct transactions, and apply transactions to the database tables. These processes are spawned from a pool of parallel query slaves. The following is a list of the processes, along with a description of their purpose:

■ The READER process reads redo as it arrives from the primary and loads it into a memory structure in the shared pool called the LCR cache.

■ The PREPARER processes turn the redo in the lcr cache into logical change records (LCR) as well as identifying dependencies between the LCRs.

■ The BUILDER process takes individual LCRs and builds complete transactions.

■ The Analyzer process takes the transactions completed by the Builder process and computes dependencies between them.

■ The COORDINATOR process monitors the dependencies between transactions and correctly schedules the application of those transactions with the apply slaves.

■ The APPLY processes accept transactions from the Coordinator process and physically apply the changes to the database tables.

Later, we will discuss how we can view each process and what that process is currently working on.

Stopping and Starting SQL Apply

The first step in starting up logical apply is to bring the database to an open state. Once the standby database is open, you can start logical apply by issuing the following statement as sys:

```
alter database start logical standby apply;
```

This statement will spawn all six processes involved in SQL Apply and will read redos from archived redo logs as they are registered with the logical standby. To start SQL Apply and have it immediately apply changes as they arrive (real-time apply) from the primary, issue the following statement:

```
alter database start logical standby apply immediate;
```

Before shutting down the standby database, or before changing attributes of the SQL Apply engine, you should first stop logical apply. The following statement stops the apply engine:

```
alter database stop logical standby apply;
```

Monitoring SQL Apply Progress

Once you start SQL Apply, you will most likely want to first check the processes to see what action they are performing. This can be done by querying the V$LOGSTDBY view. This view displays one row for each process that is part of the apply engine and gives a description of what that process is doing, as well as what SCN that process has worked on. The following query returns each process name, the highest SCN that it has worked on and its current status:

```
select type, high_scn, status from v$logstdby;
```

When querying the V$LOGSTDBY view, pay special attention to the HIGH_ SCN column. This is an indicator that progress is being made as long as it is changing each time you query the V$LOGSTDBY view.

Another place to gain information of current activity is the V$LOGSTDBY_ STATS view, which provides state and status information. All of the options for the DBMS_LOGSTDBY.APPLY_SET procedure have default values, and those values (default or set) can be seen in the V$LOGSTDBY_STATS view. In addition, a count of the number of transactions applied or transactions ready will tell you if transactions are being applied as fast as they are being read. Other statistics include information on all parts of the system.

The DBA_LOGSTDBY_PROGRESS view describes the progress of SQL apply operations on the logical standby databases. Here's an example:

```
SELECT APPLIED_SCN, APPLIED_TIME, READ_SCN, READ_TIME,
NEWEST_SCN, NEWEST_TIME
FROM DBA_LOGSTDBY_PROGRESS;
```

The APPLIED_SCN indicates that any transactions below that SCN have been committed and applied. The NEWEST_SCN column is the highest SCN that the standby has received from the primary database. When the value of NEWEST_SCN and APPLIED_SCN are the same, all available changes have been applied. If your APPLIED_SCN is below NEWEST_SCN and is increasing, SQL apply is currently applying changes. The READ_SCN column reports the SCN that the SQL Apply engine will start at, should it be restarted.

To view a list of archivelogs that are no longer needed on the standby, you must first execute the following procedure:

```
execute dbms_logstdby.purge_session;
```

This procedure updates the DBA_LOGMNR_PURGED_LOG view with a list of archivelogs that are no longer needed.

Protecting the Logical Standby from User Modifications

At this point, everyone should be asking the same question: If the logical standby is open and users can connect, what is stopping the users from trashing the tables being maintained by the logical standby? That's a good question. If you refer back to our "Creating a Logical Standby" section, one command that we left out is the following:

```
alter database guard all;
```

This statement protects the logical standby tables and prevents users from doing updates to the logical standby. The ALTER DATABASE GUARD SQL statement comes with three keywords:

- **ALL** All non-sys users cannot modify tables being maintained by SQL Apply, nor can non-sys users create new objects on the logical standby.

- **STANDBY** All non-sys users cannot modify tables being maintained by SQL Apply, but they can create new objects on the logical standby.

- **NONE** The database guard is disabled and all updates are allowed.

Users with the logstdby_administrator privilege are allowed to modify the database guard at the database level. But changing the guard at the database level can be dangerous. If only temporary corrections need to be made, it is better to temporarily disable the guard for the session only. To do this, issue the following statement:

```
alter session disable guard;
```

Once done with the modifications, reenable the guard for your session:

```
alter session enable guard;
```

Recovering from Errors

Whenever the SQL Apply engine encounters an error while applying a SQL statement, the Apply engine will stop and give the DBA the opportunity to correct the statement and restart SQL Apply. The error and the statement that stops the Apply engine are logged in a view called DBA_LOGSTDBY_EVENTS. Before we start discussing how to skip transactions, let's first cover some of the dangers. A DBA's number one concern is to keep the data on the logical standby in sync with what exists on the primary. If the SQL Apply engine receives an error during a DDL transaction, it is safe for us to issue a compensating transaction manually and then skip the failed transaction. However, if it is a DML transaction that receives an error, we should proceed very cautiously. For instance, let's suppose that transaction *x* consists of 500 inserts and 27 updates. If one of the inserts receives an error during apply and we then skip that single insert, we have logically corrupted the entire

transaction. In general, how we recover from DDL transaction errors versus DML
transactions errors can be very different.

Recovering from a DDL Transaction

One common type of DDL transaction that can fail is one that involves physical
modification, such as CREATE TABLESPACE commands. It is important to note that
the DB_FILE_NAME_CONVERT and LOG_FILE_NAME_CONVERT parameters do
not function on a logical standby. If the directory structure between the primary and
standby are the same, DDL transactions that create files will succeed without error.
However, if the directory structure between the primary and standby are different,
the DDL transaction will fail because the CREATE FILE will fail.

HA Workshop: *Recovering from a Failed DDL Transaction*

Workshop Notes

In this workshop we will examine the procedure needed to recover from a failed
DDL transaction.

Step 1.   Run the following query to determine the failing SQL statement:

```
select event_time, commit_scn, event, status
from dba_logstdby_events
order by event_time;
```

Step 2.   Disable the database guard for our session so we can modify the logical
standby.

```
alter session disable guard;
```

Step 3.   Issue a compensating transaction on the logical standby. For instance,
issue the CREATE TABLESPACE command that failed, but use the correct file
specification.

Step 4.   Reenable the database guard for your session:

```
alter session enable guard;
```

Step 5.   Restart logical apply with a clause that will cause the failed transaction
to be automatically skipped.

```
alter database start logical standby apply skip failed transaction;
```

In some rare occasions you might find it necessary to use the above procedure to skip a failed DML statement. You should fully understand how skipping that statement will affect the entire transaction and should validate your data afterward.

Recovering from a Failed DML Transaction

In general, a failed DML statement indicates that the table associated with the DML is not correctly in sync with the one on the primary. The table could have gotten out of sync by a user modifying the table on the logical standby or by defining skips on that object. Your best option for failed DML transactions is to instantiate the table so that it is once again in sync with the primary. You can use the following procedure to accomplish the table instantiation:

1. First we must stop logical standby apply.

   ```
   alter database stop logical standby apply;
   ```

2. Use the DBMS_LOGSTDBY.INSTANTIATE_TABLE procedure to put the table back in sync with the primary. The values passed to the DBMS_LOGSTDBY.INSTANTIATE_TABLE procedure are schema name, table name, and database link name.

   ```
   exec dbms_logstdby.instantiate_table('MTSMITH','MTS1','Orlando_
   dblink');
   ```

3. Restart logical standby apply.

   ```
   alter database start logical standby apply;
   ```

Changing the Default Behavior of the SQL Apply Engine

No matter how well intentioned, default values will not cover all possible situations. Depending on your transaction profile, you might find it necessary to fine-tune the default values for several components of the SQL Apply engine. The different parameters are all modified by using the DBMS_LOGSTDBY.APPLY_SET procedure. Below are some of the more common attributes of the apply engine you might find yourselves needing to change.

- **MAX_SGA** The number of megabytes that the SQL Apply engine will use to cache change records. This is considered the LCR cache.

- **MAX_SERVERS** The number of parallel query slaves that will be used for the SQL Apply engine. The default is 9, or the number specified by the PARALLEL_MAX_SERVERS PARAMETER, whichever is lower.

■ **TRANSACTION_CONSISTENCY** The level of transaction consistency maintained during the application of redo from the primary. Valid values are

■ **FULL** Transactions are applied to the logical standby database in the exact order in which they were committed on the primary database.

■ **READ_ONLY** Transactions can be committed out of order, but user queries on the standby database will return consistent results.

■ **NONE** Transactions are applied out of order from how they were committed on the primary database. Because there is no guarantee of transaction order, this mode should not be used during reporting operations.

The DBMS_LOGSTDBY.APPLY_SET procedure takes as the first value the parameter that is being changed, with the second value being what that parameter will be set to. For example, to allocate 70MB of memory to the LCR cache, we would modify the MAX_SGA using DBMS_LOGSTDBY.APPLY_SET as below. Please note that you must always stop SQL Apply prior to making any changes. The changes will take effect once you restart SQL Apply.

```
exec dbms_logstdby.apply_set('MAX_SGA',70);
```

To set TRANSACTION_CONSISTENCY to READ_ONLY, issue the following statement:

```
exec dbms_logstdby.apply_set('TRANSACTION_CONSISTENCY','READ_ONLY');
```

If you would like to return the parameters to their default values, you simply need to run the DBMS_LOGSTDBY.APPLY_UNSET procedure. For example, to put MAX_SGA back to the default value, you would issue the following statement:

```
exec dbms_logstdby.apply_unset('MAX_SGA');
```

Additional DBMS_LOGSTDBY Procedures

So far, we have seen how to use DBMS_LOGSTDBY to instantiate a table and to set and unset SQL Apply initialization parameters. But this package contains quite a bit more than just those two procedures. Let's look at some of the more popular procedures that you are likely to use in your day-to-day management of a logical standby.

DBMS_LOGSTDBY.SKIP Procedure

By default, all SQL statements and objects not owned by sys are maintained on the logical standby. In some cases, you might want to skip specific objects or schemas. For instance, if you have a development schema that developers use to develop new applications, you might not want those changes applied to the logical standby. Or, you might have a table that is used as a scratch pad, which doesn't need to be maintained on the logical standby. Skipping objects that are of no interest has the side effect of increasing performance.

To skip a schema or object or type of statement, we use the DBMS_LOGSTDBY.SKIP procedure. That procedure is defined as

```
DBMS_LOGSTDBY.SKIP (
statement_option          IN VARCHAR2,
schema_name               IN VARCHAR2,
object_name               IN VARCHAR2,
proc_name                 IN VARCHAR2);
```

A full list of valid values for the STATEMENT_OPTION parameter can be obtained in PL/SQL Packages and Types Reference 10*g* Release 1 manual.

The following example shows how to skip a specific table for a certain schema:

1. Stop logical apply.

    ```
    alter database stop logical standby apply;
    ```

2. Define which table to skip using the SKIP procedure:

    ```
    exec dbms_logstdby.skip('SCHEMA_DDL','MTSMITH','TEST1',null);
    exec dbms_logstdby.skip('DML','MTSMITH','TEST1',null);
    ```

3. Restart logical apply.

That covers how to skip a table, but what about a whole schema? We can use wildcards to indicate that the filter applies to all objects in a certain schema. For example, to skip all tables in the MTSMITH schema:

```
exec dbms_logstdby.skip('SCHEMA_DDL','MTSMITH','%',null);
exec dbms_logstdby.skip('DML','MTSMITH','%',null);
```

To undo the skips that you have defined, you simply use the DBMS_LOGSTDBY .UNSKIP procedure. This procedure takes the same parameters with the exception of the PROC_NAME, which doesn't exist.

DBMS_LOGSTDBY.SKIP_ERROR Procedure

Remember that the SQL Apply engine will stop whenever it receives an error while applying any SQL statements. In some rare cases, there may be a class of errors that you are willing to ignore. You can instruct the SQL Apply engine to ignore a class of errors and continue apply by using the DBMS_LOGSTDBY.SKIP_ERROR procedure. The procedure is defined as

```
DBMS_LOGSTDBY.SKIP_ERROR (
    statement_option        IN VARCHAR2,
    schema_name             IN VARCHAR2,
    object_name             IN VARCHAR2,
    proc_name               IN VARCHAR2);
```

To have the SQL Apply engine skip any nonschema DDL against a particular table, define the skip as follows:

1. Stop logical standby apply.

   ```
   alter database stop logical standby apply;
   ```

2. Define what type of errors should be skipped using the SKIP_ERROR procedure.

   ```
   exec dbms_logstdby.skip_error('NON_SCHEMA_DDL','MTSMITH','%',null);
   ```

3. Restart logical apply.

Once again, to unskip any skip errors that you have defined, simply use the DBMS_LOGSTDBY.UNSKIP_ERROR procedure with the same parameters minus PROC_NAME.

DBMS_LOGSTDBY.SKIP_TRANSACTION Procedure

New to Oracle Database 10*g* is the ability to start the SQL Apply engine and have it skip the last failed transaction, provided that we have issued a compensating transaction. In previous releases, users had to skip a specific failed statement using the DBMS_LOGSTDBY.SKIP_TRANSACTION procedure. This procedure will still be of some use in Oracle Database 10*g*, and we would be remiss for not mentioning it. The following example shows how to skip a specific statement that caused SQL Apply to stop. The procedure is defined as

```
DBMS_LOGSTDBY.SKIP_TRANSACTION (
    XIDUSN NUMBER           STRING,
    XIDSLT NUMBER           STRING,
    XIDSQN NUMBER           STRING);
```

The steps to skip a transaction are

1. Obtain the XIDUSN, XIDSLT, AND XIDSQN values for the failing transaction by using the DBA_LOGSTDBY_EVENTS view:

```
SELECT EVENT,XIDUSN, XIDSLT, XIDSQN FROM DBA_LOGSTDBY_EVENTS
WHERE EVENT_TIME = (SELECT MAX(EVENT_TIME) FROM DBA_LOGSTDBY_EVENTS);
```

2. Temporarily bypass the database guard so you can make a compensating transaction to the logical standby database.

```
alter session disable guard;
```

3. Execute the compensating transaction.

4. Enable the database guard.

```
alter session enable guard;
```

5. Skip the failed DDL statement by using the DBMS_LOGSTDBY.SKIP_ TRANSACTION procedure.

```
exec dbms_logstdby.skip_transaction(4,17,233);
```

6. Restart the SQL Apply engine.

Performing a Role Transition Using Switchover

First, let's define a role transition so that we are all on the same page. A database can operate in one of two modes in a Data Guard configuration: primary or standby. When we change the role of either a primary or standby, we call this a *role transition*. We have two methods that we can use to change the roles: switchover and failover. Which one you use is a very important decision. Choosing the wrong one can result in extra work on the part of the DBA to get the configuration back in sync, although a lot of that work has been eliminated with the advent of Flashback Database, which we will discuss in the section "Using Flashback After a Failover."

A switchover allows a primary and standby to reverse roles without any data loss and without any need to re-create the previous primary. In contrast, a failover implies data loss and can result in the need for the old primary to be re-created. Switchovers are normally performed for planned maintenance. For example, if the primary host needed to replace a faulty CPU that required downtime, we could perform a switchover and have users automatically redirected to the new primary. The impact to the user base could be greatly reduced, thus increasing our availability.

A switchover can be performed using either a physical or logical standby. However, there are some issues you should be aware of. If you have a configuration with a primary database, a physical standby, and a logical standby, and you perform a switchover to the logical standby, your physical standby will no longer be a part of the configuration and must be re-created. In the same scenario, if you perform a switchover to the physical standby, the logical standby remains in the configuration and does not need to be re-created. For this reason it can be stated that a physical standby is a better option for a switchover candidate than a logical standby when multiple standby types exist in the configuration.

The secret to successfully performing a switchover is proper planning and testing. Following is a list of items that should be considered prior to performing a switchover:

- First and most important, verify that the initialization parameter for both the primary and the standby support both roles. Pay special attention to the VALID_FOR attributes to the LOG_ARCHIVE_DEST_n parameter, as this will play greatly into the switchover.

- Verify that the primary and standby host each have TNS aliases that point to one another and that those aliases function correctly. Also, verify that those functioning aliases are the ones used in the LOG_ARCHIVE_DEST_n parameters.

- For a fast and efficient switchover, disconnect all user connections. If that is not feasible, restrict the user activity as much as possible. It is possible to failover user connections if they have connected via an OCI application and the proper transparent application failover setup has been performed.

- Verify that both the primary and standby temporary tablespaces are populated with tempfiles.

- Have the standby, either physical or logical, applying changes from the primary. Verify that the application of redo is current with the primary. Using the real-time apply method will speed up the switchover.

- If the primary is a RAC database, you must shut down all instances but one.

HA Workshop: *Performing Switchover with a Physical Standby*

Workshop Notes
Once you have reviewed the above recommendations, you are ready to perform the switchover. We highly recommend testing switchover in your test environment prior

to attempting it on your production system. This testing will root out any small configuration errors and make the production event smooth and painless.

Step 1. On the primary database, query the V$DATABASE view to verify that the SWITCHOVER_STATUS column indicates that a switchover is possible.

```
select switchover_status from v$database;
```

If SWITCHOVER_STATUS returns a value of TO_STANDBY, everything is good. If the query returns SESSIONS ACTIVE, you should perform the SWITCHOVER command with the SESSION SHUTDOWN clause.

Step 2. Convert the primary database into a physical standby.

```
alter database commit to switchover to physical standby;
```

If the SWITCHOVER_STATUS column in Step 1 returned SESSIONS ACTIVE, issue the following command:

```
alter database commit to switchover to physical standby with session shutdown;
```

Step 3. Shut down and restart the old primary as a new standby.

```
shutdown immediate;
startup mount;
```

Congratulations, you now have two standbys.

Step 4. When we converted the primary to a standby, we generated a marker in the redo stream and sent that marker to the standby. That marker states that no more redo has been generated. As soon as the standby receives and recovers that marker, it is eligible to become a primary database. Query the SWITCHOVER_STATUS column of V$DATABASE on the standby to ensure that the marker has been recovered and it is ready for the switchover to primary.

```
select switchover_status from v$database;
```

If SWITCHOVER_STATUS returns TO_PRIMARY, the marker has been recovered and you can proceed with the SWITCHOVER TO PRIMARY command. If the status is SESSIONS ACTIVE, you should either disconnect active sessions or issue the SWITCHOVER command with the SESSION SHUTDOWN clause. If the status states NOT ALLOWED, the marker has not been received and recovered by the standby, and switchover cannot proceed.

Step 5. Convert the standby to a primary database.

```
alter database commit to switchover to primary;
```

Or, if the SWITCHOVER_STATUS returned SESSIONS ACTIVE:

```
alter database commit to switchover to primary with session shutdown;
```

Step 6. Shut down and restart the new primary database.

```
shutdown immediate;
startup;
```

At this point, the switchover process is complete. If you have configured the VALID_FOR attribute to the LOG_ARCHIVE_DEST_n parameter, your new primary is already configured to send redo to the new standby. If you so desire, you can start managed recovery on the new primary to have it begin applying changes. If you performed the switchover to do maintenance on the primary host, you can shut down the new standby and perform the required maintenance. Before shutting down the standby, you should consider the protection mode you are in on your new primary and make sure that the conditions for that protection mode are satisfied.

HA Workshop: *Performing Switchover with Logical Standby*

Workshop Notes
After validating the requirements, we are ready to switch over to our logical standby. As we stated earlier, we highly recommend testing the switchover in a test environment prior to performing in production to root out any small configuration errors.

Step 1. On the primary database, query the SWITCHOVER_STATUS column of the V$DATABASE view to see if a switchover is allowed.

```
select switchover_status from v$database;
```

If the SWITCHOVER_STATUS column states TO STANDBY, TO LOGICAL STANDBY, or SESSIONS ACTIVE, your configuration is ready to perform the switchover.

Step 2.   New to Oracle Database 10*g* is the ability to prepare the primary database and logical standby for a switchover, thus reducing the time to complete the switchover. On the primary, issue the command to prepare the primary for the conversion to a logical standby.

```
alter database prepare to switchover to logical standby;
```

Step 3.   On the logical standby, issue the command to prepare it to become a primary database. This command instructs the logical standby to begin transmitting the LogMiner dictionary to the current primary that will soon be the new standby. Depending on the size of the LogMiner dictionary, this command could take a few minutes to complete.

```
alter database prepare to switchover to primary;
```

Step 4.   At this point, we need to query the SWITCHOVER_STATUS column of V$DATABASE on the primary to see if the receipt of the LogMiner dictionary from the standby has completed. Once the status states TO LOGICAL STANDBY, we are ready to proceed.

Step 5.   On the primary database, issue the statement to convert the primary into a logical standby.

```
alter database commit to switchover to logical standby;
```

This command will wait for all current transactions to complete and will stop any new transaction from occurring. If the statement is taking some time to complete, check V$TRANSACTION and end any long-running transactions.

Step 6.   On the logical standby query, check the SWITCHOVER_STATUS column of V$DATABASE to see if the logical standby has recovered all of the information from the primary, including the marker that indicates that the switchover is occurring. Once the SWITCHOVER_STATUS column states TO PRIMARY, issue the statement to convert the logical standby into a primary database.

```
alter database commit to switchover to primary;
```

There is no need to bounce either the new primary or new logical standby database. Optionally, you can start the SQL Apply engine on the new logical standby.

Performing a Role Transition Using Failover

Hopefully, we find you reading this section at your leisure and not with a disaster occurring around you. Ideally, everything mentioned in this section should be a part of your disaster recovery plan and it should have been tested to the *n*th degree. A failover implies that the primary database is unavailable and that, depending on our protection mode, the possibility of data loss exists. A failover is where being prepared means more than anything else in the world.

The decision to failover, in most cases (and depending on your company structure), will be made along with management. The role of the DBA is to provide the best option, that being one that incurs the least amount of interruption and data loss. For instance, if the primary database fails, it might be faster to restart the primary database and perform crash recovery than to perform a failover to a disaster site. If the primary is unable to be restarted and multiple standbys exist, the DBA will have to decide which one is the best option. In a configuration that contains both a physical and logical standby, we should always consider the physical standby as the best option, as a logical standby can contain a subset of the primary database's data. The DBA must also consider which standby is transactionally closest to the primary database, thus taking the least amount of time to failover.

Failover First Steps

Prior to performing the actual failover commands that convert the standby into a primary, we need to first perform some actions that will ensure that we have as much data as possible from the primary. We also need to prepare the standby to assume the role of a primary, making the transition smoother. Items that we should address are

- First and foremost, attempt to get all unapplied data off of the primary host and onto the standby host. This could include any archivelogs that did not get transferred.

- Ensure that any temporary tablespaces on the standby are populated with tempfiles.

- If the standby will become a RAC primary, make sure that all but one instance are down.

- Remove any delay setting for recovery of redo from the primary.

- Change the protection mode of the standby database to maximum performance.

HA Workshop: *Failover to a Physical Standby*

Workshop Notes
The following steps are to be used when performing a failover to a physical standby.

Step 1.   Resolve any gaps that may exist on the standby. Query the V$ARCHIVE_ GAP view on the standby database to identify any gaps. Attempt to resolve the gaps by copying archivelogs from the primary host or from other standbys. Copy any archivelogs to the standby host that have a higher sequence number than the last one to arrive at the standby chosen for failover.

Step 2.   Any archivelogs that have been copied to resolve a gap need to be registered in the standby controlfile. Register the archivelogs with the following command on the standby:

```
alter database register physical logfile '/database/10gDR/arch/1_217.arc';
```

Step 3.   Perform terminal recovery on the standby by issuing managed recovery with the FINISH keyword. The following command is to be used if you have standby redo logs that are configured and active:

```
alter database recover managed standby database finish;
```

   If you do not have standby redo logs, or they are not active, you must enter the following command:

```
alter database recover managed standby database finish skip standby logfile;
```

Step 4.   Once the terminal recovery command completes, convert the standby into a primary database by entering the following command:

```
alter database commit to switchover to primary;
```

Step 5.   Restart the new primary database.

```
shutdown immediate;
startup;
```

Step 6.   Back up the new primary database.

HA Workshop: *Failover to a Logical Standby*

Workshop Notes

It's important to note that when failing over to a logical standby, the old primary and any physical standby will no longer be a part of the Data Guard configuration. However, in most cases, any other logical standby databases in the configuration can still participate in the configuration. The example below illustrates how to failover to a logical standby that has no other logical standbys within the configuration.

Step 1.   Use the DBA_LOGSTDBY_LOG view to determine if the logical standby is missing any archivelogs. Copy missing archive logs or archivelogs that are higher than the last sequence received by the logical standby to the standby host.

Step 2.   Register any missing archivelogs that have been copied to the standby host with the following command:

```
alter database register logical logfile '/database/10gDR/arch/1_127.arc';
```

Step 3.   Query the DBA_LOGSTDBY_PROGRESS view to determine when all available transactions have been applied. When the NEWEST_SCN value equals the APPLIED_SCN value, all data has been applied.

```
select applied_scn, newest_scn from dba_logstdby_progress;
```

Step 4.   Activate the logical standby, making it the new primary.

```
alter database stop logical standby apply;
alter database activate logical standby database;
```

Step 5.   Back up the new primary database.

Using Flashback After a Failover

Prior to Oracle Database 10*g* when a failover occurred, the old primary database could no longer be a member of the Data Guard configuration and had to be re-created. This was an expensive operation, as it involved at lot of time and resources. By using Flashback Database, we can bring the old primary back in time to the point just before where the failure occurred and bring it back into the configuration as a standby. Then, using switchover, we can change roles, thus bringing the primary database back to the original site.

HA Workshop: *Performing a Flashback After a Failover*

Workshop Notes

The following steps assume that the old primary database had flashback enabled and that you have performed a failover to a physical standby.

Step 1. On the new primary, run the following query to determine at what SCN it became the new primary:

```
select to_char(standby_became_primary_scn) from v$database;
```

Step 2. Bring the old primary database to the mount state and flashback to the SCN retrieved in Step 1.

```
flashback database to scn <SCN obtained in step 1>;
```

Step 3. On the old primary, disable Flashback Database, as the flashback logs will no longer be valid.

```
alter database flashback off;
```

Step 4. On the old primary, create a standby controlfile.

```
alter database create standby controlfile as '/tmp/standby.ctl';
```

Step 5. Using an operating system command, copy the standby control to the location that is specified by the initialization parameter CONTROL_FILES.

Step 6. Mount the old primary/new standby.

```
startup mount;
```

Step 7. Enable Flashback Database.

```
alter database flashback on;
```

Step 8. On the new primary, enable an archive destination that points to the new primary.

```
alter system set log_archive_dest_state_2=enable;
```

Step 9.   On the new standby/old primary, start managed recovery.

```
alter database recover managed standby database disconnect;
```

Once the new standby is in the configuration, you can use the switchover process to bring the primary database back to the original site.

Data Guard Broker and Clients

Let's think back to what we have covered so far. We learned

- How to create both a physical and logical standby

- How to configure log transport services

- How to create standby redo logs

- How to manage both a physical and logical standby

- How to perform role reversals.

When we created a physical or logical standby, we had to configure around 28 parameters. Remember all of the syntax and options associated with DBMS_LOGSTDBY package? Switchover to a single physical standby takes around eight different commands. What if we told you that creating a physical or logical standby was just a matter of a few clicks? How about if we told you that a switchover or failover could be reduced to a single command or push of a button? How can it be, you say? Our reply: the Data Guard broker.

The Data Guard broker is a centralized framework that creates, automates, and manages all aspects of a Data Guard configuration. This broker can be accessed locally or remotely by using either of the two clients: the command-line interface (CLI) or the Data Guard page of the new OEM. Once you are connected, you have the ability to change any attribute of the configuration as well as monitor progress and perform health checks. Truly a wonderful thing!

The three main components of the Data Guard broker are the two interfaces or clients and the Data Guard Monitor process. The Data Guard GUI and CLI interfaces allow you to monitor and manipulate the configuration. The Data Guard Monitor is a background process that exists for each database in the configuration. When you make a change via one of the two interfaces, the DMON process is what interacts with the database to effect the actual change. The DMON process also reports back the health of the configuration. All of the information that the DMON process needs to maintain the configuration is stored in metadata files located in each ORACLE_

HOME. As the DMON processes communicate with each other across an Oracle Net link, they replicate any changes to the configuration to all metadata files in all ORACLE_HOMES.

The CLI Interface

Before we start using the CLI, we need to satisfy a few requirements. First, the physical or logical standby must have been created, as the CLI does not have the ability to create a standby (only the Data Guard GUI does). In addition, both the primary and standby databases must have been started with the DG_BROKER_ START parameter equal to True (this spawns the DMON process) and be using an spfile.

To spawn the command-line interface, enter the following command at the operating system prompt:

```
dgmgrl
```

With our ORACLE_SID and ORACLE_HOME environment variables set for the local primary database, enter the following at the dgmgrl prompt:

```
DGMGRL> connect sys/Not4U
```

Now that we are connected, we are ready to create the Data Guard configuration. The first step in creating the configuration is to define the primary database. Once that has been defined and saved, we will create the standby database objects.

```
DGMGRL> create configuration 'MyDR' as
>primary database is 'Orlando'
>connect identifier is Orlando_hasun1;
```

In this command, Orlando is the value of the DB_UNIQUE_NAME and Orlando_hasun1 is the Oracle Net alias.

Once we have been returned to the prompt, we can use the SHOW CONFIGURATION command to view what we have created thus far.

```
DGMGRL> show configuration
```

To add a standby database to the configuration, we use the ADD DATABASE command. In the following command, it's important to note that Nashville is the value of the standby DB_UNIQUE_NAME parameter, while Nashville_hasun2 is the Oracle Net alias.

```
DGMGRL> add database 'Nashville' as
>connect identifier is Nashville_hasun2
>maintained as physical;
```

So, we have successfully created our Data Guard broker configuration. At this point we start watching the primary and standby databases, waiting for the magic to happen. But nothing is different. What the heck? That's because you have to enable the configuration in order for the broker management to begin. To enable the configuration, use the appropriately named ENABLE CONFIGURATION command.

```
DGMGRL> enable configuration;
```

Once our configuration is enabled, we can once again use the SHOW CONFIGURATION command to see the results of all of our hard work.

```
DGMGRL> show configuration;

Configuration
  Name:            MyDR
  Enabled:         YES
  Protection Mode: MaxPerformance
  Databases:
    Orlando    - Primary database
    Nashville - Physical standby database
Current status for "DRSolution":
SUCCESS
```

As we can see, our configuration is complete and currently enabled. But having a running configuration wouldn't be any fun unless we have knobs to turn. Let's illustrate how to turn a few of the knobs.

One of the many things we can do with the broker is change the state of either the primary or standby database. We can change the state of the database to be offline or shutdown, stop log transport or log apply, or open in read-only. In the following example, we show how to change the standby of the physical standby to the read-only mode for reporting purposes by editing the broker database object.

```
DGMGRL> edit database 'Nashville' set state='READ-ONLY';
Succeeded.
```

To return the physical standby to the recovery mode, we change the state once again.

```
DGMGRL> EDIT DATABASE 'Nashville' SET STATE='ONLINE';
Succeeded.
```

The ONLINE state returns the database back to its default state of log apply on.

One common use of the broker is to provide non-DBA support staff a method of performing complex operations without the need to know all of the SQL*Plus commands. One good example is a switchover or failover. Using the broker is a very effective means of providing an easy interface for push-button role transfers to staff that do not necessarily understand all of the underlying concepts and procedures. Let's illustrate how easy a switchover can be performed. You might remember that the switchover process via SQL*Plus we discussed earlier took about eight commands.

```
DGMGRL> SWITCHOVER TO "Nashville";
Performing switchover NOW. Please wait...
```

Once the broker completes the switchover process, we are given the following response:

```
Switchover succeeded. New primary is "Nashville"
```

Using the Data Guard GUI

Today's community of computer geeks can generally be separated into two groups: those that love the command line and those that long for the GUI. Up to this point we have only serviced the needs of one of these two groups (our prejudice, we must admit). Now the time has come to play fair and delve into the Data Guard GUI.

First, let's cover how to navigate to the Data Guard GUI page within the new OEM interface. This section assumes that you have Grid Control installed and at least your primary database listed as an available target. To reach the Data Guard GUI page, click on the Targets tab, and from the Targets tab click on the Database tab. On the Database tab, you should see your primary database listed. Click on the primary database link to go to the primary database home page. On the primary database home page, click on the Administration tab, where you will find a link to Data Guard under the High Availability section.

If we are using a primary database in which no broker configuration has been created, we are presented with the Add Standby page shown in Figure 7-1. From this page we can create a standby and broker configuration. By clicking on the Add a Standby link we can start the standby creation wizard. If your primary database already has an existing broker configuration—that is, created with the CLI interface—you will not see the page in Figure 7-1.

After clicking on the Add a Standby link, we are presented with the page shown in Figure 7-2. This page allows us to create a physical standby or a logical standby, or add an existing physical or logical standby to a Data Guard configuration. It's important to note that if you wish to have a RAC standby database, you must create it manually and add it as an existing standby. Once the RAC standby has been added, the Data Guard GUI can handle all aspects of configuration and management. For our example, we will choose to create a new physical standby.

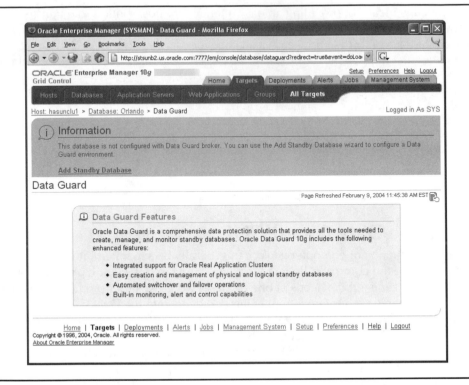

FIGURE 7-1. *Add a standby*

The next page that we are presented with allows us to choose to perform a hot backup of the primary database using RMAN or to use an existing backup that was created during a previous standby creation performed by the Data Guard GUI. For our example, we will choose a live backup of the primary database, as shown in Figure 7-3.

When performing the live backup of the primary database, the Data Guard GUI will store the backup files in a working directory prior to sending to the standby host. The page, shown in Figure 7-4, allows us to define the working directory. In

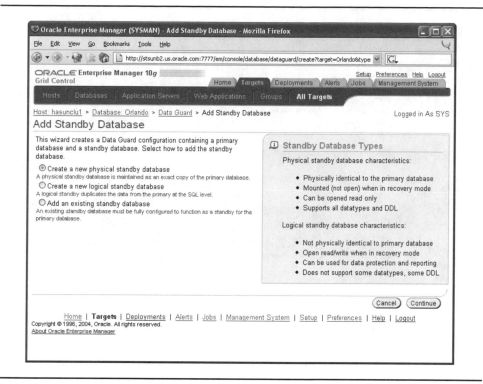

FIGURE 7-2. *Standby Wizard: standby type*

addition, we can choose to save the backup for future standby creations. If we choose to save the backup, we will be presented with the backup if we choose the Use an Existing Backup option shown in Figure 7-3. If preferred credentials are not currently defined for the primary database, we are prompted to enter them.

The next page, shown in Figure 7-5, allows us to set the standby SID name, enter the login information for the standby host, and choose host and ORACLE_ HOME for the standby. The SID name can be the same as the primary database, but is often set differently. Choosing a SID that describes its location or purpose is generally preferred. When choosing the standby host and ORACLE_HOME, we are

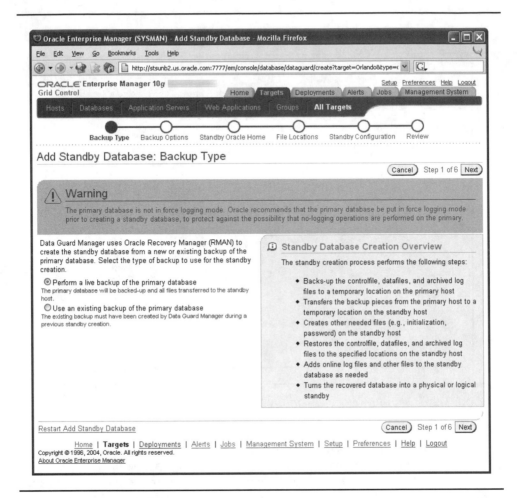

FIGURE 7-3. *Standby Wizard: backup type*

prompted with all hosts and homes that are currently listed as targets within
Enterprise Manager and have an operating system that is the same as the primary.

Next, we are given the chance to define if we want the backup of the primary
database to be transferred to the standby host via either the FTP or HTTP protocols,
or if we want to place the backup on a network share such as NFS. We will transfer

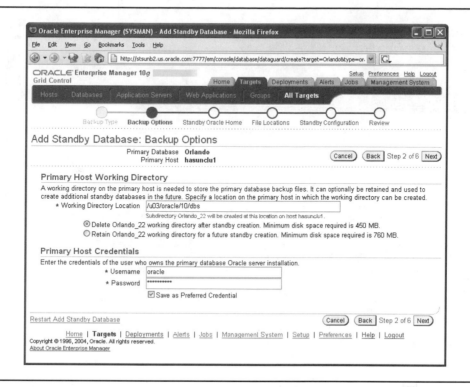

FIGURE 7-4. *Standby Wizard: backup configuration*

the backup via the FTP protocol, as shown in Figure 7-6. We are also asked to
define the location in which to place the standby datafiles. A good best practice is
to have the directory structures be exactly the same as defined on the primary so
as to avoid confusion during role transitions. However, it's acceptable to place the
files into a different directory structure. We must also define the directory where
the standby Oracle Net configuration files are located. This will allow the Data
Guard GUI to add entries to those files.

In the final configuration page, shown in Figure 7-7, we are asked to give the
standby a unique name within the Data Guard configuration as well as define
the Enterprise Manager target name. Also included on this page is the ability to
define the directory where archivelogs will be stored on the standby host.

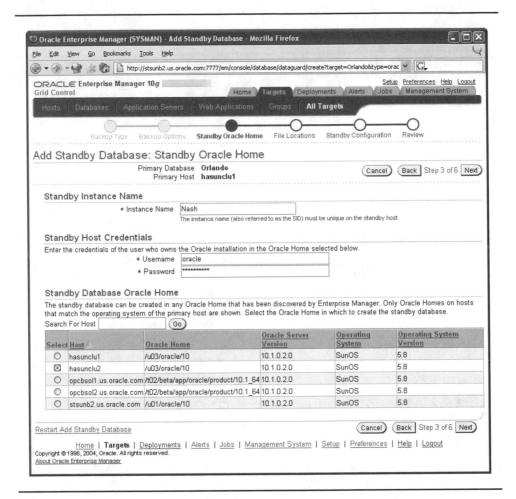

FIGURE 7-5. *Standby Wizard: standby Oracle home*

The last page in the creation process, shown in Figure 7-8, allows us to review our choices. If we would like to modify any values we can simply click the Back button and adjust the value. By selecting the Finish button, we are instructing the Data Guard GUI to proceed with the creation of the standby.

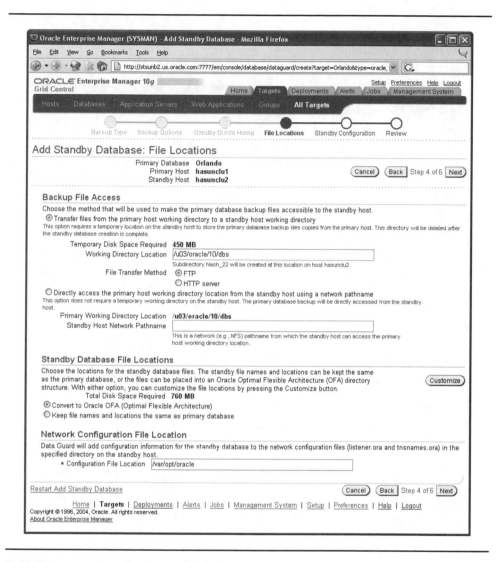

FIGURE 7-6.   *Standby Wizard: file locations*

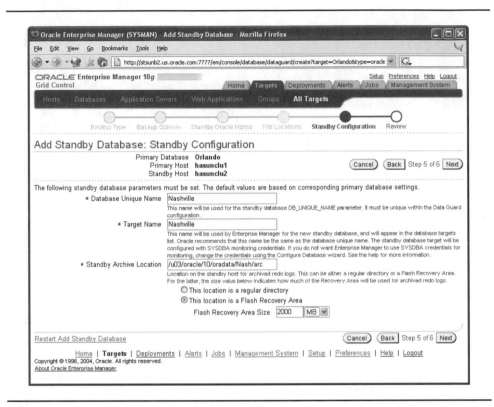

FIGURE 7-7. *Standby Wizard: standby configuration*

The first step in the standby creation process is the creation of an Enterprise Manager job, shown in Figure 7-9. Several preliminary steps are performed and the Enterprise Manager job is submitted. Once it is submitted, we are returned to the main Data Guard page shown in Figure 7-10. The status of the standby will show as Creation in Progress. You can view the status of the creation process by selecting the Creation in Progress link.

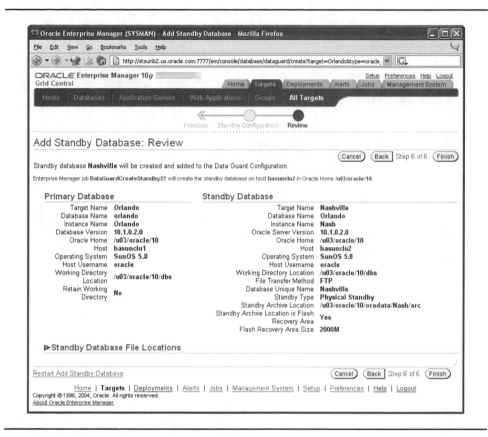

FIGURE 7-8.   *Standby Wizard: confirmation*

Once the creation process has completed, you will be brought to the main Data Guard page, which lists the primary database and all configured standby databases, as shown in Figure 7-11.

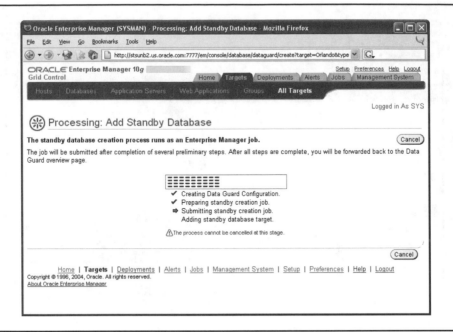

FIGURE 7-9. *Standby Wizard: job creation*

From the Data Guard page, we can proceed to modify and monitor the Data Guard environment. For instance, suppose that we want to change the state of the standby from the mounted state running recovery to the open read-only state to allow reporting. To do this, make sure the Standby Radio button is selected and then click on the Edit button. This brings us to the standby database properties page, as shown in Figure 7-12. From this page, we can choose the state in which to place the standby and apply.

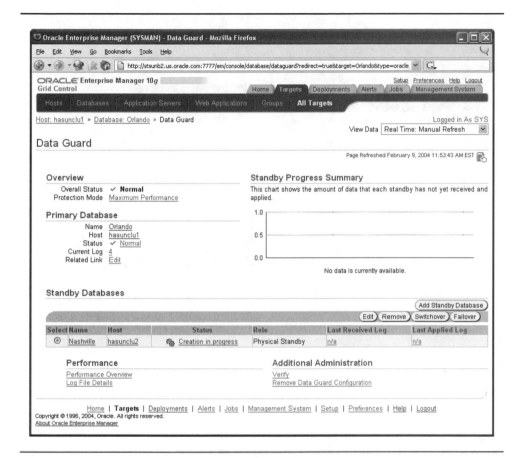

FIGURE 7-10. *Data Guard Overview page: creation in progress*

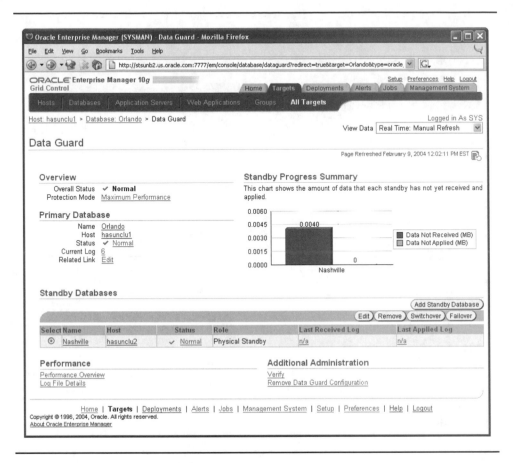

FIGURE 7-11. *Data Guard Overview page*

To edit the standby role properties of the standby, simply click on the Standby Role Properties link. This presents us with the page shown in Figure 7-13. On this page we can define such items as redo apply delay, log transport mechanism used to ship to the standby, and the use of real-time apply. After modifying any of the values clicking Apply causes them to go into effect.

FIGURE 7-12. *Standby Database Properties page*

Once you have your Data Guard configuration up and running, you might want to view specific details about the performance—we discussed several queries that could be used to do this via SQL*Plus. The Data Guard GUI also provides an excellent view of the performance characteristics of your Data Guard configuration. From the main Data Guard page, shown in Figure 7-11, select the Performance Overview link. This brings us to the page shown in Figure 7-14. From this page, we can get a detailed view of all online redo log progress in the configuration at an interval that we define.

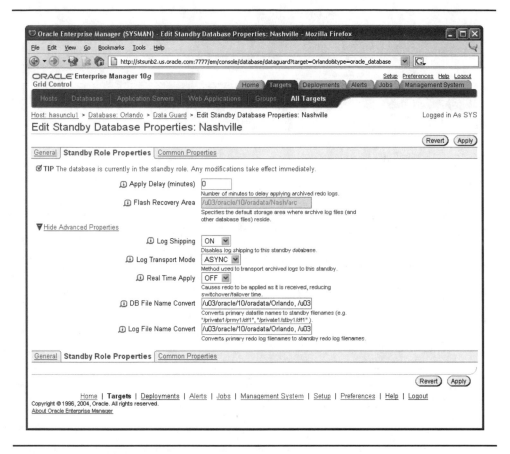

FIGURE 7-13. *Standby Role Properties page*

Finally, The Data Guard GUI provides you with a very fast and complete method to verify your Data Guard configuration. The verify operation performs numerous checks of both the broker configuration and the primary and standby databases. To perform a verification, go to the main Data Guard page shown in

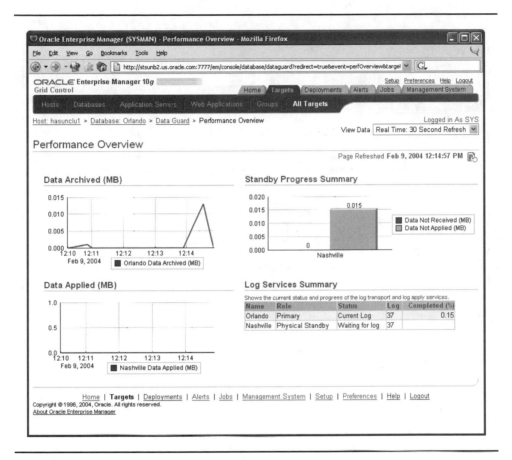

FIGURE 7-14. *Performance overview*

Figure 7-11 and select the Verify link under Additional Administration. The verification process will begin immediately, as seen in Figure 7-15. Once it completes, it will alert you to any issues that need to be corrected.

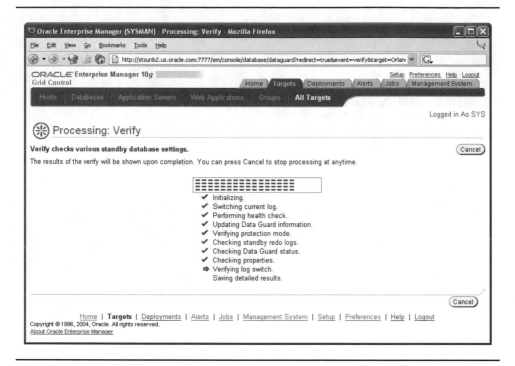

FIGURE 7-15. *Configuration verification*

CHAPTER
8

Backup and Recovery for High-Availability Environments

o this point we have concentrated on the primary tools for achieving a sturdy high-availability (HA) database: RAC, Data Guard, and internal database features. These are technologies widely associated with HA-specific environments, and are typically researched, proofed, and rolled out by DBAs with specific HA requirements spelled out in front of them.

This chapter is a little different. Everyone takes backups (well, almost everyone). Everyone spends a certain amount of time fiddling with scripts that back up the database files in case of one kind of failure or the other. Backing up a database, it is commonly believed, is not an HA technique—backups are the fallback when the database has already gone down, is unavailable, and there is no other choice but to wait for the files to restore from a backup location. The very nature of backups is to accept that occasionally the database goes down. One could argue that, with a successfully integrated RAC and Data Guard solution in place, backups are an antiquated notion of the past.

We are here to change that perception.

The Importance of Media Backups

An analysis of backup and recovery issues that get opened with Oracle Support Services revealed an interesting point: in situations where backups existed for recovery, a full restore of the entire database was initiated 40 percent of the time. In other words, when a hardware failure or a data corruption occurred, the DBA initiated a restore of every datafile in the database.

Folly! Certainly in some cases a full restore of the database may be required due to the nature of the problem. But a survey of the reported issues showed us that, in most cases, a single datafile, or a subset of datafiles, would have sufficed to resolve the issue, saving hours of lost time with the entire database down. Why the whole database restore? Typically, it was trained reaction by the DBA who has been conditioned to believe that there is only one kind of way to recover the database, and that is to recover the entire database. Often, the database restore is scripted, and the DBA is simply dot-slashing a .sh file that was built back in the days of Oracle 7.3.4.

In defense of this technique, it is very simple. There is no gray area surrounding the restore and recover decisions. There is a clear road map to completion of the recovery, after which the database will be up. But if that were the case, if it were that simple, *why do they keep calling Oracle Support for help?* Let's just drop the shtick and allow the fact that recovery situations are sticky, sweaty, nervous times for the DBA—particularly for the HADBA who is committed to uptime. And when things get murky, a black and white database restore looks very appealing, regardless of downtime exceptions. So what is to be done?

First, we must realize that media backups are a required component of any HA strategy. RAC provides us with load balancing and protection against node failure. Data Guard guarantees our system against site failure and complete disaster scenarios. But RAC nodes still share the same datafiles, so there is still the possibility of datafile corruption that affects all nodes in the cluster. And Data Guard failover is expensive, so we try to avoid it at all costs—do we failover when a single datafile goes belly up? No, there are times when good old-fashioned backups still serve a purpose.

While backups still serve a critical function, the full database restore and recovery must be avoided at all costs. For the HADBA, full database restore from backup is the kiss of death for availability. Better to failover to the Data Guard (DG) standby system and then reinstantiate the primary, than to waste valuable time with a full database restore and recovery. But, having a sound backup strategy means having access to files for single file restore, or a subset of datafiles. Given a specific recovery scenario, the best approach may be a file restore instead of DG failover. And, given new Oracle capabilities in Oracle Database 10g, this file restore can happen faster than ever before.

To take full advantage of media backups, Oracle Recovery Manager (RMAN) is a requirement for any legitimate HA strategy. No longer the painful little utility best eschewed by seasoned DBAs empowered with tried and true shell scripts, RMAN now comes equipped with the kind of functionality that makes it a necessary HA partner. There is simply nowhere else to turn for the kind of killer features that RMAN brings to the table. RMAN has been developed specifically to assist in HA environments, so it not only integrates with RAC, Data Guard, and Oracle Flashback Technologies—it complements the entire HA stack beautifully, making all components greater than their sum.

This chapter is dedicated to getting the most from an RMAN backup strategy, and not just for recovery but for assisting with load balancing, maintaining uptime, and minimizing downtime, as well as chipping in with RAC and DG maintenance.

RMAN: A Primer

It is worth spending a moment to come to terms with the underlying architecture of an RMAN backup, and how it is different from an OS copy. To do so, it is best to know exactly what RMAN is: a client utility, like export or SQL*Loader. RMAN comes installed with the Database Utilities suite with every Oracle database. As such, it can be installed at a client system that has no database, and can be used to connect remotely to any number of databases. This is becoming less common, but it is worth pointing out: RMAN makes a SQL*Net connection to the Oracle database that needs to be backed up.

Typically, the connection from RMAN to the database is a local connection, because RMAN is running from the same environment as the database—same ORACLE_HOME, same ORACLE_SID. But there are times that require a tns alias to the database be set up in the tnsnames.ora file, in which case RMAN does not require the same environment as the database—it will connect via the listener, same as a remote SQL*Plus connection, for instance.

Let's get some vocabulary out of the way:

- **Target database** In RMAN, the database you are currently attempting to back up or recover is the target.

- **RMAN executable** The RMAN executable is the client utility itself, made up of both the RMAN executable and the recover.bsq (the library file).

- **Recovery catalog** The recovery catalog is a set of tables, indexes, and packages that are installed into a user schema of an Oracle database. These tables store information about RMAN backups that occur for all the target databases in your enterprise.

- **Catalog database** The catalog database is the database you choose to house the recovery catalog schema.

- **Auxiliary database** In situations where you use RMAN to create a clone of your target database, you will make a connection to the clone as the auxiliary database.

The list above provides a good road map of the components in play during any RMAN operation (say, a backup). The connection topography can be seen in Figure 8-1. From the RMAN prompt, you make a connection to the target. If you use a catalog, you make the connection to the catalog as well; typically, the catalog connection is going to be using a net service name (TNS alias). This is because you cannot make two local connections to two different databases, and you should never put the recovery catalog in the target database. If you are performing a cloning operation, you would also make a connection to the auxiliary database.

The RMAN utility is nothing more, really, than a command syntax interpreter. It takes as input simple commands to back up or restore, and turns them into remote procedural calls that are passed as PL/SQL packages at the target database. These packages, dbms_backup_restore and dbms_rcvman, are found in the sys schema and have complementary duties. dbms_rcvman accesses the controlfile to build file lists and dictates work flow in the backup job. This backup job is then passed to dbms_backup_restore for actual file access for backups or restore. And that is all we need to know about that, for now!

RMAN and the Controlfile

RMAN has unprecedented access to information about the target database, and this access provides the unprecedented features that make RMAN backups so

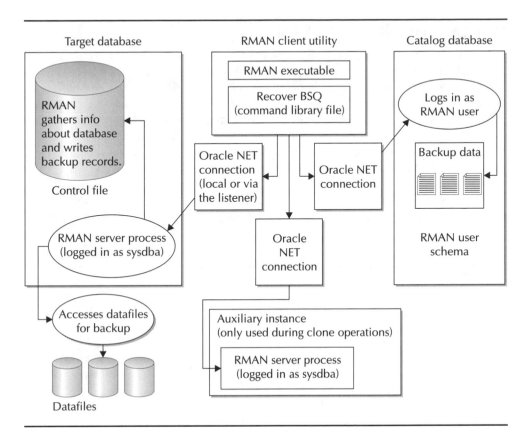

FIGURE 8-1. *Network topography of an RMAN operation*

compelling. First and foremost, RMAN makes a server process connection to the target database as a sysdba user; therefore, RMAN has access to the best source of all important information in the database: the controlfile. RMAN checks the controlfile for information about the datafiles, and compiles backup lists based on the number and size of the files. The controlfile also guides RMAN with operations concerning archivelogs: RMAN automatically adjusts for existing archivelogs and backs up only those that are complete. Then RMAN can delete all archivelogs in all destinations (except those that are listed as a service in the database—that is, archivelogs created at a standby system).

In addition to accessing the controlfile for information about what to back up and what to restore, after RMAN performs an operation, it also records the data about the backup itself in the controlfile. This data includes information about what files have been backed up, and when, along with checkpoint information and the names of the *backup pieces* (the output files created by a backup).

RMAN and the Data Block

After gathering the required data from the controlfile, RMAN performs a backup by initializing one or more channel processes. These channel processes access the datafiles and stream the Oracle data blocks from the files into memory buffers within the Oracle Process Global Area or PGA (of the target database: the database is backing itself up). Once a buffer is filled, the channel process does a memory-to-memory write of each data block from the input buffer to an output buffer. Once the output buffer fills, the entire buffer is written to the backup location. Figure 8-2 illustrates the RMAN architecture, including controlfile access.

The fact that RMAN has access to the Oracle data block pretty much sums up why RMAN is so invaluable. Nearly everything good that comes from RMAN comes from the fact that the data blocks are pulled through the Oracle memory window

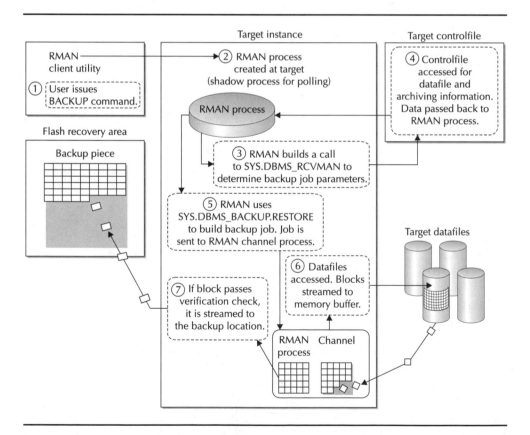

FIGURE 8-2. *RMAN backup architecture*

and then streamed to the backup location. When the memory write occurs from input buffer to output buffer, RMAN checks the block for corruption and reports all corruptions, aborting the backup—and the result is no corrupt blocks in the backup. At the same time, RMAN checks to see if the block is even worth streaming to backup: if the block has never been initialized, RMAN simply eliminates the block so that it does not take up space in the backup. It is at this time, as well, that RMAN can check the block header for an incremental System Change Number (SCN), and determine if the block should be backed up during an incremental backup (more on this in the section "Backing Up the Available Database").

There is so much good stuff to say about RMAN, there's simply no room in this chapter to cover all the territory. The basics have already been described:

- RMAN uses the controlfile to guide a backup or recovery, and records its own data in it.

- RMAN backs up the database at the data block level, streaming them through a memory buffer to perform checks.

From here on out, it's time to concentrate on what RMAN can do for the HADBA.

RMAN Command-Line Usage

As a stand-alone client utility, RMAN has an above average command syntax (naysayers, away!). Want proof? You can go to any Oracle database, version 9.0.1 or higher, and do the following:

```
bash>rman target /
rman>backup database;
```

You will get a backup of your database. Granted, the backup will be in the wrong place—without any parameters, the default location is $ORACLE_HOME/ dbs. But you will have a usable backup, after typing four words. Likewise, if you ignored our earlier pleas for no full database restore, you can do the same thing to restore your database (if your database is mounted off a current controlfile):

```
rman>restore database;
```

This command will look at the controlfile to determine which files need to be restored, as well as which backup is best used for the restoring. The simplicity saves you from knowing where the backups are or when they were last taken (or, really, from even knowing what the schematic layout of the datafiles might be at the time of restore).

There are many good sources of RMAN command-line syntax available; we don't have the space to go into the details here. Check out the Oracle Press's own *Oracle9i RMAN Backup and Recovery*, or the *Oracle 10g RMAN* reference guide itself.

RMAN from Enterprise Manager

If you use EM to back up your database, you are using RMAN and you may not even know it. EM puts a GUI, wizardly face on backup and restore operations; if you look behind the curtain, though, EM is merely building RMAN blocks and then executing them from the local copy of RMAN at the target database.

The RMAN interface through Enterprise Manager has had a welcome facelift in Oracle Database 10g, but there still exists functionality for which you must return to the command line in order to harness. We suggest, then, that you familiarize yourself with the RMAN command prompt. Then you can go back to EM and use it for what it is best at: backup job scheduling.

RMAN from EM Database Control

For each database, you can connect to the Enterprise Manager Database Control console and navigate to the maintenance page. There you will see a header entitled "Backup/Recovery." Underneath, you will see the different backup and recovery operations that you can do from EM: schedule backups, perform recovery, manage current backups, and configure backup and recovery settings (including recovery catalog settings). One important note: If you are looking for a GUI interface to Oracle Flashback Technologies, Flashback Database can be found under the "Perform Recovery" heading in Enterprise Manager. More on this in Chapter 9.

- **Schedule backups** From this page, you provide host credentials, and then you can schedule a job to run your RMAN backups based on your provided parameters

- **Perform recovery** This wizard guides you through the steps to perform different types of recovery.

- **Manage current backups** This console provides all of the functionality required to do backup housekeeping, as detailed later in this chapter.

- **Configure backup settings** Here you can make changes to permanent configuration parameters.

- **Configure recovery settings** This interface actually provides an excellent window into the myriad different settings the HADBA can use to tightly control recoverability, from setting a mean time to recovery, to turning on archivelog mode, to configuring for Flashback Database.

- **Configure recovery catalog settings** Here you can specify the location of the recovery catalog and register the target database, if you need to.

HA Workshop: *Schedule a Backup Job from Enterprise Manager Database Control*

Workshop Notes

This workshop will go through the steps to schedule a job for backing up a database in archivelog mode using EM.

Step 1.   From EM Database Control, go to the maintenance page and click on Schedule Backup Job. The first page wants to know if you will back up to disk or tape, and whether you want to use an Oracle suggested backup strategy or a custom built strategy. In this exercise, we use a custom strategy and will back up to disk, as shown in Figure 8-3. Provide the host credentials—this is the username and

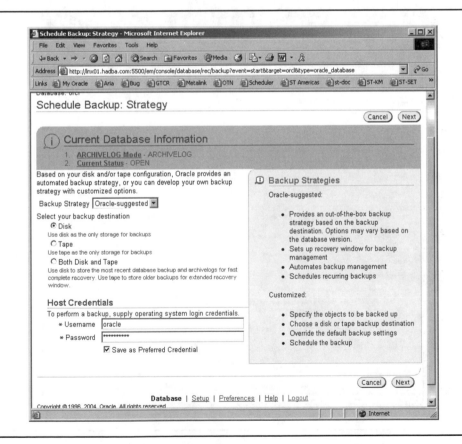

FIGURE 8-3.   *Choosing a backup strategy*

password of the OS user who will run the job. We suggest using Oracle, or whatever name you gave to the Oracle software owner. Then click Next.

Step 2.   Outline the backup strategy. Choose a full, online backup; this will take a backup of the entire database while the database is up and running (requires archivelog mode). Also, choose to back up all archivelogs on disk, and choose to delete archivelogs after they are backed up. (Our selections are previewed in Figure 8-4.) Then click Next.

Step 3.   Specify a location for the backups on disk. If you have already created a flashback recovery area, it will be the only option here. Click Next.

FIGURE 8-4.   *Backup strategy*

Step 4. Schedule the backup job. In Figure 8-5, we have created a backup to run at 2:00 A.M. every day, for an indefinite time into the future.

Step 5. Review the backup job details, then submit the job by clicking on Submit. You can review the job immediately by clicking on View Job, or return to it later by going to the bottom of the Maintenance page and, under Related Links, choosing Jobs.

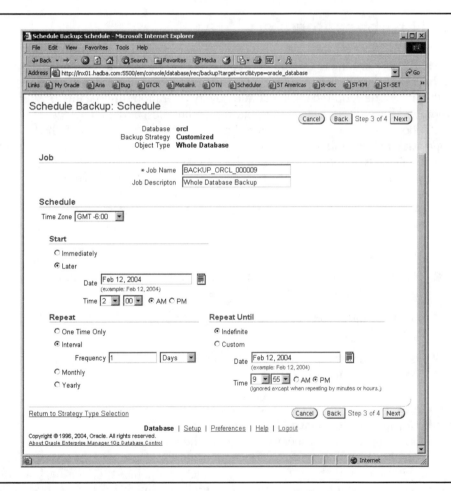

FIGURE 8-5. *Scheduling the backup job*

Preparing an RMAN Backup Strategy

RMAN performs invaluable services to achieve high availability, even if you are not using RAC or Data Guard and merely looking for simple, straight-forward solutions for the unclustered, stand-alone database running on a modest server. While RMAN provides perhaps the single most powerful out-of-the-box backup experience in the market, to fully unlock its potential, you need to spend a few moments configuring RMAN to work for you.

The Flashback Recovery Area

The flashback recovery area (FRA) is not a requirement for using RMAN, but it should be. New to Oracle Database 10*g*, the recovery area is a specific location on disk that you set up to house all the Oracle recovery files. *Recovery files* refers to all files that might be required for a media recovery operation: full datafile backups, incremental backups, datafile copies, backup controlfiles, and archivelogs. The FRA also functions as a repository for mirrored copies of online redo log files, the block change tracking file, and a current controlfile. If set up, flashback logs for using the Flashback Database option also live in the FRA (see Chapter 9).

The concept behind the FRA is to simplify the management of your backup and recovery duties by consolidating the requisite files into a single location that Oracle and RMAN can then micromanage, while the DBA moves on to other important HA duties. This simplification is based on some underlying principles of a solid backup strategy that focuses on availability:

- At least one copy of important datafiles, if not the entire database, should be kept on disks that are locally accessible to the database.

- Backups past a certain age should be moved to tape based on storage pressure on local disks.

- Long-term backup management should be almost completely automatic, based on business rules.

The FRA that you set up can be either a directory on a normal disk volume or it can be an Automatic Storage Management (ASM) disk group (see Chapter 3 on ASM setup and usage). You specify the size of the FRA as an init parameter. When determining how large to make your FRA, consider the types and number of files that you will be putting there. This, of course, gets to the heart of your backup and recovery strategy (which we have not discussed yet) from an HA perspective. Let's just say, for now, that what you need is space for two complete copies of your database and a few days worth of archivelogs, and then add 20 percent on top of that.

The FRA is determined by two initialization parameters: db_recovery_file_dest and db_recovery_file_dest_size. The first determines the location and the second, the size. These can be set in your init.ora file, if you still use one, or in the spfile via an 'alter system set...' command.

With a flashback recovery area configured, you are not required to set any other log_archive_dest_n parameter for archivelogs; by default, with an FRA, Oracle will default log_archive_dest_10 to the FRA. It should be noted, as well, that with an FRA in use, you cannot use log_archive_dest or log_archive_duplex_dest—but, of course, you rid yourself of these outdated parameters long ago...right?

FRA functionality comes on the tails of two other Oracle technologies: Oracle Managed Files (OMF), the means by which init.ora parameters determine the size, name, and function of database files; and Automatic Storage Management, the technology that allows Oracle to manage disk volumes for easy DBA management of disk space. You can use the FRA without using OMF and ASM, but they work very well together to provide a complete management solution for all files related to Oracle. For the HADBA, using these three technologies in tandem provides the best of all worlds: availability, manageability, and top-notch performance.

HA Workshop: *Configure the Flashback Recovery Area*

Workshop Notes
The flashback recovery area is determined by initialization parameters. In this workshop, we are adding a recovery area to a running, operational database.

Step 1. Determine the size you need for your recovery area. For this example, we are setting up a strategy to account for 24 hours of archivelogs and two full copies of the entire set of datafiles.

```
SQL> select sum(bytes) from v$datafile;
SUM(BYTES)
----------
 891289600
```

Then get the total size of archivelogs over the last 24 hours.

```
SQL> select sum(blocks*block_size) bytes from v$archived_log
  2  where completion_time > sysdate-1;
    BYTES
----------
  81971200
```

You can also gather the total size of the archivelogs based on the number of archivelogs that are currently listed as available on disk. To confirm the status of archivelogs, you would need to run 'crosscheck archivelog all' from the RMAN command prompt first.

```
SQL> select sum(blocks*block_size) bytes from v$archived_log
  2  where status = 'A';
    BYTES
----------
  81971200
```

We then multiply our database size by 2, and then take the sum of the datafile and archivelog values, and multiple by 1.2 to get a 20 percent increase from this size to cover file header blocks and other files that may exist in this space:

$$((891289600 * 2) + 81971200) * 1.2 = 2237460480$$

Based on this calculation, we can now set our db_recovery_file_dest_size value in the spfile.

```
SQL> ALTER SYSTEM SET DB_RECOVERY_FILE_DEST_SIZE = 2237460480
SCOPE=BOTH SID='*';
```

Step 2.   Determine the location for your recovery area. For this example, we are using a simple directory name on an existing mounted volume, u02. We reviewed the volume at the OS level to ensure that enough space existed for our recovery area size, determined above:

```
df -k
```

Then it is merely a matter of setting the value of our init parameter.

```
SQL> ALTER SYSTEM SET DB_RECOVERY_FILE_DEST = '/u02/fra/'
SCOPE=BOTH SID='*';
```

Final Notes on the Flashback Recovery Area
A few closing remarks on the FRA before we move on with our RMAN configuration:

■   **Using ASM**   If you use ASM for your FRA, you should be mindful of any mirroring that you have established for the disk group in question. For instance, if you have set up a two-way mirror for the disk group, your FRA size value must only be half the size of the total disk group size.

- **Using OMF**   If you use OMF, it is worth noting that it's not really a good idea to set your db_recovery_file_dest to the same location as the db_file_create_dest or db_file_create_online_log_dest_n parameters. This is for performance as well as data protection purposes. Oracle will actually throw a warning if you set these to the same value.

- **Sharing the FRA Across Multiple Databases**   The same flashback recovery area can be used by multiple databases. This can provide significant advantages, particularly for a Data Guard configuration, but also if you have a large ASM disk group and multiple databases on the same system. It can come in handy, as well, when it comes time to clone production for test purposes. Here's the catch: either all the databases that share the FRA have a different value for db_name, or a different name for the value db_unique_name.

Permanent Configuration Parameters

So we have set up the location for our backups. Next we have to configure the parameters of the backup itself. In the old days of RMAN—in version 8.1.7 or lower—every single backup job you ran from RMAN had to be configured at the time of job execution. So if you wanted to parallelize the backup across four channels, and you wanted to set a backup piece size, and you wanted to go to a tape device residing on your media management server, the job would look something like this:

```
run {
allocate channel sbt1 type 'sbt_tape'
parms = "env=(nb_ora_server=linx02)" maxpiccesize = 8G;
allocate channel sbt2 type 'sbt_tape'
parms = "env=(nb_ora_server=linx02)" maxpiecesize = 8G;
allocate channel sbt3 type 'sbt_tape'
parms = "env=(nb_ora_server=linx02)" maxpiecesize = 8G;
allocate channel sbt4 type 'sbt_tape'
parms = "env=(nb_ora_server=linx02)" maxpiecesize = 8G;
backup database format = 'FULL_DB_%U'
filesperset = 4;
}
```

Rest assured, if you come from 8*i* and you have a pile of RMAN scripts you still want to use, this script will still run successfully in Oracle Database 10*g*. However, starting with 9*i*, Oracle acknowledged that certain parameters of a backup are the same across every backup job, and should be stored permanently for use each time. The ability to set values for RMAN execution that can be used by all subsequent jobs is referred to as *permanent configuration parameters*. Permanent configuration parameters are set at the RMAN command prompt using the configure command.

To list the current configuration parameters, you can type **show all** at the RMAN prompt:

```
RMAN> show all;
using target database controlfile instead of recovery catalog
RMAN configuration parameters are:
CONFIGURE RETENTION POLICY TO REDUNDANCY 1; # default
CONFIGURE BACKUP OPTIMIZATION OFF; # default
CONFIGURE DEFAULT DEVICE TYPE TO DISK; # default
CONFIGURE CONTROLFILE AUTOBACKUP OFF; # default
CONFIGURE CONTROLFILE AUTOBACKUP FORMAT
    FOR DEVICE TYPE DISK TO '%F'; #default
CONFIGURE DEVICE TYPE DISK PARALLELISM 1
    BACKUP TYPE TO BACKUPSET; # default
CONFIGURE DATAFILE BACKUP COPIES
    FOR DEVICE TYPE DISK TO 1; # default
CONFIGURE ARCHIVELOG BACKUP COPIES
    FOR DEVICE TYPE DISK TO 1; # default
CONFIGURE MAXSETSIZE TO UNLIMITED; # default
CONFIGURE SNAPSHOT CONTROLFILE NAME TO
'D:\ORACLE\ORA10\DATABASE\SNCFBETA10.ORA'; # default
CONFIGURE ARCHIVELOG DELETION POLICY TO NONE;
```

With permanent configuration parameters, you can set up job control information that will exist for all backups of the database. Thus, for the backup job mentioned above, you could instead configure it like this:

```
configure default device type to 'sbt_tape';
configure channel device type 'sbt_tape'
  parms = "env=(nb_ora_server=linx02)";
configure channel device type 'sbt_tape' maxpiecesize = 8G;
configure device type 'sbt_tape' parallelism 4;
```

Having done so, the script for running the backup each subsequent time would simply be

```
backup database format = 'FULL_DB_%U';
```

NOTE
Why didn't we configure the format as a permanent configuration? The format we are using implies a full database backup, and there may come a time when we want to use our permanent config parameters to take an incremental backup to tape.

HA Workshop: *Setting Permanent Configuration Parameters for High-Availability Backup Strategy*

Workshop Notes

This workshop will set up the parameters for a backup strategy that maximizes the functionality of RMAN to assist in your HA environment. The actual backup commands, as well as restore/recover commands, can be found in HA Workshops later in the chapter.

Step 1. Establish the default device as disk, and configure the disk channels.

```
Configure default device type to disk;
Configure device type disk parallelism 2 backup type to copy;
Configure retention policy to recovery window of 7 days;
Configure backup optimization on;
configure controlfile autobackup on;
```

Step 2. Establish tape channels so that the recovery area files can be aged out to the tape device.

```
configure channel device type 'sbt_tape'
    parms = "env=(nb_ora_server=lnx01, nb_ora_class=oracle)";
configure device type sbt parallelism 2;
```

> **NOTE**
> *Your PARMS clause will depend on your media management product. Refer to the documentation from your media manager to know what RMAN must pass to the tape device in order to successfully push the backup stream to tape.*

Caring for Your Controlfile

The permanent configuration parameters can be applied to every backup of the target database because they are stored in the target database controlfile. You can always view the parameters by looking at V$RMAN_CONFIGURATION (note that this view is not populated with default configuration parameters).

RMAN adds an increased amount of reliance on the presence of a controlfile for its continual operation: the cfile is the lookup table for what to back up and restore—it is the lookup table for determining where the RMAN backups reside and when they were taken, and it is now the home of our backup job controls. As such, we must be just a little nervous about the health of the controlfile. Here's why.

The most important thing is to have an accessible backup of the controlfile *that includes data from your most recent backup.* In other words, the controlfile needs to be backed up after the successful completion of your database and archivelog backup. By default, RMAN backs up the controlfile whenever it notes that the system datafile is being backed up. The problem with this controlfile backup is that it is initiated at the same time as the datafile backup, so by its very nature it does not contain information about the backup in which it is contained.

One way to accomplish competent cfile backups is to set the permanent configuration parameter Controlfile Autobackup to On (see "HA Workshop: Setting Permanent Configuration Parameters for High-Availability Backup Strategy"). When enabled, this parameter will automatically take a controlfile backup to the flashback recovery area or a specified location (on disk or tape) after every backup operation.

This backup comes at a very small cost—the controlfile is typically only a few megabytes in size. The controlfile autobackup has a few features that are extremely desirable to us in an HA environment. First, this autobackup cfile will always contain the RMAN backup metadata that is most recent. Second, the autobackup cfile will be written in a format that is immediately recognizable by RMAN—RMAN will be able to find the autobackup controlfile, even when all it knows about the database it is trying to restore is the DBID.

When turned on, the default location for the controlfile autobackup is the flashback recovery area. In the absence of an FRA, the location for disk backups is $ORACLE_HOME/dbs directory. If you configure the default device type to tape, then

What is the snapshot controlfile?

You may have noticed when reviewing the RMAN configuration parameters that there is the option to rename the snapshot controlfile. The snapshot controlfile is a copy of the controlfile that RMAN utilizes during long-running operations (such as backup). RMAN needs a read-consistent view of the controlfile for the backup operation, but by its nature the controlfile is extremely volatile. Instead of putting a lock on the controlfile and causing all kinds of database enqueue problems, RMAN makes a copy of the cfile called the snapshot controlfile, and uses it instead of the actual controlfile. The snapshot is refreshed at the beginning of every backup. You can relocate the snapshot if it makes sense in your environment (such as making it accessible to all nodes in a RAC cluster), but for the most part it does no harm to leave it in the $ORACLE_HOME/dbs directory.

this backup goes to tape. If you back up to disk, lack an FRA, and want to set the controlfile autobackup to a smarter location than the dbs directory, it is done this way:

```
configure controlfile autobackup format = '/u02/backup/cf_%F';
```

The only requirement is that the format contain the %F format so that the backup is recognizable to RMAN during a restore operation.

Backing Up the Available Database

It's time to get into the meat of things, and that means taking backups of our database that emphasize availability. What does that mean, exactly? Well, backing up for availability requires that you envision your recovery requirements prior to establishing the backup strategy. It means looking at the different types of failures that your media recovery strategy must account for, and then preparing in advance for as fast a recovery as possible.

The High-Availability Backup Strategy

The HA backup strategy is based on a few guiding principles:

- A complete restore of the database must be avoided at all costs.

- Datafile recovery should take minutes, not hours.

- User errors should be dealt with using Flashback Technology, and not media recovery.

- Backup operations should have minimal performance drain on normal database operations.

- Backup maintenance should be automated to fit business rules.

When you consider these guiding principles, they lead us toward a specific configuration for our backups in the HA environment.

Whole Datafile Backups

The centerpiece of our backups must be, of course, backups of the Oracle datafiles. You can ignore your temporary tablespace temp files; RMAN does not consider them when backing up, and neither should you. They are built from scratch every time you open the DB anyway. Every other file needs a complete, whole backup taken.

RMAN Backupsets Using the backup Command   RMAN's specialty, leading up to version Oracle Database 10*g*, was taking a backup using a format called the backupset. The backupset was an RMAN-specific output file that was a multiplexed catchall for all the datafiles of the database, streamed into a single backup piece (think of a backupset as a logical unit, like a tablespace; think of a backup piece as a physical unit, like the datafile). This is an extremely efficient method for getting a backup taken that minimizes the load by eliminating unused blocks. This is the *only* way RMAN can back up to tape.

The only problem with backupsets is that you have to stream the blocks from the backupset through the Oracle memory area, through input/output buffers, and then back to the datafile locations—then rebuild any empty blocks from scratch. So the restore takes a little time. No big deal, if you are restoring from tape; the tape restore is the bottleneck, anyway.

Parallelization and Multiplexing for RMAN Backups

We've spoken briefly about allocating multiple channels to run an RMAN backup. When two or more channels are allocated for a single backup operation, this is referred to as *parallelization*. When two or more channels are allocated, RMAN breaks up the entire workload of the backup job into two relatively equal workloads, based on datafile size, disk affinity, and other factors. Then the two jobs are run in parallel, creating two separate backupsets. Datafiles cannot span backupsets, so if you allocate two channels to back up a single datafile, one channel will sit idle.

Parallelization increases the resource load used by RMAN during the backup, from disk I/O to memory to CPU, so the backup will run faster but also eat up more resources on your target database server. Typically, as well, it makes little sense to parallelize to a high degree if your backup location is serialized—say, you are backing up to a single disk, or to a single tape device. Particularly for tape backups, it makes little sense to parallelize channels to a single tape, as you simply increase the bottleneck at the access point to the tape.

Multiplexing, on the other hand, refers to the number of files that are included in a single backupset. During a backup of type backupset, RMAN will stream data from all the files included in the backup job into a single backupset. This leads to efficiencies at the time of the backup, as all files can be accessed at the same time. However, be cautious of multiplexing, as having a high degree of multiplexing can lead to problems during restore. Say you have a backupset with 10 files multiplexed together in the backupset. During restore of a single datafile, RMAN must read the entire backupset from tape into a memory structure to gather information about the single datafile. This means the network activity is extremely high, and the restore is very slow for a single file. Multiplexing does not apply to backups of type copy, as the backup product is a full-fledged copy of each datafile.

The moral of this story:

1. Parallelize based on the number of backup locations available. If you have four tapes, allocate four channels.

2. If you multiplex datafiles into the same backupset, attempt to multiplex files that would be restored together.

RMAN Datafile Copies to Disk   RMAN can also take copies of the Oracle datafiles. It still uses the memory buffers during the backup, to take advantage of corruption checking, but empty blocks are not eliminated—and the end result is a complete, block-for-block copy of the datafile. You can only do this to disk; it doesn't make sense to do it to tape because backupsets are far more efficient.

The benefit of datafile copies is that, given a restore operation, the copy can quickly be switched to by the Oracle database, instead of physically restoring the file to the datafile location. The restore goes from minutes (or hours) to mere seconds. Talk about a desirable feature for availability: we can begin to apply archivelogs immediately to get the file back up to date.

The problem, of course, is that you need the disk space to house a complete copy of the datafiles in your database. Of course, this is becoming less and less of a problem as Storage Area Networks (SANs) become commonplace, and disk prices continue to drop. But, given a multiterabyte database, using disk-based copies might prove impossible.

We recommend that in Oracle Database 10g, you take advantage of disk-based copies whenever possible. Using local datafile copies is the best way to decrease the mean time to recovery (MTTR), which is the goal of any HADBA. And creating them using RMAN means you have all the benefits: corruption checking, backup file management, block media recovery, and so forth. If you don't have space for copies of all your files, prioritize your files based on those that would be most affected by an extended outage, and get copies of those files. Send the rest directly to tape.

Incremental Backups

After you figure out what to do about getting your full datafile copies taken, its time to consider the use of incremental backups. RMAN provides the means by which to take a backup of only those data blocks that have changed since the last full backup, or the last incremental. An incremental strategy allows you to generate less backup file product, if you have limited disk or tape space. Using incremental backups during datafile recovery is typically more efficient than using archivelogs, so you usually improve your mean time to recovery as well.

If you have the ability to do so, taking full database backups every night is preferable to taking a full backup once a week, and then taking incrementals. The first step of any recovery will be to restore the last full datafile backup, and then begin the process of replacing blocks from each subsequent incremental backup. So if you have a recent full backup, recovery will be faster. Incremental strategies are for storage-minded DBAs who feel significant pressure to keep backups small due to the size of the database.

RMAN divides incremental backups into two levels: 0 and 1 (if you used incremental backups in RMAN9*i* and lower, levels 2–4 have been removed because they really never added much functionality). A level 0 incremental backup is actually a full backup of every block in the database; a level 0 is the prerequisite for any incremental strategy. Specifying a level 0 incremental, versus taking a plain old backup, means that RMAN records the incremental SCN: the marker by which all blocks will be judged for inclusion in an incremental backup. The incremental SCN is not recorded when level 0 is not specified when the backup is taken.

After you take your level 0 backup, you are free to take as many level 1 backups as you require. During a level 1 backup, RMAN determines if a block has been modified since the level 0 backup. If so, the block makes the pass from the input buffer to the output buffer, and ends up in the backup piece. When complete, the level 1 backup is a pile of blocks that, by itself, is a significant subset of the actual datafile it represents (depending on your database volatility, of course). By default, the level 1 will check back to the last incremental backup, meaning if you take a level 1, and then another level 1, the second will only back up blocks since the first level 1, instead of checking back to the level 0 (full). This is depicted in Figure 8-6.

Incrementally Updated Backups   In Oracle Database 10*g*, Oracle introduces the ability to leverage incremental backups for fast recovery via incrementally updated backups. In a nutshell, RMAN now allows you to apply an incremental backup to a copy of the datafiles on an ongoing basis, so that the copy is always kept as recent as the last incremental backup. Theoretically, then, you could switch to the datafile copy, apply archivelogs since the last incremental backup, and be back in business.

The benefits are enormous: now you can mimic taking a new, full copy of the datafiles every night without the overhead of such an operation. You also extend the lifespan of your full datafile copy, as you can theoretically apply incremental backups to the copy forever without taking a new full copy of the file.

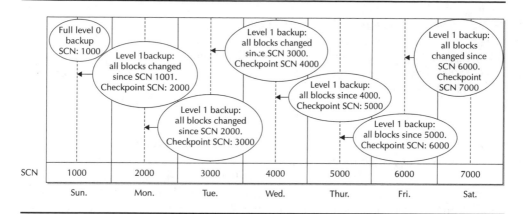

FIGURE 8-6. *Incremental backups for a week*

The requirements are minimal for incrementally updated backups:

1. You need to tag your full, level 0 backup so that it can be specified for the incremental apply.

2. You can only apply an incremental to a copy, and not a backupset.

3. The incremental backup must be taken with the keywords "for recover of copy."

HA Workshop: *Using Incrementally Updated Backups*

Workshop Notes
This workshop assumes you configured your permanent parameters as they were outlined in the previous workshop. This will mean you have your default device type set to disk, and the default backup type is copy (instead of backupset). We also assume the presence of a flash recovery area to handle file naming, organization, and so forth.

Step 1. Take the full, level 0 backup. Be sure to tag it, as this is how we refer to it during the application of the incremental backup. Be sure there is enough space in the recovery area to house full copies of all your datafiles.

```
backup incremental level 0  tag 'INC_4_APPLY' database;
```

> **NOTE**
> *Because we set our default backup type to copy,*
> *and we set parallelism to 2, we will only be creating*
> *two file copies at a time in the preceding command.*
> *If you want your backup to access more datafiles*
> *at the same time, increase disk parallelism to a*
> *higher value.*

Step 2.   Take the level 1 incremental backup. If this is production, you should schedule your level 1 to meet business needs. Every night is a very common approach. If you are merely testing incremental application at this time, be sure to run some DML changes against your database after making the level 0 backup, and before running the level 1. Switch the logfiles a few times, as well, to give some distance between the two backups.

```
backup incremental level 1 for recover of copy
tag 'INC_4_APPLY' database;
```

Step 3.   Apply the incremental backup to the datafile copies of your database.

```
recover copy of database with tag 'INC_4_APPLY';
```

After applying the first incremental level 1, you can script the incremental backup and the incremental application to the backup copy so that you apply the latest incremental backup immediately after taking it.

Using Block Change Tracking for Better Incremental Performance   If you do decide to use incremental backups in your recovery strategy, you should take note of a new performance feature for incrementals that has been introduced in Oracle Database 10*g*. This new feature is called *block change tracking*, and it refers to an internal Oracle mechanism that, when switched on, will keep track of all blocks being modified since the last level 0 backup. When the incremental level 1 backup is taken, RMAN looks at the block change tracking file to determine which blocks to back up.

Prior to Oracle Database 10*g*, the only way that RMAN could determine which data blocks to include in a level 1 incremental backup was to read every block in the database into an input buffer in memory and check it. This led to a common misconception about incremental backups in RMAN: that they would go significantly faster than full backups. This simply didn't hold up to scrutiny, as RMAN still had to read every block in the database to determine its eligibility—so it was reading as many blocks as the full backup.

With block change tracking, the additional I/O overhead is eliminated almost entirely, as RMAN can now read only those blocks required for backup. Now, there is a little bit of robbing Peter to pay Paul, in the sense that block change tracking incurs a slight performance degradation for the database. But if you plan on using incremental backups, chances are you can spare the CPU cycles for the increased backup performance and backup I/O decrease.

To enable block change tracking, you simply do the following:

```
ALTER DATABASE ENABLE BLOCK CHANGE TRACKING;
```

Alternatively, if you are not using a flashback recovery area, you can specify a file for change tracking:

```
ALTER DATABASE ENABLE BLOCK CHANGE TRACKING USING FILE '/dir/blck_change_file';
```

You turn off change tracking like so:

```
Alter database disable block change tracking;
```

It should be noted that after you turn change tracking on, it does not have any information about block changes until the next level 0 backup is taken.

Backing Up the Flashback Recovery Area

With datafile copies, incremental backups, and archivelogs piling up in the flash recovery area, it's time to start thinking about housekeeping operations. First, though, it's important to recognize the powerful staging functionality that the FRA provides. With all backups first appearing in the FRA, the process of staging those backups to tape has been greatly simplified.

RMAN now comes equipped with a command to back up the recovery area:

```
backup recovery area;
```

This backs up all recovery files in the recovery area: full backups, copies, incrementals, controlfile autobackups, and archivelogs. Block change tracking files, current controlfiles, and online redo logs are not backed up. This command can only back up to channel type SBT (tape), so it will fail if you do not have tape channels configured. This is why we recommended them in the HA Workshop "Setting Permanent Configuration Parameters for High-Availability Backup Strategy." For more on tape backups, see the section "Media Management Considerations."

Alternatively, if you want the same functionality but you do not use a flashback recovery area, you can use

```
backup recovery files;
```

This has the same effect: full backups, copies, incrementals, cfile autobackups, and archivelogs are backed up. This can only go to tape, so have SBT channels configured.

Backup Housekeeping

More often than not, backups are never used. This is a good thing. However, we leave quite a trail of useless files and metadata behind us as we move forward with our backup strategy. So we must consider housekeeping chores as part of any serious HA backup strategy. Outdated backups clog up our flashback recovery area and take up needed space on our tapes, and the metadata inexorably builds up in our RMAN catalog, making reports less and less useful with every passing day. Something must be done.

Determine, Configure, and Use Your Retention Policy

Lucky for us, that something became much simpler in Oracle Database 10*g*. Backup maintenance had already become simple in Oracle9*i* when a retention policy was properly configured. The retention policy refers to the rules by which you dictate which backups are obsolete, and therefore eligible for deletion. RMAN distinguishes between two mutually exclusive types of retention policies: redundancy and recovery windows.

Redundancy policies determine if a backup is obsolete based on the number of times the file has been previously backed up. Therefore, if you set your policy to REDUNDANCY = 1 and then back up the database, you have met your retention policy. The next time you back up your database, all previous backups are obsolete, because you have one backup. Setting redundancy to 2, then, would mean that you keep the last two backups, and all backups prior to that are obsolete.

The recovery window refers to a time frame in which all backups will be kept, regardless of how many backups are taken. The recovery window is anchored to sysdate, and therefore is a constantly sliding window of time. So, if you set your policy to a "Recovery Window of 7 Days," then all backups less than seven days old would be retained, and all backups older than seven days would be marked for deletion. As time rolls forward, new backups are taken and older backups become obsolete.

You cannot have both retention policies, so choose one that best fits your backup practices and business needs. There is a time and a place for both types, and it always boils down to how you view your backup strategy: is it something that needs redundancy to account for possible problems with the most recent backup, or do you view a backup strategy as defining how far back in time you can recover?

After you determine what policy you need, configuration is easy: use the configure command from the RMAN prompt and set it in the target database controlfile. By default, the retention policy is set to redundancy 1.

```
CONFIGURE RETENTION POLICY TO REDUNDANCY 1; # default
```

You change it with simple verbiage:

```
RMAN> CONFIGURE RETENTION POLICY TO RECOVERY WINDOW OF 7 DAYS;
new RMAN configuration parameters:
CONFIGURE RETENTION POLICY TO RECOVERY WINDOW OF 7 DAYS;
new RMAN configuration parameters are successfully stored
```

After you configure the policy, it is simple to use. You can list obsolete backups and copies using the report command, and then when you are ready, use the delete obsolete command to remove all obsolete backups. Note that RMAN will always ask you to confirm the deletion of files:

```
RMAN> report obsolete;
RMAN> delete obsolete;
RMAN retention policy will be applied to the command
RMAN retention policy is set to redundancy 1
using channel ORA_DISK_1
Deleting the following obsolete backups and copies:
Type                    Key    Completion Time    Filename/Handle
--------------------    ------ ----------------   --------------------
Backup Set              11     12-JAN-04
  Backup Piece          9      12-JAN-04          /U02/BACKUP/0DFBCJ5H_1_1

Do you really want to delete the above objects (enter YES or NO)?
```

You can automate the delete obsolete command, so that a job can perform the action at regular intervals and save you the effort. To do so, you have to include the force keyword to override the deletion prompt:

```
delete force noprompt obsolete;
```

Retention Policies and the Flashback Recovery Area

The flashback recovery area is self-cleaning. (You know, like a cat, only without those disturbing leg-over-the-head in-front-of-the-television moments.) What this means is that as files build up in the FRA and storage pressure begins to appear, the FRA will age out old files that have passed the boundaries of the retention policy you implemented. Take an example where you have a retention policy of redundancy 1. You take a full database backup on Monday. On Tuesday, you take a second full database backup. On Wednesday, you take a third full database backup. However, there is not room for three full backups in the FRA. So the FRA checks the policy, sees that it only requires one backup, and it deletes the backup taken on Monday—and the Wednesday backup completes.

An important note about this example: with redundancy set to 1, you still must have enough space in your FRA for two whole database backups. This is because RMAN will not delete the only backup of the database before it writes the new one, because the possibility exists for a backup failure and then you have *no* backups. So before the Monday backup is truly obsolete, the Tuesday backup has to exist in its entirety, meaning you have two backups.

If the FRA fills up with files, but no files qualify for deletion based on your retention policy, you will see an error and the backup that is currently underway will fail with an error:

```
RMAN-03009: failure of backup command on ORA_DISK_2 channel
at 11/04/2003 15:44:56
ORA-19809: limit exceeded for recovery files
ORA-19804: cannot reclaim 471859200 bytes disk space from 1167912960 limit
continuing other job steps, job failed will not be re-run
```

A full FRA can be a far more serious problem than just backup failures. If you set up your FRA as a mandatory site for archivelog creation, then the ARCH process can potentially hang your database waiting to archive a redo log to a full location. By all estimations, it behooves the HADBA to keep the FRA open for business.

Stage the Flashback Recovery Area to Tape

So our goal is to keep a copy of our database in the FRA, as well as maintain our retention policy that requires more than a single backup of the database be available for restore. The way to accomplish this, of course, is to back up the FRA to tape. The retention policy that you configure applies to all backups, whether they be on disk or tape. However, if you use the FRA as a staging area that is frequently moved to tape, you will never be required to clean up the FRA. Your maintenance commands will always be run against the backups on tape. When you back up the recovery area, you free up the transient files in the FRA to be aged out when space pressure occurs, so the errors noted above don't impair future backups or archivelog operations.

Take our script from the HA Workshop "Using Incrementally Updated Backups," and modify it to include an FRA backup and a tape maintenance command to delete obsolete backups from tapes (remember, our retention policy is set to a recovery window of seven days):

```
backup incremental level 1 for recover of copy
tag 'INC_4_APPLY' database;
recover copy of database with tag 'INC_4_APPLY';
backup recovery area;
delete obsolete device type sbt;
```

Performing Recovery

Here's one of our favorite sayings: every DBA has a backup strategy—few of them, however, have a recovery strategy. Our advice here is not to be the cliché. Make sure you understand your recovery options, and that they are tested once in a while. Maintaining availability through the failure event requires that you have the knowledge and trust in your backups to take immediate action that is not a knee-jerk reaction that leads to further downtime due to the recovery itself. The key, as always, is not to initiate a full restore of the database in a blind panic.

Database Recovery: Restore and Recover

Recovering from some sort of failure (database corruption, hardware loss, and so forth) typically involves two distinct steps for an Oracle database: restore and recovery. Datafile *restore* refers to the act of getting a copy of the lost or broken file back in place from the backup. *Recovery* refers to the process of applying archived redo log changes to the restored file.

As we've said a few times throughout this chapter, the goal is to avoid a full database restore. When you encounter an error, it is critical that you come to terms with the full extent of the problem, and be mindful of overreacting. Think first to restore a single datafile back for recovery. You can always bring the file or group of files manifesting the problem first and recover them, and then investigate for other possible problem files.

This approach is assisted in a huge way by the backup approach we have espoused so far: incrementally updated datafile copies that live in the FRA. Because the files exist on disk, and are independent of each other (that is, not multiplexed into a single backup piece), you can perform restore and recovery piecemeal without slowing down the overall performance.

Stream through a day's worth of archivelogs two or three times, however, and you will probably realize that a piecemeal approach does have its downside. So trying to diagnose the entire problem prior to recovery is extremely useful.

If you are taking backupset-type backups directly to tape, restoring a single datafile from the backupset is going to be extremely expensive. RMAN must restore the entire backup piece from tape before it can extract just the blocks for the single datafile. So multiplexing multiple files into the same backupset can be very costly at the time of recovery. Better, then, to set filesperset=1, which will slow down the backup but provide the most flexibility during restore.

Full Database Recovery

Okay, there are times when it's absolutely required. In those cases, the code is simple and straightforward. Note that the following code for restoring the database assumes that you have the current controlfile and the target database is mounted.

If there is no controlfile, you should see the section below, "Recovery from Complete Loss (No Controlfile)."

```
restore database;
recover database;
```

If you need to specify a point in time in the past to recover to:

```
run {set until time = '04-NOV-03 12:00:00';
restore database;
recover database; }
```

Datafile or Tablespace Recovery

The most common form of recovery should be datafile recovery. To perform datafile recovery, you must offline the datafile prior to restoration. You can do this from the SQL prompt, or from within RMAN (shown next). These recovery commands assume the database is still open and running.

```
rman>sql 'alter database datafile 8 offline';
```

Then, from the RMAN prompt, you issue your restore and recover command. To save yourself typing, you can refer to the files by their file number instead of name.

```
sql>select file#, name from v$datafile;
rman>connect target /
rman> run { restore datafile 8;
 recover datafile 8;
 sql 'alter database datafile 8 online';}
```

The same basic structure is used for tablespaces:

```
rman> run { sql 'alter tablespace users offline';
restore tablespace users;
recover tablespace users;
sql 'alter tablespace users online'; }
```

Recovery from Complete Loss (No Controlfile)

If the controlfile has been lost along with the rest of the database, you have a few different options, depending on what your controlfile backup strategy is. If you took our advice and configured RMAN for controlfile autobackup, then you have a few steps to run through.

HA Workshop: *Recovering from a Complete Loss*

Workshop Notes

This workshop guides you through the restoration and recovery of an Oracle database that has been completely lost. This example shows how to recover using RMAN when there is no RMAN catalog and no controlfile detailing our backups, so we must employ the controlfile autobackup feature. What is not covered here is the reinstallation of the Oracle software itself. If your complete loss included the ORACLE_HOME for your Oracle Database 10*g* install, you would also need to reinstall the software, and apply any patches that existed, prior to following this procedure.

Step 1.   Determine the DBID of the lost database.

This can be done by checking the location where you have been putting your controlfile autobackups. If you use a flashback recovery area, check the FRA directory structure for <sid>->autobackup->date->autobackup_name.

```
pwd
/u02/flash_recovery_area/beta10/autobackup/2003_11_04
ls
O1_MF_S_509209441_ZTJ5228D_.BKP
```

In this filename, the fourth number string is your database ID, 509209441.

Step 2.   Start up nomount a default instance for your database.

```
ORACLE_SID=beta10;export ORACLE_SID
sqlplus "/ as sysdba"
sql> startup force nomount
```

This opens an instance with default System Global Area (SGA) parameters.

Step 3.   Restore your spfile.

```
rman target /
rman> restore spfile from autobackup;
rman> shutdown immediate;
rman> startup nomount;
```

Step 4.   Restore the controlfile, and then mount the database.

```
rman> restore controlfile from autobackup;
rman>alter database mount;
```

> **Step 5.**   Restore the datafiles, and perform media recovery.
>
> ```
> rman> restore database;
> rman> recover database;
> rman> alter database open resetlogs;;
> ```

Recovery Using the Incrementally Updated Datafile Copy

There is no extra step required to use the incrementally updated datafile copies for restore operations. They will be used automatically because their incremental update time will show them to be the most recent copies of the files. Cool, huh?

Block Media Recovery

So we get to the one feature of RMAN that is absolutely too cool for words: block media recovery (BMR). BMR refers to RMAN's ability to restore from backup a single data block, and then perform media recovery on that single block. This is huge, people. Ora-1578? No problem. Plug in the file number and block number from the 1578 error, and RMAN will go to the last backup, get the one block showing corruption, restore it, and then scroll through the archivelogs to see if any of the redo need be applied to the block. Here's the kicker: the file that has the corrupt block remains available through the recovery process. Wait, it gets better. The segment that contains the corrupt block is available during the recovery process. In other words, you can continue to use the table that has a corrupt block, as long as you don't try to select from the bad block. Talk about high availability! It doesn't get any better than this.

Usage is simple. Take your average ora-1578 error:

```
ORA-1578: ORACLE data block corrupted (file # 7, block # 1234)
```

Note the file number and block number, and plug them into the RMAN command:

```
blockrecover datafile 7 block 1234;
```

You can specify multiple blocks:

```
blockrecover
    datafile 7 block 1234
    datafile 10 block 3265;
```

Media Management Considerations

RMAN is a fully functional backup utility that provides unparalleled functionality, particularly in a high-availability environment. However, there is one thing RMAN cannot do by itself: back up directly to tape. To back up directly to tape, RMAN must pass the stream of data blocks to a media management layer (MML), which can redirect the data flow to a media management server that controls your tape devices.

The SBT Interface

The media management layer is provided by a third-party vendor, and is written specifically to receive data from an RMAN backup session and redirect it to tape. Common media management products include Veritas NetBackup, Legato Networker, HP Omniback, and Tivoli Data Protection. These vendors provide an Oracle integration file called the SBT library, which gets loaded by RMAN into the Oracle memory stack when a tape channel is allocated for backup. There are two ways that RMAN can locate the library file provided by the media management vendor: the file can be symbolically linked in the $ORACLE_HOME/lib directory, or you can call the sbt_library as a parameter in the channel allocation command.

Prior to version 9*i*, Oracle looked to load the SBT library by initializing the file $ORACLE_HOME/libobk.so (or libobk.a, libobk.sl, depending on the operating system). This file is merely a symbolic link file that is re-created to point to the actual SBT library file provided by the vendor. By default, this pointed to a dummy sbt library file provided by Oracle, libdsbtsh8.so. This file allowed you to allocate a tape channel and then back up to disk, so that tape channels could be tested and debugged. To use the default SBT interface, you had to set the environment variable BACKUP_DIR to a disk location. In Oracle9*i* and Oracle Database 10*g*, you no longer have a libobk.so file by default. This file will only exist in the $ORACLE_HOME/lib directory if it is created by your media management provider.

Instead, you now specify the sbt library file as a value in the PARMS specification of your tape channel allocation. This is the recommended approach by Oracle, as it is more specific and requires less work in the Oracle software stack.

```
configure channel device type sbt
parms= "SBT_LIBRARY=/fullpath/libraryfilename";
```

Many media management vendors still employ the usage of the libobk.so symbolic link. Refer to your vendor documentation to find out.

If you want to test out tape channel usage using the Oracle-provided default SBT interface, you can specify it at the PARMS line, as noted above, and then you provide an additional ENV variable for the place on disk you would like to write the tape backup to:

```
configure channel device type sbt
parms= "SBT_LIBRARY=oracle.disksbt,
env = (BACKUP_DIR=/u02/backup);
```

You should know that it is not a good idea to take your production-level backups using the disk sbt file. This gives you all the drawbacks of backing up to tape and none of the benefits of backing up to disk. It is merely a troubleshooting or proofing exercise.

Backing Up Directly to Tape

We have talked already about using the flashback recovery area as a staging area for backups: the backups go to disk first, and then after a predetermined amount of time elapses, we move the backups to tape. However, it may be that in your environment, you require that backups go directly to tape.

Configuration for backing up directly to tape is pretty straightforward. Change your default device to SBT. Configure your SBT channels to contain the proper PARMS values to match your media management setup. Determine your level of parallelization and multiplexing. Then you schedule your backups.

```
configure default device type to sbt;
configure channel device type sbt parms =
    "SBT_LIBRARY=/fileloc/libobk.so,
    ENV=(NB_ORA_SERV=linx01, NB_ORA_CLASS = oracle)";
configure device type sbt parallelism 4;
configure channel device type sbt filesperset=4;
```

Determining Parallelization and Multiplexing

Parallelization refers to the number of tape channels you allocate simultaneously for an RMAN backup. Multiple channels run simultaneously to speed up the backup process. However, there are seriously bad side effects during restore that occur if your allocated channels during backup outnumber the tape devices that will house the backup pieces. If you allocate two channels, and you have only one tape device, then the two backup sets will be interspersed together on the same tape. On restore, unless you are restoring the entire database, you will have to read through a lot more tape to get access to all the writes that are required for the restore.

The same problem applies to multiplexing. If you do not limit the number of files that go into each backupset (filesperset greater than 1), you will have to wait longer for a single file restore. During the restore, RMAN will have to read the entire backupset into a memory buffer at the target database to determine which blocks are needed for the one file being restored. So, the more files you multiplex, the longer you will have to wait and the more network bandwidth is used during the restore of a single datafile.

So the best possible scenario is one in which you have dozens of tape devices that you can write to simultaneously during a backup, so that you can set a higher level of parallelization during backup where only one backupset is being written to any one tape at a time. Then you set filesperset=1 at the time of backup, so that every backupset only contains one file. If this is not possible in your environment, try coming to terms with some middle ground for your multiplexing solution. One channel per tape device is pretty much set in stone, so what you are determining is a cost-to-return ratio between how long you can run your backup, and how long it will take to restore a file during recovery.

RMAN and Data Guard

The relationship between RMAN and Data Guard is based on the technology that underpins the Data Guard product: the standby database. As you learned in Chapter 7, the Standby Database stands at the center of the DG environment: a complete duplicate copy of the production database mirrored to a similar hardware configuration (this, of course, refers to a physical standby database). RMAN backups can be used to build the standby database—in fact, there is functionality built directly into RMAN to do so.

Using RMAN to Build the Standby Database

A common use of Oracle backups in any environment is to move them to a new location and open them as a clone copy of the database for test and development purposes. It's a good way to get some value out of backups, other than merely a "just in case" fallback. In RMAN, the ability to clone a database has been built into the command-line interface as the duplicate command, and is quite simple:

```
duplicate target database to <clone_db_name>;
```

Then this command has been extended to support the creation of a standby database using RMAN backups:

```
duplicate target database for standby;
```

Of course, that is the icing on the cake: there is a certain amount of prep work required to create the standby database from RMAN backups. When performing the duplication, RMAN makes the connection to the target database (the primary database) and to the catalog (if you use one), and then a third connection to the auxiliary database. The auxiliary database is the database that will become the standby database. Figure 8-7 shows the topology required for a standby creation, given RMAN backups to a tape media server. What is important to note about the duplication process is that the auxiliary database instance must exist before duplication can start, and the auxiliary instance must have access to the RMAN backups.

If the backups have been taken to a media management server accessible by the target node and the auxiliary node, there is little problem with the requirements. The only trick you must remember involves permissions to backups

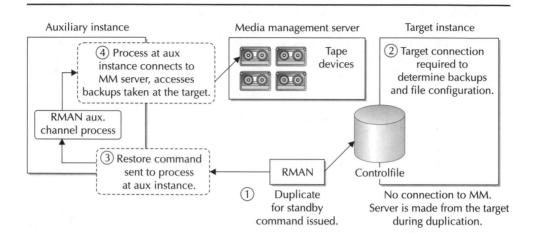

FIGURE 8-7. *Anatomy of a duplicate for standby operation*

at the media management server. Typically, computer systems are registered at the media management server as *clients* and the backups are encoded with a *client name* at the time of backup. So, when you attempt to access backups at the auxiliary node that were taken from your target node, you might expect the server to respond that "no such backups exist." To resolve the issue, you pass the name of the target server from the auxiliary server, like so:

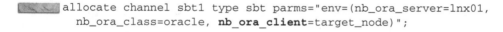
```
allocate channel sbt1 type sbt parms="env=(nb_ora_server=lnx01,
    nb_ora_class=oracle, nb_ora_client=target_node)";
```

NOTE
This example shows the syntax for passing a client name if you are using Veritas NetBackup for Oracle. Other media managers have different ways of handling client to client restores. Consult your media management vendor's documentation.

Flashback Recovery Area and the Standby Database

If you want to use backups that exist in your target node flashback recovery area, things get handled a little differently. To provide access to the FRA, you can NFS mount the FRA at the standby location. If the FRA is on a shared volume formatted with Oracle Clustered File System (OCFS), you can also give direct access to the FRA, so long as the standby node has access to the shared volume. Or, if it makes sense in your environment, you can always copy the entire FRA over from your target node to the standby node.

There are a lot of good reasons to allow sharing of the flashback recovery area between your primary database and your standby database, as noted in Chapter 7. From the configuration perspective, it allows RMAN to have access to disk-based datafile backups, which typically are the most recent and require the least amount of archivelog recovery to bring up to speed with the primary database. This is particularly true if you use incrementally updated backups as described above.

HA Workshop: *Use RMAN to Create a Standby Database*

Workshop Notes
This exercise creates a standby database on the same server as the primary database. The ORACLE_SID for the standby is stby, but the db_name will be the same as the primary: beta10. We will use both the db_file_name_convert and log_file_name_convert parameters, and we will perform media recovery.

Step 1. Use RMAN to create a standby controlfile.

```
ORACLE_SID=beta10
export ORACLE_SID
rman
RMAN> connect target /
RMAN> backup current controlfile for standby
   format= '/space/backup/stby_cfile.%U';
```

You will need to specify a point in time after you created this standby controlfile, so perform a few log switches and then record the last log sequence number from v$archived_log.

```
SQL> alter system switch logfile;
SQL> alter system switch logfile;
SQL> select sequence# from v$archived_log;
```

Step 2. Build your standby database directory structures.

```
mkdir /space/oracle_user/OraHome1/oradata/stby
mkdir /space/oracle_user/OraHome1/oradata/stby/arch
cd /space/oracle_user/OraHome1/admin
mkdir stby
cd stby
mkdir pfile bdump udump cdump
ls
```

Step 3.   Copy the target init.ora file to the auxiliary location. If your target database uses an spfile, you will need to create a pfile from the spfile in order to capture parameters to move over.

If you use an spfile at your target:

```
Sql> connect /@beta10 as sysdba
create pfile='/space/oracle_user/OraHome1/admin/stby/pfile/init.ora'
from spfile;
```

If you use an init.ora file at your target:

```
cp /space/oracle_user/OraHome1/admin/beta10/pfile/init.ora
   /space/oracle_user/OraHome1/admin/stby/pfile/init.ora
```

Step 4.   Make all necessary changes to your stby init.ora file.

```
Control_files=
   '/space/oracle_user/OraHome1/oradata/stby/control01.dbf'
Background_dump_dest=/space/oracle_user/OraHome1/admin/stby/bdump
user_dump_dest=/space/oracle_user/OraHome1/admin/stby/udump
log_archive_dest_1=
   'location=/space/oracle_user/OraHome1/oradata/stby/arch'
standby_archive_dest=
   'location=/space/oracle_user/OraHome1/oradata/stby/arch'
lock_name_space='stby'
remote_login_passwordfile=exclusive
db_file_name_convert=('beta10', 'stby')
log_file_name_convert=('beta10', 'stby')
```

Step 5.   Start up the stby instance in nomount mode.

```
ORACLE_SID=stby
export ORACLE_SID
sqlplus /nolog
sql>connect / as sysdba
sql>startup nomount
pfile=/space/oracle_user/OraHome1/admin/stby/pfile/init.ora
```

Step 6.   Configure your network files for connection to stby. After making any changes to your listener.ora file, be sure that you bounce your listener or the change will not take effect.

```
lsnrctl
LSNRCTL>stop
LSNRCTL>start
```

```
The tnsnames.ora file should have an entry like this:
STBY =
  (DESCRIPTION =
    (ADDRESS_LIST =
      (ADDRESS = (PROTOCOL = TCP)(HOST = cervantes)(PORT = 1521))
    )
    (CONNECT_DATA =
      (SID = stby)
      (SERVER = DEDICATED)
    )
  )
```

The listener.ora file should have an entry like this:

```
SID_LIST_LISTENER =
  (SID_LIST =
    (SID_DESC =
      (GLOBAL_DBNAME = beta10)
      (ORACLE_HOME = /space/oracle_user/OraHome1/)
      (SID_NAME = stby)
    )
  )
```

Step 7.   From RMAN, connect to the target and auxiliary instance and run the duplicate command.

```
ORACLE_SID=beta10
export ORACLE_SID
rman
RMAN>connect target /
RMAN> connect auxiliary sys/password@stby
RMAN>run {
  set until sequence = 789 thread = 1;
  duplicate target database for standby
  dorecover;}
```

RMAN and the Logical Standby Database
As we learned in Chapter 7, it is no longer required in Oracle Database 10g that the primary database be quiesced (inactive) in order to take a backup for a logical standby database. Instead, we create a physical standby database, then make the conversion. See Chapter 7 for more information on creating a logical standby database.

Using the Physical Standby Database to Create Backups

If you have a physical standby database configured, you can put it to work for you. RMAN can connect to the standby database and take the backups at the standby. These backups can then be used to restore files at the primary database. Using this functionality, you can offload the disk I/O and memory utilization associated with running backups at your production server. Doing so provides yet another way to maintain an extremely high level of availability by eliminating the impact of backup processing.

You have to use a recovery catalog in order to back up your database files from the standby. By using the catalog, you can connect to the standby database, take the backups, and have them recorded in the catalog. Then, when you connect to the primary database and the catalog, RMAN will have access to the metadata about the backups taken at the standby.

The trick to performing backups at the standby is to know the nature of the standby databases, and the nature of RMAN backups. A standby database is an exact replica of the primary database, meaning it has the same database ID (DBID) as the primary. RMAN uses the DBID to identify unique databases in the recovery catalog. So, when RMAN connects to the standby, it considers it to be the primary database in most ways, with the same exact file structure and content. So a file backed up at the standby is a file that can be restored to the primary, as they are identical.

Don't let us lead you on thinking that you are somehow "faking out" RMAN when you connect to the standby. RMAN is standby aware; it knows when it's connected to a standby, and acts accordingly. For instance, if you use a db_file_name_convert parameter at your standby to rename files to new locations, RMAN knows that it backed up a file from, say, /u02/oradata on the standby, but that it must restore the file to, say, /u04/oradata on the primary.

The backups that you need to be mindful of will be archivelog backups. Naturally, a copy of every archivelog must by rule exist at the standby database for recovery. So, you can back up the archivelogs from the standby. That's not the issue. The issue is archivelog cleanup—typically, an archivelog backup strategy employs the delete input option, which removes archivelogs after they have been backed up. But if you back up from the standby, the archivelogs will never be removed from the primary. You will have to employ another script to delete archivelogs from the primary database site.

HA Workshop: *Back Up Directly to Tape from the Standby*

Workshop Notes

This workshop assumes that you have a physical standby database configured, with archivelogs streamed to the standby site via a Data Guard configuration. This workshop steps through a process of backing up datafiles directly to tape; we also address archivelog backup and cleanup at both sites (primary and standby).

Step 1. Configure your media management layer, then configure your tape backup channels. For media manager configuration, see "Media Management Considerations." This step needs to be performed at both the primary and standby database. You should configure the SBT channels on the standby to reflect the client name of the primary, so that the backups taken at both sites are organized and stored the same at the media management server.

```
rman target / catalog rman/password@rman_cat_db
rman> configure default device type to sbt;
rman> configure channel device type sbt parms =
    SBT_LIBRARY=/fileloc/libobk.so,
    ENV=(NB_ORA_SERV=lnx01, NB_ORA_CLIENT = lnx02)";
rman> configure device type sbt parallelism 4;
rman> configure channel device type sbt filesperset=4;
```

Step 2. Back up the controlfile and spfile from the primary database site, and then clean out archivelogs based on a time frame of retention.

```
rman target / catalog rman/password@rman_cat_db
rman> backup current controlfile;
rman> delete archivelog completed before sysdate-7;
```

Step 3. Back up the database and archivelogs from the standby site.

```
connect target sys/password@standby_db catalog rman/password@rman_cat_db
backup database plus archivelogs not backed up 2 times;
delete archivelogs completed before sysdate-7;
```

Backup Using the Standby Database with a Flashback Recovery Area

If you have employed an FRA, the workshop above changes little. If you share an FRA between your standby and primary sites, you get the best of both worlds: you can run the backup at your standby database; the backups end up in your FRA, and are immediately usable by the primary database. You still need to connect to the primary to back up the controlfile and spfile.

If your standby and your primary have separate FRA areas, you lose a lot of functionality of the FRA for the primary site. This is because any backups you take to the standby FRA would have to be manually copied to the primary database FRA prior to restore. Better, in that situation, to take your backups directly to tape, so that you can connect your primary directly to the tape device and run the restore.

Design Your Backup Strategy to Fit Your Specifics
There is considerable room for tweaking your backup strategy to include your standby database as a partner. For example, you could have an FRA on the standby that is not shared by the primary until a restore is actually required; then, you remount the volume at the primary site. This type of solution would require a certain amount of hardware support, obviously, but the options are wide open. So, think through what fits your needs.

A Note on Recovery
When performing a restore operation at your primary using backups taken at the standby, be sure you connect to the primary database as the target, and then the recovery catalog. After doing so, restore and recovery will proceed normally, with no special modifications.

RMAN and RAC

RMAN is an excellent partner for any RAC environment, regardless of the RAC configuration. If you use raw partitions, RMAN is an excellent choice for the backup, as there are no tricky offsets for the dd command, and no chance of error. RMAN accesses the datafiles on the raw partitions via the Oracle memory buffer, so every block is read correctly and written correctly. If you use the Oracle Cluster File System (OCFS), RMAN is just as adept at backing up the datafiles.

RMAN certainly simplifies the backup and recovery strategies in any environment, even RAC. That being said, it is worth noting some unique backup and recovery challenges of the cluster database.

RMAN Configuration for the Cluster

There are configuration decisions that must be made prior to implementing an RMAN backup strategy for the RAC database. These decisions are predicated on how the backup will proceed, and then how the recovery will proceed.

RMAN makes an Oracle Net Service connection to a node in the database. This connection must be a dedicated connection that is not configured for failover or load balancing across the cluster. In other words, RMAN does not connect to the cluster—it connects to one node in the cluster. All RMAN server processes related to job building, controlfile access, and controlfile updates will reside at the node of connection. However, when you allocate channels for a backup job to occur, you can allocate channels at each node in the cluster by specifying a connect string in the channel allocation command.

```
allocate channel x1 type sbt connect sys/password@node1;
allocate channel x2 type sbt connect sys/password@node2;
```

And so on. In this way, you can distribute the workload of a backup operation across the nodes of the cluster. The decision to put a single node in charge of backup operations, or to share the work across all (or some) nodes, is an architectural decision you must make based on how you use the nodes in your cluster. It might make sense in some environments to restrict backup overhead to a less-used node in the cluster; likewise, if you have a well-tuned load-balancing technique for all nodes, distributing the backup workload evenly might make the most sense. We discuss the consequences further, as it pertains to datafile and archivelog backups, later in this chapter.

The Snapshot Controlfile in RAC Environments

You will need to move the snapshot controlfile to a shared location, if you plan on running backups from more than one node. If you do not move the snapshot to a shared file system like OCFS, then you must make sure that the local destination is identical on all nodes. To see the snapshot controlfile location, you can use the show command:

```
rman> show snapshot controlfile name;
```

To change the value, use the configure command.

```
rman> configure snapshot controlfile name to
        '/u02/oradata/grid10/snap_grid10.scf';
```

Datafile Backup

Datafiles can be backed up from any node in the cluster, as they are shared between instances anyway. So, you can run a datafile backup from any node, or from all nodes, and not run into any problems.

If you are backing up to tape, you must configure your third-party SBT interface at each node that will have channels allocated for backup. If you only back up from a single node, then only that node will have to be configured with the media management layer. But if you allocate channels across all nodes, the media management layer must be configured at each node.

If you are backing up to disk without using a flashback recovery area, you would most likely want to configure a shared disk location on which to write your backups, so that if a node is lost, the backups taken at any node will be available to any other node. You could do this through NFS mounts, if you do not use OCFS.

Archivelog Backup

Archivelog backup strategies are where it gets a little sticky. This is because every node generates its own thread of archivelogs, which typically pile up on the local disks of each node. Because RMAN connects to only one node, but reads a shared controlfile that lists all archivelogs, RMAN will fail when it tries to back up archivelogs that exist on unreachable disks of other nodes.

```
RMAN-6089: archived log <name> not found or out of sync with catalog
```

Chapter 4 provided an overview of configuring archivelogs for the RAC cluster. Depending on which solution you chose, the backup of those archivelogs will differ.

Archivelogs Going to Shared OCFS Volume   This is, by far, the simplest and most elegant solution for archivelogs in a RAC/Linux environment. If you archive logs from all nodes to a shared volume running Oracle Clustered File System, you can connect to any node in your cluster and be able to back up archivelogs that are produced by every node. If you use this methodology, the RMAN backup command is simple, and you can allocate a channel at each node to perform archivelog backups (for load sharing only), or you can use a single node.

```
backup archivelog all delete input;
```

The delete input command means that after RMAN backs up the archivelogs, it will delete those files that it just backed up. See more in the "Archivelog Housekeeping with RMAN" section below for archivelog maintenance.

Archivelogs Available via NFS Mounts   If you have set up a configuration that archives logs from each node to every other node, you still should be able to back up the archivelogs from any node. Using this methodology, you can run your backup with channels allocated all at a single node, or you can spread the load out across all nodes for load balancing.

If you use NFS to archive logs from every node to a single *repository* node, the repository node must serve as the node to which RMAN connects for backups. In such an environment, you would need to allocate all the channels for archivelog backup at the same repository node for the channel processes to have access to all the archivelogs required for backup.

Archivelogs to Local Disks Only   If you choose to stay in the stone age of clustering, and continue to produce archivelogs for each thread only at the local node level, you will be required to allocate backup channels at each node in order to perform an archivelog backup. This is not that big of a deal, really, except that there are significant consequences during recovery. We talk about that in the recovery section coming up.

Archivelog Housekeeping with RMAN   The archivelog backup command will check v$archived_log for all archivelogs with a status of A (for available), and then back them up. If the archivelog record has a status of D (deleted) or X (expired), then RMAN will not attempt to back up that archivelog. There is a widely held misperception that RMAN determines which archivelogs to back up by checking the log_archive_ dest for available files. This is not the case. RMAN uses views in the controlfile to determine the status and availability, and these views can only be updated by RMAN. So if you clean out archivelogs at the OS level (instead of using RMAN), the archivelog backup will fail as it tries to back up nonexistent files, and will give the same RMAN-20242 error mentioned above when trying to back up archivelogs inaccessible on other nodes.

It is highly recommended that you use RMAN to clean up after your archivelogs even if you don't use RMAN to back them up. Not only does RMAN mark the status of the archivelogs in the controlfile (something you can *only* do with RMAN), but RMAN will also never delete an archivelog while it is being written by the ARC*n* process. It knows more about the archivelogs than any other utility.

If you use RMAN to back up archivelogs, we highly recommend using the delete input command at some level to automate archivelog cleanout. That said, you may want to back up archivelogs, but not delete them immediately—in the case of recovery, obviously, it's best to have them on disk, not tape. What you can do is automate a process that backs up archivelogs older than a certain number of days, and then deletes them:

```
backup archivelog until sysdate-7 delete input;
```

This will back up archivelogs older than seven days, then delete them. If you want to back up archivelogs up to the current point, but delete ones older than seven days, you can do that also, but it takes two separate commands:

```
backup archivelog all;
delete archivelog completed before sysdate -7;
```

The only problem with this approach is that if you run it every day, you will get approximately seven copies of every archivelog backed up to tape. This is because you back up all the archivelogs every day, but only delete any of them after seven days. So you can specify how many times to back up archivelogs, after which they will be skipped. Then you issue your delete command:

```
backup archivelog not backed up 2 times;
delete archivelog completed before sysdate -7;
```

You have now achieved archivelog maintenance nirvana: you back up every archivelog to tape twice, you keep the last few days' worth on disk, and you delete permanently from all backup locations archivelogs that are older than seven days.

From the RAC perspective, archivelog housekeeping follows all guidelines outlined above. In addition, remember that you may have issues of accessibility if you generate archivelogs at different nodes—make sure that you follow the same channel allocation rules you follow for backup when performing maintenance commands.

Thinking Forward to Recovery

The single-node connection that limits RMAN's connection to the RAC database determines how recovery proceeds. While the restore of the database files can occur from any node in the cluster, recovery is a different beast altogether. RMAN connects to a single node in the cluster, issues the recover command, and then goes looking for archivelogs to perform recovery. This session needs archivelogs from every thread in the cluster, meaning that it is looking locally at the node for archivelogs from every node. Figure 8-8 shows what the DBA at Horatio's Woodscrew Company did wrong in Chapter 1, and why his recovery caused so many headaches: he had each archivelog thread generated only at the local node.

There are multiple ways to deal with this situation. We recommend, again, that you run your RAC cluster on an Oracle Cluster File System (OCFS) configuration. With OCFS in use on your shared disk volumes, you can configure all the archivelog destinations for each node to a shared location that is visible to all nodes. If you use a flashback recovery area, put the FRA on the shared OCFS disk pronto: life will be very, very good to you (FRA on CFS is discussed next).

If you are not using CFS, and instead are using uncooked volumes for your shared disk location, you no doubt have decided against putting your archivelogs on the raw partitions because of the administrative impossibility of it all. Instead, all of your archivelogs are being created locally at each node; or you have implemented an NFS multiple archive destination solution to stream a copy of all archivelogs to each node—or to a single recovery node.

The secret to successful recovery when you have archivelogs on cooked, local file systems is the ability to successfully NFS mount the log archive destination of all

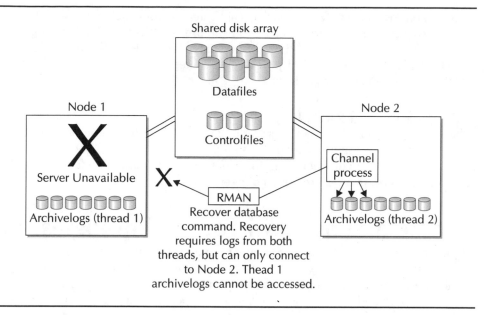

FIGURE 8-8.   *The doomed archivelog configuration*

nodes by the single node that is performing recovery. With node failure a real issue in most environments, here are your rules to live by:

1. You need to push your archivelogs from each node to *at least one other node*. Otherwise, you've given yourself a single point of failure.

2. Ensure that every log_archive_dest that you have configured for each node is uniquely named, so that you can NFS mount it from any other node.

3. Use RMAN to back up your archivelogs. RMAN can always write archivelogs to whatever location you specify, and when it does, these archivelogs are usable by the recovery session RMAN implements. So you can worry a little less about your complicated archiving strategy.

Flashback Recovery Area for RAC

It is extremely advantageous to use the flashback recovery area, but even more so in a clustered environment. The FRA can ease the headaches associated with multithread archivelog generation, as well as provide simplicity during stressful recovery situations. With a shared FRA (using OCFS), you can set your log_archive_dest of each node to a shared location that is accessible by all other nodes. You can also employ a backup strategy where backups are spread across each node, and the backups still go to a single location, or you can use a single-node backup strategy. With the FRA in place, you can have the backups accessible to all other nodes if a node failure occurs, regardless of your backup strategy. The benefits are simplicity in design and availability as the goal.

Tape Backups and RAC Nodes

Whether you use an FRA or not, it is worth noting that if you plan on backing up to tape, you should configure your vendor's media management interface at each node in the cluster. Even if you back up from a single node, if that one node fails, you may need to perform a restore from a different node.

Oracle and Split-Mirror Technologies

We decided to include this section simply because more and more database administrators are walking away from meetings knowing that split-mirror technologies are about to seriously impact their day-to-day life. And split mirrors are being leveraged, more and more, as sites for backups to occur, so it's worth mentioning split-mirror technology in this RMAN chapter.

The Split-Mirror Configuration

If you haven't been subjected to this yet, let's sum up: *split-mirror technologies* refers to vendor solutions that use a specific hardware configuration that mirrors all writes to a disk volume. At certain intervals, the mirrors are broken, such that the writes continue to one of the volumes, but the second volume is frozen in time at the moment of the split.

Meanwhile, a third volume is "resilvered" with the primary volume, so that a mirror exists again. The split mirror sits idle, waiting for a possible failure to occur, in which case the system administrator can failover to the broken mirror, making it the primary volume. After a predetermined amount of time ticks by, the primary and the third volume are split, and the second mirror is "resilvered" back to the primary. See Figure 8-9 for a look at this solution.

The benefits of this technology are, essentially, the following:

- The failover to the split-mirror volume, in case of a problem at the primary, is immediate.

- The need for backups is eliminated, as a fallback always exists that is immediately accessible.

- If backups are needed, they can be taken from the split mirror, so there is no hit at the primary volume site.

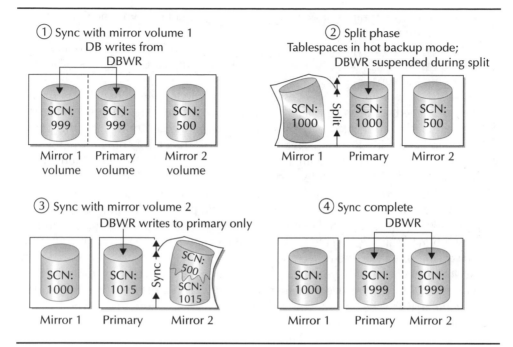

FIGURE 8-9. *Sync and split fail-safes*

To use split-mirror technology successfully with an Oracle database, it is required that, prior to the mirror split, every tablespace in the database be placed into hot backup mode first. This is required because, despite what the vendor tells you, the mirror split is not a singular event. It is more like peeling a banana: it starts in one place, and progresses to the end. While fast, it is not occurring at the same time across the entire volume. Therefore, it is possible that a write is occurring to the primary volume database, but the write only occurs at the bottom of the unpeeled secondary volume.

To cope with this problem, the hot backup gives Oracle a safety valve, in the form of "before image" data blocks in the redo stream. That way, if the split-mirror copy of a datafile is copied back to the primary to perform recovery, any corruption due to the mirror peel will be overwritten during the recovery of the file at the primary.

RMAN Backups from the Split Mirror

With increasing frequency, it is becoming apparent to DBAs with split-mirror investments that an additional layer of protection is required, in the form of RMAN backups of the database. With an idle copy of the database simmering on the back burner of the split mirror, a light bulb appears above the DBAs head: he or she should just mount the split-mirror drive onto a different server, and take the RMAN backup from the split mirror directly to tape (or a different disk volume that can be mounted on the primary).

Great idea! Sounds simple enough, right? Well... there's a few tricky points that need to get worked out first; otherwise, you will have the case of the mysteriously disappearing backups.

Here's the problem: RMAN accesses the controlfile to determine what to back up, and after the backup is complete, it updates the controlfile with the details of the backup. If you are connected to a split-mirror copy of the controlfile, it is this copy that gets updated with the details about the backup. So then, of course, when you go to resilver the split volume with the primary, the controlfile is overwritten with the data in the primary controlfile, and the backup data is lost forever.

The solution, you figure, is to use a recovery catalog when you back up at the split mirror. A sound, logical decision: after the backup is complete, the split volume controlfile is updated with the backup records, which are then synchronized to the catalog. Then it's simply a matter of syncing the catalog with the primary volume so that the backups can be used. Too cool!

So let's say you do this: you back up from the secondary volume, you sync the backup records to your recovery catalog, and then you connect RMAN to the primary volume database and to the catalog. You perform a resync. And this is where things get really, really weird. Sometimes, when you try to perform an operation, you get the error

```
RMAN-20035: invalid high recid
```

Other times, things work just fine it seems, but the backups you took at the split-mirror database have disappeared from the recovery catalog.

The problem, now, has become the internal mechanism of how RMAN handles record building in the controlfile and the recovery catalog. Every record that is generated gets a record ID (RECID), which is generated at the controlfile. When the backup occurs at the split-mirror DB, the controlfile gets its high RECID value updated, and this info gets passed to the catalog. But the recid at the primary database controlfile has not been updated, necessarily. So when you connect to the catalog and the primary DB, if the catalog's high recid is higher than the one in the controlfile, you get the "invalid high recid" error. If the recid in the catalog is lower than the recid of the primary database controlfile, RMAN initiates an update of the catalog that effectively eliminates all the records since the last sync operation with the primary cfile. Poof! Backup records from the split volume are gone.

The solution to this problem is to set the controlfile at the split mirror to become a backup controlfile. If RMAN detects that it is backing up from a noncurrent controlfile (backup or standby), it does not increment the recid in the catalog, so that the records are available after a resync with the current controlfile at the primary database.

HA Workshop: *Configure RMAN to Back Up from the Split Mirror*

Workshop Notes

This workshop assumes that you put all the tablespaces into hot backup mode (a requirement) during the period of the split. After the split, you connect the split volume to a new server that has Oracle Database 10*g* installed, and you now want to take an RMAN backup. Because RMAN will give an error if files are in backup mode, you will need to manually end backup for every file, as shown. It's best to write a script for this. This workshop also assumes that you split the archivelog destination and bring it across to the clone at the same time for archivelog backup.

Step 1. Mount the database on the clone server, and prepare the controlfile for RMAN backup.

```
startup mount;
alter database datafile 1 end backup; --- you will need to do this for
every file
recover database using backup controlfile until cancel;
cancel
exit
```

Step 2. Connect RMAN to the clone instance (as the target), and to the recovery catalog, and run the datafile backup.

```
rman target /
rman> connect catalog rman/password@rman_cat_db
rman> backup database plus archivelog not backed up two times;
```

Step 3. Connect RMAN to the production database (as the target) and the catalog, and perform a sync operation and archivelog cleanup, and then back up the controlfile.

```
rman target /
rman> connect catalog rman/password@rman_cat_db
rman> resync catalog;
rman> delete archivelog completed before sysdate -7;
rman> backup controlfile;
```

Use DG Instead

The bottom line, from our perspective, is that if you can interject yourself into the conversation about hardware configuration before the decision is made, you should encourage your sys admins to look into a Data Guard configuration instead of sync and split hardware modeling. If the entire purpose of the sync and split is for the hardiness of the Oracle database, you probably would save money and add other functionality by switching to a DG model instead. A combined Data Guard, RMAN, and Flashback Database configuration will provide the same functionality as split-mirror technology, without the proprietary hardware costs. You still get disaster recovery, off-loaded backup I/O, and a fallback database position that is quickly implemented. But you can lay it all down on commodity-priced servers.

CHAPTER
9

Oracle Flashback: Surviving User-Induced Trauma

328 Oracle Database 10g High Availability

 edia recovery, as outlined in Chapter 8, provides us with safeguards against all kinds of unforeseeable problems—block corruption, hardware failure, even complete database loss. But what you may have noticed is that Chapter 8 didn't talk at all about the largest cause of media recovery operations: user error.

We know. We *know*. User-induced outages are the most frustrating, because we expect humans to catch their own mistakes, whereas hard drives and motherboards all fail. They just do. But user errors happen, too, and the HADBA must do something about them.

User errors can be roughly defined as errors caused by a human mistake, rather than a software or hardware malfunction: table updated with wrong values, table dropped, table truncated. They are the kinds of errors that, in our honest moments, we realize that everyone makes, but in the heat of an outage, we need to know *who* did *what* and just how soon can they be verbally reprimanded by someone important.

Prepared for the Inevitable: Flashback Technology

As an HADBA, though, our energies our best spent preparing for the inevitable user-induced problem. And media recovery should not be our first line of attack; typically, user error is not something that we can recover from because the action is not interpreted as an error by the database. "Delete * from scott.emp" is not an error; it's a perfectly legitimate DML statement that is duly recorded in the redo stream. So if you restore the datafile and then perform recovery, all you will do is, well, delete * from scott.emp again. Point-in-time recovery can be a solution, but not for the HADBA committed to avoiding full restore of the database—way too much outage. Tablespace-point-in-time-recovery (TSPITR) offered a toned-down version of media recovery for user error, but it still required a full outage on the tablespace, had huge space demands for a temporary clone instance, and didn't work for all objects.

To make up for the frightening lack of options afforded a DBA when faced with user-induced database trauma, Oracle introduces in Oracle Database 10g the concept of Flashback Technology. Flashback Technology refers to a suite of features that allow a multitude of different ways to survive user errors. They have as a unifying concept only the simple idea that user errors occur, and recovering from them should be simple and fast. The Flashback features are

- Flashback Query
- Flashback Table

- Flashback Drop
- Flashback Database

Flashback Query

If you recognize Flashback Query from Oracle9*i*, you're right: there was some Flashback Query functionality that existed in Oracle 9*i*. In Oracle Database 10*g*, that functionality has been expanded and simplified to allow you better access. Read: no more PL/SQL interface. Now, it's all built in into SQL so you don't have to program a PL/SQL block to look at historical versions of a row.

Flashback and the Undo Segment: A Love Story

The first two types of flashback—Flashback Query and Flashback Table—have their functionality based entirely on technology that has existed in the Oracle database for years: the undo segments (or the segments formerly known as rollback). Undo segments exist in order to undo transactions that have not been committed. In the past, a committed transaction could not be undone because the associated before image of the row in the rollback was freed up to be overwritten.

This is still true: when you commit a transaction, the extent in the undo segment that contains the before image of the row is freed up to be overwritten. However, changes in the way undo space was used in Oracle 9*i* mean that all new transactions look for unused space in the undo tablespace before overwriting previously used segments. Even then, it always goes to the oldest remaining extents first. This means that before images of rows in the database last far longer than they ever have in the past.

This is all very good news, and in Oracle 9*i* and later, Oracle put it to use with the Flashback Query. Now the DBA can actually control how long he or she wants the undo extents to remain before they are overwritten. After doing so, we can put undo to good use—to help us undo committed transactions that were mistakes.

The ability to query or change objects back to a certain time in the past is predicated on how long our undo extents can remain in the undo tablespace before they are overwritten. Undo extents are used by new transactions based on space pressure in the undo tablespace. Basically, Oracle will not overwrite undo extents until it has exhausted all other possibilities first—that is, until every extent in the undo tablespace has been utilized. Then, it finds the oldest extent and overwrites it. The threshold for how far back you can use a Flashback Query or Flashback Table is set by how long Oracle can go from the time a transaction is committed until the time that undo extents for that transaction get overwritten. The period from committed transaction to undo extent being overwritten is the flashback window.

There are plenty of factors that go into determining the flashback window, but the most important is your transaction load. You can view statistics for undo usage with the view V$UNDOSTAT. Each row in this view represents the number of undo blocks utilized for a ten-minute period. Running a few analyses of this view through peak usage should provide a decent template by which to guide your settings for undo.

Setting Undo Parameters for Flashback Query and Flashback Table

The guidelines for using Flashback Query demand that you first have automatic undo enabled—no rollback segments are allowed. (Okay, that's a lie. It is feasible to use flashback operations with old-school rollback segments, but Oracle discourages it and so do we. There is no reason to try and set up rollback segments manually anymore.) Oracle is best left to control undo management using new algorithms that emphasize retention of transactional history—algorithms that do not exist in rollback segments. Therefore, you need to set UNDO_MANAGEMENT = AUTO in the pfile or spfile. Second, set your UNDO_TABLESPACE parameter to point to which tablespace will handle undo duties. Finally, you set UNDO_RETENTION = value in seconds. This sets the desired length of time to keep undo segments around.

Performing Flashback Query

Performing a Flashback Query of a table is simple, now that it has been integrated into SQL. All you need to know is the time in the past when you would like to view the contents of a table, and then you plug it into your query:

```
select scr_id, head_config from ws_app.woodscrew as of timestamp
  to_timestamp('2003-12-01 09:40:00','YYYY-MM-DD HH:MI:SS')
where scr_id=1001;

    SCR_ID HEAD_CONFIG
---------- --------------------
      1001 Phillips
      1001 Phillips
```

You can also use an SCN qualifier, if you know the System Change Number (SCN) of the change you are looking for:

```
select scr_id, head_config from ws_app.woodscrew
as of scn 751652 where scr_id=1001;

    SCR_ID HEAD_CONFIG
---------- --------------------
      1001 Slot
      1001 Slot
```

Flashback Versions Query with Enterprise Manager

Implementing Flashback Query—and its relatives, Flashback Transaction Query and Flashback Versions Query—is far simpler when you use Enterprise Manager (EM). EM allows you to quickly turn a Flashback Query into an operation that can undo a user-induced error, whether through a Flashback Table or through applying the undo SQL for the bad transaction.

Enterprise Manager combines the best features of multiple technologies to provide a user interface that helps you get answers quickly. Underneath the covers, it uses transaction queries to build a more complete investigation into what logical errors have occurred. The first of these is flashback version query, which also is referred to as row history. Version query provides the ability to look at every version of a row that existed within a specified time frame. So, you provide a query to look at a row, and a time frame that you want to review, and Oracle returns a list of every iteration that row has been through. This allows you to see a row morph over time in order to determine what may be at the root of the problem.

HA Workshop: *Exploring Flashback Versions Query*

Workshop Notes

This workshop requires a few tables be built, and populated with a few dummy rows, so that you can watch Flashback Versions Query in action. Here is the DDL and DML for the Woodscrew table and indices. We also build a secondary table with rows for future use in Flashback Drop and Flashback Database. You are obviously not compelled to use our simplistic little test here, and could easily test with existing dummy tables in your system.

```
create table woodscrew (
scr_id          number not null,
manufactr_id    varchar2(20) not null,
scr_type        varchar2(20),
thread_cnt      number,
length          number,
head_config     varchar2(20));

alter table woodscrew add primary key
 (scr_id, manufactr_id) using index;

create index woodscrew_identity on woodscrew
(scr_type, thread_cnt, length, head_config);

create table woodscrew_inventory (
 scr_id          number not null,
```

```
manufactr_id      varchar2(20) not null,
warehouse_id      number not null,
locale            varchar2(20),
count             number,
lot_price     number);

insert into woodscrew values (
1000, 'Tommy Hardware', 'Finish', 30, 1.5, 'Phillips');
insert into woodscrew values (
1000, 'Balaji Parts, Inc.', 'Finish', 30, 1.5, 'Phillips');
insert into woodscrew values (
1001, 'Tommy Hardware', 'Finish', 30, 1, 'Phillips');
insert into woodscrew values (
1001, 'Balaji Parts, Inc.', 'Finish', 30, 1, 'Phillips');
insert into woodscrew values (
1002, 'Tommy Hardware', 'Finish', 20, 1.5, 'Phillips');
insert into woodscrew values (
1002, 'Balaji Parts, Inc.', 'Finish', 20, 1.5, 'Phillips');
insert into woodscrew values (
1003, 'Tommy Hardware', 'Finish', 20, 1, 'Phillips');
insert into woodscrew values (
1003, 'Balaji Parts, Inc.', 'Finish', 20, 1, 'Phillips');

insert into woodscrew_inventory values (
1000, 'Tommy Hardware', 200, 'NORTHEAST', 3000000, .01);
insert into woodscrew_inventory values (
1000, 'Tommy Hardware', 350, 'SOUTHWEST', 1000000, .01);
insert into woodscrew_inventory values (
1000, 'Balaji Parts, Inc.', 450, 'NORTHWEST', 1500000, .015);
insert into woodscrew_inventory values (
1005, 'Balaji Parts, Inc.', 450, 'NORTHWEST', 1700000, .017);
commit;
```

Step 1.　Open up the Oracle Database 10*g* Enterprise Manager console and click on Administration | Schema | Tables. This opens up a view of all tables in the schema of the user you have logged in as. You can change this to the owner of the Woodscrew table by changing the Schema to the user and then clicking on Go. Then you can select the Woodscrew table and, from the drop-down list from Actions, choose View Data. Note in Figure 9-1 that the value for column HEAD_CONFIG is "Phillips" for all rows.

Step 2.　Change rows in the table to reflect a different head configuration for the woodscrews.

```
update woodscrew set head_config= 'Slot'
where scr_id=1001;
commit;
```

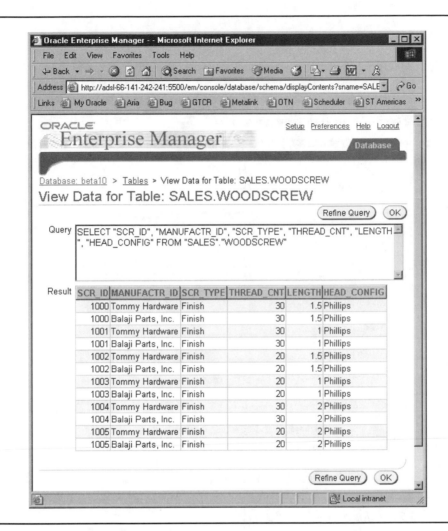

FIGURE 9-1. *Navigating to the table and viewing contents*

Step 3.   View the new data in the table. From Tables, select the Woodscrew table, choose View Data from the Actions drop-down list, and then click Go. Note in Figure 9-2 that two rows now have "Slot" instead of "Phillips."

Step 4.   It has been determined that the screws with scr_id 1001 are *not* slot-headed, but rather Phillips. There has been a logical corruption introduced into the database. Let's review a single row and see what versions the row has been through.

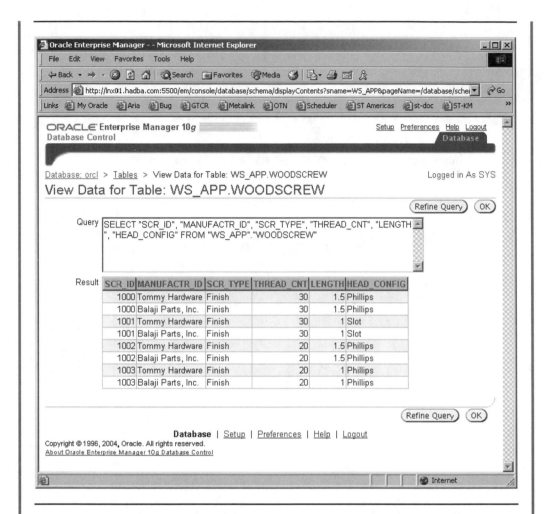

FIGURE 9-2. *Slot-headed screws*

From the Tables view, select the Woodscrew table; then from the Actions list, choose Flashback by Row Versions and then click Go.

Step 5. From here, we need to provide the parameters of our Flashback Query. First, choose all columns by selecting Move All under Step 1. Under Step 2, we need to specify a clause that isolates a single row. We will use the following WHERE clause:

```
where scr_id=1001 and manufactr_id='Tommy Hardware'
```

We then choose the time frame for our row history exploration. You can choose to Show All Row History or specify a specific time frame. All Row History shows all versions of the row that still exist in the undo tablespace. In Figure 9-3, we see the results of our query, with the transaction that updated the two rows.

Step 6. From this view, we can continue with the wizard and perform a flashback of the table. But we now know all the different operations that have occurred against this row in the database.

Step 7. If you want proof that Enterprise Manager is working hard for you, click back to the Recovery: Row History Filter page. At the bottom is a button for Show Flashback Versions Query SQL, as shown in Figure 9-4. Click on this button and take a look at the SQL you are blissfully ignoring.

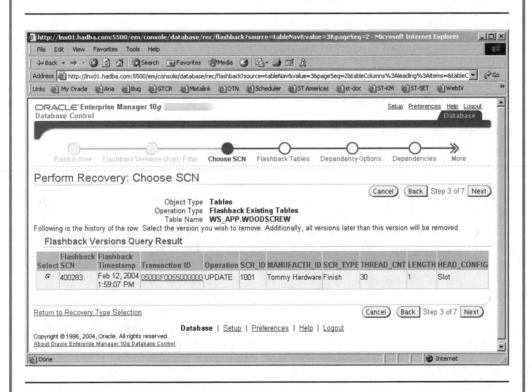

FIGURE 9-3. *All versions of the row*

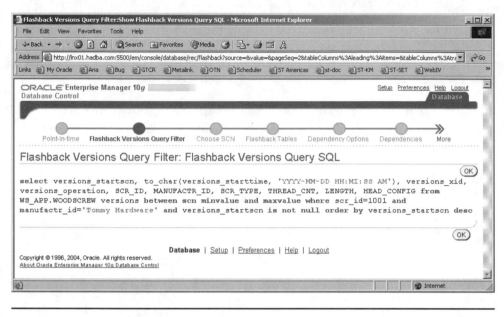

FIGURE 9-4. *Flashback Versions Query SQL*

Flashback Transaction Query

There's always more than one way to skin a cat, and there's more than one way to organize a manhunt for bad data in the database. Flashback Transaction Query allows you to look at all changes made by a specific transaction, or all transactions in a certain time frame. Then you can go in and undo just a subset of the transaction, instead of the entire transaction being undone and then redone.

Again, the best way to use Transaction Query is through Enterprise Manager. Save yourself the grief and log into the EM Console for the database and use the same set of operations described in the HA Workshop "Exploring Flashback Versions Query."

Flashback Transaction Query is compelling because it allows the HADBA to review a bad transaction in its entirety, even though the window into the error may be only a single row. For instance, if we found a row of our Woodscrew table had been deleted, we could look up that row in Flashback Versions Query. Then, we can get the Transaction ID for the DELETE operation and see how many other rows were deleted at the same time. This provides a means by which to get a look at the full scope of the problem.

But we can also take it a step further, as Oracle has built into Enterprise Manager the ability to review the UNDO SQL statement for each row affected in the transaction.

So, for the delete against Woodscrew, each deleted row would be displayed with an INSERT statement that would replace the missing row in the table. In this fashion, you can correct an error without necessarily undoing the entire transaction—perhaps you meant to delete one row, but your SQL was incorrect and you deleted two rows. With EM, you can undo one delete and leave the other in place. Let's take a look.

HA Workshop: *Explore Flashback Transaction Query*

Workshop Notes
This workshop is an extension of the workshop "Exploring Flashback Versions Query" in the previous section. The same Woodscrew table is used.

Step 1.   Introduce a fault into the Woodscrew table.

```
SQL> delete from woodscrew where scr_id='1001';
commit;
```

Step 2.   Someone querying for a one-inch finish woodscrew manufactured by Tommy notices that the screw has been deleted from the database, even though these are still offered by the company to customers. What happened? We turn to the EM Administration I Schema I Tables page. Choose the owner of the Woodscrew table and click on Go.

Step 3.   Select the Woodscrew table; then from the Actions list, choose Flashback Transaction History and click Go.

Step 4.   Choose all columns, and then put a WHERE clause in to set the boundary of our inquiry. We will use the WHERE clause of the user who encountered the fault:

```
where scr_id=1001 and manufactr_id='Tommy Hardware'
```

   Then choose a time frame (we use All Row History for this example) and click Next.

Step 5.   You are looking at a row history report, as you would for Flashback Row History. To review the transaction, click on the transaction ID for the DELETE operation. You are now looking at the entire transaction that included the delete of our specified row, as shown in Figure 9-5. What is useful is that we can note here any other rows that were also impacted by this transaction, to determine if we need to fix just the one row or multiple rows.

Step 6. You will also note in Figure 9-5 that the undo SQL is provided for each row change that occurred as part of the transaction. This allows us to undo part of the transaction instead of the entire transaction, if desired. We can simply cut and paste the undo SQL into SQL*plus to undo the corruption.

```
SQL> insert into "WS_APP"."WOODSCREW"
("SCR_ID","MANUFACTR_ID","SCR_TYPE",
"THREAD_CNT","LENGTH","HEAD_CONFIG")
values
('1001','Tommy Hardware','Finish','30','1','Slot');
```

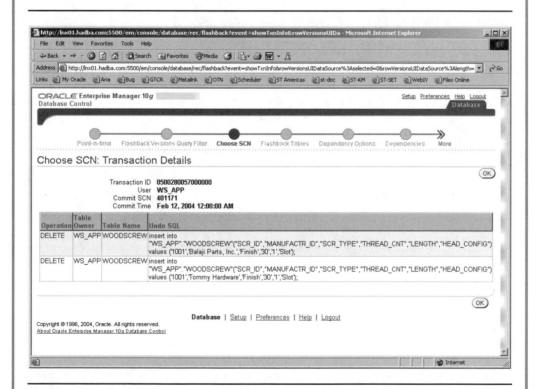

FIGURE 9-5. *Transaction information*

Flashback Table

Perhaps the most compelling of the Flashback Technologies is the ability to simply revert a table to a previous point in time in a simple and straightforward fashion. The ability to perform point-in-time recovery on a table or group of tables has often been the grounds by which entire clone databases are built—just so that a single table could be extracted and then imported back into production. Those days are long gone, we're happy to say!

Flashback Table employs the same mechanisms as Flashback Query—with information stored in the undo segments, Oracle can rewind a database one transaction at a time to put the table back the way it was at a specified time in the past. Because Flashback Table depends on undo, the same restrictions apply: you can only flashback a table as far back as the undo segments allow you.

In addition to undo, the ability to flashback a table requires you to enable row movement for the table. Row movement was initially put in place as a function of partitioned tables, which allowed an updated row to move to the appropriate partition if the update changed the partition key value. Flashback Table employs row movement to assist in the rewind operations.

```
alter table woodscrew enable row movement;
```

Flashback Table cannot save you from all user errors. Certain DDL operations that occur against a table cannot be undone; most importantly, you cannot flashback a table to before a truncate table operation. This is because a truncate does not produce any undo—that is why truncate exists, versus a delete * from table. Also, Flashback Table cannot be used for a dropped table (use Flashback Drop for that—see the section "Flashback Drop").

Enabling Row Movement and Flashback Table

It is critical that you foresee possible Flashback Table candidates and enable row movement as soon as possible. You cannot enable row movement and then flashback the table to a point prior to enabling row movement. Such an operation will get you this error:

```
ORA-01466: unable to read data - table definition has changed
```

In other words, you cannot wait until you need to flashback a table, and then enable row movement as part of the flashback operation. Instead, you would probably want to use Flashback Transaction Query to manually undo each row change.

Performing the Flashback Table from SQL

With row movement enabled, you can move forward with normal operations on the table. Then, when a user-induced corruption occurs in the table, you can use SQL at the command line to perform the Flashback Table:

```
flashback table sales.woodscrew to timestamp
to_timestamp('2003-12-01 13:30:00','YYYY-MM-DD HH24:MI:SS')
```

Alternatively, you can use SCN if you know the SCN (through investigation via Flashback Query, for example):

```
flashback table sales.woodscrew to scn 751652;
```

Like Flashback Query, the performance of a Flashback Table operation is dependent on the amount of data that has to be rewound, and how far back you are rewinding. The more data that has to be undone, the longer the operation will take. But this will always be faster than the performance you can achieve by trying to perform a point-in-time recovery of the table by other methods: you can try tablespace point-in-time recovery, or you can try to restore the tablespaces to a different instance, and then export the table from the clone instance and import it back into production. Nothing can come close to Flashback Table.

Flashback Table with Enterprise Manager

There is functionality inside Enterprise Manager to utilize the Flashback Table feature. The added strength of EM for Flashback Table is the ability to first explore the table via Flashback Row History to determine exactly to what time you want to flash back. If you already know the exact time for flashback, using SQL at the command line would be just as simple as using the Flashback Table Wizard in EM. EM does, however, provide a way to determine what dependencies are at play.

HA Workshop: *Explore Flashback Table*

Workshop Notes
In this workshop, we will "accidentally" delete all the rows from the Woodscrew table, and then flashback the entire table to the point in time right before the DELETE transaction took place.

Step 1.   View the data in Woodscrew. Because of previous exercises, it might be worthwhile to truncate the table and then reinsert the records manually using the original population script (as shown earlier in the "Explore Flashback Versions

Query" HA workshop). Make sure you have all eight rows. Also, make sure you enable row movement prior to inserting the fault:

```
alter table woodscrew enable row movement;
```

Step 2.   Insert the fault. We will delete all the rows in the table using a SQL*Plus DELETE statement. Afterward, use the View Data action item in EM to view the empty table.

```
delete from woodscrew;
commit;
```

Step 3.   From EM | Administration | Schema | Tables, choose the Woodscrew table. Then, from the Action list choose Flashback Table and then click Go. This takes you into a Perform Recovery Wizard, which first asks you to "Specify the point in time to which to recover." Because we don't already know when the delete took place, choose to evaluate row changes and transactions—the first choice. Click on Next.

Step 4.   You will now see a familiar screen—the Flashback Versions Query interface. Here, we have to set our columns and a WHERE clause to narrow down our search. Because the delete affected all rows, we can choose a single row to review here. We will use the same row as in previous workshops.

```
where scr_id=1001 and manufactr_id='Tommy Hardware'
```

Now we can see the information about the DELETE operation that whacked our poor Woodscrew table, as shown in Figure 9-6.

Step 5.   You can click on the transaction ID to review the entire delete. However, of more importance to us is the Flashback SCN column, which shows us the SCN to set to undo the DELETE operation. With the appropriate DELETE transaction checked from the list, simply clicking on Next will automatically choose the flashback SCN specified on this screen.

Step 6.   On Step 4 of 7 in the Flashback Table Wizard, Oracle allows you to specify any logically related objects that should be rewound to the same SCN as this table. Oracle will automatically honor all constraints that exist for the table, but you may have logically related tables that should be flashed back. If so, this is your opportunity to specify them. In our example, we do not have any related tables, so click Next.

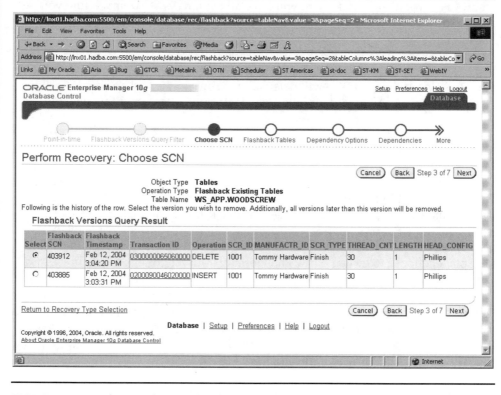

FIGURE 9-6. *The row history for the DELETE operation*

Step 7. Voila: we are magically transported to Step 7 of 7, where we see the summary of the action that will take place. Most useful here are the Show Row Changes and Show SQL buttons options, which will show what rows will be changed and what SQL will be executed by EM on your behalf. Click on Submit. If there is any problem, or if you just feel better about it, you can cut the EM-generated SQL into a SQL*Plus session to run the Flashback Table.

```
FLASHBACK TABLE SALES.WOODSCREW TO SCN 804109;
```

Flashback Drop

Flashback Drop allows you to "undrop" database objects. No longer will you have users desperate for the entire database to be restored to a point in the past because they thought they were on the dev instance instead of prod.

There's nothing all that dramatic about how Flashback Drop has been implemented. In Oracle Database 10g, when you drop a table, it merely gets renamed to a system-identifiable string, but the segment remains in the tablespace it was dropped from. It will remain there until you undrop the object or purge it manually, or until the tablespace runs of out space for regular objects. If space pressure exists in the tablespace, Oracle will begin to age out dropped objects from oldest to newest.

When you drop an object, Oracle doesn't just rename the object itself. All dependent objects move to the Recycle Bin as well: indices, triggers, and constraints. Therefore, when you undrop the table, its entire dependent chain comes back with it.

The Recycle Bin

The Recycle Bin is a virtual directory of all dropped objects in the database: nothing more than a list of objects that have been dropped but not purged. The Recycle Bin is a logical container, and does not require a specific storage location—actual storage for all dropped objects is in the tablespace the object was in prior to drop. Take an example: user matt drops the table ws_app.woodscrews. The Woodscrews table is in the tablespace WS_APP_DATA, but its two indices are in the WS_APP_IDX tablespace. When Woodscrews is dropped, the table is renamed to an internal name, and so are the two indices that existed on the table. Both appear in the DBA_RECYCLEBIN view. However, the actual Woodscrews table segment still exists in the WS_APP_DATA tablespace, and the indices still exist in the WS_APP_IDX tablespace. They are logically part of the Recycle Bin, but physically exist in the same place they always have.

The Recycle Bin is quickly viewed via data dictionary views:

- USER_RECYCLEBIN

- DBA_RECYCLEBIN

Purging the Recycle Bin

Manually eliminating dropped objects from the Recycle Bin is not necessary. Objects are purged from the Recycle Bin as the space is required by other segments in the tablespace. In other words, dropped objects continue to take up space in a tablespace until other objects in that tablespace run out of free space elsewhere. Then, the first dropped object is the first object to be purged. Oracle automatically looks to purge indices before tables, so that actual data is the last thing to be lost. Recycle Bin objects will also be dropped before a tablespace autoextends, if autoextend is on.

The new PURGE command exists to purge the Recycle Bin. You can purge by user, by object, by tablespace, or the entire bin.

```
purge table sales.woodscrews;
purge index sales.woodscrews_pk_idx;
purge tablespace sales;
purge recyclebin;
```

> ### How long do objects live in the Recycle Bin?
> A valid question, but the answer of course is: it depends. No, really. It depends. The real question you probably want to hear is, can I control how long an object lives in the Recycle Bin? The answer to this question is no.
>
> You cannot force an object to remain in the Recycle Bin, if space pressure exists in the tablespace of the dropped object. Even with autoextend on, the dropped object is purged before the TS extends. So, if you want to determine a certain lifespan on objects in the Recycle Bin, either you will be left to make the tablespace overly large to accommodate drops, or you can manually manage the Recycle Bin and purge those objects you don't want to keep in order to leave space for those you do.
>
> You can, therefore, shorten the stay of an object in the Recycle Bin. But you cannot force something to remain, given a shortage of tablespace room.

Undropping Objects in the Recycle Bin

Getting objects back from the Recycle Bin is pretty simple—a simple SQL command renames the object back to its original name, along with any dependent objects.

```
flashback table ws_app.woodscrews to before drop;
```

Of course, sometimes it's not that simple. For instance, if you have multiple dropped objects with the same name, then you would have to refer to the object by its new and improved Recycle Bin name.

```
SQL> select object_name, original_name, droptime, dropscn from user_recyclebin;
OBJECT_NAME                      ORIGINAL_NAME
-----------------------------    ---------------
DROPTIME             DROPSCN
-------------------- ----------
RB$$48623$INDEX$0                PK_WOODSCREW
2004-01-12:15:21:26  1241651
RB$$48622$TABLE$0                WOODSCREW
2004-01-12:15:21:26  1241652
SQL> flashback table " RB$$48622$TABLE$0" to before drop;
```

Note the quotes around the Recycle Bin object name. These are required due to special symbols in the name.

If you have dropped an object and then created a new object with the same name, you can still flashback the first object. There is syntax in the Flashback SQL to rename the object when you pull it from the Recycle Bin.

```
flashback table ws_app.woodscrews to before drop rename to woodscrews_history;
```

HA Workshop: *Explore Flashback Drop and the Recycle Bin*

Workshop Notes
Time to drop our Woodscrew table and review the Recycle Bin contents. While this can be done at the command line, our workshop will show how to undrop a table using EM.

Step 1. Drop the Woodscrew table. From EM | Administration | Schema | Tables, change the schema to the owner of the Woodscrew table. Select the Woodscrew table from the list of tables, and then click on the Delete button. A confirmation screen asks if you are sure about the drop, and you can click Yes.

Step 2. View the list of tables. Note that Woodscrew is no longer in the list. Click on the Recycle Bin link in the lower right-hand corner of the screen. First, under Search, enter the Schema Name of the owner of the Woodscrew table and click on Go.

Note that in Figure 9-7 the table Woodscrew is in the Recycle Bin, along with the primary key index and the WOODSCREW_IDENTITY index. Also worth note is the button on the right titled View Content. This button allows you to look at the rows in the dropped table to determine if it is the correct object to be flashback dropped.

Step 3. Click the radio button next to the Woodscrew table, and then click the Flashback Drop button. You will get a standard warning asking if you are sure.

Step 4. The next page (see Figure 9-8) offers you the ability to rename the undropped object. After you click Next, you get the impact analysis from EM explaining what exactly Flashback Drop will do.

Step 5. Click on Submit. Confirmation tells us the selected tables have been restored from the Recycle Bin. You can confirm this by navigating back to EM | Administration | Schema | Tables and choosing the schema of the Woodscrew owner. The Woodscrew table will be back in place.

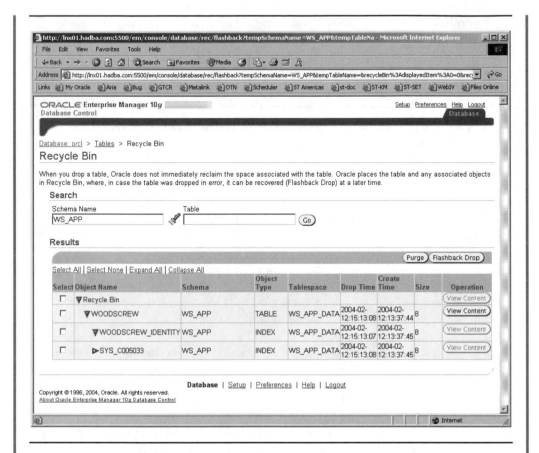

FIGURE 9-7. *The Recycle Bin of user WS_APP*

Step 6. Delete the Woodscrew table again. Click on Recycle Bin and find the dropped table again, as outlined in Step 2 above. Select Woodscrews, and then click on Purge (next to Flashback Drop).

Step 7. A confirmation screen asks you if you want to purge the selected objects and their dependents. Click on Continue. The Recycle Bin of the SALES user is now empty of the Woodscrew table and its indices. They have been permanently removed from the database.

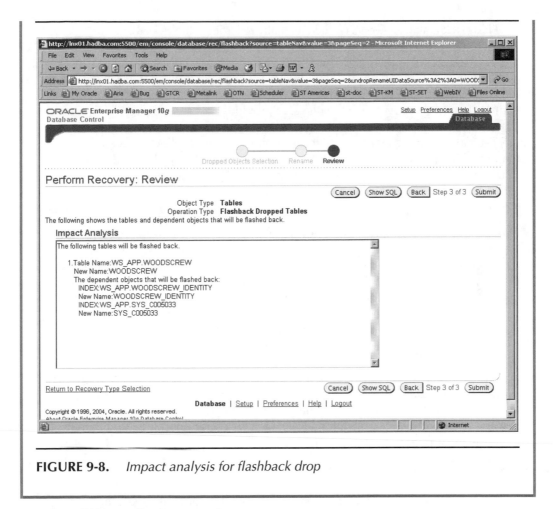

FIGURE 9-8. *Impact analysis for flashback drop*

Flashback Database

The most revolutionary Flashback Technology may also be the one that gets used the least often. Flashback Database provides the ability to quickly rewind the entire database to a previous point in time. This operation has as its end result that which you would get from doing point-in-time recovery using RMAN or user-managed recovery. However, Flashback Database does not require the restore of all of the database's datafiles from the most recent backup, followed by a roll-forward using all the archivelogs that have accumulated since that backup. By avoiding these costly operations, Flashback Database can perform a point-in-time recovery in a fraction of the time typically required for such an operation.

Flashback Database works by incrementally recording all blocks that have changed at a timed interval. These flashback "checkpoints" then provide the points to which the database can be "rewound." After rolling back to the flashback checkpoint, archivelogs can be used to then roll forward to the exact time or SCN specified by the FLASHBACK DATABASE command. So, the operation uses new technology as well as the old standby, the archivelogs, to provide a fast way to perform point-in-time-recovery.

Typically, there is less archival to be applied after a flashback checkpoint than must be applied to the last backup (typically taken every night, vs. every few minutes for flashback logs), so the recovery stage of flashback is very quick.

Flashback Logs

Flashback Database implements a new type of log, called the flashback log, which is generated by the database at regular intervals and accumulates in the flashback recovery area (FRA) you created in Chapter 8. You must have an FRA for Flashback Database; the logs cannot be created anywhere else. The flashback log contains a copied image of every block that has been changed since the last flashback log was generated. These blocks can then be reinstated into the database when a FLASHBACK DATABASE command is issued in order to rewind the database back to its state at the time specified in the FLASHBACK command.

Because entire blocks are being dumped to the flashback logs, they can accumulate very quickly in extremely active databases. Setting an appropriately sized FRA is crucial to the success of meeting your Flashback Database needs. In addition, you can manually turn off flashback logging for certain tablespaces that could be manually re-created after a Flashback Database operation, and thereby decrease the amount of logging that occurs.

```
alter tablespace ws_app_idx flashback off;
```

You can turn it back on at any time, but it is worth noting that you cannot rewind backward through a flashback logging gap for the tablespace you turned off.

```
alter tablespace sales_idx flashback on;
```

Any tablespace that has flashback logging turned off for any period of time within the FLASHBACK DATABASE command would need to be offlined prior to performing the Flashback Database.

Flashback Retention Target

The lifespan of flashback logs correlates directly to how far back in time you would like to have the Flashback Database option. By default, the flashback logs will be kept long enough so that you can always flashback 24 hours from the current time. If this is too long or too short of a time, you can change it with an init parameter:

```
alter system set db_flashback_retention_target=720;
```

The value is specified in minutes (720 would be 12 hours).

HA Workshop: *Configure for Flashback Database*

Workshop Notes
This workshop will walk you through the primary steps required to configure the database initially for using flashback logging for Flashback Database operations.

Step 1. Shut down the database and start up mount. The database must be mounted but not open.

```
SQL> select status from v$instance;
```

In addition, check to make sure the database is in archivelog mode. Archivelog mode is required for Flashback Database.

```
SQL> archive log list;
Database log mode              Archive Mode
Automatic archival             Enabled
Archive destination            USE_DB_RECOVERY_FILE_DEST
Oldest online log sequence     62
Next log sequence to archive   64
Current log sequence           64
```

Step 2. Set the flashback retention target to your desired value. We will use 12 hours as the window.

```
alter system set db_flashback_retention_target=720
SCOPE=BOTH SID='*';
```

Step 3. Set the values for db_recovery_file_dest and db_recovery_file_dest_size (flash recovery area parameters). Note that if you have already set these for your RMAN backup strategy as outlined in Chapter 8, you should review the parameters now. Flashback logs increase FRA usage significantly. It would behoove you to at least double the given size of the FRA.

```
SQL> ALTER SYSTEM SET DB_RECOVERY_FILE_DEST_SIZE = 2335825920
SCOPE=BOTH SID='*';
```

```
SQL> ALTER SYSTEM SET DB_RECOVERY_FILE_DEST = '/u02/fra/'
SCOPE=BOTH SID='*';
```

Step 4.   Turn flashback logging on. This is done in the same fashion as turning archivelog on—with an ALTER DATABASE command when the database is mounted but not open.

```
alter database flashback on;
```

Step 5.   Turn flashback logging off for any tablespaces that you deem do not require it.

```
alter tablespace sales_idx flashback off;
```

Step 6.   Open the database.

```
alter database open;
```

Flashback Database: Tuning and Tweaking

So, you've determined that Flashback Database provides you with a fallback position you desire for your database, and you have determined how far back you want your fallback position to be. You've set your db_flashback_retention_target. Now, the question comes up: how do I know if I have enough space in my flashback recovery area to handle the volume of flashback logs being generated? And, for that matter, how much flashback logging is occuring?

Using V$FLASHBACK_DATABASE_LOG

One thing at a time. First, Oracle provides built-in analysis for you to use in determining if you need to increase the size of your flashback recovery area (FRA). After you enable flashback logging, Oracle begins to keep track of the amount of flashback logging that is occuring, and stores it in the view V$FLASHBACK_DATABASE_LOG. This view actually provides an estimate for the total flashback size:

```
select estimated_flashback_size from v$flashback _database_log;
```

Note that this view gives the size for flashback logs, not for all users in the FRA, so you will need to add this value to whatever size you need for archivelogs and RMAN backups. This estimated value only gets better with age, meaning that as the database runs through its day-to-day (and then month-to-month) operations, Oracle can provide a better estimate of the size. So, it is a good idea to check back in with this estimator to find out if you still have the right specifications in place.

V$FLASHBACK_DATABASE_LOG also provides you with the actual oldest time that you can flashback the database to, given the current size of the FRA and the currently available flashback logs. You can use this as another indicator of space issues in the FRA.

```
select oldest_flashback_scn, oldest_flashback_time
from v$flashback_database_log;
```

Using V$FLASHBACK_DATABASE_STAT

Oracle has built a monitoring view so that you can keep your trained HADBA eye on flashback logging activity. V$FLASHBACK_DATABASE_STAT provides you with information on flashback data generated over the course of a period of time (typically, a one-hour window extending back from sysdate). In addition to showing how much flashback logging occurred, this view posts the redo generated and the actual database data generated over the same period.

```
select * from v$flashback_database_stat;
<output>
```

HA Workshop: *Perform Flashback Database*

Workshop Notes

It's time to give it a test drive. We are going to introduce a fault that cannot be handled by any of the other less intrusive forms of flashback: the table truncate. Because the truncate does not produce any redo, we cannot do a Flashback Table. So we are forced to do a flashback of the entire database.

Step 1.   First, get the current SCN from the database. Because we are simply testing, we can prepare for the test by getting the current SCN prior to putting the fault into the database.

```
SQL> select current_scn from v$database;
CURRENT_SCN
----------------
885524
```

Step 2.   Introduce the fault.

```
SQL> truncate table woodscrew;
Table truncated.
```

Step 3.   Shut down the database, and then remount. The database must be mounted and not open for flashback.

```
SQL> connect / as sysdba
Connected.
SQL> shutdown immediate;
Database closed.
Database dismounted.
ORACLE instance shut down.
SQL> startup mount;
```

Step 4.   Issue the FLASHBACK command.

```
SQL> flashback database to scn 885524;
Flashback complete.
```

Step 5.   Open the database read-only to confirm that the table has been flashed back to the appropriate SCN.

```
SQL> alter database open read only;
Database altered.
SQL> connect sales/sales;
Connected.
SQL> select count(*) from woodscrew;
  COUNT(*)
----------
        12
```

Step 6.   Open the database with resetlogs.

```
SQL> connect / as sysdba
SQL> shutdown immediate;
SQL> startup mount;
SQL> alter database open resetlogs;
```

Flashback Database: Opportunity for Different Uses

One of the most interesting things about Flashback Database is that the full set of uses won't be apparent to everyone until after it has been around a while. Flashback Database is quite literally a rewind button for the database. You can flashback to a certain point, and open the database read-only to have a look. If you haven't gone back far enough, you can do another flashback. Then, you can also use the database's existing "fast-forward" button—database recovery using archivelogs—to move forward, if you have flashed back too far into the past. So, when trying to come to terms with a user-induced trauma, you can move back and forth in the database until you isolate the perfect moment to open the database.

Flashback Database as a Historical Data Extraction Tool

Take the preceeding HA Workshop, "Perform Flashback Database." At Step 6, after we opened the database read-only and confirmed that the Woodscrew table was back, we opened the database with resetlogs. This would be required in most cases where we simply needed to get the database back up and operational in as little time as possible. All data generated after the flasback time would be sacrificed on the database altar.

But, there is another option. If you can live without the lost table until you can schedule emergency downtime (at end of business day, for instance), then you might be able to get the Woodscrew table back and not be forced to lose data from any other tables in the database. To do this, you would flashback until the appropriate time and then open the database read-only. Then, instead of opening resetlogs, you would use export to do a table-level dump of the Woodscrew table. After the export completed, you would only have to issue a RECOVER DATABASE command, and Oracle would fast forward to the time of the clean shutdown, and you could open the database and be back in business. There would have to be an outage of the entire system for the duration of the export, but it can be a decent trade-off to get data from a lost table and still retain the rest of the database data up to the current time.

Flashback Database for Standby Database Reinstantiation

Another intriguing possibility for Flashback Database comes in relation to the standby database function of your Data Guard implementation. The standby database can also be flashed to a previous time. Therefore, if you failover to the standby to overcome a logical failure, you can flashback the standby if the failure has already been propagated from the primary database.

Perhaps more compelling, Flashback Database can be used for standby database reinstantiation. When a failover occurs from the primary to the standby, in the past you have been forced to use backups to restore a copy of the new primary back to the old primary and make it a standby, and then fail back over. Now, you can instead use Flashback Database on the old primary to move it back to the exact SCN at which the standby database was at prior to activation. Then you set up the flow of archivelogs from the new primary to the old primary and give it a new standby controlfile, and you are back in business in minutes.

PART
IV

Distributed Database Solutions

CHAPTER
10

Oracle Streams for
High Availability

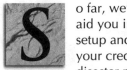o far, we've offered some exposure to internal database features that aid you in the struggle for availability. You have been through the setup and administration of a RAC environment. You have confirmed your credentials as a true paranoid by configuring a Data Guard disaster protection scheme. You've got your media backups humming along with RMAN, and you've tested out the Flashback technologies to save you from your users. All of these solutions armor you against downtime, working together to provide a complete high-availability solution for your database.

But there's this other thing. This kinda new thing. This kinda cool thing. It does not act like any of the HA technologies we've espoused to this point. It can complement any of them, or be used in their stead. It provides a slightly different approach to availability that emphasizes distribution of database activities. Oracle calls it Streams.

Streams, as a term, actually applies to a larger set of functionality within Oracle that has nothing to do, at its core, with availability. Streams is really a queuing technology, referred to frequently as *advanced queuing*. The queuing nature of Streams resembles any queuing architecture that you may already have been exposed to: it is a publish/subscribe approach to event management. But on top of the queue structure, you can create a robust and extremely advanced solution for data sharing and load balancing that distributes data across multiple independent and available databases.

When used in this fashion, Streams typically gets called Streams replication, and while it is primarily a data-sharing technology, it can be used as a highly customizable availability solution. But we should make something very clear: Streams is not an "out of the box" experience. Streams requires a larger ongoing commitment to the specifics of your environment than any other HA solution that we have described this far. However, with a little elbow grease and some ingenuity, Streams may just be the future of your HA world.

Given the complexity of Streams, we will keep things very simple in this chapter, and cover the primary topics of importance where Streams can be used for availability. For all other Streams topics, we defer to Oracle's complete Streams documentation set as referenced in the bibliography.

Streams at a Glance

The Streams technology lies on top of a queuing architecture. At its most basic, Streams is a methodology for gathering events, storing them in a queue, and then publishing those events to different subscribers. The power of this, from our perspective, is that Streams captures *events* from the redo log being produced by an Oracle database. As such, Streams has access to every database change that occurs, and can pass that information to another database—propagating, or replicating, the database changes, across the network to multiple databases.

When Streams is configured, an Oracle background process, known as a capture process, will read through the redo stream and gather the DML and DDL statements that it finds. Streams converts these statements into a specific format called a logical change record (LCR). When it comes from the redo log, an LCR is an atomic row change, and it's important to note that a transaction can be made up of one or more LCRs, depending on how many rows are affected by the transaction. Once converted into an LCR, Streams stores the DML or DDL event in a queue table. From this queue table, the LCRs can be propagated to another queue table in the same database or a different database. Finally, an apply process translates the LCR and applies it to the corresponding database object in the new database. Figure 10-1 illustrates this model.

What's important to note here is that Streams is turning DML and DDL operations from your database redo log into logical records that can be passed to another database. In the process of making the pass, you (as the DBA) are provided the opportunity to filter, manipulate, or change the logical record to meet your business demands. The power of this lies in your ability to very closely control how data is propagated from one database to another.

Hey, Isn't This What Advanced Replication Is For?

Yes. advanced replication does almost exactly what Streams does (although without all the control). Replication, however, is trigger-based; this means that if you want to replicate a particular object from one database to another, you must set up a trigger

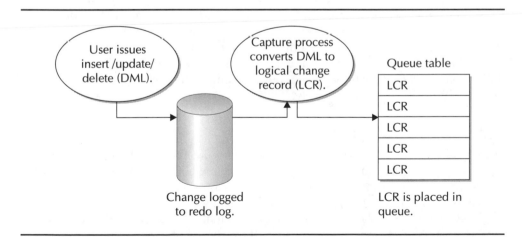

FIGURE 10-1. *Streams translates the redo stream into LCRs in a queue table*

on the table to fire on each DML action. The trigger then adds the same row to a stage table. This stage table gets its contents pushed periodically to another database. This process can be very expensive.

Streams, on the other hand, utilizes the records about DML that are already being recorded in the redo log, so no further activity at the source database is required. You can turn on Streams replication for one object or the entire database. The workload falls almost entirely to the destination database, which must translate the redo logs from the source into LCRs and then queue/dequeue and apply them. So, Streams can replicate data in a much more efficient manner than advanced replication, in addition to providing a better level of control over the process.

Streams divides the workload into three separate operations (more or less): capture, propagation, and apply.

Streams Capture Process

The capture process is responsible for executing the first stage of a Streams configuration. The capture process must check the DML and DDL records in the redo log and evaluate them for possible capture. The evaluation process checks against the rule set that has been set up for the capture process. Rules are database objects that you set up to determine what type of change events you want to extract from the redo logs. Based on the rule set, the capture process extracts the appropriate changes and converts them into LCRs, and queues the LCR into the queue table.

Local vs. Downstream Capture

New to Oracle Database 10*g*, you can now move the capture process away from the source database. Up to this point, the capture had to take place at the source database. But Oracle Database 10*g* now gives you the ability to push the archivelogs from the source database to another database (in the same fashion as you would with a Data Guard configuration), and then initiate the capture process at the downstream location. In this way, you push the entire Streams environment away from the source database completely.

Streams Propagation

The capture process is responsible for placing the LCRs that it captures into a queue table. From the queue table, the LCRs can be consumed by an apply process, or they can be propagated to another queue. The other queue can be local or remote—remote being the key to using Streams for availability.

Propagation takes place via propagation jobs that you configure. Propagation jobs are just database jobs, detailed using DBMS_JOB, but they have certain characteristics that make them unique. The most important characteristic is that a propagation job can evaluate a rule set, in much the same way as the capture process, so that only certain LCRs are propagated to the next queue.

Streams Apply Process

After the capture process defines and enqueues the LCRs from the redo stream, and after the propagation job has moved the LCRs from the source database to the queue table at the destination database, it is time to do something. Ultimately, the LCR that represents a change to a table needs to be applied to the copy of the table at the destination. For this, Oracle has an apply process. The apply process reads the queue table, and based on its rule set, determines which of the LCRs it needs to consume. By consume, we mean take the LCR and apply the change to an object.

There is a considerable amount of flexibility and configurability built into the apply process of Streams. You can configure a rule set for apply (as you can for the capture process and propagation jobs) so that you have further filtering options. The apply process can use rules to determine if an LCR is applied directly to its associated object, or if you want to pass the LCR to an intermediary procedure. If you pass the LCR to a procedure, you can encode changes to the data, such as modifying a datatype or adding a value to a new column, before the LCR gets applied. As you might imagine, this provides an unparalleled way of morphing data from an OLTP database to a data warehouse, or to modify data to test a new application.

Rules, Rules, Rules

As you may have noticed, there's a lot of talk about rules in Streams. Everything obeys rules of operation, but for Streams, a rule is actually a specific thing. Literally, rules are objects that reside in the Oracle database. You use DBMS_RULES to define a rule, and to modify it. Rules are organized into rule sets. A rule set can be referenced by a capture process, a propagation job, or an apply process in order to determine which records will be used by the Streams configuration at each step of the process. The capture process uses a rule set to determine which records in the redo log are converted to LCRs and placed in the queue table. The propagation job uses a rule set to determine which LCRs in a queue are moved to the remote queue table. The apply process will reference a rule set to determine who will consume the LCRs in the queue table.

The same rule set can be referenced by the capture, propagation, and apply agent. Conversely, each capture, propagation, or apply agent can have more than one rule set. Rule sets are typically defined as positive rule sets, or negative rule sets. Positive rule sets indicate a set that informs the process of what to include when reviewing records. For example, a positive rule set will inform the capture process to capture all rows for the table woodscrew_orders. A negative rule set will inform the process of what should be excluded during a review of records. For instance, a negative rule set may tell the capture process to exclude row changes for woodscrew_orders table that have an order date prior to January 2002. In this example, then, the capture process is informed by its positive rule set to capture DML for woodscrew_orders, but the negative rule set then discards records that have an ORD_DATE < 01-01-2002.

Through rule creation, you can very closely control the exact nature of all data that gets propagated and applied via Streams. We will not delve too deep into all the possibilities, but understand that rules are the foundation of successful Streams replication.

Streams for High Availability

As we've tried to make clear, Streams is not inherently a high-availability technology. The reason for its existence is more about event management systems than anything else. Downhill from event management comes the ability to replicate data very effectively using Streams. This data replication can occur locally—the source and destination database are the same. More likely, the replication takes place between a local source and a remote destination. This type of replication allows for a distributed database environment that allows local copies of centralized data, coupled with the power of data duplication for protection, and user load balancing across multiple databases.

Streams Replication and Replica DBs

The distributed nature of Streams replication provides us with a unique availability solution. With Streams, a complete copy of a database can be created at a remote site. In this way, it will look very similar to a logical standby database, and that is a fair assessment. However, Streams replication provides more flexibility than the logical standby database. Streams can be set up to exclude certain objects from replicating at the destination, so you are provided performance and space gains.

Streams replication also provides for the possibility of updating production databases at the destination site, and having the changes propagated back to the source. In this way, the disaster failover system also doubles as a secondary load-balancing system, where you can offload certain activities that might interfere with production systems.

The Replica Database

When you use Streams to maintain a copy of a database, the destination database is referred to as a *replica* database, as opposed to a standby database. The replica database differs significantly from the standby in its open and usable nature, and in that the database structure can be significantly different than the source database—even to the point that the database objects are different. With Streams, you can manipulate the incoming LCRs from the source database such that they are inserted into tables with different physical structures. In this way, you can have the same data living in two different formats and used in different ways.

In the case of a disaster at the source database, you can redirect users to the replica database in much the same way you would a standby database. The primary difference between a replica and a standby is that a replica does not contain an exact copy of the system or sysaux tablespaces. The data dictionary of the replica is unique to itself, and the objects that you replicate are unique as well. Only the rows moving from the source are the same.

Setting Up Streams Replication

Streams replication requires a significant amount of planning and configuration. You need to determine what you will be replicating, and to where. With Oracle Database 10*g*, there is also the determination of using local or downstream capture. After the planning, it's time to perform the configuration itself at both the source database and the destination database.

Planning for Streams Replication

There are a series of decisions that must be made prior to the replication configuration. These steps determine the nature of the replication setup that you will implement.

Determining Your Replication Set

You first need to determine which objects you will be replicating from your source to your destination database. Obviously, if you are creating a full replica database, every DML statement in the redo stream of the source will be converted to an LCR for application at the destination (except for DML against system and sysaux objects, of course).

However, if you want to take advantage of Stream's flexibility, it might make more sense to carefully choose those items that are of absolute importance in case of a disaster, and exclude those database objects that can be sacrificed. In situations where you have an extremely large production database, you may be forced to cut development environments, simply to save room and bandwidth at the destination database.

Because of the way in which Streams records LCRs in the queue, and then interprets them for application, you will get better performance if each table in your replication set has a primary key. The primary key is the default means by which the apply process can resolve the LCR into a change at the destination table. In the absence of a primary key, Streams will use a unique key that has a NOT NULL value in one of its columns. Short of that, it will need to record the value of each field in the row change. As you might imagine, this becomes more and more

expensive. So, think about your data structure, and whether there are good keys for
Streams replication.

Determining Your Replication Sites
Once you have determined what you will replicate, you have to determine where
you will be replicating to. The site of the replica database will reflect your decisions
about how to balance the distance of pushing the LCRs over the Internet with the
need to create a physical distance between the primary and disaster recovery database.
In addition to location, you have to determine what type of system will house the
replica; if you have a RAC cluster that you are protecting, obviously another RAC
cluster would be ideal. But you do not have to match the replica to the primary
database with exact physical structure or components. It might make sense from a
cost perspective to house the replica in a smaller system, where you can limp along
at a reasonable level until you can get the primary systems back up and operational.

Determining the replica database system is a sort of "chicken and egg" situation,
when combined with the decision to be made about what to replicate. Obviously, if
you have a like system for the replica and source, a full database replica would be
more feasible than, say, if your source is a multinode RAC with a monstrous SAN,
and the replica is a single-node system with mostly local storage.

Local or Downstream Capture?
You need to determine if you will be performing the capture of LCRs from the
source database redo logs local at the source, or downstream, at the destination
database. Downstream configuration provides a better disaster recovery solution,
as it would require that you push the archivelogs from the source to the destination
prior to performing a capture. This means you also have an extra set of the archivelogs
just in case you need them for the source. When you use downstream capture, the
capture process only looks at archivelogs. When you use a local capture process,
the local capture process has access to the online redo logs, and will use them and
archivelogs whenever necessary.

Downhill capture also means that you limit almost the entire configuration and
administration task set to the replica database. At the source, you merely configure
the push of the archivelogs to the source. That's it. The rest of the work is done at
the destination site (capture and apply). This also means that a propagation job
will not be required, as you can establish the same queue table for the capture and
apply processes.

Determining the Role of the Destination Database
You need to establish how the destination (replica) database will be used. It is
feasible to imagine that the replica database will not be configured for any users,
but will merely sit idle until a disaster occurs. Of course, if you've been provided

the opportunity to have the resources sit idle, then perhaps a logical (or better yet, a physical) standby database configuration would be more appropriate for you. Streams gets its strength from the fact that you can use the replica database even as it performs its disaster recovery role.

If you do have the replica database open for business, you need to know how, exactly, it will be open to users. Will you allow DML against the replica objects from the production? Or will it only be used for reporting purposes (queries, but not DML)? This is a critical distinction. If you want to set up the replica to serve as a load balancer for the source, you must reconfigure in your head the entire architecture of the Streams environment. Now, you must see that you have two sources and two destinations. You will need to configure Streams to go back and forth to both locations. You will also need to configure some form of conflict resolution, in case users at both databases simultaneously update the same row. (We discuss conflict resolution later in this chapter in the "Conflict Resolution" section.)

If the replica objects from the source will only be used for reporting, you do not have to make these kinds of considerations, and your life will be much easier. However, keep in mind that a logical standby database is a much easier way to configure a reporting copy of the production database. Both logical standby and Streams replicas can be open and used for reporting even as changes are applied. The difference, of course, is that you can better control the set of replicated objects with Streams. But a logical standby will always be a simpler solution.

Configuring Streams Replication

Once you have planned how your replication environment will work, it is time to get to the business of configuration. In this section, we will discuss the ins and outs of local capture and remote propagation of LCRs, which is the most common form that Streams replication takes. Later in this chapter, we concentrate more on downstream capture for Streams replication.

We also assume that you want to configure Streams such that you can make changes to replicated objects at both databases—in other words, both databases will be a source and a destination database for the same set of tables. Quite frankly, this is the most compelling reason to use Streams as an availability solution. But doing so is an extreme complicater. Such is life.

init.ora Parameters

The first order of business is to configure the initialization parameters for both the source and destination database. There are seven primary values to be concerned with, as they directly affect Streams functionality:

■ **COMPATIBILE**   Must be set to 10.1.0 for all the newest new.

- **GLOBAL_NAMES**   Must be set to True. This is required to identify all databases in the Streams configuration uniquely.

- **JOB_QUEUE_PROCESSES**   You will need to set this to at least 2. Better to have 4 or 6.

- **OPEN_LINKS**   The default is 4, which is fine—just don't set this any lower.

- **SHARED_POOL_SIZE**   Streams uses the shared pool for staging the captured events as well as for communication if you capture in parallel. If no STREAMS_POOL_SIZE is set, the shared pool is used. Streams needs at least 10MB of memory, but can only use 10 percent of the shared pool. So, if you choose not to use a Streams pool, you will need to set the shared pool to at least 100MB.

- **STREAMS_POOL_SIZE**   You can specify a pool that is used exclusively by Streams for captured events, parallel capture, and apply communication. By setting this parameter, you will keep Streams from muddying the already murky shared pool, and stop it from beating up on other shared pool occupants. Of course, by setting this, you also dedicate resources to Streams that cannot be used by other processes if Streams goes idle for any reason. You should set this parameter based on the number of capture processes and apply processes—that is, the level of parallelism: 10MB for each capture process, 1MB for each apply process. We always suggest generosity over scrooging—start at 15MB and go up from there.

- **UNDO_RETENTION**   The capture process can be a source of significant ORA-1555 (snapshot too old) errors, so make sure you set the undo retention to a high enough value. Oracle suggests starting at 3600 (1 hour). You will have to monitor your undo stats to make sure you have enough space in the undo tablespace to keep the hour of undo around (see Chapter 9 for more on undo retention).

Setting Up Replication Administrator Users
After you make the necessary modifications to the init file, you need to create users that will be responsible for replication administration. Can you use an existing user to own the Streams replication admin space? Absolutely. Do we recommend it? No. Make a new, clearly defined user at both the source and the destination. This user will be granted specific privileges that will control the capture, propagation, and apply movement. This user won't own the objects being replicated, but will just perform the queuing of the LCRs to the appropriate places.

Streams Pool vs. Shared Pool

As part of the init parameter changes, you need to determine how Streams will use the SGA for staging LCRs. By default, the shared pool is used. However, you can isolate Streams memory utilization to a new memory pool in Oracle Database 10g, called the Streams pool. The decision to use a Streams pool must be based on the level of activity you expect to see in your Streams environment. When Streams uses the shared pool, it is sharing the memory resources with many other Oracle processes. This can be beneficial, as the shared pool can move resources around based on demand. However, it can also mean that Streams is causing you to lose performance on objects that would have otherwise remained pegged—SQL execution plans, PL/SQL blocks, and so forth. Using a Streams pool dedicates resources to Streams, and this means that Streams won't walk all over anyone; it also means that when Streams runs idle, the memory resources in the Streams pool will also be idle.

In general, we suggest a Streams pool. As long as you spend the time it takes to monitor Streams memory usage, you can effectively tune the pool to match usage, and keep Streams out of everyone else's way.

Putting the Databases in Archivelog Mode

Of course (of course!) your production database is running in archivelog mode, but the replica database may not be in archivelog mode. It is only required if you will be allowing users to update production tables at the replica, and you will need to capture rows and move them back to production.

Configuring the Network

You will need to ensure that there is connectivity between the production and replica databases. You will also need to create all necessary TNS aliases in order to facilitate Oracle Net connectivity between the two databases. Then, you build your database links to connect the Streams administrator at each site to the Streams administrator at the other site.

Enabling Supplemental Logging

You need supplemental logging if you do not have a primary key or a unique NOT NULL constraint on the replicated table. Supplemental logging adds the values of every column in the row to the LCR, so that the record can be appropriately applied at the destination.

```
ALTER TABLE ws_app.woodscrew_inventory
   ADD SUPPLEMENTAL LOG DATA (ALL) COLUMNS;
```

You can also add supplemental logging for the entire database (note that you may have already done so when you configured your database for LogMiner in Chapter 2):

```
ALTER DATABASE ADD SUPPLEMENTAL LOG DATA;
```

Creating Streams Queues

The next step is to create the queue table that will serve as the queue for captured and propagated LCRs. Typically, you can create a single queue that is used both for locally captured LCRs and LCRs that are propagated from other source databases. You need to create a queue at each database; it is highly recommended that you give the queue tables at each database a different name (such as ws_app01_queue and ws_app02_queue).

```
BEGIN
DBMS_STREAMS_ADM.SET_UP_QUEUE(
queue_table => 'stream_admin.ws_app01_queue_table',
queue_name => 'stream_admin.ws_app01_queue');
END;
/
```

Creating a Capture Process

At both databases, you need to create a capture process and associate it with a rule set. The DBMS_STREAMS_ADD_<object>_RULES procedures will do all of this with a single block. You can add rules at the TABLE, SUBSET, SCHEMA, or GLOBAL level with the associated ADD_TABLE_RULES, ADD_SCHEMA_RULES, and so forth. The only one that is not completely clear here is ADD_SUBSET_ RULES—this is for creating a capture process for a subset of rows within a table. In our examples, we are setting up Streams for the ws_app schema in our database.

```
BEGIN
DBMS_STREAMS_ADM.ADD_SCHEMA_RULES(
schema_name => 'ws_app',
streams_type => 'capture',
streams_name => 'ws_app01_capture',
queue_name => 'ws_app01_queue',
include_dml => true,
include_ddl => true,
include_tagged_lcr => false,
source_database => NULL,
```

```
inclusion_rule => true);
END;
/
```

This example creates a capture process named ws_app01_capture and associates it with the ws_app01_queue we created previously. It creates a positive rule set with two rules: capture all DML for the ws_app schema, and capture all DDL for the ws_app schema. You will need to create a capture process at both the production and replica databases. When you create a capture process in this fashion, Streams automatically sets an instantiation SCN for all objects in the schema you have specified.

The instantiation SCN is the starting point for Streams replication to begin. It specifies where in the redo stream to begin looking for change events for the replication set and then convert them to LCRs.

Instantiating the Replica Database

At some point, you will need to move the data from the primary database to the replica. It is not expected that you will have Streams replication set up before any data exists in any of the databases. Rather, it is assumed that one of the databases will hold a significant amount of data that will have to be moved to the replica at the beginning of the replication process. The act of moving the data to the replica, and informing Streams where in the redo history to start, is referred to as *instantiation*.

First you need to move the data from the source to the destination. Transportable tablespaces, export, RMAN duplication—do whatever you have to do to get the objects moved from the source to the destination. Our examples will use original export/import (as opposed to the new Data Pump exp/imp); the benefit of using export/import is that it will capture the instantiation SCN set when you create your capture process, and move it over with the copy of the data. This is the starting point in the local queue at the destination database for the apply process to begin taking LCRs for the replication set and applying them to the destination database objects.

Creating a Propagation

Once we have our capture processes configured, and we have instantiated our schema, we next establish the propagations that will be used to push LCRs from the ws_app queue at each database to the queue at the other database. We must specify the source queue and the destination queue, with the destination queue suffixed with a database link name, shown here:

```
BEGIN
DBMS_STREAMS_ADM.ADD_SCHEMA_PROPAGATION_RULES(
schema_name => 'ws_app',
streams_name => 'ws_app01_propagation',
```

```
source_queue_name => 'stream_admin.ws_app01_queue',
destination_queue_name => 'stream_admin.ws_app02_queue@STR10',
include_dml => true,
include_ddl => true,
include_tagged_lcr => false,
source_database => 'ORCL',
inclusion_rule => true);
END;
/
```

This code will create a propagation at our source that moves LCRs from the local ws_app01_queue to the remote ws_app02_queue at the destination. It creates a positive rule set with two rules: push all LCRs that contain DML for the ws_app schema, and push all LCRs that contain DDL for the ws_app schema. Remember that with a multisource replication environment, where we will propagate in both directions, we need to set up a propagation job at both databases, with reverse values for source and destination queues.

Creating an Apply Process
The procedure to create an apply process comes in the same flavors as the capture process; in fact, you'll notice that you use the same procedure to create an apply process that you do to create a capture process. You simply change the STREAMS_ TYPE from capture to apply, like this:

```
BEGIN
DBMS_STREAMS_ADM.ADD_SCHEMA_RULES(
schema_name => 'ws_app',
streams_type => 'apply',
streams_name => 'ws_app02_apply',
queue_name => 'ws_app02_queue',
include_dml => true,
include_ddl => true,
include_tagged_lcr => false,
source_database => 'STR10',
inclusion_rule => true);
END;
/
```

This should look very familiar by now. You have created an apply process named ws_app01_apply, which looks to the ws_app02_queue for LCRs to be applied. It creates a positive rule set with two rules: DML for the ws_app schema, and DDL for the ws_app schema.

Creating Substitute Key Columns, If Necessary

If you are replicating a table that does not have a primary key, you will need to inform Streams which columns will act as a primary key for the sake of replication. For instance, if the DBA down at Horatio's Woodscrew Company wants to replicate the woodscrew_inventory table, he would need to set a substitute key in Streams— woodscrew_inventory has no primary key.

```
BEGIN
DBMS_APPLY_ADM.SET_KEY_COLUMNS(
object_name => 'ws_app.woodscrew_inventory',
column_list => 'scr_id,manufactr_id,warehouse_id,region');
END;
/
```

For any columns that are referenced as the substitution key for replication, you will need to enable supplemental logging at the source database as well.

Configuring for Conflict Resolution

If you have a multisource replication environment, where rows in the same objects can be updated at both sites, you will need to consider the need for conflict resolution. If necessary, you will need to configure your conflict handlers at this time. Conflict resolution, and its configuration, is detailed in the next section, "Conflict Resolution."

Throwing the Switch

After you have done all of these configuration steps, you are ready to "throw the switch" and enable the Streams environment to begin capturing, propagating, and applying the changes in your database.

First, enable the capture process at both databases (you would do this for the capture process at both databases, although we only code list for one).

```
BEGIN
DBMS_CAPTURE_ADM.START_CAPTURE(
capture_name => 'ws_app01_capture');
END;
/
```

You do not need to enable the propagation you have created—propagation agents are enabled by default. So then it is time to enable the apply processes at both databases.

```
BEGIN
DBMS_APPLY_ADM.START_APPLY(
apply_name => 'ws_app02_apply');
END;
/
```

After you have enabled the capture and apply processes, the Streams environment has been configured and will now be capturing new changes to the ws_app schema objects, moving them to the other database and applying them.

Conflict Resolution

A Streams replication environment is not complete until you have determined what kind of conflict resolution you need, and created conflict handlers to, you know, handle them. A conflict occurs in a distributed database when two users at different databases are attempting to modify the same record with different values. For instance, at each database a user updates the woodscrew_order table to change the order count value for the same order by the same customer. Which value should the Streams environment accept as the correct value? The determination of which record to keep and which to reject is known as conflict resolution.

There are four distinct types of conflicts that must be accounted for, depending on your application:

- Update conflicts
- Uniqueness conflicts
- Delete conflicts
- Foreign key conflicts

Update Conflicts

Our previous example is an update conflict: two users at different databases are updating the same record at roughly the same time. For a moment, each database has a different value for the ORD_CNT for a particular customer order for screws. However, as the apply process moves the LCR for that row from the other database, Streams will find that the row has been updated already, and will signal the conflict.

Update conflicts are the most unavoidable types of conflicts in a distributed model where the same tables are being modified at each location. Oracle has built-in conflict handlers for update conflicts that you can implement using the DBMS_ APPLY_ADM package. These are set up as apply handlers that get called when a conflict is detected, as in the following example for the woodscrew_orders table:

```
DECLARE
cols DBMS_UTILITY.NAME_ARRAY;
```

```
BEGIN
cols(1) := 'scr_id';
cols(2) := 'ord_cnt';
cols(3) := 'warehouse_id';
cols(4) := 'region';
DBMS_APPLY_ADM.SET_UPDATE_CONFLICT_HANDLER(
object_name => 'ws_app.woodscrew_orders',
method_name => 'OVERWRITE',
resolution_column => 'scr_id',
column_list => cols);
END;
/
```

You have to create a conditional supplemental log group for all columns that you list as being checked as part of this conflict handler—in this example, the SCR_ID, ORD_CNT, WAREHOSUE_ID, and REGION columns.

```
ALTER TABLE ws_app.woodscrew_orders ADD SUPPLEMENTAL LOG GROUP log_
group_ws_ord ('scr_id','ord_cnt','warehouse_id', 'region');
```

Uniqueness Conflicts

A uniqueness conflict can often be referred to as an *insert* conflict, as an insert is the most common trigger: two rows are inserted into the table at different databases with the same primary key value. The primary key constraint does not trigger an error until the LCR is moved from the other database. A uniqueness conflict can occur, as well, if the primary key is updated or changed for an existing record.

Uniqueness conflicts should be avoided, instead of resolved. Uniqueness conflicts can be avoided by sticking to two unbending application rules: unique string creation is appended with the GLOBAL_NAME from each origination database, and the application cannot modify a primary key value once created. By sticking to those rules, you will guarantee no unique conflicts in your replication environment.

Delete Conflicts

A delete conflict is triggered when a row is deleted that was also deleted or updated at the other database. As with uniqueness conflicts, it is best to avoid delete conflicts instead of coding to resolve them. At the application level, deleted rows from the application should instead be marked for delete at the application, then pooled together and run in batch format. You can also restrict deletions to the primary database, such that no deletes can occur at a secondary (replica) site.

Foreign Key Conflicts

Foreign key conflicts occur when an LCR is being applied at a database that violates a foreign key constraint. This is primarily a problem in Streams environments with more than two source databases, where it would be possible that two different source databases are sending LCRs to a third database. If the first source sends a record that references a foreign key value that was generated at the second source, but the second source hasn't sent its foreign key generation yet, the third database will trigger a foreign key conflict.

HA Workshop: *Configuring Streams Replication*

Workshop Notes

This workshop will configure Streams replication for the ws_app schema that we have been using for examples throughout this book; that is, we will be replicating the woodscrew, woodscrew_inventory, and woodscrew_orders tables in the ws_app schema. We will be configuring schema-level replication, so if you are following along at home, we suggest you drop the ws_app schema you have and rebuild it from scratch with just the three tables and their indices. Then, reinsert the base rows as described in Chapter 1. Because of Streams restrictions, we will not be replicating partitioned tables or IOTs. For more on Streams restrictions, see the Oracle Database 10g Streams documentation.

The workshop will configure a bidirectional, multisource Streams environment where data can be entered at the primary and replica database. The primary will be known as ORCL; the replica is STR10. The ws_app schema already exists in ORCL, and we will have to instantiate the existing rows at STR10.

The first phase of this workshop requires us to prepare both databases for Streams replication. The second phase sets up propagation of row changes from our primary database to our new replica (from ORCL to STR10). In the third phase, we will set up Streams to replicate back from STR10 to ORCL (making this a bidirectional multisource Streams environment).

Step 1. Put all databases in archivelog mode.

```
SQL> archive log list

Database log mode              No Archive Mode
Automatic archival                Disabled
Archive destination               USE_DB_RECOVERY_FILE_DEST
Oldest online log sequence        303
Current log sequence          305

SQL> show parameter recover;
NAME                            TYPE        VALUE
---------------------------------------------------------------
db_recovery_file_dest           string      /u01/product/oracle/
                                            flash_recovery_area
```

```
db_recovery_file_dest_size      big integer    2G

SQL> shutdown immediate;
SQL> startup mount;
SQL> alter database archivelog;
SQL> alter database open;
```

Step 2. Change initialization parameters for Streams. The Streams pool size and NLS_DATE_FORMAT require a restart of the instance.

```
SQL> alter system set global_names=true scope=both;
SQL> alter system set undo_retention=3600 scope=both;
SQL> alter system set job_queue_processes=4 scope=both;
SQL> alter system set streams_pool_size= 20m scope=spfile;
SQL> alter system set NLS_DATE_FORMAT=
     'YYYY-MM-DD HH24:MI:SS' scope=spfile;
SQL> shutdown immediate;
SQL> startup
```

Step 3. Create Streams administrators at the primary and replica databases, and grant required roles and privileges. Create default tablespaces so that they are not using SYSTEM.

```
---at the primary:
SQL> create tablespace strepadm datafile
'/u01/product/oracle/oradata/orcl/strepadm01.dbf' size 100m;

---at the replica:
SQL> create tablespace strepadm datafile
---at both sites:
'/u02/oracle/oradata/str10/strepadm01.dbf' size 100m;
SQL> create user stream_admin
    identified by stream_admin
    default tablespace strepadm
    temporary tablespace temp;
SQL> grant connect, resource, dba, aq_administrator_role to stream_admin;
SQL> BEGIN
        DBMS_STREAMS_AUTH.GRANT_ADMIN_PRIVILEGE (
        grantee  => 'stream_admin',
        grant_privileges => true);
        END;
        /
```

Step 4. Configure the tnsnames.ora at each site so that a connection can be made to the other database.

```
---In $ORACLE_HOME/network/admin for the ORCL instance:
STR10 =
  (DESCRIPTION =
    (ADDRESS_LIST =
      (ADDRESS = (PROTOCOL = TCP)(HOST = lnx01)(PORT = 1521))
    )
    (CONNECT_DATA =
      (SERVER = DEDICATED)
      (SERVICE_NAME = str10)
    )
  )
---In $ORACLE_HOME/network/admin for the STR10 instance:
ORCL =
  (DESCRIPTION =
    (ADDRESS_LIST =
      (ADDRESS = (PROTOCOL = TCP)(HOST = lnx01)(PORT = 1521))
    )
    (CONNECT_DATA =
      (SERVER = DEDICATED)
      (SERVICE_NAME = orcl)
    )
  )
```

Step 5.   With the tnsnames.ora squared away, create a database link for the stream_admin user at both ORCL and STR10. With the init parameter global_name set to True, the db_link name must be the same as the global_name of the database you are connecting to. Use a SELECT from the table global_name at each site to determine the global name.

```
SQL> select * from global_name;
SQL> connect stream_admin/stream_admin@ORCL
SQL> create database link STR10
     connect to stream_admin identified by stream_admin
     using 'STR10';
SQL> select sysdate from dual@STR10;
SLQ> connect stream_admin/stream_admin@STR10
SQL> create database link ORCL
     connect to stream_admin identified by stream_admin
     using 'ORCL';
SQL> select sysdate from dual@ORCL;
```

Step 6.   If you have not already done so, build the ws_app schema in ORCL. (See Chapter 2 for the ws_app schema build scripts.) We are providing the DDL for the three tables here to remind you of the structures, in case you are reading and not doing right now.

```
SQL> create table woodscrew (
 scr_id           number not null,
 manufactr_id     varchar2(20) not null,
 scr_type         varchar2(20),
 thread_cnt       number,
 length           number,
 head_config      varchar2(20),
 constraint pk_woodscrew primary key (scr_id, manufactr_id)
 using index tablespace ws_app_idx);
SQL> create index woodscrew_identity on woodscrew
     (scr_type, thread_cnt, length,head_config)
      tablespace ws_app_idx;
SQL> create table woodscrew_inventory (
 scr_id           number not null,
 manufactr_id     varchar2(20) not null,
 warehouse_id     number not null,
 region           varchar2(20),
 count            number,
 lot_price  number);
SQL> create table woodscrew_orders (
 ord_id           number not null,
 ord_date         date,
 cust_id          number not null,
 scr_id           number not null,
 ord_cnt          number,
 warehouse_id     number not null,
 region           varchar2(20),
 constraint pk_wdscr_orders primary key (ord_id, ord_date)
 using index tablespace ws_app_idx);
```

Step 7.   Add supplemental logging to the ws_app tables. This is required both for the conflict resolution for the tables and for the woodscrew_inventory table that does not have a primary key. We will later identify a substitution key that will operate as the primary key for replication.

```
SQL> Alter table ws_app.woodscrew add supplemental log data
     (ALL) columns;
SQL> alter table ws_app.woodscrew_inventory add supplemental log data
     (ALL) columns;
SQL> alter table ws_app.woodscrew_orders add supplemental log data
     (ALL) columns;
```

Step 8.   Create Streams queues at the primary and replica database.

```
---at ORCL (primary):
SQL> connect stream_admin/stream_admin@ORCL
```

```
SQL> BEGIN
  DBMS_STREAMS_ADM.SET_UP_QUEUE(
  queue_table  => 'stream_admin.ws_app01_queue_table',
  queue_name   => 'stream_admin.ws_app01_queue');
  END;
  /
---At STR10 (replica):
SQL> connect stream_admin/stream_admin@STR10
SQL> BEGIN
  DBMS_STREAMS_ADM.SET_UP_QUEUE(
  queue_table  => 'stream_admin.ws_app02_queue_table',
  queue_name   => 'stream_admin.ws_app02_queue');
  END;
  /
```

Step 9. Create the capture process at the primary database (ORCL).

```
SQL> BEGIN
  DBMS_STREAMS_ADM.ADD_SCHEMA_RULES(
  schema_name        =>'ws_app',
  streams_type       =>'capture',
  streams_name       =>'ws_app01_capture',
  queue_name         =>'ws_app01_queue',
  include_dml        =>true,
  include_ddl        =>true,
  include_tagged_lcr =>false,
  source_database => NULL,
  inclusion_rule  => true);
  END;
  /
```

Step 10. Instantiate the ws_app schema at STR10. This step requires the movement of existing rows in the ws_app schema tables at ORCL to ws_app schema tables at STR10. We will be using traditional import and export to make the movement take place. The benefit of using export/import is that the export utility will take the instantiation SCN generated when you built the capture process above, and document it with each object in the dump file. Then, when you import, the instantiation SCN will be recorded with the new objects that are built. This saves us some steps, mercifully.

Note, as well, that when we instantiate STR10, we have to prebuild the tablespace ws_app_data and ws_app_idx, then build the ws_app user.

```
---AT ORCL:
exp system/123db file=wsapp.dmp log=wsappexp.log object_consistent=y
owner=ws_app
```

```
---AT STR10:
---Create ws_app tablespaces and user:
create tablespace ws_app_data datafile
'/u02/oracle/oradata/str10/ws_app_data01.dbf' size 100m;
create tablespace ws_app_idx datafile
'/u02/oracle/oradata/str10/ws_app_idx01.dbf' size 100m;
create user ws_app identified by ws_app
default tablespace ws_app_data
temporary tablespace temp;
grant connect, resource to ws_app;

imp system/123db file=wsapp.dmp log=wsappimp.log fromuser=ws_app
touser=ws_app streams_instantiation=y

Import: Release 10.1.0.1.0 - Beta on Tue Jan 27 14:10:08 2004
Copyright (c) 1982, 2003, Oracle.  All rights reserved.
Connected to: Oracle10i Enterprise Edition Release 10.1.0.1.0 - Beta
With the Partitioning, OLAP and Data Mining options

Export file created by EXPORT:V10.01.00 via conventional path
import done in US7ASCII character set and AL16UTF16 NCHAR character set
import server uses WE8ISO8859P1 character set (possible charset conversion)
. importing WS_APP's objects into WS_APP
. . importing table                 "WOODSCREW"            12 rows imported
. . importing table          "WOODSCREW_INVENTORY"          4 rows imported
. . importing table            "WOODSCREW_ORDERS"          16 rows imported
Import terminated successfully without warnings.
```

Step 11. Create a propagation job at the primary database (ORCL).

```
SQL> BEGIN
  DBMS_STREAMS_ADM.ADD_SCHEMA_PROPAGATION_RULES(
  schema_name            =>'ws_app',
  streams_name           =>'ws_app01_propagation',
  source_queue_name      =>'stream_admin.ws_app01_queue',
  destination_queue_name =>'stream_admin.ws_app02_queue@STR10',
  include_dml            =>true,
  include_ddl            =>true,
  include_tagged_lcr     =>false,
  source_database        =>'ORCL',
  inclusion_rule         =>true);
  END;
  /
```

Step 12. Create an apply process at the replica database (STR10).

```
SQL> BEGIN
DBMS_STREAMS_ADM.ADD_SCHEMA_RULES(
```

```
schema_name          =>'ws_app',
streams_type         =>'apply',
streams_name         =>'ws_app02_apply',
queue_name           =>'ws_app02_queue',
include_dml          =>true,
include_ddl          =>true,
include_tagged_lcr   =>false,
source_database      =>'ORCL',
inclusion_rule       =>true);
END;
/
```

Step 13. Create substitution key columns for the table ws_app.woodscrew_ inventory at STR10. This is required for any table that does not have a primary key. The column combination must provide a unique value for Streams.

```
SQL> BEGIN
DBMS_APPLY_ADM.SET_KEY_COLUMNS(
object_name      =>'ws_app.woodscrew_inventory',
column_list      =>'scr_id,manufactr_id,warehouse_id,region');
END;
/
```

Step 14. Configure conflict resolution at the replica site (STR10). The conflict handlers will be created for each table. Because this is a replica, we assume that in the event of a conflict, the primary database is always the correct value. Thus, we will set this up so that the incoming record will always overwrite the existing value.

```
DECLARE
cols DBMS_UTILITY.NAME_ARRAY;
BEGIN
cols(1) := 'scr_type';
cols(2) := 'thread_cnt';
cols(3) := 'length';
cols(4) := 'head_config';
DBMS_APPLY_ADM.SET_UPDATE_CONFLICT_HANDLER(
object_name       =>'ws_app.woodscrew',
method_name       =>'OVERWRITE',
resolution_column=>'scr_type',
column_list       =>cols);
END;
/

DECLARE
cols DBMS_UTILITY.NAME_ARRAY;
BEGIN
```

```
cols(1)  := 'scr_id';
cols(2)  := 'ord_cnt';
cols(3)  := 'warehouse_id';
cols(4)  := 'region';
DBMS_APPLY_ADM.SET_UPDATE_CONFLICT_HANDLER(
object_name       =>'ws_app.woodscrew_orders',
method_name       =>'OVERWRITE',
resolution_column=>'scr_id',
column_list       =>cols);
END;
/


DECLARE
cols DBMS_UTILITY.NAME_ARRAY;
BEGIN
cols(1)  := 'count';
cols(2)  := 'lot_price';
DBMS_APPLY_ADM.SET_UPDATE_CONFLICT_HANDLER(
object_name       =>'ws_app.woodscrew_inventory',
method_name       =>'OVERWRITE',
resolution_column=>'count',
column_list       =>cols);
END;
/
```

Step 15.   Enable the capture process at the primary database (ORCL).

```
BEGIN
DBMS_CAPTURE_ADM.START_CAPTURE(
capture_name => 'ws_app01_capture');
END;
/
```

Step 16.   Enable the apply process at the replica database (STR10).

```
BEGIN
DBMS_APPLY_ADM.START_APPLY(
apply_name => 'ws_app02_apply');
END;
/
```

Step 17.   Test propagation of rows from primary (ORCL) to replica (STR10).

```
AT ORCL:

insert into woodscrew values (
```

```
1006, 'Balaji Parts, Inc.', 'Machine', 20, 1.5, 'Slot');

AT STR10:

connect ws_app/ws_app
select * from woodscrew where head_config = 'Slot';
```

Step 18.   While it may seem logical, you do not need to add supplemental logging at the replica. This is because the supplemental logging attribute was brought over when we exported from ORCL and imported into STR10 with STREAMS_INSTANTIATION=Y. If you try to create supplemental logging, you will get an error:

```
ORA-32588: supplemental logging attribute all column exists
```

Step 19.   Create a capture process at the replica database (STR10).

```
BEGIN
DBMS_STREAMS_ADM.ADD_SCHEMA_RULES(
schema_name        =>'ws_app',
streams_type       =>'capture',
streams_name       =>'ws_app02_capture',
queue_name         =>'ws_app02_queue',
include_dml        =>true,
include_ddl        =>true,
include_tagged_lcr  =>false,
source_database => NULL,
inclusion_rule  => true);
END;
/
```

Step 20.   Create a propagation job from the replica (STR10) to the primary (ORCL).

```
BEGIN
DBMS_STREAMS_ADM.ADD_SCHEMA_PROPAGATION_RULES(
schema_name            =>'ws_app',
streams_name           =>'ws_app02_propagation',
source_queue_name      =>'stream_admin.ws_app02_queue',
destination_queue_name=>'stream_admin.ws_app01_queue@ORCL',
include_dml            =>true,
include_ddl            =>true,
include_tagged_lcr     =>false,
source_database        =>'STR10',
inclusion_rule         =>true);
END;
/
```

Step 21. Create an apply process at the primary database (ORCL).

```
BEGIN
DBMS_STREAMS_ADM.ADD_SCHEMA_RULES(
schema_name          =>'ws_app',
streams_type         =>'apply',
streams_name         =>'ws_app01_apply',
queue_name           =>'ws_app01_queue',
include_dml          =>true,
include_ddl          =>true,
include_tagged_lcr   =>false,
source_database      =>'STR10',
inclusion_rule       =>true);
END;
/
```

Step 22. Create substitution key columns for woodscrew_inventory at the primary database (ORCL).

```
BEGIN
DBMS_APPLY_ADM.SET_KEY_COLUMNS(
object_name    =>'ws_app.woodscrew_inventory',
column_list    =>'scr_id,manufactr_id,warehouse_id,region');
END;
/
```

Step 23. Create conflict resolution handlers at ORCL. Because this is the primary, we set a 'DISCARD' resolution type for rows that are generated at STR10 and conflict with rows generated at ORCL. This completes our conflict resolution method, which resembles a site priority system. All rows generated at ORCL overwrite rows generated at STR10; all rows generated at STR10 that conflict with rows at ORCL will be discarded.

```
DECLARE
cols DBMS_UTILITY.NAME_ARRAY;
BEGIN
cols(1) := 'scr_type';
cols(2) := 'thread_cnt';
cols(3) := 'length';
cols(4) := 'head_config';
DBMS_APPLY_ADM.SET_UPDATE_CONFLICT_HANDLER(
object_name      =>'ws_app.woodscrew',
method_name      =>'DISCARD',
resolution_column=>'scr_type',
column_list      =>cols);
```

```
END;
/

DECLARE
cols DBMS_UTILITY.NAME_ARRAY;
BEGIN
cols(1) := 'scr_id';
cols(2) := 'ord_cnt';
cols(3) := 'warehouse_id';
cols(4) := 'region';
DBMS_APPLY_ADM.SET_UPDATE_CONFLICT_HANDLER(
object_name       =>'ws_app.woodscrew_orders',
method_name       =>'DISCARD',
resolution_column=>'scr_id',
column_list       =>cols);
END;
/

DECLARE
cols DBMS_UTILITY.NAME_ARRAY;
BEGIN
cols(1) := 'count';
cols(2) := 'lot_price';
DBMS_APPLY_ADM.SET_UPDATE_CONFLICT_HANDLER(
object_name       =>'ws_app.woodscrew_inventory',
method_name       =>'DISCARD',
resolution_column=>'count',
column_list       =>cols);
END;
/
```

Step 24.   Set the instantiation SCN at ORCL for the apply process. Because we are not moving an instantiation over from STR10 with an export dump file, we will have to manually set the instantiation SCN using DBMS_APPLY_ADM. Here, we use the current SCN. You can do this while connected to either the source or the destination; here, we are connected to the source for this phase—STR10. Thus, we push the instantiation SCN to ORCL using the stream_admin user's database link.

```
DECLARE
  iscn NUMBER;
BEGIN
 iscn := DBMS_FLASHBACK.GET_SYSTEM_CHANGE_NUMBER();
 DBMS_APPLY_ADM.SET_SCHEMA_INSTANTIATION_SCN@ORCL(
    source_schema_name        =>'ws_app',
    source_database_name       =>'STR10',
    instantiation_scn          =>iscn,
```

```
      recursive                =>true);
END;
/
```

Step 25.   Enable capture at the replica database (STR10).

```
BEGIN
DBMS_CAPTURE_ADM.START_CAPTURE(
capture_name => 'ws_app02_capture');
END;
/
```

Step 26.   Enable the apply process at the primary database (ORCL).

```
BEGIN
DBMS_APPLY_ADM.START_APPLY(
apply_name => 'ws_app01_apply');
END;
/
```

Step 27.   Test propagation of rows from the replica database (STR10) to the primary database (ORCL).

```
AT STR10:

SQL> connect ws_app/ws_app
SQL> insert into woodscrew values (
  1007, 'Balaji Parts, Inc.', 'Machine', 30, 1.25, 'Slot');

AT ORCL:

SQL> connect ws_app/ws_app
SQL> select * from woodscrew where head_config = 'Slot';
```

Step 28.   Find a cold refreshment and congratulate yourself! You have configured a bidirectional multisource Streams replication environment.

Downstream Capture of LCRs

The previous examples have all used a local capture process during the Streams environment configuration. As we mentioned previously, you can also configure Streams for downstream capture. New to Oracle Database 10g, downstream capture is a way of pushing the Streams environment completely downhill to the destination database.

Downstream capture requires that you set up a log transport service from the source to the destination database, as you would do for a Data Guard configuration (see Chapter 7 for more on log transport services). When the archivelogs arrive at the destination database, a capture process at the destination database uses LogMiner to review the archivelogs and extract records into LCRs that are then placed in a queue at the destination.

This allows us to forgo the usage of a propagation job, as the LCRs are queued into a location that is directly accessible by the destination database's apply process. Downstream capture also means that we have moved the entire environment, other than log transport, away from the source database. This can be extremely advantageous in many environments where the source database may need to be cleared of the administration of the Streams processes and database objects. Downstream capture also provides an extra degree of protection against site failure, as we are automatically creating another set of archived redo logs.

The downside is that you are pushing the entire archivelogs across the network, instead of just a subset of the data that a Streams propagation would push. You also sacrifice a degree of recoverability, as the downstream capture can only review archivelogs for records. When there is a local capture process at the source, the capture process can scan the online redo log for records, so there is a quicker uptime on record changes for the replication set.

Downstream capture also has a few restrictions that are avoided by using local capture. These restrictions come from moving a physical file to the destination; this requires a degree of operating system and hardware compatibility between the source and destination sites. When you propagate LCRs using a propagation job, you are sending logical records that have been freed of OS restrictions; with downstream capture, you are copying physical files from one location to another. So you have to have the same OS at both sites, although not the same OS version. You also need the same hardware architecture—no 32-bit to 64-bit transfers allowed.

HA Workshop: *Configuring Streams for Downstream Capture*

Workshop Notes
This workshop will outline the steps for downstream capture of changes to the ws_app schema. We will be grossly overlooking aspects that are covered in other parts of this book (such as log transport configuration). For this workshop, we will concentrate on configuring the destination database, STR10, to capture changes that originate at the source database, ORCL.

Step 1. Ensure that there is network connectivity between the source and primary databases via tnsnames.ora entries.

Step 2. Configure log transport at the source (ORCL) to the destination (STR10). See Chapter 7 for log transport configuration.

Step 3. At both the source and destination, set the parameter REMOTE_ARCHIVE_ ENABLE to True.

```
alter system set remote_archive_enable=true scope=both;
```

Step 4. Build Streams administrators at both databases. You can avoid a Streams administrator at the source, but you still have to grant certain privileges to an existing user. Instead, just build the Streams admin and call it even.

```
SQL> create user stream_admin
     identified by stream_admin
     default tablespace strepadm
     temporary tablespace temp;
SQL> grant connect, resource, dba, aq_administrator_role to stream_admin;
SQL> BEGIN
        DBMS_STREAMS_AUTH.GRANT_ADMIN_PRIVILEGE (
          grantee  => 'stream_admin',
          grant_privileges => true);
        END;
        /
```

Step 5. Build a database link from the Streams admin at the destination to the Streams admin at the source.

```
SQL> create database link ORCL
     connect to stream_admin identified by stream_admin
     using 'ORCL';
SQL> select sysdate from dual@ORCL;
```

Step 6. Create a queue at the destination (STR10), if one does not exist.

```
SQL> BEGIN
  DBMS_STREAMS_ADM.SET_UP_QUEUE(
  queue_table  => 'stream_admin.ws_app02_queue_table',
  queue_name   => 'stream_admin.ws_app02_queue');
  END;
  /
```

Step 7. Create the capture process at the destination (STR10).

```
BEGIN
DBMS_CAPTURE_ADM.CREATE_CAPTURE(
```

```
queue_name => 'ws_app02_queue',
capture_name => 'ws_app_dh01_capture',
rule_set_name => NULL,
start_scn => NULL,
source_database => 'ORCL',
use_database_link => true,
first_scn => NULL,
logfile_assignment => 'implicit');
END;
/
```

Step 8.   Add the positive rule set for the capture process at STR10.

```
BEGIN
DBMS_STREAMS_ADM.ADD_SCHEMA_RULES(
schema_name => 'ws_app',
streams_type => 'capture',
streams_name => 'ws_app_dh01_capture',
queue_name => 'ws_app02_queue',
include_dml => true,
include_ddl => false,
include_tagged_lcr => false,
source_database => 'ORCL',
inclusion_rule => true);
END;
/
```

Step 9.   Instantiate the ws_app schema at the destination database (STR10). This will follow the instantiation rules and procedures listed in the previous HA Workshop, "Configuring Streams Replication."

Step 10.   Create an apply process at the destination database (STR10). This will reference the queue that you set up in Step 6.

Step 11.   Follow through with all further configuration required from the previous HA Workshop, such as enabling capture and apply processes.

Administration of Stream Processes

After you have configured the Streams environment between your two (or more) databases, it is time to consider the ongoing administration that will be required to keep the environment healthy and operational. Like any other availability solution, Streams can operate without much user intervention after you have it set up correctly. The difference, unfortunately, is that it is much easier to misconfigure Streams—

there are just so many moving parts. You need to spend a certain amount of time monitoring Streams to ensure that the LCRs are being queued and dequeued successfully at each database. This means keeping a trained eye on the error logs, as well as any performance views that we discuss below. You also need to make sure that you have a sanity check to ensure that the two environments are staying in sync. If the network connection goes down, for instance, there may be some restarting and resyncing of Streams propagation.

Unfortunately, it is outside the scope of this humble chapter to provide all the management techniques for Streams. You will need to dig into the Streams documentation for Oracle for more information. Here are some of the highlights of the data dictionary and v$views available for Streams:

- DBA_APPLY

- DBA_APPLY_ERROR

- DBA_CAPTURE

- DBA_PROPAGATION

- DBA_RULES

- V$BUFFERED_QUEUES

Completely Removing a Streams Configuration from the Database

Starting in Oracle Database 10g, Oracle provides a means by which you can remove an entire Streams environment from a database. The procedure is part of the DBMS_STREAMS_ADMIN package, and it will remove all the pieces and parts you've configured for Streams. It will not remove the Streams admin user, however. This will need to be done afterward. You will need to run the procedure at all databases involved in a Streams replication scheme.

```
SQL> execute DBMS_STREAMS_ADM.REMOVE_STREAMS_CONFIGURATION();
```

Streams Summary

While we haven't spent much time summarizing in previous chapters, we wanted to provide some parting news here. Streams is an extremely large and complex technology set that can be configured to serve innumerable purposes in your enterprise. Its primary use is as an events management system—it is for controlling the lifespan of events in a publish/subscribe model. Due to its architecture, it provides an extremely powerful engine for configuring a replicated database across a distributed environment. Because of this replication functionality, there exists the ability to utilize Streams replication as a high-availability partner for disaster recovery and load balancing.

Streams is complicated, however. Because it is so flexible, it has many moving parts that the database administrator must take responsibility for. It is best, usually, to consider Streams as part of the application development environment. This is because an application typically has to be Streams aware for it to work correctly. There are restrictions on datatypes, there are bandwidth issues, there are performance considerations, and data rearchitecting may be required in order to have a successful Streams implementation.

We say this not to stop you from using Streams, but to get you in the loop. Streams is extremely powerful. But it does not deploy over a weekend, or even over a week. It requires extensive planning and testing.

One final note: the Streams documentation from Oracle Corporation weighs in at over 1,000 pages, when you take the entire document set as a whole. This chapter represents less than 4 percent of that total. In other words, consider Streams the iceberg and this chapter the tip. You want to be fully informed when it comes to the concepts and administration of Streams, so make sure you get the full document set and read all of it. Or most of it. Okay, at least some of it.

CHAPTER
11

Oracle Net
Configuration for
Failover

critical piece in the high-availability puzzle is a piece that is often taken for granted: the client configuration. With each release, Oracle has attempted to move more and more of the configuration on to the server side, lessening the need to configure the client. In the traditional world of Oracle and SQL*Net configurations, a client-side tnsnames.ora is configured, which tells the client which host to connect to, on what port, and what instance to look for once the connection arrives. In Oracle Database 10*g*, it is possible to make connections without the benefit of even using a tnsnames.ora on the client, using the Easy Connect Net Naming Method.

Nevertheless, the client machine is where it all begins, as it is at the client where the connection is first initiated. As such, how the client is configured to connect can still play a critical role in determining the availability, or perceived availability, of the application. We saw in Chapter 6 how services are used at the server side to segment workloads and assign nodes. We will now see how this configuration works together with the client and listener configurations.

Definitions

Let's begin our discussion by defining some terms, before we dive into the configuration details. You will hear many terms bandied about regarding various failovers, and load-balancing configurations, so a basic understanding of these terms is necessary. What is *Transparent Application Failover*? What is *listener load-balancing* vs. *client-side load-balancing*? What is *connect-time failover*? What is the meaning of life? These are the questions that haunt us, and keep us awake at night, and more specifically, keep the HA DBA awake at night, so we will attempt to answer them here.

Connect-Time Failover

We begin with connect-time failover, which is defined as a failed initial connection attempt that must be retried against a different address. Consider the following entry in a client's tnsnames.ora:

```
GRID =
  (DESCRIPTION =
    (ADDRESS = (PROTOCOL = TCP)(HOST = rmscvip1.us.oracle.com)(PORT = 1521))
    (ADDRESS = (PROTOCOL = TCP)(HOST = rmscvip2.us.oracle.com)(PORT = 1521))
    (CONNECT_DATA =
      (SERVICE_NAME = grid)
    )
  )
```

Given the above entry for the alias called GRID, when a client attempts to connect, the first address in the list will be the one initially tried—in this case, rmscvip1. Should the initial connection attempt to rmscvip1 be unsuccessful, the next address in the list will be tried. This is known as a connect-time failover. You can add as many entries to the list as you have available nodes to accept connections. Note also that the entries in the list do not have to be RAC nodes. The above may apply in a Streams or advanced replication environment, or one of the entries in the list may be a standby database—either physical or logical, as long as there is an available service defined and running on that node. The other criteria, of course, is that the addresses in the list will all allow the client to get to the data that is needed by the application. In the case of a RAC environment, we know that the data is always the same, as it is the same database. In the case of Streams, advanced replication, and physical or logical standby, whether or not the data is accessible depends on how these options are configured.

Transparent Application Failover

Transparent Application Failover, or TAF, refers to the failover of a connection that has already been made when a node or instance goes down. This is controlled by the parameter FAILOVER=ON, in the tnsnames.ora. By default, this parameter will be set to on, if not defined. Setting it to OFF will disable failover. When it is enabled, there are two types of failover, defined as part of the FAILOVER_MODE parameter: session (the default), or select. With TYPE=SESSION, should an instance fail after a session is connected, that session will be failed over to another available address in the list, without the user needing to reconnect. However, any SQL statements that were in progress will need to be reissued. With TYPE=SELECT, if the session fails over in the middle of a query, the query will be restarted after the failover. Consider the following modification to the CONNECT_DATA section of the tnsnames.ora file:

```
(CONNECT_DATA =
      (SERVICE_NAME = grid)
      (FAILOVER_MODE =
        (TYPE = SELECT)
        (METHOD = BASIC)
      )
  )
```

In this case, should a failure occur, the failed over session will keep track of the number of rows retrieved so far, so that when the query is restarted, the session will discard those rows that have already been returned.

Note that the query still must start over from the beginning; so if we had returned 9,000 out of 10,000 total rows, when the query is reissued it will have to go through those 9,000 rows again. The user or application will start to see a response again once we hit row number 9,001—at this point, new rows will be returned to the application. However, it will not be necessary to reissue the query. With DML statements, such as insert, update, or delete statements, an error will be returned if the statement is in progress during failover, and uncommitted transactions will be rolled back. In this case, the session is still failed over, so that the statements can be reissued without the need to reconnect.

Preconnect vs. Basic

In our example entry in the tnsnames.ora, we specified METHOD=BASIC. What this means is that the initial connection is made to only one node. In such a case, should a failure occur, it will take some additional time to failover the connection as it must reconnect to the next node in the list. With METHOD=PRECONNECT, at the initial connection, a session will be opened against all addresses in the list, with only one actually being used, but the others already connected. The advantage of this is that if a failure occurs, the failover will be quicker, since a connection is already opened on the alternate node(s). The disadvantage is that the preconnected sessions on the alternate node(s) are still consuming memory resources on the other nodes, and in most cases this might be considered a wasted resource since you would generally expect these sessions will not be needed.

Client-Side Load Balancing

Client-side load balancing is determined by configuring the tnsnames.ora with multiple addresses in the description, with the parameter LOAD_BALANCE=YES, as in this example:

```
GRID =
    (DESCRIPTION =
      (ADDRESS = (PROTOCOL = TCP)(HOST = rmscvip1.us.oracle.com)(PORT = 1521))
      (ADDRESS = (PROTOCOL = TCP)(HOST = rmscvip2.us.oracle.com)(PORT = 1521))
      (LOAD_BALANCE = yes)
      (CONNECT_DATA =
        (SERVICE_NAME = grid)
      )
    )
```

In this entry, the addresses will be tried at random by the client, because the LOAD_BALANCE entry is set. So the first entry in the list will not always be the first one tried. The client will randomly pick an address to try, without regard to the availability of the node or to how heavily loaded the node may be. The choice is done at random, with the expectation that if all clients are randomly picking an address to connect to, the resulting distribution of the load should be fairly even.

Server-Side Load Balancing

Server-side load balancing (also known as listener load balancing), on the other hand, is a bit more intelligent. It is controlled by the REMOTE_LISTENER parameter in the server parameter file. The REMOTE_LISTENER parameter in the spfile should be pointing to a TNSNAMES entry on *each server node*, which in turn will list the IPs and ports of all available listeners in the cluster. The following is an example:

```
LISTENERS_GRID =
  (ADDRESS_LIST =
    (ADDRESS = (PROTOCOL = TCP)(HOST = rmscvip1.us.oracle.com)(PORT = 1521))
    (ADDRESS = (PROTOCOL = TCP)(HOST = rmscvip2.us.oracle.com)(PORT = 1521))
  )
```

The REMOTE_LISTENER parameter is then set to LISTENERS_GRID in the spfile:

```
*.remote_listener='LISTENERS_GRID'
```

As such, any connections coming in to a node can be redirected to another node by the listener, without any special client-side configuration. Since the load balancing is done on the server, the listener can take into account the load on the individual nodes, and direct new connections to the node with the least load. Client-side load balancing will *not* override this in any way. If REMOTE_LISTENER is defined as above, and combined with client-side load balancing, the client will first randomly pick an address from the client tnsnames.ora to connect to. Once that choice is made, and communication is initiated with the listener at that address on the server, the listener will then check the load (based on CPU load, by default) and may decide to either accept the connection or redirect it to another node with less load.

How Is the Load Balanced?

It is easy enough to say that the listener directs connections to the node with the least load, but how is that determined? The truth of the matter is that the algorithms used are not published, and are fairly complex. However, at a high level, the CPU runqueue length is used by default to determine the load. The rate at which PMON updates the listeners with this information varies, depending on whether meaningful changes in the load or number of sessions have occurred, or whether the state of one of the instances has changed. Changes in the load are only considered meaningful if they are proportionately great, based on the overall capacity of the system. These "meaningful" changes may trigger PMON to refresh the information, but if not, it may be as long as 10 minutes between updates.

This may or may not be the best way to distribute the load, however. Therefore, it is possible to change that using an undocumented parameter in the listener.ora. By setting the parameter PREFER_LEAST_LOADED_NODE_<listener_name>= OFF, we suggest that the listener base its connection redirects on session_count, rather than the runqueue length. An example of this parameter is as follows:

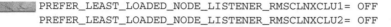

```
PREFER_LEAST_LOADED_NODE_LISTENER_RMSCLNXCLU1= OFF
PREFER_LEAST_LOADED_NODE_LISTENER_RMSCLNXCLU2= OFF
```

This parameter may be helpful in situations where multiple nodes in the cluster have just been rebooted, and thus have an equal load. Combine this with a mid-tier application that initiates many connections in a short period of time, and you may have a situation where PMON does not have time to update the runqueue information before all of the connections have come in. In this case, all or most of the connections may be established to a single node, instead of being properly balanced out. This is avoided by setting the above parameter to OFF, which not only causes us to look at the number of sessions as the first piece of the puzzle, but also allows the listener to utilize its knowledge of established session information in between PMON updates, so that the information is not outdated. Thus, if a login storm occurs, with many sessions connecting in the span of a minute or less, the listener will track these connections and will be able to distribute the load accordingly, based on current and accurate session information.

NOTE
JDBC Connections, using both the Thin and Thick drivers, can take advantage of their own specific failover methods using "Fast Connection Failover." Fast Connection Failover works in conjunction with the Oracle Notification Services (ONS) in a RAC environment to allow for application_level connection retries and also load-balancing support. Though this is generally outside the scope of responsibility of the HA DBA, we refer you to Chapter 8 of the Oracle® Database JDBC Developer's Guide *and Reference for an introduction to Fast Connection Failover.*

Net Configuration

Now that we have gotten the definitions (and more) out of the way, we can look more at the specific configuration of these options. We saw some examples of different tnsnames entries, enabling the various features discussed. We will now discuss some of the mechanics of configuring these various pieces.

Using GUI Tools to Generate Configuration Files

Net configuration files can be generated manually by creating your own local tnsnames.ora file, or you can use a variety of different tools to walk you through the configurations. In Oracle Database 10g, probably the simplest way to accomplish this is to use the DBCA to create the services, as we described in Chapter 6. After the DBCA has done its work, you can take the tnsnames.ora files generated on the server and distribute them out to the appropriate clients. Note, however, that you probably do not want the entire server-side tnsnames.ora to be sent out to every client, because every service will be defined in that file. Instead, you can take that information specific to a service/application, and create a tnsnames.ora for a specific set of clients and distribute it that way. This will prevent, for example, clients who normally connect to the accounts payable service from instead trying to connect to the OLTP service.

Aside from the DBCA, you can also run the netmgr (Net Manager) or netca (Net Configuration Assistant) at the client, to step you through the creation of a basic tnsnames.ora file at the client site. Again, once you have a file set up for a specific service, or set of users, you can distribute the tnsnames.ora to multiple clients in need of access to that specific service.

Easy Connect

Oracle Database 10g allows for a simpler client configuration, in that in some cases it is not necessary to have a TNSNAMES file at all. This is possible using Oracle Net Easy Connect. In doing so, the client may connect by simply specifying the connect string in the form of //<vipname:port>/<service_name>. Note that it is not necessary to specify the port if you are using port 1521. This type of connection is possible only with Oracle Database 10g and later clients. A connection using the Easy Connect syntax will connect you to any available node that the service is running on, regardless of the VIP that is specified. For example, the following client connection to the grid_callcenter service could be made to either of the nodes available for the service, even though the VIP for node1 is specified:

```
connect scott/tiger@//rmscvip1/grid_callcenter
```

or

```
connect scott/tiger@//rmscvip1:1521/grid_callcenter
```

Using the Easy Connect syntax in Oracle Database 10g Release1, instead of a tnsnames.ora file, means that you will not be able to take advantage of advanced features, such as TAF or client-side load balancing. However, the listener load balancing is still possible.

Environments Suitable for TAF

The primary environment suited for use of transparent application failover is a RAC environment, because we can always be assured that when failing over to another node, we are still accessing the same data as before—because it is the same database. However, TAF can also be used in other environments, such as physical or logical standby environments, replication environments, and Streams environments. Determining the suitability depends on how these environments are used.

For example, with a standby database, it is possible to have users failover transparently, as we mentioned in Chapter 7, when the database is switched over to the standby. This depends, however, on how quickly the switchover takes place, and also on the settings for RETRIES and DELAY, as discussed next. With logical standby and replicated environments, it is possible for clients to failover as well, without necessarily having to perform a switchover, because in both cases (logical standby and replication) the target databases for failover are open. However, successful select failover would depend on the availability of the data at the target sites, as the propagation of data to a replicated site or a logical standby does not necessarily have to be synchronous.

In the following HA Workshop, we will take the most common case—that of implementing transparent application failover in a RAC environment, and demonstrate the configuration and testing of TAF to verify the setup. The same principles can be applied to other environments as well.

HA Workshop: *Configuring and Testing TAF*

Workshop Notes
This workshop will walk you through the creation of a tnsnames.ora file with select type failover enabled, and then test the failover of an in-flight query when the instance where the query started goes down.

Step 1. Create the tnsnames.ora file on an Oracle Database 10*g* client machine, similar to the following:

```
GRID =
  (DESCRIPTION =
    (ADDRESS = (PROTOCOL = TCP)(HOST = rmscvip1.us.oracle.com)(PORT = 1521))
    (ADDRESS = (PROTOCOL = TCP)(HOST = rmscvip2.us.oracle.com)(PORT = 1521))
    (LOAD_BALANCE = yes)
    (CONNECT_DATA =
      (SERVICE_NAME = grid)
      (FAILOVER_MODE =
        (TYPE = SELECT)
        (METHOD = BASIC)
```

```
         (RETRIES = 30)
         (DELAY = 5)
       )
     )
   )
```

Step 2.   Connect to the grid service from the client machine:

```
sqlplus scott/tiger@grid
```

Step 3.   Confirm which node you are connected to, and the failover method, with the following query, run from a sysdba session on the server:

```
SQL> select inst_id, username, failover_type, failover_method, failed_over
  2  from gv$session where username = 'SCOTT';
  INST_ID USERNA FAILOVER_TYPE FAILOVER_METHOD FAILED_OVER
---------- ------ ------------- --------------- ------------
        2 SCOTT  SELECT        BASIC           NO
```

From the above, we can see that our user SCOTT connected to instance 2, the FAILOVER_TYPE is select, and the session has not yet failed over.

Step 4.   Create or populate a table with a large amount of data—enough so that a long-running query can be performed (long enough that we can shut down instance 2 in the middle). In our case, we have granted select on DBA_OBJECTS to SCOTT, and created a table called TEST_TAF as select * from SYS.DBA_OBJECTS:

```
Create table TEST_TAF as select * from SYS.DBA_OBJECTS;
```

Step 5.   Connect as sysdba again to instance 2, in another session, and *prepare* to issue a SHUTDOWN ABORT, but do not press ENTER yet.

Step 6.   Toggle back over to user Scott's session on the client. Execute a query against the TEST_TAF table from within Scott's session:

```
select * from test_taf where object_name like 'D%';
```

Step 7.   As soon as the query begins, switch back over to your sysdba connection to instance 2 and execute the SHUTDOWN ABORT command.

Step 8.   After a brief pause, your query from within your client session (as user Scott) should continue on. On instance 1, open up another sysdba connection and run the same query as before to get the session information for Scott.

```
SQL> select inst_id, username, failover_type, failover_method, failed_
over  from gv$session where username = 'SCOTT'

  INST_ID USERNA FAILOVER_TYPE FAILOVER_METHOD FAILED_OVER
---------- ------ ------------- --------------- ------------
        1 SCOTT  SELECT        BASIC           YES
```

Note that the session now resides on INST_ID 1, and the FAILED_OVER column says YES.

> **NOTE**
> *The DELAY parameter in the above configuration tells us to wait five seconds after the failure is first noted, and then to attempt to reconnect. RETRIES tells us to retry this 30 times, with a five-second delay each time. The length of the pause you see in Step 7 will depend on how far the query has gotten, and will also depend on these parameters. If neither parameter is set, your session may error out rather than failing over as expected.*

Listener Configuration

One of the most important differences in the configuration of Oracle Net in Oracle Database 10g is the fact that the listener in a RAC environment must be configured to listen on the virtual IP (VIP), rather than the actual IP address of the node. For those who may be familiar with RAC Guard in 9.2, or Parallel Fail Safe (OPFS) in previous releases, this is not a new concept, except to say that this is now an enforced configuration rather than an optional choice. However, this is still a new concept to most RAC users, and, of course, it is also new to those of you who are new to RAC altogether.

Another difference is the name used by the default listener. In past releases, it was fairly certain that 9 times out of 10, you were using a listener that was simply called LISTENER. However, in a RAC environment with a shared home (that is, a single home on a cluster file system), you only have a single listener.ora. You cannot, therefore, have two listeners both called LISTENER. Thus, it has become standard practice to name the listener for each node using the convention LISTENER_<NODENAME>. The default RAC and DBCA configuration in Oracle Database 10g will use that convention.

Why a Virtual IP?

So, why must we use a virtual IP address in a RAC environment in Oracle Database 10g? We touched on the reasoning briefly in earlier chapters, but we will go into more detail here. The simple answer to this question is "TCP timeouts." So, now that we have answered this question, we can move on, right? No? Okay, let's discuss this a bit more.

TCP Timeouts

TCP timeouts, believe it or not, play a huge piece in the perceived availability of applications. When a node in a RAC environment goes down, or in any high-availability environment with multiple addresses to attempt, there is no way for the client to know this. If a client is connecting using a TNS alias, or a service that allows connection to multiple nodes, the client may unknowingly try its first connection attempt to the node that is down. This in and of itself is not a problem, as there are supposed to be multiple addresses in the list. As such, when the client fails to get a response from the first address in the list, the next address will be tried, until the connection succeeds. The problem lies with the time that it takes to go to the next address in the list. How long does the client wait to determine that the host it is trying to reach is not accessible? The time can range anywhere from a few seconds to a few minutes, and in some environments this is simply unacceptable. If a node goes down for several hours, days, or weeks, the database may still be humming along just fine, with x number of nodes still accessing the database. However, some clients may always be trapped into making the initial connection attempt to the down node, and therefore be stuck in front of a (seemingly) interminable hourglass while the connection is timing out, prior to being rerouted to the next address in the list.

Reigning in TCP Timeouts at the OS   Unfortunately, this time is something that is generally outside of the control of Oracle. In addition, it varies from client to client, and operating system to operating system. It is controlled by the operating system timeout values on the client side, so making modifications to all clients can be cumbersome since there may be many clients and many variations to configuration changes that need to be made. Further, changing the timeout values may also result in adverse consequences on other applications that the clients are running, if other applications rely on a higher TCP timeout value for whatever reason.

To make matters worse, the behavior may not be consistent. If client-side load balancing is enabled, it is quite possible that some connections will succeed immediately on their first attempt, because they just happened to randomly connect to a node that is available. At other times, however, the connection time increases, because the client randomly and unwittingly picks the down node for its first connection attempt. The result of this is confusion and frustration at the client side, even though from the database perspective, everything is functioning as it should.

Giving the HA DBA Control Over TCP Timeouts   Enter the virtual IP address, or VIP. By using a virtual IP address, Oracle eliminates the problem with TCP timeouts on the initial connection, without the need to make any changes to a single client machine. This is done by enforcing client connections to first come in on the virtual IP address for all connections. When all nodes are functioning properly, each VIP is running on its assigned node, and connections are directed to the appropriate listener and service. When the unthinkable happens, and a node fails (gasp!), CRS will kick in, and the VIP for that node will actually be brought online on one of the remaining nodes of the cluster, where it can respond to a ping and also to connection attempts. It is important to note that this VIP will *not* now be accepting connections to the database. However, since the IP address is available, it will be able to respond to a connection attempt immediately. The response given to the client would normally be in the form of an ORA-12541, advising that there is no listener available. This is because the node where the VIP now resides has its own listener, but it is listening on its own VIP—not the VIP of any other nodes. The client, receiving the message back that there is no listener, will then be able to immediately retry, using the next IP in the ADDRESS_LIST, rather than waiting up to two minutes for the timeout we would normally expect. Thus, a connect-time failover has still occurred, but the connection attempt succeeds within a matter of a few seconds. The actual ORA error is masked, so that the client never sees it.

Bibliography

his bibliography is organized by chapter, and then by topic within the chapter (where such divisions apply). You will notice that we relied very heavily on the Oracle documentation set for this book. Such is the price of the bleeding edge publication. You can get HTML or PDF versions of the Oracle Database 10*g* documentation from OTN at the following URL:

http://otn.oracle.com/documentation/database10g.html

Other documents include technical white papers, which can be referenced from Oracle Technology Network (OTN). OTN is one of the richest online resources for Oracle information, and we suggest that you get signed up if you haven't already. You can download software for testing purposes, and some of Oracle's best and brightest have ongoing columns.

Some articles are from Metalink, the Oracle Support web site. These articles require that you have a support contract with Oracle to download them.

Chapter 2: RDBMS Features for Availability

Most sources for Chapter 2 come directly from the Oracle documentation set itself, and the Administrator's Guide mostly. Other sources include white papers available on OTN and some technical notes that will only be available if you have a Metalink account with Oracle Support.

Enterprise Manager

- Choi, Phil, et al. *Oracle Enterprise Manager Grid Control Installation and Basic Configuration 10*g *Release 1 (10.1),* Oracle Corporation, December 2003.

This quick guide provides detailed memory and disk requirements, OS compatibilities, and other critical first-look information when you are deciding how (or if) to use EM Grid Control.

Data Architecting for Availability

- Kyte, Thomas. *Effective Oracle by Design,* Berkeley: McGraw-Hill/Osborne, August 2003.

The best source of data architectural advice on the market.

- Niemiec, Richard J. *Oracle9i Performance Tuning Tips & Techniques,* Berkeley: McGraw-Hill/Osborne, May 2003.

If you've caught Mr. Niemiec at IOUG or OracleWorld, you know his knowledge runs deep, and he's harnessed his team at TUSC for another excellent tome on perf/tune.

Partitioning

■ Baylis, Ruth, et al. *Oracle® Database Administrator's Guide 10g Release 1 (10.1)*, Oracle Corporation, December 2003.

Chapter 16 is the primary source of reliable and accurate information on partitions.

■ Cyran, Michele, et al. *Oracle Database Concepts, 10g Release 1 (10.1)*, Oracle Corporation, December 2003.

Chapter 18 is the conceptual platform for understanding the terms and structures for partitioning. You should start here for foundational understanding.

■ "Partitioned Indexes: Global, Local, Prefixed and Non-Prefixed." Available online from http://metalink.oracle.com, Reference DocID 69374.1. [Referenced on February 2, 2004]

The most concise explanation of partitioned indices that is available anywhere.

Index-Organized Tables

■ Baylis, Ruth, et al. *Oracle® Database Administrator's Guide 10g Release 1 (10.1)*, Oracle Corporation, December 2003.

Chapter 14 provides a succinct introduction to the use and admin of IOTs.

Materialized Views

■ "Oracle9*i* Materialized Views," Oracle white paper. Available online from http://otn.oracle.com/products/oracle9i/pdf/o9i_mv.pdf, May 2001. [Referenced on February 2, 2004]

The most important pieces of this excellent paper cover summary management and the succinct explanation of query rewrite.

■ Lane, Paul, et al. *Oracle® Data Warehousing Guide, 10g Release 1 (10.1)*, Oracle Corporation, December 2003.

Chapters 8 and 9 will give a complete picture of the minutae of mviews, including all the exceptions and restrictions that exist. In addition, Chapter 17 provides in-depth coverage of the command-line implementation of SQL Access Advisor—for those of you who simply cannot abide by EM.

Online Reorganization

■ Baylis, Ruth, et al. *Oracle® Database Administrator's Guide 10*g *Release 1 (10.1),* Oracle Corporation, December 2003.

Chapter 14 provides a succinct introduction to the usage of DBMS_REDEFINITION used for table reorgs.

■ "Maximum Availability Architecture," Oracle white paper. Available online from: http://otn.oracle.com/deploy/availability/pdf/MAA_WP.pdf, February 2003. [Referenced February 2, 2004]

We started here for a lot of different things, but the section on table reorganization is succinct and provides useful examples.

Resource Manager and the Scheduler

■ Baylis, Ruth, et al. *Oracle® Database Administrator's Guide 10*g *Release 1 (10.1),* Oracle Corporation, December 2003.

Chapter 24 covers Resource Manager in all its specificity. Chapters 25–28 cover the Scheduler, with Chapter 25 helping with a transition away from DBMS_JOB.

LogMiner: Transaction Extraction

■ Rich, Kathy, et al. *Oracle® Database Utilities 10*g *Release 1 (10.1),* Oracle Corporation, December 2003.

Chapter 19 provides excellent coverage of using LogMiner at the SQL interface level to gain access to LogMiner. Our coverage is short and, admittedly, rather lean on specifics.

Transportable Tablespaces

■ Baylis, Ruth, et al. *Oracle® Database Administrator's Guide 10*g *Release 1 (10.1),* Oracle Corporation, December 2003.

Chapter 8 covers the nitpicking details of transporting tablespaces in general, as well as using cross-platform transportation.

Chapter 3: Tuning Your Database for Availability

Primary sources for the information in this chapter are Oracle white papers available on OTN.

Intelligent Infrastructure

■ Hansell, Daniela, et al. "The Self-Managing Database: Automatic Health Checking and Monitoring," Oracle white paper. Available online from: http://otn.oracle.com/products/oem/pdf/SMHealth.pdf, October 2003. [Referenced March 11, 2004]

ADDM (Automatic Database Diagnostic Monitor)

■ "The Self-Managing Database: Automatic Performance Diagnosis," Oracle white paper. Available online from: http://otn.oracle.com/products/manageability/database/pdf/twp03/TWP_manage_automatic_performance_diagnosis.pdf, November 2003. [Referenced March 11, 2004]

Advisor Central

■ "The Self-Managing Database: Automatic SGA Memory Management," Oracle white paper. Available online from: http://otn.oracle.com/products/manageability/database/pdf/twp03/TWP_manage_automatic_shared_memory_management.pdf, November 2003. [Referenced March 11, 2004]

Automatic Storage Management (ASM)

■ "Automatic Storage Management Technical Overview," Oracle white paper. Available online from: http://otn.oracle.com/products/manageability/database/pdf/asmwp.pdf, November 2003. [Referenced March 11, 2004]

Chapter 4: RAC Setup and Configuration

Cluster Ready Services (CRS)

■ Pruscino, Angelo, et al. "Oracle Real Application Clusters 10*g*: The Fourth Generation," Oracle white paper. Available online at: http://otn.oracle.com/tech/grid/collateral/10gRAC.pdf, [Referenced March 11, 2004]

■ "CRS and 10*g* Real Application Clusters." Available online from: http://metalink.oracle.com. Reference DocID 259301.1, [Referenced on March 11, 2004]

Configure a Linux/RAC Cluster

- Notes on configuring a Firewire cluster available online at:
  http://oss.oracle.com/projects/firewire/dist/documentation/Hardware,
  [Referenced March 11, 2004]
  http://oss.oracle.com/projects/firewire/dist/files/README, [Referenced
  March 11, 2004]

Preparing for the CRS Install

- Austin, David, et al. *Oracle® Real Application Clusters Installation and
  Configuration Guide,* December 2003.

Chapter 5 covers necessary preinstall steps for installing CRS/RAC on Linux.

The Actual CRS Install Itself

The primary sources for this chapter are the online documentation, in addition to
some information from Oracle white papers available on OTN. Chapter 7 covers
steps for the actual install process itself.

Installing the RDBMS

Chapter 8 covers installation of the RDBMS and DB creation.

Chapter 5: Database Administration in a RAC Environment

Adding and Removing Cluster Nodes

- Austin, David, et al. *Oracle® Real Application Clusters Administrator's
  Guide,* December 2003.

Chapter 5 discusses the process of adding/removing nodes in a RAC environment.

Monitoring RAC Metrics Using AWR

- Austin, David, et al. *Oracle® Real Application Clusters Deployment and
  Performance Guide,* December 2003.

Chapter 3 of the RAC Deployment and Performance Guide provides details on
performance views in a RAC environment, as well as RAC statistics and events.

Chapter 4 of the RAC Deployment and Performance Guide discusses the use of Enterprise Manager to monitor performance in a RAC environment.

Patching in a RAC Environment

- Pruscino, Angelo, et al. "Oracle Real Application Clusters 10*g*: The Fourth Generation," Oracle white paper. Available online at: http://otn.oracle.com/tech/grid/collateral/10gRAC.pdf, [Referenced March 11, 2004]

Chapter 6: Utility Computing: Applications as Services

The primary sources are online documentation, as well as internal papers.

Services

- Austin, David, et al. *Oracle® Real Application Clusters Administrator's Guide,* December 2003.

Chapter 4 in the RAC Administrator's Guide covers the administration of services, concepts, adding, modifying, and more.

Appendix B of the RAC Administrator's Guide has a complete reference for the SRVCTL command-line utility.

Oracle Cluster Registry (OCR)
Chapter 3 discusses ocrconfig and backing up/restoring the OCR.

Chapter 7: Oracle Data Guard: Surviving the Disaster

The primary sources are exclusively the online documentation when it comes to Data Guard. They represent complete and detailed coverage of all the information for the Oracle Database 10*g* Data Guard product.

Integrating Data Guard with other High-Availability Features

- Baird, Cathy, et al. *Oracle® High Availability Architecture and Best Practices 10*g *Release 1 (10.1),* Oracle Corporation, December 2003.

The definitive answer when it comes to tying together Data Guard with other HA features such as RAC.

The Data Guard Broker and Clients

■ Day, Rhonda, et al. *Oracle® Data Guard Broker 10*g *Release 1 (10.1)*, Oracle Corporation, December 2003.

Everything you ever wanted to know about how to create and control a broker configuration. A very detailed examination of all available broker options that can make your job easier.

Data Guard Administration Guide—The Source

■ Schupmann, Viv, et al. *Oracle® Data Concepts and Administration 10*g *Release 1 (10.1)*, Oracle Corporation, December 2003.

A detailed look at all things Data Guard. This should be your first stop if you have a question.

Enterprise Manager

■ Choi, Phil, et al. *Oracle Enterprise Manager Grid Control Installation and Basic Configuration 10*g *Release 1 (10.1)*, Oracle Corporation, December 2003.

A must-read to install and configure this great upgrade for Oracle Enterprise Manager.

Chapter 8: Backup and Recovery for High Availability Environments

The sources here are rather limited, and as with most chapters there is heavy reliance on Oracle documentation for Oracle Database 10*g*.

RMAN: A Primer

■ Freeman, Robert, et al. *Oracle 9*i *RMAN Backup and Recovery*, Berkeley, McGraw-Hill/Osborne, September 2002.

This is an excellent resource for a foundational understanding of RMAN, with a strong slant toward conceptual understanding and architectural explanation. You might recognize the workshop format, as it is the same one used in our HA book.

Preparing an RMAN Backup Strategy

■ Romero, Antonio, et al. *Oracle® Database Backup and Recovery Basics 10*g *Release 1 (10.1),* Oracle Corporation, December 2003.

The basics cover configuration of both the permanent configuration parameters and the flashback recovery area setup, particularly Chapter 3.

Backups for the Available Database

■ Romero, Antonio, et al. *Oracle® Database Backup and Recovery Advanced User's Guide 10*g *Release 1 (10.1),* Oracle Corporation, December 2003.

Chapter 6 covers media management, more about the flashback recovery area, as well as setting up the auxiliary instance and the snapshot controlfile.

■ Romero, Antonio, et al. *Oracle® Database Backup and Recovery Basics 10*g *Release 1 (10.1),* Oracle Corporation, December 2003.

Chapter 4 covers the creation and usage of incrementally updated backups. This chapter also covers backing up the flashback recovery area to tape.

Backup Housekeeping

■ Romero, Antonio, et al. *Oracle® Database Backup and Recovery Basics 10*g *Release 1 (10.1),* Oracle Corporation, December 2003.

Chapter 6 covers maintenance operations.

Performing Recovery

■ Romero, Antonio, et al. *Oracle® Database Backup and Recovery Basics 10*g *Release 1 (10.1),* Oracle Corporation, December 2003.

See Chapter 5 for straightforward examples of restore and recovery operations with RMAN.

■ Romero, Antonio, et al. *Oracle® Database Backup and Recovery Basics 10*g *Release 1 (10.1),* Oracle Corporation, December 2003. Chapter 8 covers topics such as recovering to a new host and block media recovery.

Media Management Considerations

■ Freeman, Robert, et al. *Oracle 9*i *RMAN Backup and Recovery,* Berkeley, McGraw-Hill/Osborne, September 2002.

This book has excellent coverage of linking RMAN to media management on multiple vendor products, including Veritas Netbackup, Legato Networker, HP Omniback, and Tivoli Data Protection. The exact nature of the operations is explained conceptually in Chapter 4.

RMAN and Data Guard

■ Freeman, Robert, et al. *Oracle 9i RMAN Backup and Recovery*, Berkeley, McGraw-Hill/Osborne, September 2002.

Chapter 17 provides excellent examples of creating physical standby databases in Oracle9*i* (not much has changed).

■ Schupmann, Viv, et al. *Oracle Data Guard Concepts and Administration, 10*g *Release 1 (10.1)*, Oracle Corporation, December 2003.

Appendix D covers the creation of the physical standby using RMAN.

RMAN and RAC

■ Freeman, Robert, et al. *Oracle 9i RMAN Backup and Recovery*, Berkeley, McGraw-Hill/Osborne, September 2002.

Chapter 18 covers the critical information concerning RMAN and RAC, including a detailed account of archivelog setup in a pre-OCFS world. There are two excellent workshops that cover duplicating from RAC to a single-node database, and creating a single-node standby from a RAC database.

■ Austin, David and Bauer, Mark. *Oracle Real Application Clusters Administrator's Guide, 10*g *Release 1 (10.1)*, Oracle Corporation, December 2003.

Chapters 6 and 7 both provide in-depth coverage of setting up RMAN on your cluster, and provide significant coverage of archivelog backup and maintenance.

Oracle and Split Mirror Technologies

■ Romero, Antonio. Oracle® Database Backup and Recovery Advanced User's Guide 10*g* Release 1 (10.1), Oracle Corporation, December 2003.

Chapter 7 covers the basics of using split mirrors for backups. However, this model assumes that you are merely using the split mirror as the backup itself, instead of connecting to this backup and taking an RMAN media backup.

■ Vengurlekar, Nitin, Maestas, Steve, and Haisley, Stephan. "Exploiting EMC Timefinder and Oracle Recovery Manager," Oracle white paper. Available online from: http://otn.oracle.com/deploy/availability/pdf/RMAN8i_BCV.pdf. [Referenced February 17, 2004]

This is the best document on using RMAN to take a backup from a split-mirror backup that is currently available to the public. It references old versions of all software involved, but the principles and concepts are still applicable.

Chapter 9: Oracle Flashback: Surviving User-Induced Trauma

As one would expect with such a new technology, there is little information generated at this time, beyond what you can find in this book.

■ Romero, Antonio. Oracle® Database Backup and Recovery Advanced User's Guide 10*g* Release 1 (10.1).

Chapter 9 covers the use of flashback commands from the RMAN command prompt, as well as from SQL*Plus.

■ Bednar, Tammy. "Flashback Technology: Recovering from Human Errors," Oracle white paper, November 2003. Available online from: http://otn.oracle.com/deploy/availability/pdf/TWP_HA_ FlashbackOverview_10g_111503.pdf. [Referenced February 17, 2004]

This is an excellent overview in a brief 13 pages.

Chapter 10: Oracle Streams for High Availability

The Streams documentation is expansive, and we found that we had three documents from Oracle Corporation open at the same time, and would have to switch back and forth frequently to get all the information required. If you are serious about Streams configuration for replication, you will need to read all of the documentation. There's just no way around it. Then, get the pdf files below and keep them handy.

■ Urbano, Randy. *Oracle Streams Concepts and Administration, 10*g *Release 1 (10.1),* Oracle Corporation, December 2003.

Along with the Streams Replication Guide, this is hands-down the most important document to have at your side during Streams testing and development. There is no one or two chapters to single out here: you will read this entire thing, most likely. If you want an overview of Streams as an availability partner, go to Chapter 7.

■ Urbano, Randy. *Oracle Streams Replication Administrator's Guide, 10*g *Release 1 (10.1),* Oracle Corporation, December 2003.

This documentation covers the implementation of Streams for replicating data from database to database (or even within a database itself). It is required reading. You should know that much of the Streams knowledge is taken for granted, so you will need to review the Streams Admin Guide, as well.

Chapter 11: Oracle Net Configuration for Failover

Definitions

■ Polk, Jennifer. *Oracle® Database Net Services Administrator's Guide,* January 2004.

Chapter 2 covers connect-time failover, transparent application failover, and load balancing.

Easy Connect

■ Polk, Jennifer. *Oracle® Database Net Services Administrator's Guide,* January 2004.

Chapter 8 covers Discussion of Naming Methods and connection syntax.

Why a Virtual IP?

■ "Performance problems with Failover When TCP Network Goes Down (No IP Address)." Available online from: http://metalink.oracle.com Reference DocID 249213.1 [Referenced on March 11, 2004]

Index

INTERNATIONAL CONTACT INFORMATION

AUSTRALIA
McGraw-Hill Book Company
Australia Pty. Ltd.
TEL +61-2-9900-1800
FAX +61-2-9878-8881
http://www.mcgraw-hill.com.au
books-it_sydney@mcgraw-hill.com

CANADA
McGraw-Hill Ryerson Ltd.
TEL +905-430-5000
FAX +905-430-5020
http://www.mcgraw-hill.ca

**GREECE, MIDDLE EAST, & AFRICA
(Excluding South Africa)**
McGraw-Hill Hellas
TEL +30-210-6560-990
TEL +30-210-6560-993
TEL +30-210-6560-994
FAX +30-210-6545-525

MEXICO (Also serving Latin America)
McGraw-Hill Interamericana Editores
S.A. de C.V.
TEL +525-1500-5108
FAX +525-117-1589
http://www.mcgraw-hill.com.mx
carlos_ruiz@mcgraw-hill.com

SINGAPORE (Serving Asia)
McGraw-Hill Book Company
TEL +65-6863-1580
FAX +65-6862-3354
http://www.mcgraw-hill.com.sg
mghasia@mcgraw-hill.com

SOUTH AFRICA
McGraw-Hill South Africa
TEL +27-11-622-7512
FAX +27-11-622-9045
robyn_swanepoel@mcgraw-hill.com

SPAIN
McGraw-Hill/
Interamericana de España, S.A.U.
TEL +34-91-180-3000
FAX +34-91-372-8513
http://www.mcgraw-hill.es
professional@mcgraw-hill.es

**UNITED KINGDOM, NORTHERN,
EASTERN, & CENTRAL EUROPE**
McGraw-Hill Education Europe
TEL +44-1-628-502500
FAX +44-1-628-770224
http://www.mcgraw-hill.co.uk
emea_queries@mcgraw-hill.com

ALL OTHER INQUIRIES Contact:
McGraw-Hill/Osborne
TEL +1-510-420-7700
FAX +1-510-420-7703
http://www.osborne.com
omg_international@mcgraw-hill.com

BIBLIO RPL Ltée
G – JUIL. 2005